A

VOCABULARY

OF THE

KASHMÍRÍ LANGUAGE

Owing to the antiquity and rarity of this book, certain pages are regrettably absent, and readability is compromised due to the blurring of the original text. If you possess any insights regarding the availability of these missing sections, kindly inform us. Your assistance is crucial in ensuring the completion of this significant work for the benefit of future generations.

A VOCABULARY OF THE KASHMÍRÍ LANGUAGE

IN TWO PARTS

KASHMÍRÍ-ENGLISH,
AND
ENGLISH-KASHMÍRÍ

WILLIAM JACKSON ELMSLIE

GYAN

Published by

Gyan Publishing House
5, Ansari Road
Daryaganj, New Delhi-110002
Phone: 011-47034999, 9811692060
E-mail: books@gyanbooks.com

Distribution Network
gyanbooks.com
India, USA, Canada, UK, Australia

ISBN: 978-93-6780-162-8 (PB)

First Published, 1872

2nd Impression 2024

Printed at: Gyan Press, Delhi.

A VOCABULARY OF THE KASHMÍRÍ LANGUAGE IN TWO PARTS
Author: WILLIAM JACKSON ELMSLIE

A

VOCABULARY

OF THE

KASHMÍRÍ LANGUAGE.

A

VOCABULARY

OF THE

KASHMÍRÍ LANGUAGE.

In Two Parts:

KASHMÍRÍ-ENGLISH,

AND

ENGLISH-KASHMÍRÍ.

BY

WILLIAM JACKSON ELMSLIE,

M.A., M.D., F.R.C.S.E., ETC.,

MEDICAL MISSIONARY TO KASHMIR.

LONDON:

CHURCH MISSIONARY HOUSE,

SALISBURY SQUARE, FLEET STREET.

1872.

PREFACE.

THE author hopes that this small Vocabulary of the Kashmírí Language, while interesting to the comparative philologist, will be found useful to the English traveller in Kashmir.

The materials composing this little work were collected by the author while discharging his duties as a Medical Missionary to the inhabitants of the valley.

Several short lists of Kashmírí words have appeared from time to time in the Transactions of the Asiatic Society of Bengal, but they are more interesting to the philologist than practically useful to the traveller, from there being no corresponding lists of English words with their equivalents in Kashmírí.

Scattered up and down in the book will be found some original information respecting Kashmir and its people.

As Kashmírí is a colloquial language, it was deemed advisable to insert the different forms of the same word met with in conversation.

The work is doubtless far from being complete, and probably

contains not a few errors, from the fact, that the language, as now spoken, has not been reduced to writing.

But if this work should serve as a stepping stone to something more complete and accurate, the author will regard himself as well repaid for his labour.

W. J. E.

Edinburgh,
February, 1872.

DIRECTIONS FOR READING.

A is sounded as u in 'but.'

Ȧ is an a pronounced low down in the throat.

Á is sounded as a in 'ark.'

Ã is pronounced like a drawling a.

B is equal to the English b.

Ch is sounded as ch in 'church.'

D is sounded like an English d, but a little more dentally.

Ḍ is sounded by rolling the tongue back upon itself and making it strike the roof of the mouth.

E is equal to a in 'cape.'

É is equal to a in 'cape.'

Ĕ is sounded like e in 'pet.'

F is equal to the English letter. The Kashmírís are prone to sound f as ph.

G is sounded as the hard English g.

H is sounded as in English.

I is equal to i in 'pin.'

Ĭ is equal to i in 'pin.'

Í is sounded like ee in 'queen.'

J is equal to the English letter.

K is sounded as in English.

L is sounded as in English.

M is equal to the English letter.

N is equal to the English letter.

O is sounded as o in 'mote.'

Ó is sounded as o in 'mote.'

Ŏ is equal to o in 'top.'

P is sounded as in English.

R is pronounced as a Scotchman sounds the English R.

Ṛ is pronounced by rolling the tongue back upon itself and making it strike the roof of the mouth.

S is sounded as in English.

T is sounded as in English, but a little more dentally

Ṭ is pronounced by rolling the tongue back upon itself and making it strike the roof of the mouth.

U is sounded as u in 'put.'

Ú is sounded as u in 'rule,'

V is equal to the English letter.

W is sounded as in English.

Y is sounded as in English.

Z is equal to the English letter.

ENGLISH-KASHMĪRĪ.

A.

Abandon, *v.* trâwun.

Abate, *v.* galun.

Abdomen, *n.* yaḍ, shikaṁ, waḍur.

Abies Smithiana, *n.* súngal, púsṭúl (Himalayan spruce).

Ability, *n.* kúwat, hĕkit, bal.

Able, to be, hĕkun.

Abolished, *adj.* chĕhit.

About (numerically) is rendered by the affix *ah.*

About a month, rĕtah.

Abound, *v.* seṭhah ásun.

Above, *prep.* pĕṭ, pĕṭh.

Abscess, *n.* phĕphar-wĕphar, phĕphur.

Abstain, *v.* sakre karinyi.

Abstemious, *adj.* shoṅt.

Abstinence, *n.* sakré, pál.

Abundance, *n.* hurir, tsirir, suchh.

Abundant, *adj.* hur, t ur, seṭhah.

Abuse, *n.* lyĕk, lánatána, yihánat, ládana, tabra, lĕk.

Abuse, to, *v.* lánatána karinyi, yihânat karinyi, ládana karinyi, tabra kaḍun, tabra wanun, lĕk kaḍinyi, lĕk tsárinyi.

Abyssinian, *n.* Habush.

Accept, *v.* kabul karun, mánun.

Accident, *n.* ittifák, milatsár.

Accidentally, *adv.* hanga tah manga.

Acclivity, *n.* thazar.

Accomplice, *n.* sharík, jora.

Accomplish, *v.* sherun, pukhta karun.

According to, *prep.* barábar, hyu.

Account, *n.* hisáb.

Accusation, *n.* gráo, háts.

Accuse, *v.* gráo karun, háts karun.

Acer, *n.* tílpatar, kílpatar, kanur.

Achillea millefolium, *n.* momádrú, chopándíga.

Acid, *adj.* tsauk.

Acid, to be, tsŏkun

Acidity, *n.* tsoker.

Acorus calamus, *n.* warch, barí.

Acquaintance (knowing), *n.* parzán, zán.

Acquainted, *adj.* ágah.

Across, *prep.* ápor.

Acute, *adj.* truk.

Address, *n.* neb.

Adhatoda vasica, *n.* pekkar, báñsa, vasa, bahikat.

Adiantum caudatum, *n.* washán, hansuráj.

Adiantum capillus veneris, *n.* dumtúlí (maiden hair fern).

Adiantum venustum, *n.* washán, hansuráj.

Admirable! *interj.* wah! wah!

Admonish, *v.* nasíhat karinyi.

Admonition, *n.* nasíhat.

Adopted, *adj.* mangatah.

Adorn, *v.* sambálun, sherun.

Adultery, *n.* khap-khap, tsóts, harám, harámkárí.

Adultery, to commit, *v.* khapun, tsóts karun.

Advice, *n.* nasíhat, tadbír.

Advise, *v.* nasíhat karinyi.

Adze, *n.* túr, tór.

Affliction, *n.* dŏkh.

Afflicted, *adj.* dãdlad, dãdkóṭ.

Afraid, *v.* naṭun.

After, *prep.* patah.

Afternoon, in the, *adv.* peshnan.

Afterwards, *adv.* tamih patah.

Again, *adv.* phírit, báz, beyih, dúbárah, paut phírit.

Agaricus campestris, *n.* mánskhel (common mushroom).

Agate, *n.* yesham, dágal.

Age, *n.* umar, vélah, vãüs, umr, wens.

Agent, *n.* drál, makím, gumáshta.

Agitated, (of water) *v.* grótsun.

Agony, *n.* dód.

Agree, *v.* mánun, samakhun.

Agriculture, *n.* grestil.

Ailment, *n.* dód.

Aim, *n.* nishána.

Aim, *v.* nishána karun.

Air, *n.* wáo, ákásh, shínyí.

Alarm, *n.* khóts.

Alas! *interj.* háe, afsús, aphós, wãe wãe.

Alder, *n.* srol, sawálí, sílein.

Alive, *adj.* zinda.

All, *adj.* sárí, sóruí, sór.

All at once, *adv.* aki laṭi.

Allium sativum, *n.* lasám, thom.

Almond-tree, *n.* bádám-kul.

Almond, *n.* bádám.

Alms, *n.* krai.

Alnus sp. *n.* srol, sawáli, sílein.

Alone, *adj.* kunui, kun.

Also, *adv.* tih, níz.

Although, *conj.* yadante, yód.

Always, *adv.* dohai, zah, hardam.

Am, *v.* chhus, chhas.

Amaranthus Anardana and Gangeticus, *n.* ganhár.

Amaranthus cruentus, *n.* bustán afroz.
Amethyst, *n.* gunafsh.
Among, *prep.* manz.
Amulet, *n.* tãwiza.
Amygdalus Persica, *n.* Súnú, tsúnú (Peach).
Anagallis cœrulea, *n.* anású.
And, *conj.* bĕyih, tah.
Andromeda ovalifolia, *n.* ratankáṭ.
Anemone obtusiloba, *n.* ratanjog.
Angel, *n.* yam.
Anger, *n.* tsak.
Angry, *v.* tsak yinyi, tsak khasinyi, róshun.
Animal, *n.* jánwar.
Anise, *n.* zyur?
Ankle, *n.* tsúnun, goḍ.
Anklet, *n.* goḍakur.
Annoyance, *n. m.* dŏkh.
Anoint, *v.* mathun, malun, manḍun.
Another, *adj.* beyák, beák, doyum.
Answer, *n.* jawáb, wŏttar, wád.
Answer, *v.* wádwád karun.
Ant, *n.* riai, re, riyai.
Ant-hill, *n.* ré-ól.
Antelope, *n.* harna, rús?
Antimony, *n.* surma.
Anus, *n.* gohistán, pon, pharj, mekad, ásan, tsŏt.
Anvil, *n.* yiran.
Anxiety, *n.* aṭkal.
Any one, *pron.* kihn.
Any where, *adv.* kunyi.

Apart, *adj.* byun.
Aperture, *n.* khajar.
Apology, *n.* híth, zárapára.
Apostle, *n.* shĕch anawun.
Apparel, *n.* pheran, poshák.
Apparent, *adj.* nŏn.
Appetite, *n.* bochhé.
Apple, *n.* tsúnṭ, trel, trela?
Apple-tree, *n.* tsunṭ-kul, trela-kul.
Apple (of throat) *n.* hírigŏgul.
Applied, *v.* lagun.
Apply, *v.* lágun.
Apricot, *n.* tser, tséra, khubání, phaṭeng.
Apricot-tree, *n.* tséra-kul.
April, *n.* Rabi' u-l-Akhir or Rabí' u-s-sáni (the fourth month of the Mussulman year), Wahek, Wáhyik, Baisáka.
Approve, *v.* mánun.
Aquarius (sign), *n.* Qunyib.
Arable land, *n.* wáimats zamín.
Arch, *n.* gumbaz.
Archer, *n.* tír-tráwunwol.
Are, *v.* chhih.
Aries (sign), *n.* Mísh.
Aristolochia rotunda, *n.* bekh záfrán.
Artemisia Indica and vestita, *n.* tataur, púnjan, banjírú.
Arm, *n.* mats, nur, máts, gúl, matsh, nãr.
Armour, *n.* shashtar, joshan, jabajáma.
Arm-pit, *n.* kats.

Army, *n.* lashkar, fauj, sína.
Arrange, *v.* sherun, sambálun.
Arrangement, *n.* sher.
Arrival, *n.* wasúl.
Arrive, *v.* wátun, pilun.
Arrive, to cause to, *v.* wátanáwun.
Arrow, *n.* kán, tír, náwak, bán.
Art, *n.* hunur.
Art, *v.* chhuk, chhak.
Artemisia elegans, *n.* jhau, lasaj.
Artemisia indica, *n.* Afsantín Mastárú.
Artemisia sacrorum and vulgaris, *n*, tatwen.
Artery, *n.* rag.
Artifice, *n.* hailah.
Arundo donax, *n.* nái.
As, *adv.* & *conj.* yuth, zan.
As-so, *adv.* yuth-tyuth.
Ascardis, *n.* Khólah.
Ascend, *v.* khasun.
Ascend, to cause to, *v. t.* khárun (chaṛháná).
Ascend, to make to, *v.* khásun.
Ascender, *n.* khasawun.
Ascent, *n.* thazar.
Ascertain, *v.* málum karun.
Ascertaining, *n.* zán.
As far as that, *adv.* tŏtámat.
As for as, *prep.* támat.
Ash, *n.* síjú, chíjlá, chúj (Fraxinus xanthoxylloides), húm, hamú (Fraxinus floribunda).
Ashamed, *adj.* sharminda, khajal.
Ashamed, *v.* mandachhun.
Ashamed, to feel, *v.* mandachhun, mandachh yun.
Ashamed, to make, *v.* mandachháwun.
Ashes, *n.* súr.
Ash-pit, *n.* tsoṭ.
As if, *conj.* zan.
Ask, *v.* mangun, pritshun.
Ask alms, *v.* béchun.
Asleep, *adj.* shungmut.
Asparagus filicinus, *n.* alípalí.
Asparagus racemosus, *n.* sejpán.
Ass, *n.* khar, kharin, khaḍ.
Assafœtida, *n.* yang, yangú, yanga (ferula assafœtida).
Assault, *n.* yala.
Assemble, *v.* samun, sumburun.
Assembled, *adj.* sumburmut.
Assembly, *n.* biṭh, anjuman.
Assist, *v.* tárun.
Assistance, *n.* madad, kumbak, yárí.
Associate, *v.* samakhun.
Astonish, *v.* tambalun.
Astonished, *adj.* khírah, hãrán.
Astrology, *n.* zitish, jotish.
Astrologer, *n.* zitish.
Astronomy, *n.* jotish.
Asylum, tsalan-shái.
Attach, *v.* lágun.
Attentively, *adv.* wárah.
Aucklandia Costus, *n.* kŏṭ.

August, *n.* Shábán, Bádirpet, Bãdirú.

Aunt, *n.* pihchain, mámain más, pŏp.

Auspicious, *adj.* phrúts.

Autumn, *n.* harud.

Avarice, *n.* lalach, shúmí, shúmrí.

Awake, *adj.* hoshiyár.

Awake, *v. i.* wuzun, hoshiár gatshun, níndarih wuthun.

Aware, *adj*, ágah.

Awl, *n.* ár, ãr.

Axe, *n.* tabar, makaz, makuts, túr.

B.

Back, *n.* thár, trak, trek, pusht, máo, khoḍatsur.

Back, *adv.* pat, phírit.

Back side (podex), *n.* tsakij.

Backwards, *adv.* patkun.

Bad, *adj.* yach, zubún.

Badly, *adv.* yachh.

Badness, *n.* yachhar.

Bag, *n.* thela, thílí, gótsur, túbra, bustúr, bastúr.

Bake, *v.* búzun.

Baked, *adj.* buzmut.

Baked clay, *n.* katir.

Baker, *n.* kándar, kándaryain.

Balance, *n.* trakur, tárats, háyúk, tól.

Ball, *n.* ḍiyung, hál, gogul.

Balsamina impatiens, *n.* bantil, tatúra, trúal (balsam).

Bandage, *n.* gand, pãtau, dáj, dajitur, dajiryel, paitawa, daij.

Bank, *n.* but, lub, baut, buṭh, boñt, bál, bauṭh.

Banker, *n.* sarráf, saráf.

Banquet, *n.* sál.

Bar, *n.* hangkal, poh.

Bárahsing, *n.* hángul, mimyamar.

Barber, *n.* naid, náí.

Barberry, *n.* enkasing.

Bare, *adj.* kun, nethanun.

Bark (of tree), *n.* dĕl.

Bark, *v.* wórun.

Barking-deer, *n.* kákur.

Barley, *n.* wushka, kisar.

Barren, *adj.* hánṭ.

Barren woman, *n.* hãnṭ, kàir.

Barrera ushna, *n.* ushna.

Basket, *n.* ṭokur, ḍákir, phaut, kranjul, páj, phatú, zen.

Basket-maker, *n.* kányul.

Bashfulness, *n.* haiya, mandachh.

Basin, *n.* bána, thál, tasht.

Bassia latifolia, *n.* mahora, mahwa-mowa.

Bat, *n.* ráta krúl.

Bath, *n.* hammám, ghusal, shrán, sinán.

Bathe, *v.* ghusal karun, shrán karun, sinán karun.

Bath-man, *n.* hammámi.

Beak, *n.* tónt, sanyer.

Beam, *n.* virám. dãr.

Bean, *n.* bãgla.

Bear, *n.* háput, hápits, hápúts, wándúr.
Bear, *v.* prasun, zyun.
Bear fruit, *v.* phalun.
Beard, *n.* dãr, resh.
Beat, *v.* márun, layun, dŏg dyun, chob dinyi, már dyun.
Beaten, *adj.* márah.
Beating, *n.* chób, már, layinah, dŏg.
Beautiful, *adj.* shúbawun, mãrmund.
Beautiful, *v.* shúbun.
Beautiful woman, *n.* náznín.
Bed-clothes, *n.* wurun.
Be, to, *v.* sapadun, sapun, ásun, zarun, lagun, banun.
Because, *conj.* kyázi.
Become, *v.* gatshun, banun.
Becoming, *adj.* shúbawun.
Becoming, *v.* shúbun.
Bee, *n.* bumbur, tilur, mánch tilur, manch-tilar.
Beef, *n.* bauḍ máz (literally the large flesh).
Bee-hive, *n.* gan.
Bees' wax, *n.* syut, kush.
Before, *adv.* bónṭh.
Before, *prep.* bronta kanyi, bonṭ, bronṭ, bronṭah kanyih.
Befriend, *v.* dost sapadun, yár sapadun, mithar sapadun.
Beg, *v.* mangun.
Beget, *v.* zowaráwun.
Beggar, *n.* fakír, rísh, bechanwol.
Begin, *v.* gŏḍ karinyi.
Beginning, *n.* ágház, ágáz, gŏḍ.
Beginning, in the, *adv.* godanyi.
Behind, *prep.* & *adv.* pat, patah.
Belch, *n.* ḍákur, ḍãkur.
Belch, *v.* ḍákur karun, ḍákur tráwun, ḍãkur khasun, ḍãkur yun (the last two with dative of person).
Belching, *n.* ḍákur, ḍãkur.
Belief, *n.* ímán, báwar, pats.
Believe, *v.* pats karinyi pats tháwinyi, báwar karun, ímán anun.
Bell, *n.* rŏnyí, gariyál.
Bellows, *n.* daman-basta.
Belly, *n.* yaḍ.
Belly-band, *n.* bál tang.
Beloved, *adj.* ṭoṭ, dilband.
Below, *prep.* & *adv.* bŏn, tal.
Bend, *v.* namun, numráwun.
Beneath, *prep.* tal.
Benefit, *v.* tárun.
Benevolence, *n.* ratsar.
Benevolent action, *n.* ratsar.
Berberis, *n.* enkasing.
Beside, *prep.* nish, nishi (the i is for emphasis), nishih.
Betrothal, *n.* ganḍun.
Betula Bhojputra, *n.* búrjrí (Birch).
Betula tartarica, *n.* bhojpatr, the birch.
Bewailing, *adj.* wadawun.
Big, *adj.* bauḍ.

Big-bellied, *adj.* yaḍa bauḍ.
Big, to be, *v.* baḍun.
Big-toe, *n.* nyuṭ, nyauṭ, nyeṭ.
Bile, *n.* tilapyut.
Bill (bird's), *n.* tónt.
Bind, *v.* basta karun, ganḍun, walun, wŏlun.
Binding, *n.* shruk.
Birch, *n.* búrjrí (Betula Bhojputra).
Bird, *n.* jánwar, pánkhí, úpháún, tsíri.
Bird cherry, *n.* zamb-chule (Prunus Padus).
Birth, *n.* prasun.
Birth-place, *n.* zenajáe.
Biscuit, *n.* yáj.
Bit, *n.* reza, hana, tukra, chhal, tilyim.
Bitch, *n.* húin.
Bite, *v.* buchhun, tsúp hyun, tsápun.
Bitter, *adj.* ṭuṭh, ṭyuṭ, khar, ṭuṭ.
Bitter, *v.* ṭiṭhun.
Black, *adj.* mishkín, kruhun, krĕhun, mushik.
Black bird, *n.* kastúr.
Blacksmith, *n. m.* khár.
Blacksmith's wife, *n.* khárabáí.
Bladder, *n.* peshábuk ṭhela, múṭaragúts.
Blade, *n.* patar.
Blame, *n.* gráó, ãb.
Blandishments, *n.* nakhra.
Blanket, *n.* durma.
Blemish, *n.* sháṁat.
Blind, *adj.* ŏn. To be blind, ŏn sapanun.
Blister, *n.* bastah.
Block (of wood), *n.* munḍ.
Blood, *n.* rath, rat. To draw or take blood, rath kaḍun.
Blood stone, *n.* pitáwul.
Bloom, *v.* phólun, kherun, phulun.
Bloom, to cause to, *v.* phólanáwun.
Blossom, *v.* phólun, kherun.
Blossom, to cause to, *v.* phólanáwun.
Blow, *n.* thápur, daug, chhŏk, dug.
Blow, *v.* phukh dyun.
Blow (as a flower), *v.* phŏlun.
Blow (of the wind), *v.* yun, gatshun, wothun, phŏkun.
Blowing, *n.* phukh.
Blue, *adj.* nyul.
Blunt, *adj.* mŏnḍ.
Boa constrictor, *n.* ájdá.
Boar, *n.* sór.
Boast, *v.* thĕkun.
Boasting, *n.* láf.
Boat, *n.* náó, baháts, khúch, ḍúnga, shikárí, tsaṭawár, parinda, tsákawár, larináo, bagí. These are the names of the different kinds of boats sailing on the Kashmir lakes and rivers.
Boatman, *n.* hánj, hánz.

Boatman's work, *n.* hánjí.
Body, *n.* maur, pán, tan.
Boil, *v.* grakun, ranun, šíwun.
Boiling, *n.* chháo, pák.
Boiling, *adj.* zalawun.
Boletus igniarius, *n.* bulgar janglí.
Bone, *n.* ádij, ustakhán.
Bone (rounded head of), *n.* adyul.
Book, *n.* kitáb, púthí.
Bookbinder, *n.* jildagur.
Boot, *n.* mas.
Borax, *n.* wáwat.
Border, *n.* daúl.
Bore, *v.* tsombun.
Born, *v.* nauwun, zyun.
Borrow, *v.* wazum hyun, kiráe hyun.
Bosom, *n.* nál, kuchh.
Both, *adj.* dŏn, dóshawa.
Bottle, *n.* ábgínah.
Bottle maker, *n.* shishigar, kátsagur.
Bound, *adj.* basta.
Bound, *v.* lagun.
Bow, *n.* renz, hárinj, góna, kamán, hárij, dúnyí.
Bowels, *n.* roda, andrum.
Bowl, *n.* khós.
Bowstring, *n.* yonyí, gon.
Boy, *n.* nĕchu, shúr, lŏkuṭ, bálak.
Bracelet, *n.* bungir, kaur, gul, kátsabungir, athakur, dodabungir, phalibungir, katsakar, shishí, gunus, kúr, kánkain, kangun.
Bracelet-maker, *n.* bungarigur.
Bracelet-seller, *n.* bungiriwóin.
Brahmin, *n.* gór, báchibaṭ, Brahmun.
Bragging, *n.* láf.
Brain, *n.* menga, kā̃ḍ, was, kauḍhí, kóḍ.
Bramble, *n.* chhánch, kaldach, amb.
Branch, *n.* lanḍ, lā̃nḍ, kón, lang, har.
Brass, *n.* lóí, sartal.
Brassica rapa, *n.* gunglú, gugchí (turnip).
Brave, *adj.* phailwán.
Braying (of ass), *n.* ṭáng.
Brazier (portable) *n.* kángrí, kángar, manan.
Bread, *n.* anapán, tsŏt, tsŏṭh.
Break, *v.* phuṭarun, phuṭun, tshanun.
Breakfast, *n.* kój, koj, chasht.
Breakfast-time, at, *adv.* kā̃jis.
Breakfast-time, *n.* kanjis, kanj.
Breast, *n.* wách, wach, sína, bab, mŏn, tan, wachh.
Breath, *n.* prán, shah, dam, phŏk, phrak, sháh.
Breathe, *v.* sháh hyun, sháh khárun.
Breathe with difficulty, *v.* khamun.
Breathless, *adj.* damjádá.

Breathless, *v.* khamun.
Breathlessness, *n.* shánsh, hanharáí, phrĕk.
Bribe, *n.* rúshwat, kauts.
Brick, *n.* sir, sír.
Brickmaker, *n.* seri-karanwol.
Bridle, *n.* lákam, wag.
Bridge, *n.* kadal.
Brimful, *adj.* sarshár.
Bring, *v.* nyun, anun.
Bring down, *v.* wálun.
Bring forth, *v.* prasun.
Bring in, *v.* tsánun.
Brink, *n.* bŏt.
Broad, *adj.* paná.
Broken, *adj.* khŏnḍ, chák.
Broken finely, *adj.* tsun.
Bronchocele, *n.* gaḍur.
Brother, *n.* bhoyi, báí, bóí.
Brother-in-law, *n.* hahar.
Brother's daughter, *n.* báwaz.
Brother's son, *n.* báphthir.
Brother's wife, *n.* báí kákin.
Bruiser, *n.* indar-muhul.
Brushmaker, *n.* kanganyigur.
Bubo, *n.* kaṭsabror, kaṭsawádir.
Bucket, *n.* nauṭ.
Buffalo, *n.* baṅs, srahḍah, mãnsh, mánsha-kauṭ, mahesh.
Build, *v.* ladun.
Builder, *n.* dosil.
Builder's wife, *n.* dosil-báí.
Bull, *n.* dánd, hakhur, wreshib, hakhuḍ.
Bulrush, *n.* pits, yira (typha augustifolia and typha latifolia).
Bunch, *n.* gúrun, guran.
Bunch of grapes, *n.* dacha-gúrun.
Bupleurum marginatum, *n.* kálízewar.
Burden, *n.* bor, bár.
Burglar, *n.* tsúr, sanyitsúr.
Burglary, *n.* san.
Burn, *v.* dazun, zálun.
Burn, to cause to, *v.* zálanáwun.
Burner of dead bodies, *n.* káwúj.
Burning, *n.* rih, tatzar.
Burning, *adj.* dazwawun.
Burning, place of, *n.* shumshán, áwarĕn.
Burnt bread, *n.* phuhur.
Burst, *v.* phaṭun, pháṭawun.
Bury, *v.* dŏbarun.
Bush, *n.* thur, kuj.
Business, *n.* kóm, kartúl.
But, *conj.* wali, amá, lekin.
Butcher, *n.* púj, pújain.
Butter, *n.* thauí, thainyi, thaiṅg, thanyi, gyau, thain.
Butter-milk, *n.* gurus.
Buttock, *n.* mandul, sukúj.
Buy, *v.* molyi hyun.

C

Cabbage, *n.* hák-wák.
Cabinet-maker, *n.* torkachhán.

Cæsalpinia sepiaria, *n.* kando, úrí.
Cake, *n.* krãr.
Calamity, *n.* baláe.
Calf, *n.* wúts, watsir, wutz, wutzhir.
Calf (of leg), *n.* graz, grŏz.
Call, *n.* álau, nád.
Call, *v.* álau dyun, nád dyun.
Call to prayers, *n.* báng, malah-báng.
Camel, *n.* unṭh, unṭ, unṭín, wúnt, wúntinyi.
Cancer (sign), *n.* Kurukauṭ.
Candle, *n.* shama, soyat.
Cannabis sativa, *n.* bhang bangí (Indian hemp).
Canopus, *n. m.* árandotí.
Canthus (of eye), *n.* nók.
Cap, *n.* kalposh, kalapósh.
Cap-maker, *n.* topigur, topagar.
Capricorn (sign), Makur.
Capsicum annuum, *n.* matitsa wángrú (red pepper).
Caravan, *n.* karwánah.
Caravansary, *n.* watalar.
Caraway seeds, *n.* zyur.
Card, to (of cotton), *v.* donun.
Cardamom, *n.* ail.
Care, *n.* parwah, parwa.
Carefulness, *n.* sŏr.
Carnelian, *n.* pyul.
Carpenter, *n.* chhán.
Carpenter's wife, *n.* chhánabái.
Carpet, *n.* satarand, watharun, kál.
Carpet-maker, *n.* kálbáf.
Carrot, *n.* gázar, mormúj, balmúj, kách (daucus carota).
Carry away, *v.* nyun.
Caruncula lachrymalis, *n.* mish.
Cash, *n.* nakad, dayár, danna, pãñsah.
Cast, *v.* tshunun, tráwun.
Cast down, *v.* tráwun.
Caste, *n.* krám.
Castle, mar, kalai.
Cat, *n.* brãr, brór, lãsh.
Catch, *v.* raṭun.
Cat's-eye stone, *n.* lasan.
Cattle-dealer, *n.* nakháa.
Cause to fall, *v.* hárun.
Cave, *n.* gŏph.
Cavern, *n.* gŏph.
Cavity, *n.* zud, khŏd.
Cedar (deodar), *n.* divadár, rãyil.
Cedar-Himalayan, *n.* diár, deodár (cedrus deodara).
Cedrela toona, *n.* dawí, drab, túni (the toon tree).
Cedrus deodara, *n.* diár, deodár, divadár, rãyil.
Ceiling, *n.* tálau.
Celosia cristata, *n.* máwal (cockscomb).
Celtis caucasica, *n.* brímdú, brúmíj, brimla.
Centipede, *n.* kanahaiping.
Cerasus vulgaris, *n.* glás, gilás (cherry).
Cerebellum, *n.* tun-koḍ.
Cerebrum, *n.* mauṭ-koḍ.

Ceremony, *n.* rít.
Certain one, *pron.* falãnyi.
Certainty, *n.* pats.
Chadar, *n.* tsadir-wádir.
Chaff, *n.* tŏh, tuh, kŏsh, kúsh, kum.
Chaff (rice) *n.* kisr.
Chain, *n.* kánkal, zanjír.
Chair, *n.* kúris, sandal.
Chalk, *n.* sep, kain.
Chamber, *n.* kuṭh, manḍan, kuṭ.
Chamois, *n.* gurál.
Chance, by, *adv.* hanga-tah-manga.
Change, *n.* adala-badal.
Change, *v.* adala-badal karun.
Chapter, *n.* báb.
Character, *n.* mód.
Charcoal, *n.* yangar, káyiri tsínyi, tsinya.
Charity, *n.* daram.
Charm, *n.* mãnthár, tãwiza, matsaband, doi khár.
Chattering woman, *n.* ṭairṭair, cháirchàir.
Cheap, *adj.* srúg, sraug.
Cheat, *v.* brám dyun.
Checkmate, *n.* shahmát.
Checkmate, *v.* mát karun, mát dyun.
Checkmated, *v.* hárun, mát sapadun, hár sapadinyi.
Cheek, *n.* mŏkh, mŏk, rŏkh, buṭh, múganḍ.
Cheerful, *adj.* prasand, khosh, wanda khosh.
Cheese, *n.* tsáman.
Chenopodium, *n.* mustakh.
Cherish, *v.* rachhun.
Cherry, *n.* glás, gilás.
Chestnut, *n.* khúprah, hának dún.
Chest, *n.* wachh, sína, wach.
Chew, *v.* tsápun.
Chicken, *n.* kŏkirpút, kokur-pút, pút, puts.
Chief, *n.* tsút, sarkash, arbáb.
Chief of Police, *n.* kutawál.
Chief, *adj.* zyuṭ.
Child, *n.* nechú, shur, bálak.
Childless, *adj.* áputr.
Chilimchi, *n.* bãtí.
Chin, *n.* hŏngainyi, hongaiṅ.
China, *n.* Chín.
Chisel, *n.* baun.
Chisel (carpenter's), *n.* pun.
Choice, *n.* kabúl.
Choose, *v.* kabúl karun.
Chrysopogon glaucoptis, *n.* shilighá.
Chunar, *n.* búnyi.
Cichorium intybus, *n.* kásni, hand, gúl.
Cinnamomum albiflorum, *n.* taj, tamála, patra, tejpat, patraj.
Circle, *n.* gardi.
Circulate, *v.* pherun, pherná-wun.
Circumstances, *n.* wuiṅ, hál.
City, *n.* nagar, shahr.
Civility, *n.* tamíz.

Claim, *n.* dáwá.
Clang, *n.* jhan.
Clarified butter, *n.* gyau.
Clavicle, *n.* aiharanḍ.
Claw, *n.* panjih, bók.
Claw, *v.* kashun.
Clay, *n.* miṭ.
Clean, *adj.* sáf, srán, pák, shrúts, srúts, pawithar.
Clean, *v.* shrúts karun, chhalun, tsaṭun.
Clear, *adj.* khol, hóú.
Cleave, *v.* pháṭawun.
Clerk, *n.* kitaba-lĕkhanwol.
Clerodendron siphonanthus, *n.* arnah.
Clever, *adj.* azmomuth, gáṭul, kámikár, truk.
Climb, *v.* khasun.
Cling, *v.* wáṭh sapadun.
Clock, *n.* sá,at, gur, gàir.
Clod, *n.* ḍela, tuj.
Close, *adj.* nizík.
Close, *v.* waṭun, band karun.
Shut or close the box, sanduk band kar.
Shut the door, darwaza dih.
Closing, *n.* thup.
Cloth, *n.* kapur.
Cloth-dresser, *n.* purzagur.
Clothe, *v.* walun, sunun walanáwun, sunáwun, tsunun, tsunáwun, práwun.
Clothe, to cause to, *v.* walanáwun.
Clothing, *n.* poshák.
Clothes, *n.* pheran, poshák.
Cloth-merchant, *n.* bazzáz.
Cloud, *n.* aubur, banlás, ŏbur, abar, míg, abr, meg.
Clove, *n.* róng.
Club, *n.* ḍáng, ḍus, tsoṭa, lúr.
Club (used in playing hockey on horseback) ṭúkin.
Club-bearer, *n.* chobdár, loriwol.
Cluster, *n.* hil.
Coal (live), *n.* tungul.
Coal-black, *n.* tsinyih.
Coarse, *adj.* phúr, mauṭ, vyut, trakúr, kuḍur.
Coat of mail, *n.* jabajáwa.
Cobbler, *n.* tsomor.
Cock, *n.* kŏkur.
Cock-crowing, *n.* kokur-báng.
Cockscomb, *n.* máwal, mawur (Celosia cristata).
Coffee, *n.* kahwah, mogil cháí.
Coil, *n.* wuṭhin, táo.
Coil, *v.* wuṭhun.
Colchicum illyricum, *n.* talkh shirin.
Cold, *adj.* shuhul, turun, shatíl, túl.
Cold, *n.* túr.
Cold season, *n.* harúd.
Collar, *n.* trauṭh, hunzura, nál.
Collar bone, *n.* ãhiranḍ, aiharanḍ.
Collect, *v.* súmráwun, barun.
Collected, *adj.* sumburmut.

Collector, *n.* amal karanwol, tahsíldar, sumráwunwol.
College, *n.* tsáṭáhál.
Collyrium, *n.* tul, ashud.
Colour, *n.* rangi, rang.
Colour-materials, *n.* phal.
Column, *n.* tham.
Comb, *n.* kangú, kangain.
Comb, *v.* kangú dyun.
Come ! exclam. woló !
Come, imper. walah.
Come, *v.* yun.
Come back, *v.* phírit yun.
Come down, *v.* wasun.
Come in, *v.* atsun.
Come into remembrance, *v.* yun yád.
Come out, *v.* nerun.
Comet, *n.* laṭitáruk, tájtáruk.
Come together, *v.* sumun.
Comfort, *v.* wanda khosh karun dilas tasallí dyun.
Comfortable, *adj.* dil-khosh, wanda-khosh, man-prasand.
Comforted, *adj.* madárá.
Command, *n.* hukm, yel.
Command, *v.* hukm dyun, hukm karun.
Commencement, *n.* gŏḍ, goḍain.
Commit (an action), *v.* karun.
Commit to the custody of, *v.* hawálah karun.
Commit to the charge of, *v.* himáyit karinyi, sipárish karinyi.
Common, *adj.* jorah, sharík.
Companion, *n.* yár, mithir, rafík, sãthí, sãth.
Compare, *n.* hishir karun.
Compassion, *n.* lol.
Compassionate, *adj.* ágah, bakhwún.
Compel, *v.* zoras set anun.
Complain, *v.* gráo karun, krak karinyi, faryád karinyi.
Complaint, *n.* nálish, gráo, bárau.
Complete, *adj.* gáṭul, pukhta.
Complete, *v.* párun.
Compliment, *n.* khoshák, prasandák, salám, bandagí, namaskár, abíd.
Compliment, *v.* salam karun, bandagí karinyi, abíd karinyi.
Compose, *v.* karun.
Computation, *n.* grand.
Conceal, *v.* khaṭun, khaṭit tháwun.
Concealed, *adj.* khaṭit.
Concord, *n.* militsár.
Condemn, *v.* hukm karun.
Condition, *n.* hál.
Conduct, *v.* wat háwinyi.
Conductor, *n.* wata-háwuk.
Cone (of fig-tree), *n.* cháng.
Confectioner, *n.* halawói, halwáí.
Confederate, *n.* milasár.
Confess, *v.* ánkár karun.
Confidant (female's), *n.* vĕs.

Confide, *v.* pats karinyi.
Confidence, *n.* pats.
Confident, *adj.* táwakal, sántúsh.
Confine, *v.* kaid karun.
Confirm, *v.* mukarrar karun.
Confounded, *adj.* mandachho mut, sharminda, hairán.
Confuse, *v.* mandachháwun.
Confusion, *n.* hairání.
Congratulate, *v.* mubárak karun.
Conjunctivitis, *n.* trŏsher, trŏshur.
Connection, *n.* paiwand.
Connive, *v.* sharík sapadun, milasár sapadun, yár sapadun, mithar sapadun.
Conquer, *v.* zenun, galba karun, tsor karun.
Conqueror, *n.* tsor karanwol, galba karanwol.
Conscious, *adj.* gáṭúl, khabardár.
Consider, *v.* bozun, vetsárun.
Consideration, *n.* fikr.
Consign, *v.* pushurun, pushráwun.
Console, *v.* dilása karun.
Constipation, *n.* kabzbandí.
Consult, *v.* salah karun, mashwara karun.
Contained, *v.* vetsun.
Contempt, *n.* yihánat.
Contented, *adj.* prasand, khosh.
Contention, *n.* harahar, har.
Contentment, *n.* santuk.
Contiguous, *adj.* nízík.
Continue, *v.* rozun.
Continually, *adv.* dohai.
Convalescent, *v.* balun.
Convallaria, *n.* bekh-zambak, bekh-sumbul.
Convenient, *adj.* nesbat, hishir.
Conversation, *n.* kat-bát, katha bátha, kathah.
Converse, *v.* kat-bát karinyi.
Convey, *v.* wátanáwun.
Conveyer, *n.* wátanáwawun.
Conveying, *adj.* wátanáwawun.
Convict, *v.* hukm karun.
Conviction, *n.* háts.
Convince, *v.* shakk kaḍun.
Convoy (guard), *n.* watahawuk.
Cook, *n.* wáza.
Cook, *v.* ranun, pákawun, grĕkanáwun.
Cook, to cause to, *v.* pákanáwun, ranáwun.
Cook-house, *n.* wazagar.
Cooking pot, *n.* lej, lyúl.
Cooking range, *n.* chŏka.
Cooking vessel, *n.* lyul, lij.
Copper, *n.* trám.
Coppersmith, *n.* misgur, ṭhánṭhir.
Copy, *n.* rúp, súrat.
Coquet, *v.* nakhra karinyi.
Coquetry, *n.* nakhra.
Cork, *n.* ṭhán.
Cork, *v.* ṭhán, dyun.
Coral, *n.* ludir.

Coral necklace, *n.* ludirimál.
Cordially, *adv.* manah set, dil o jánah set.
Coriander-seed, *n.* dányiwal.
Coriaria Nepalensis, *n.* balel, tadrelú.
Corn, *n.* hárí, galla.
Corner, *n.* kúnj, kún, kúnch.
Corner (of mouth), *n.* práts.
Corn field, *n.* dãr.
Cornus macrophylla, *n.* ḳasír.
Corpse, *n.* murda, maith, hap, shau, meṭ, mait, lásh.
Corrupt (to bribe), *v.* rúshwat karun.
Corrupt, *v.* kharáb karun.
Corylus avellana, *n.* findak, bindak.
Corylus Colurna, *n.* wínrí.
Cost, *n.* kharj.
Costos, *n. m.* kŏṭ.
Cotoneaster obtusa and rotundifolia, *n.* lehan, lín, kháriz.
Cottage (small), *n.* páhar.
Cotton, *n.* kapas, phamb, sithar, kapá.
Cotton carder, *n.* dún, dúm, káḍhí.
Cotton cleaner, *n.* dúñ, dúm, káḍhí.
Cotton plant, *n.* kapas.
Cotton thread, *n.* sátrakón.
Cough, *n.* tsás, sás, tsáñs, sáñs.
Cough, *v.* sás karun, sáñs karun.
Council, *n.* painch, majlis.
Counsel, *n.* salah, mashwara, tadbír.
Counsellor, *n.* wazírí, salah karanwol.
Count, *v.* ganzarun, ganzaráwun.
Countenance, *n.* bút.
Counterfeit, (of coin), *adj.* khauṭ.
Counting, *n.* grand.
Country, *n.* dísh, watan, zamín, butarát.
Couple, *n.* jórah.
Couple (in composition), *n.* hur.
Cousin, *n.* pitar boí, pitar binyí mámatur boí, mámatir binyí, másatur bóí, másatir binyí, pŏpatur bóí, pŏpatir binyí, piturboe.
Cousinia, *n.* krits.
Courage, *n.* dilerí, gairat.
Courier, *n.* kásid, khat ninawol.
Court (enclosure), *n.* ángun.
Court (of justice), *n.* kachhírí, kachharí.
Courtesy, *n.* tamíz.
Cover, *v.* walun.
Cover, *n.* giláf.
Covering (reed), *n.* ḍúk.
Coverlet, *n.* shihposh.
Covet, *v.* lúb karun, tama karun.
Covetous, *adj.* lálachí, tamáí.
Covetousness, *n.* lúb, tama.
Cow, *n.* gáo, kámadeyan, kámadín.

Cowardly, *adv.* lĕḍ, lánts.
Cowardly, *adj.* buzdil.
Cow-herd, *n.* gupan-gúr, dúm, gupan-rachhanwol, gau-roch, gúr, gújar, gŏpangúr.
Cowrie, *n.* hár.
Crack, *n.* prhát̤, chák, bàir, bàu̥r.
Crane, *n.* hilau, brag.
Cratægus oxyacantha, *n.* ringo, ríng (Hawthorn).
Crawl, *v.* pherun.
Cream, *n.* zĕl.
Create, *v.* paida karun, wopúdáwun.
Created, *adj.* paidah, paida.
Creator, *n.* paida-karanwol.
Creature, *n.* insán, khalkat.
Creep, *v.* sut pakun.
Crime, *n.* gunah, páp.
Cripple, *adj.* mauzur.
Crippled, *adj.* long.
Crocodile, *n.* krím.
Crocus sativus, *n.* kangan, kongs (saffron).
Crooked, *adj.* kŏb, haul.
Crooked, *v.* namun.
Crop, *n.* láganai, khal.
Cross, *v.* tarun, apor tarun.
Croton tiglium, *n.* jamal gotah, jaipál phal.
Crow, *n.* káo, shógah, kávin, káwin.
Crown, *n.* gúnḍ, táj, jega, mokaṭ.
Crown of head, *n.* tál, woḍ, khásir, khapir, áistán.
Crozophora tinctoria, *n.* nílakrai.
Crucify, *v.* súli dinyi.
Cruel, *adj.* rahmrúst.
Crumb, *n.* chapa.
Crupper, *n.* dúmij.
Crush, *v.* tseṭun, ḍagun.
Crust (of sore), *n.* krór, król.
Cry, *n.* krak, krek, bák, álau, ṭúng.
Cry, *v.* nád dyun, krak dinyi, álau dyun.
Crystal, *n.* soṭka.
Cuckoo, *n.* kukil, byol-kuk.
Cucumber, *n.* lãr.
Cucumber plant, *n.* lãr-kul.
Cucurbita maxima, *n.* al (squash).
Cultivate, *v.* láganai karinyi.
Cultivation, *n.* grestil.
Cultivator of soil, *n.* gróst, grúst.
Cup, *n.* piyálah, khos, piyála, jám, kalush, kauwul.
Cup-bearer, *n.* sharabasán.
Cupboard, *n.* khut.
Curcuma zedoaria, *n.* ámba-haldí.
Curdle, *v.* ẓyun, záorun.
Cure, *n.* iláj, wapáí.
Cure, *v.* iláj karun, wapáí karinyi.
Curl, *n.* mast, wánk.
Curl (behind ears), *n.* ḍakh.
Curse, *n.* wohau, wãnts.
Curse, *v.* wŏháwun.

Curtain, *n.* pardah, thor.
Cuscuta pedicellata, *n.* zránd, kwíklapot.
Cuscuta reflexa, *n.* midasat, ákásbil, niradhar.
Cushion, *n.* shándagund.
Custom, *n.* hāl, ádat, zápitah.
Cut, *adj.* tsuṭ.
Cut, *v.* tsaṭun, garun, kaṭun.
Cut, to cause to, *v.* tsaṭanáwun.
Cut in slices, *v.* katurun.
Cutler, *n.* roshangar, khárinyigar.
Cutter, *n.* tsaṭawun.
Cutting (from a plant), *n.* máo.
Cutting, *n.* uk.
Cymbal, *n.* tál, chhéna.
Cymbals, to play with, *v.* tál márinyi.
Cyperus longus, rotundus, *n.* múthrán.
Cypress, *n.* sarú.
Cyrus, *n.* Khosrau.

D.

Dagger, *n.* khanjar, khanjari.
Daily, *adv.* prat doho, doho prat doho.
Dalbergia sissoo, *n.* safeda.
Damage, *n.* nuksán, zarar.
Damascus, *n.* Shám.
Damp, *adj.* láwa, adur.
Damsel, *n.* kúr.
Dance, *n.* nagamah, jishna.
Dance, *v.* natsun.
Dancing-boy, *n.* bachhih.
Dancing-man, *n.* bánḍ.
Dandelion, *a.* dúdal (taraxacum officinale).
Danger, *n.* khatra, báyi, khúdashih.
Daphne Cannabina, *n.* Sannarkat.
Dark, *adj.* gauṭ.
Darkness, *n.* gaṭih, anyigaṭih.
Date (fruit), *n.* khazir, tamarí.
Date-palm, *n.* khazir-kul.
Date (of time) *n.* samwaṭ.
Datura alba, *n.* dáturr chhat.
Datura fastuosa, *n.* dáturr.
Datura stramonium, *n.* tattúr, dattúr.
Daucus carota, *n.* mormúj, balmúj, kách (carrot).
Daughter, *n.* kúr, kúḍ, komárí, kanya.
Daughter-in-law, *n. f.* nŏsh.
Day, *n.* doh, din, zaman.
Day after day, *adv.* doho pat doho.
Day before yesterday, *adv.* ótrah.
Day-break, *n.* prabát.
Day, by, *adv.* dohas.
Day-dawn, at, *adv.* kŏkarbángi, malah-bángi.
Day-time, in the, *adv.* dohas.
Dawn, *n.* subh, prabát, rets.
Dead, *adj.* múdmut, murdah, mŏrda, māt.

Dead body, *n.* lásh, maith, haph, murda, shau.

Deadly, *adj.* máranwol.

Deaf, *adj.* sakht-kan, zaur.

Deafness, gŏbir, zar, zarer.

Dear, *adj.* ṭóṭ, draug, drúg, prór (used especially about Báramúla).

Death, *n.* mót, kál, móth, marun, sháṅtún.

Debt, *n.* wazum, karz.

Debtor, *n.* wazum - hinawol, wazumwól, karzdár.

Decay, *v.* tsamathun.

Deceit, *n.* fareb, bram, máe.

Deceive, *v.* bram dyun, bram-ráwun, tambaláwun, mats-ráwun.

December (Zi-hijja, the last month of the Mussulman year), *n.* Poh.

Deception, *n.* bram, fareb, máe.

Decide, *v.* hukm karun, agnya karinyi.

Decided, *adj.* mushakhas, mu-karrar.

Decision, *n.* yatsha.

Declivity, *n.* sanyar.

Decrease, *v.* galun (ghaṭná).

Decree, *n.* hukm.

Deed, *n.* kom, kar.

Deep, *adj.* sun, saun, gútul.

Deer, *n.* surag, áho, rós, rós-kaṭ, rús, rúskaṭ.

Defame, *n.* náo kaḍun.

Defeat, *n.* hazímat, hár, dorgat, idabar, sangkaṭ.

Defeat, *v. t.* hár dinyi, hárun.

Defeated, *v.* hazímat khyun.

Defect, *n.* ãb, chunyer, kasúr, kasar.

Defendant, *n.* faryãdí.

Defender, *n.* rãch.

Deficient, *adj.* kaṃ, aḍalyuk.

Defile, *n.* nár.

Defile, *v.* lárun, mathun, dág-dár sapadun.

Deformed, *adj.* yach-shakl, yach-rúp.

Degrade, *v.* bekár karun.

Degree (rank), *n.* bajir, hash-mat.

Degrees, by, *adv.* kadama pat kadama, pairi pat pairi, padi pat padi.

Delay, *n.* tãr, tsér.

Delicate, *adj.* pishul, narm, ãyul, ãvyil.

Delicious, *adj.* myút.

Delight, *v.* khush-dil karun.

Delightful, *adj.* mudhúr, dilas-praywun.

Delirium, *n.* tambalun.

Deliver, *v.* dyun, wátanáwun mokaláwun.

Delphinium Saniculæ folium (flowers of), *n.* asbarg, ghá-fiz.

Delude, *v.* matsaráwun, dala-ráwun.

Demand, *v.* mangun, tsádun.

Demon, *n.* deo, mushrán.
Den, *n.* gŏp.
Denial, *n.* ánkár.
Depart, *v.* pyun, gatsun.
Departure, *n.* kúch.
Dependence, *n.* pats.
Depend on, *v.* pats, karinyi.
Deposit, *n.* hawála, amánat.
Depraved, *adj.* yach.
Depravity, *n.* yachhar.
Deputy, *n.* wakíl.
Descend, *v.* wasun, bŏn wasun, bŏn gatshun, tal gatshun.
Descender, *n.* wasawun, wasanwol.
Descent, *n.* sanyar.
Describe, *v.* sifat karun.
Desert, *n.* shinya.
Deserter, *n.* tsalanwol.
Deserve, *v.* lá,ik sapadun.
Desire, *n.* măl, tamanná, lól, khárah, yitsha, shauk.
Desire, *v.* yatshun, mangun.
Desirous, *adj.* lolabrut.
Desmodium tiliæfolium, *n.* chamkát, marára.
Desolate, *adj.* wairánah, khwár.
Desolate, *v.* wairán karun.
Desolation, *n.* dás.
Despair, *n.* nyerásh, na-umedí.
Desperate, *adj.* ashái-rúst, umed-rúst.
Despise, *v.* lokut tháwun, tána tána karun.
Destiny, *n.* tálai.
Destroy, *v.* márun, zaba karun.
Destructive, *adj.* naksándár, naksánlad, naksánzad.
Detachment, *n.* foj, palṭan.
Detect, *v.* mutsaráwun.
Determine, *v.* mushakhas karun.
Detriment, *n.* hárun, chhunyer.
Deutzia staminea, *n.* phurílí.
Devil, *n.* shaitán.
Devour, *v.* khyun.
Devotion, *n.* tapasia, ábádat.
Devout, *adj.* shónt.
Dew, *n.* lawa, shabnam, suradág, lauwa.
Dewlop, *n.* ghabghab.
Diamond, *n.* almás.
Diadem, *n.* gúnd.
Dice, *n.* zár.
Die, *v.* marun.
Differ, *v.* fark tháwun, tafáwat tháwun.
Different, *adj.* byun, wŏpar.
Difficult, *adj.* sakht, mushkil.
Dig, *v.* khanun, tachhun.
Digest, *v.* shrapun.
Digested, *v.* shrapun.
Digestion, *n.* shrapun.
Dignity, *n.* obre, mód.
Diligent, *adj.* shogal.
Diminish, *v.* kam sapadun, máne sapadun, kam karun, máne karun.
Dimness of vision, *n.* tsámp.
Dining-room, *n.* rawak.
Dinner, *n.* kój.

Dioscorea deltoidea, *n.* krís, knís.
Dip, *n.* gŏta.
Direction (as to relation), kun.
Dirt, *n.* mal.
Dirty, *adj.* malbúrut, mordár, mál, mokur.
Disable, *v.* bad karun, yach karun.
Disappointment, *n.* nirásh, naumedí.
Disappear, *v.* poshídah sapadun, khatit sapadun.
Discharge, *v.* tráwun, láyun, mokajár dyun, khalásí dinyi.
Disclose, *v.* mutsaráwun.
Discord, *n.* dushmani, shatrut,
Discovery, *n.* zán.
Disease, *n.* dód, yalat.
Disgrace, *n.* beyizzatí.
Disgraced, *adj.* mandachhomut.
Disguise, *n.* rúph, shakl, súrat.
Disgust, *n.* nafrat.
Disgusted, *adj.* wanda-rúdmut.
Dish, *n.* lij, chin, thál, ṭúr, rikib.
Dishevelled, *adj.* pareshán.
Dishonour, *v.* paizár dyun.
Dismiss, *v.* chhorun, tráwun, bekár karun, kámirúst karun.
Dismount, *v.* gurih pĕṭhah wasun.
Disobedience, *n.* hŏḍ.
Disorder, *n.* tarbidawaráí.
Disperse, *v.* danun, chhakaráwun.
Dispersing, *adj.* chhakaráwun chhakaráwanwol, danawun, danawól.
Disposition, *n.* mizáj.
Dispute, *v.* harahar karinyi.
Dispute, *n.* bahs, darak.
Dissolute, *adj.* búkirdúr, trakkur, yach.
Dissolve, *v.* gálun.
Distaff, *n.* salai.
Distance, *n.* dúrir, dúryir.
Distance, at a, *adv.* dúrih, dúri pĕṭh, dúrih, dúré.
Distant, *adj.* dúr.
Distinct, *adj.* byun.
Distress, *n.* fikr, sángkalaf.
Distressed, *adj.* diltang, khuts.
Distressed, *v.* kuṭhun.
Distribute, *v.* bágrun.
District, *n.* parganah, zillah.
Disturb, *v.* iztaráb karun, bekarárí karinyi.
Disturbed, *adj.* hãrán.
Ditch, *n.* khwod, khwunamut, sanyir.
Dive, *n.* gŏta.
Divide, *v.* bágrun, bágráwun, fark karun.
Divorce, *n.* talák, tráwun.
Do, to, *v.* karun.
Doctor, *n.* hakím.
Doe, *n.* minyamar, ruskaṭ.
Doff, *v.* tráwun.
Dog, *n.* hún, shánuk, phú.
Dolomiæa macrocephala, *n.* dhúp.
Dome, *n.* ḍumuṭ.

Don, *v.* práwun.

Donkey, *n.* khar.

Door, *n. m.* darwáza, bar.

Door-keeper, *n.* ḍiḍwoin, pahrawol.

Door, to shut the, *v.* bar dyun.

Double chin, *n.* ghabghab.

Doubt, *n.* shenk.

Doubt, *v.* shenk nyinyi.

Doubtless, *adv.* shenkirúst.

Dove, *n.* kúkil?

Down, *adv.* bŏn.

Downwards, *adv.* bŏn-kun.

Drag, *v.* kaḍun, lamun.

Drain, *n.* hĕnur, hindur.

Drake, *n.* batuk.

Draught (of fluid), *n.* chhun.

Draughtsman, *n.* nakkásh.

Draw, *v.* lamun.

Draw a bow, *v.* kaḍun kamán.

Draw a breath, *v.* shah kaḍun.

Drawers (trousers), *n.* paijamah, yezár.

Draw out, *v.* nĕbar kaḍun, kaḍun.

Dread, *n.* bím.

Dream, *n.* sŏpun, khwáb.

Dream, in a, *adv.* khwãbi, khwábas, manz.

Dream, *v.* sŏpun wuchhun, khwáb wuchhun.

Dregs, *n.* lum, lamb.

Dress, *n.* poshák, phĕran.

Dress another, *v.* walanáwun.

Dressed in black, *adj.* siyahposh.

Dress one's self, *v.* walun.

Dried dung, *n.* bauṭ.

Drink, *v.* chun, chhun, chyun.

Drink, to give or cause to, *v.* cháwun.

Drive, *v.* pakanáwun.

Drive out, *v.* kaḍun.

Drone (bee), *n.* bómbur.

Drop, *n.* phúr, phyur, katra, bend, dána.

Drop, *v.* pashpun, paydun, peḍun.

Drought, *n.* hŏchir.

Drown, *v.* phaṭun, phaṭáwun.

Drowned, *adj.* phaut.

Drowsiness, *n.* zŏlah.

Druggist, *n.* búhur.

Drum, *n.* nagára, nagár, ḍumḍum.

Drummer, *n.* nagár wáyanwol, ḍum-ḍum wáyanwol.

Drunk, *adj.* mast, wolyomut.

Dry, *adj.* hok, huk, hukmut, hauk.

Dry, *v.* hukhun, hukhanáwun.

Dry, to be, *v.* hŏkun.

Dual, *n.* There is no dual in Kashmírí as in Arabic, Greek, and Sanscrit.

Duck, *n.* batij.

Dumb, *adj.* káúl, tsopa.

Dung, *n.* lĕd, rĕk, molut.

Durable, *adj.* durr.

Dust, *n.* mĕts, lats, gard.

Duty, *n.* hak.

Dwell, *v.* rozun, basun, ásun.

Dwelling, *n.* gar.
Dye, *v.* rangun.
Dyeing, *n.* rang.
Dyer, *n.* rangur.
Dysentery, *n.* zahír.

E.

Each, *adj.* prat.
Eager, *adj.* yatsanwol.
Eagle, *n.* grad.
Ear, *n.* kan, káwah.
Ear-ache, *n.* kanas dód.
Ear of corn, *n.* hilyi.
Early, *adv.* subhanas, prabátas, prabátan, rets.
Earn one's living, *v.* zenun.
Earnest, *adj.* durr.
Earnest-money, *n.* sai.
Ear-ring, *n.* dejihur, kanadur, kanawã̄j, kanawol.
Earth, *n.* zamín, bútrát, búmika, mits, bútarát, darthí, gil, púthúr, bhútrát.
Earthquake, *n.* bunyúl, bukam.
Ease, *n.* sáhil, latsar, árám.
Easiness, *n.* lantsar.
East, *n.* púr, mashrik.
Easy, *adj.* suhul, ásán, sahal, sihal, laut.
Eat, *v.* khyun.
Eat, to cause to, *v.* khyáwun.
Eat, to give to, *v.* khyáwun.
Eater, *n.* khyĕwun.
Echo, *n.* shabit.
Eclipse, *n.* grahan, gruhun.
Edge, *n.* bera, bauṭh, dára (of a cutting weapon), dandir (of every thing except a cutting weapon).
Edge of eyelid, *n.* ṭárich zih, mish.
Edge of orbital cavity, *n.* khánkur.
Edwardsia mollis, *n.* janglí kits, bankeintí.
Effort, *n.* talásh, wadhyug.
Effort, to make an, *v.* zór karun.
Egg, *n.* ṭhúl, anḍ.
Egg (of louse), *n.* lichh.
Egg-plant, *n.* rã̄lwángin, or rínwángin, wángún.
Eight, *adj.* ã̄ṭh.
Eighteen, *adj.* ardah.
Eighteenth, *adj.* ardã̄hyum.
Eighth, *adj.* ã̄ṭhyum.
Eightieth, *adj.* shítyum.
Eighty, *adj.* shít.
Eighty-eight, *adj.* arashít.
Eighty-eighth, *adj.* arashítyum.
Eighty-fifth, *adj.* pántsashíṭyum.
Eighty-first, *adj.* akashítyum.
Eighty-five, *adj.* pántsashít.
Eighty-four, *adj.* tsŭshít, tsoyishít.
Eighty-fourth, *adj.* tsushítyum.
Eighty-nine, *adj.* kunanamat.
Eighty-ninth, *adj.* kunanamatyum.

Eighty-one, *adj.* akashít.
Eighty-second, *adj.* dŭshítyum.
Eighty-seven, *adj.* satashít.
Eighty-seventh, *adj.* satashít-yum.
Eighty-six, *adj.* shishít, shey-ishít.
Eighty-sixth, *adj.* shishítyum.
Eighty-third, *adj.* trashítyum.
Eighty-three, *adj.* tráshít.
Eighty-three, *adj.* treyishít.
Eighty-two, *adj.* doyishít, dŭ-shít.
Either, *conj.* nathá, yá, kháh,
Elæagnus sp. *n.* gíwáin, kan-kol.
Elbow, *n.* khŏn, khonawaṭ.
Elder, *adj.* zyuṭ (*m*) ziṭ, zichih (*f*), godanyuk, zúṭh. Elder brother, godanyuk bói, zúṭh bói.
Eldest son, *n.* kák.
Eleagnus orientalis, *n.* kankol mirich.
Elegant, *adj.* naznín, nakhral.
Elephant, *n.* haust, gazah, hust, hast.
Eleven, *adj.* kah.
Eleventh, *adj.* kahyum.
Elm, *n*, brerí, brárí, brankul, amrái, bren, bran.
Eloquent, *adj.* gáṭul, moḍir zeo.
Else, *adj.* beyih.
Emancipated, *adj.* mŏkul.
Embankment, *n.* suth.
Embrace, *v.* nálamut karun.
Embracing, *n.* nálamut.
Embroider, *v.* práwun.
Embroiderer, *n.* chikandór.
Emerald, *n.* sabza.
Eminence, *n.* labur, teng, lábur.
Emperor, *n.* pádshah, ráza.
Employ, *v.* (mashghúl kardan), shogla karun.
Empty, *adj.* tshur, khálí, chhŏnói.
Encamp, *v.* lashkarí hinz jái karinyi.
Encouraged, *adj.* madárá.
End, *n.* patolákain, sámána, anjám.
Endeavour, *v.* (koshídan) talásh karun, wadhyug karun.
Endive, *n.* haud.
Endless, *adj.* anjámavarái, anjámarust, anjámavenna.
Endurance, *n.* tseḍa.
Enemy, *n.* shathar, dushman, shithar.
Energy, *n.* kówat, bal.
English, *adj.* Angrezí.
Engrave, *v.* khanun.
Enmity, *n.* wair, shitrut, dush-maní.
Enormous, *adj.* sĕṭha bàuḍ, sĕṭha thàuḍ.
Enough! *interj.* yutuí, bas, yútoi.
Enquire, *v.* pritshun, prátshun.
Entangle, *v.* (pech kardan), walun, ganḍun, wuṭhun.

Enter, *v.* andar yun, andar gatshun, andar atsun, atsun.

Entertain, *v.* (mahmándárí kardan) patsaláz karinyi, mahmandárí karinyi.

Entertainment, *n.* sál.

Entrust, *v.* pusharun, púshiráwun, hawálah karun.

Envious, *adj.* mánir.

Envy, *n.* zidd, hasad, ḍánṭun.

Ephemeral fever (of children), *n.* zar.

Epilepsy, *n.* set, laṭh.

Epistle, *n.* khat.

Equal, *adj.* barábar, hyú, hyuk.

Equal in age, *adj.* yak jázámut, yikawaṭain.

Equipoise, *n.* pársang.

Equisetum debile, *n.* matí (Horse tail).

Erect, *adj.* thŏd.

Eructate, *v.* ḍākur khasun, dakur yun.

Eructation, *n.* ḍákur, ḍākur, ḍākar.

Eryngium planum, *n.* kandú.

Escape, *v.* tsalun, mŏkalun.

Escaped, *adj.* tsäúl.

Especially, *adj.* goḍinyi.

Essence, *n.* tsorit.

Establish, *v.* mukarrar karun, mushakhas karun.

Estate, *n.* aláka. Owner of an estate, alákadár.

Esteem highly, *v.* mánun.

Eternal, *adj.* hamesha, dohai, sadáí.

Eunuch, *n.* lánts.

Euonymus Fimbriata and Hamiltonii, *n.* síkí, pakúá, chúál.

Europe, *n.* Faringistán.

Euryale ferox, *n.* jewar.

Even, *adv.* (bhí) tih.

Even (level), *adj.* barábar, hyú.

Evening, *n.* shám, sandiya, kalachan, sandia,

Evening, at, *adv.* sháman, digaran.

Evening (in the), *adv.* sháman, digaran.

Evening-twilight, *n.* shafak.

Event, *n.* chich.

Ever, *adv.* zah, mulai, hamesha, sadáí, dohai.

Every, *adj.* prat.

Every one, *adj.* prat ak.

Everywhere, *adv.* prat sháí.

Evidence, *n.* sháhidi, gawáhí, saukhí.

Evident, *adj.* hó,ú, záhir, drashṭánt.

Evil, *n.* badí, yachhar, yachhí.

Evil doer, *n.* yach kom karawun.

Ewe, *n.* gob, lau, gaub.

Exalt, *v.* (bar dáshtan) thŏd karun, tulun.

Examination, *n.* pritsagár.

Examine, *v.* (justan) tsáḍun.

Example, *n.* haibat.

Exchange, *v.* badal dyun.
Exchanger of money, *n.* sarráf.
Exceedingly, *adv.* ámób.
Excellence, *n.* rutsar.
Excellent, *adj.* rut.
Excellently, *adv.* wárah.
Except, *prep.* síwáí, wará,í, veráí, rust, siwá, venna, magar, yátu.
Excite, *v.* (angekhtan) tulun, hurun.
Excoriate, *v.* tachhun.
Excuse, *n.* uzr, zárapar, híth.
Execute, *v.* jáí pĕṭ anun, amal karun, kóm karinyi.
Execution, *n.* (qatl) khash.
Executioner, *n.* (jallád) márawátul.
Exertion, *n.* wadhyug, talásh.
Expect, *v.* umed tháwinyi, ásha tháwinyi.
Expel, *v.* kaḍun, dúr karun.
Expense, *n.* kharj, kharjí.
Experiment, *n.* sargí.
Explain, *v.* bozanáwun, bayán karun, wanun, dapun.
Explanation, *n.* arth.
Expresser of oil, *n.* telawoin.
Extend, *v.* pilanáwun, zúth karun.
Extension, *n.* khajar.
External meatus, *n.* kanagogul.
Extinguish, *v.* tseta karun, poit karun, baḍáwun.
Extort, *v.* see 'wring.'
Extract, *v.* kaḍun.
Extraordinary, *adj.* áshtsarí, ajá,ib.
Extremely, *adv.* seṭha, ámób.
Exult, *v.* khushí karinyi, khosh sapadun, prasand sapadun.
Eye, *n.* ȧchh, nithar, ȧch, chasham.
Eye (of needle), *n.* sutsanyi poh.
Eye-ball, *n.* ȧchhgúl.
Eye-brow, *n.* búma, búmba, búmb, bum.
Eye-lashes, *n.* achhirwál, achharwál.
Eye-lid, *n.* ṭór, tár.
Eye-sight, *n.* drenṭ, gāsh.
Eye-witness, *n.* sákhí, gawáí.

F.

Faba vulgaris, *n.* kăiún.
Fable, *n.* kat.
Face, *n.* but, róe, mŏkh.
Face to face, *prep.* bronta kanyi, seda-seda.
Fàcility, *n.* lautsar, latsar.
Fade, *v.* see 'decay,' vesarun.
Fæces, *n.* goh.
Faggot, *n.* haṭ.
Fagopyrum esculentum, *n.* trúmba.
Fairy, *n.* viganí, parí.
Fairy-like, *adj.* parí-tintsál.
Faith, *n.* ímán, pats, báwar, bránt.

Faithful, *adj.* wafádár, wafá karanwol.

Faithless, *adv.* bewafá.

Falcon, *n.* pãz, buhir.

Fall, *v.* pyun, harun, pathar pyun.

Fall, to cause to, *v.* páwun.

Fall, to make to, *v.* páwun.

Falling-star, *n.* ráh.

Fallow-land, *n.* behádrao zamín, bít zamín.

Falls (of a river), *n.* shráṭ and sháṭ.

False, *adj.* apozyor, khŏṭ, apoz, brám dinawol.

Fame, *n.* khabar.

Family, *n.* shuribãts, basawin, ṭabar, kabílah.

Famine, *n.* drág, bochi.

Famous, *adj.* námósdár, neknáo, nun.

Fan, *n.* shúp.

Fancy, *n.* khayál, vetsar.

Fancy, *v.* vetsar karun.

Far, *adj.* & *adv.* dúr.

Farewell, *n.* salám, bandagi.

Farewell, to bid, *v.* salám dinyi, salám karinyi, bandagi karinyi.

Farmer, *n.* gróst.

Farrier, *n.* khár.

Fast, *n.* roza, fáka.

Fast, *v.* roza karinyi or tháwinyi.

Fat, *adj.* mauṭ, vyauṭh, vyuṭ, vyuṭh, púṭh.

Fat, to be, *v.* veṭhun.

Fat, to become, *v.* veṭhun.

Fate, *n.* prálabad, bágnai.

Father, *n.* mól, kák, bab, bába, pita, báb.

Father-in-law, *n.* hyihur, hyuhur.

Fatigue, *n.* thakun, losun.

Fatigued. *v.*, thakun.

Fatness, *n.* vechhar.

Fatten, *v.* veṭhráwun.

Fauces, *n.* gyeg.

Fault, *n.* páp, gunah, ráh.

Favour, *n.* mihrbání, daiya, niamat.

Favour, *v.* mihrbání karinyi, daiya karinyi.

Fear, *n.* bím, ḍar, khóf, baiya.

Fear, *v.* khotsun, ḍarun, baiya khyun.

Fear, to make to, *v.* khotsanáwun.

Feast, *n.* sál, bozan, ziáfat.

Feather, *n.* pakh, pak, tihir.

February, *n.* Phágun.

Feed, *v.* khen dyun, bata dyun, khyáwun.

Fell, *v.* páwun.

Fellow-traveller, *n.* set pakawun.

Female portion of a house, *n.* báts.

Fennel (sweet), *n.* bádiyáná, bãdiyána.

Ferocious, *adj.* sakht, trakúr, kaṭhun.

Ferry, *n.* nambal, ḍemb, zóḍ, gaṭ.

Ferry, *v.* tárun.

Ferryman, *n.* tárawun, táranwól, karanáv.

Fertile, *adj.* phalabarrit (of the earth), mewadár (of a tree).

Ferula Assafœtida, *n.* Yang.

Festival, *n.* íd.

Fever, *n.* tab, píḍa, tazzar, zál, túr.

Few, *adj.* manai, kam.

Fickleness, *n.* utáwul.

Ficus carica, *n.* anjír.

Ficus caricoldes, *n.* anjír.

Ficus caricordes, *n.* kirmri (species of fig).

Ficus reticulata, *n.* thaur (fig-tree).

Fidelity, *n.* wafádárí.

Field, *n.* maidán, thinya, lóganai, dór, khít, láganai, zirát.

Fifteen, *adj.* pandah.

Fifteenth, *adj.* pandãhyum.

Fifth, *adj.* pántshyum.

Fiftieth, *adj.* pántsãhyum.

Fifty, *adj.* pántsah.

Fifty-eight, *adj.* arawanzah.

Fifty-eighth, *adj.* arawanzãhyum.

Fifty-fifth, *adj.* pántsawanzãhyum.

Fifty-first, *adj.* akawanzãhyum.

Fifty-five, *adj.* pántsawanzah, pants tah pántsah.

Fifty-four, *adj.* tsŏwanzah.

Fifty-fourth, *adj.* tsŏwanzãhyum.

Fifty-nine, *adj.* kunahéṭh.

Fifty-ninth, *adj.* kunahaiṭhyum.

Fifty-one, *adj.* akawanzah.

Fifty-second, *adj.* dúwanzãhyum.

Fifty-seven, *adj.* satawanzah.

Fifty-seventh, *adj.* satawanzãhyum.

Fifty-six, *adj.* shiwanzah.

Fifty-sixth, *adj.* shiwanzãhyum.

Fifty-third, *adj.* trawanzãhyum.

Fifty-three, *adj.* trawanzah.

Fifty-two, *adj.* dowanzah.

Fig, *n.* injír.

Fight, *n.* jang, yod, laḍáí, harahar, nyáí.

Fight, *v.* jang karun, yod karun, laḍáí karinyi, harahar karinyi, nyáí karun.

Fighting, *n.* har, harahar.

Fig-tree, *n.* kirmri, thaur.

File, *n.* phihrawáo.

Filings, *n.* tsúṅ.

Fill, *v.* barun, barrun, berrit karun.

Filter, *n.* káṭ, zanjír.

Filth, *n.* múlat.

Final, *adj.* patyum.

Finally, *adv.* patolákain.

Find, *v.* labun.

Fine, *n.* chaṭi.

Fine, in, *adv.* patolákan.
Finger, *n.* anguj, ungaj.
Finger (little), *n.* kis.
Finger's breadth, *n.* khajar.
Finish, *v.* sapadáwun, párun, mokaláwun, sherun.
Fir, *n.* yãr.
Fire, *n.* nár, tĕngul, agaṅ, náratengul.
Fire, to make a, *v.* nár zálun.
Fireplace, *n.* dán, baṭh, gäij, auktsór, tsŏl, uktsŏr, dámbur, bukhãrí.
Firewood, *n.* zun, zyun, zálun, káyúr.
Firm, *adj.* dur.
Firmament, *n.* nab.
First, *adj.* gŏḍanyuk, goduk.
First, at, *adv.* gŏḍanyi.
Fir-tree, *n.* budal, yór, yãr, yãḍ.
Fish, *n.* gáḍ, goḍ, gãḍ.
Fish, *v.* gáḍ raṭinyi.
Fisher, *n.* gáḍahánz.
Fisherman, *n.* gáḍahánz, gád raṭanwol.
Fisherwoman, *n.* gáḍahánzain.
Fissure, *n.* bair, trit.
Fist, *n.* moth, musht, daug, mukál, nyuk.
Fit, *adj.* shúbun.
Fit, *v.* lagun.
Fit, to be, *v.* shúbun.
Fitted, to cause to be, *v.* shubanáwun.
Five, *adj.* pántsh.
Five fingers, *n.* panjih.
Five o'clock, *n.* dígar, dígaran.
Fix, *v.* bahanáwun.
Flag, *n.* alam.
Flame, *n.* rih, tembir, nár, agan.
Flank, *n.* hul, kamar.
Flash, *n.* wuzamal.
Flat, *adj.* hyu, barábar, satur, sum.
Flatter, to, *v.* walás, karun, khushámad karun.
Flatulence, *n.* nafak.
Flavour, *n.* swád, maza, sád.
Flea, *n.* pyush, písh.
Flee, *v.* tsalun.
Flesh, *n.* máz, sun, máta, ninyi, mámas.
Flesh (of fruit), *n.* máz.
Flexible, *adj.* hul.
Flint, *n.* zakhmakh.
Float, *v.* yírun.
Flock, *n.* tyúr, khyul.
Flog, *v.* kamcha láyun.
Flood, *n.* sail, yup, yúp, sailáb.
Flọur, *n.* óṭ.
Flourish, *v.* phulun.
Flourishing, *n.* phúlai.
Flow, *v.* pranun, wagun.
Flower, *n.* posh.
Flower, to, *v.* phólun.
Flower, to cause to, *v.* phólanáwun.
Flower-garden, *n.* poshibág.
Flower-seller, *n.* púsh.
Fly, *n.* machh.
Fly, *v.* wuḍun, wuphun.

Fly, to make to, *v*. wuḍanáwun, wuphanáwun.
Flying, *adj*. wuḍán.
Flying fox, *n*. wútsagagur, wutsah-gagur.
Flying squirrel, *n*. us-gagar.
Foal, *n*. kháryuk.
Foam, *n*. paus.
Foam, *v*. paus tráwṛun.
Fold, *v*. waṭun.
Follow, *v*. pata yun.
Fontanelle (anterior), *n*. áyistán.
Food, *n*. khurák, khen, bata, guzah.
Fool, *n*. bekal, nádán.
Foolish, *adj*. bekal, aklirust, akliwarái, aklisiwái, bozvenna.
Foolish, to become, *v*. matun.
Foolishness, *n*. bekali.
Foot, *n*. khór, khŏr, pád.
Foot (of camel or elephant), *n*, paud.
Footless, *adj*. raun.
Footman, *n*. piádah.
Footstep, *n*. púr.
Fop, *n*. thekawun.
Foppish, *adj*. thúng.
For, *prep*. bápat, khátra.
For rubbing, mathuni bápat.
Forbid, *v*. mána karun.
Forceps, *n*. wauts.
Ford, *n*. ḍemb, nambal, zód, sháṭ.
Forearm, *n*. nair, hauts, báú.
Forefinger's length, *n*. gira.
Forehead, *n*. jabín, dekah, deko.
Foreign, *adj*. begána, wapir.
Foreigner, *n*. wŏpar, parud, begána, azãníji,
Forenoon, *n*. koj, chasht.
Forest, *n*, wan, jangal.
Forfeit, *v*. cheṭ labinyi, cheṭ hinyi.
Forge, *v*. brám dyun.
Forgery, *n*. makir, ṭhagil.
Forget, *v*. mashun, mashráwun, mashrah karun.
Forgetful, *adj*. muṭh.
Forgetfulness, *n*. bul.
Forgive, *v*. ádar karun, báv karun, shafkat karun.
Forgiving, *adj*. bakhwun, bakhshawun.
Forgotten, to be, *v*. mashun.
Form, *n*. rúp, shakl, súrat.
Form, to, *v*. banáwun.
Fornication, *n*. harám, harámkárí.
Forsake, *v*. tráwun. *See* 'Throw away.'
For the sake of, *prep*. pás, khãtra bápat.
Fort, *n*. mar, kalái.
Fortieth, *adj*. tsatajihyum.
Fortnight, *n*. pach.
Fortress, *n*. kalái, gaḍ.
Fortune, *n*. tálai, bágnai, danna, dayár, daulat.
Fortune-teller, *n*. saidmakár.
Forty, *adj*. satajih.

Forty-eight, *adj.* aratājih.
Forty-eighth, *adj.* aratājihyum.
Forty-fifth, *adj.* pántsatājihyum.
Forty-first, *adj.* akatājihyum.
Forty-five, *adj.* pántsatājih.
Forty-four, *adj.* tsŏyitājih.
Forty-fourth, *adj.* tsŏyitājihyum.
Forty-nine, *adj.* kunawanzah.
Forty-ninth, *adj.* kunawanzāhyum.
Forty-one, *adj.* akatājih.
Forty-second, *adj.* dótājihyum, dŏyitājihyum.
Forty-seven, *adj.* satatájih.
Forty-seventh, *adj.* satatājihyum.
Forty-six, *adj.* shayitājih.
Forty-sixth, *adj.* shayitājihyum.
Forty-third, *adj.* tíyitájihyum, títājihyum.
Forty-three, *adj.* tíyitājih, títājih.
Forty-two, *adj.* dŏyitājih, dotājih.
Forward, *v.* guzráwun.
Forwards, *adv.* bronṭ.
Go forwards, bronṭ pak.
Come forwards, bronṭ wallah, or bronṭ yih.
Forwards, *adv.* bronṭ kun. The literal translation of this expression is towards forwards, or in the direction of forwards.
Foul, *adj.* malbúrut.
Foundation, *n.* dyón, kuris, kán, kan.
Fountain, *n.* nág, nagarád.
Four, *adj.* tsór.
Fourteen, *adj.* tsŏdah.
Fourteenth, *adj.* tsŏdāhyum.
Fourth, *adj.* tsúryum, tsoryum.
Fowl, *n.* kŏkir, kokur.
Fowl-house, *n.* mur, kokurmur.
Fox, *n.* potsalo, phenḍasháj, losh, loh, luhf, luhv.
Fragaria vesca, *n.* ingrách, yangtash (strawberry).
Fragment, *n.* reza, hana, chhal, tilyun.
Fragrance, *n.* mushk.
Fragrant, *adj.* mushka berrit, soganddár, khúshbú.
Fraud, *n.* *m.* bram, hílah, tambalun, daga.
Fraxinus floribunda, *n.* húm, hamú (ash).
Fraximus Xanthoxylloides, *n.* chíjlá, chúj, síjú (ash).
Free, *adj.* khalás, mokul, ázád.
Free, *v.* tráwun, mokaláwun.
Free, to be, *v.* mŏkalun.
Freedom, *n.* mokajár, khalásí.
Frequently, *adv.* kentsi phiri.
Fresh, *adj.* nau, táza, sabz.
Fresh, *v.* nauwun.
Fret, *v.* tsraṭ dyun.
Friday, *n.* Shukharwár, Jamát.
Fried, *adj.* buzmut.

Friend, *n.* rafík, dost, yár, mithar, vĕs.

Friendly, *adj.* mihrbán, diya karanwol.

Friendship, *n.* mitrut, dostdãri, yáraz, methri, mithrachárí.

Frighten, *v.* khotsanáwun, ḍaranáwun, kampanáwun.

Frigid, *adj.* shatíl, turun.

Fringe, *n.* yin, serish.

Fringed, *adj.* yiniwol, serishwol.

Frog, *n.* ninyimonduk, ninyimondij, mainah.

From, *prep.* nishi. From him, tas nishi.

From (lit. from upon—said of a place), *prep.* peṭhah. From Islamabad, Islámabáda peṭhah (Islámabád par se).

From here, *adv.* yitih pĕṭhah.

Frontier, *n.* saṛhad.

Frown, *v.* but tsokráwun.

Fruit, *n.* mewah, phal.

Frustrate, *v.* na-ummed karun, nirásh karun.

Fry, *v.* búzun.

Fuel, *n.* zun, zyun.

Full, *adj.* burut, labrez, berrit, traft, tráwa-tráwa.

Full (as to food), *adj.* yaḍ barit.

Funeral-pile, *n.* rázabal, áwarain, tsintabal, tsenta.

Furious, *adj.* díwána, múth, bowala, wanmath.

Furnace, *n.* gaj, náragaj.

Furniture, *n.* asbáb, sámagrí.

Furtively, *adv.* tsúrih, tsúré.

Future, *adj.* bonṭhum, yiwawun.

G.

Gain, *n.* myuts.

Gain, *v.* zenun, somráwun.

Gain a victory, *v.* póshun.

Gall, *n.* pyut.

Gall-bladder, *n.* tilapyut.

Gallows, *n.* koṭ.

Gamble, *v.* gindun, zár gindun.

Gambler, *n.* zãr, zãrí.

Gambling, *n.* zár.

Game (of hazard), *n.* zár.

Game, *n.* shikár.

Gamester, *n.* zãrí.

Garb, *n.* poshák.

Garden, *n.* poshibág, wãr, bág, dór.

Gardener, *n.* árum, bághbán, dándir, dándirain, bágwán.

Garden-plot, *n.* wãr, wãḍ.

Garland, *n.* poshan hund táj, mál.

Garlic, *n.* ruhun.

Garment, *n.* pheran.

Gate, *n.* darwáza, bar.

Gate-keeper, *n. m.* ḍíḍwoiù.

Gather (fruits and flowers), *v.* tsárun.

Gay, *adj.* khosh, prasand.

Gemini, *n.* Methum.

Generous, *adj.* ṭóṭ, bakhshanwol, dinawol.

Gentiana, *n.* jintyána, pakanbed.
Gentian, *n.* búí.
Gentle, *adj.* narmdil, wandakumal.
Gentleman, *n.* wóiń.
German, *adj.* sak.
Get, *v.* labun.
Get better (from some sickness), *v.* balun.
Ghee, *n.* ghyau.
Gift, *n.* bakhshá,ísh.
Gild, *v.* sŏn láwun.
Ginger, *n.* shónṭ.
Gipsywort, *n.* gandamgundú (Lycopus Europæus).
Girdle, *n.* kamarband, hul, ḍenṭon, lúngí.
Girl, *n.* shuri, korihan, komáryi, kúr, kanya.
Girth, *n.* tang.
Give, *v.* dyun, bakhshun.
Give birth to, *v.* zyun.
Give in charge, *v.* pushráwun.
Give, to cause to, *v.* dyáwun.
Giver, *n.* dinawol.
Glad, *adj.* khosh, prasand.
Gladness, *n.* forhat.
Glass (vessel), *n.* piyála, khós.
Gleet, *n.* tát.
Glen, *n.* nár.
Glory, *n.* prakásh.
Glove, *n.* gunús, korr.
Glue, *n.* máyí, átij.
Glutton, *n.* yiḍal, kháo, yiḍabáuḍ.
Gnat, *n.* moh.
Gnaw, *v.* tsápun.
Gnaw, to cause to, *v.* tsápanáwun.
Go, *v.* pakun, gatshun.
Go-between, *n.* manzimyór, manzimyāriń.
Go in, *v.* atsun.
Go, to make to, *v.* pakanáwun, wáyun.
Go out, *v.* nerun.
Go up, *v.* khasun.
Go wrong, *v.* ḍalun.
Goad, *n.* alabányi, alaphál, alabel, pyíhun.
Goat, *n.* tsáwúl, tsáwij.
Goat's flesh, *n.* tsáwil-máz.
God, *n.* khuda, Dáí, Bagwán, Narain, Shau.
God-chamber, *n.* ṭhokur-kuṭ.
Goitre, *n.* gaḍur.
Gold, *n.* sŏn.
Goldsmith, *n.* suniyár, sŏnar.
Gonorrhœa, *n.* tát.
Good, *adj.* ján, rút, zabar.
Good! *interj.* adz!
Goodness, *n.* rátsar.
Good fortune, *n.* fretsar.
Good-looking, *adj.* jánbut.
Goods, *n.* asbáb.
Goose, *n.* batij, batuk.
Gospel, *n.* injíl.
Grain, *n.* phaul, dána, galah.
Grain (bruised), *n.* dáchhul.
Grain (roasted), *n.* saut.
Granary, *n.* khal, gŏnyi, túda, ḍer.

Grandmother, *n.* nányí, ama, nányi.
Granulations (of a wound), *n.* ang.
Grape, *n.* dach.
Grasp, *v.* raṭun.
Grass, *n.* dyul, gása, dramun, kach, gháso.
Grass-cutter, *n.* ghãs.
Grass-shoes, *n.* púlahor.
Grateful, *adj.* shukr karawun.
Gratis, *adv.* muft, yithai, ithai, yanai.
Gratuitously, *adv.* muft, yithai.
Gratuity, *n.* bakhsháish.
Grave, *n.* kabar-wabar, gór.
Grave-clothes, *n.* kafan.
Grave-digger, *n.* goramal, malah, malakhosh.
Gravel (disease), *n.* kanyi-phalyi.
Grave-yard, *n.* mazár, malgu-zár.
Graze, *v.* gása khyun.
Great, *adj.* bāúd.
Great, to be, *v.* baḍun.
Greater, to become, *v.* hurun.
Greatness, *n.* bajar.
Grease, *n.* charab.
Green, *adj.* nyúl.
Greengrocer, *n.* árum.
Grey, *adj.* rúl.
Greyhound, *n.* tázihun.
Grief, *n.* gam, wadás, nálah, wŏsh.
Grief, to remove, *v.* gam kásun.
Grieve, *v.* gam barun, gam khyun.
Grieved, *adj.* dãdkóṭ, dãdlad.
Grind, *v.* pyuhun, guhun.
Grindstone, *n.* gralij kaiṅ.
Gripe, *n.* péch.
Grislea tomentosa, *n.* táwí, tháí.
Groan, *v.* hác karun.
Grocer, *n.* wóiṅ.
Groin, *n.* kaṭs.
Groom, *n.* mírakhŏr, sá,ís, ta-halyi, charbardár.
Gross, *adj.* vyut.
Ground, *n.* láganai, kalar, pathur.
Ground floor of a house, *n.* wauṭ.
Grow, *v.* bŏwun, khasun.
Gruel, *n.* kánz.
Guard, *v.* rátaráchí karinyi.
Guarding, *n.* rátaráchi.
Guess, *v.* menun.
Guest, *n.* póts, pauts.
Guide, *n.* wata háwúk, pesh-wá.
Gulf, *n.* áwalun.
Gum, *n.* samagh.
Gun, *n.* bandúk.
Gunpowder, *n.* shora.
Gunpowder maker, *n.* shora-gur.
Gut, *n.* andrun.
Gymnosporia spinosa, *n.* láp, patákí.
Gypsum, *n.* makol.

H.

Habit, *n.* khislat, hā̃l, bó, ádat, poshák.
Habitual, *adj.* militsár.
Hæmorrhoids, *n.* pŏṭ.
Hail, *n.* ḍóṭ, ḍóṭh.
Hair, *n.* wál, kísh, mast.
Hair, arrangement of, *n.* wáñ-kapan, tshóg.
Half, *adj.* oḍ.
Half a pound, *n.* páo.
Hallowed, *adj.* pawitar, pák.
Halt, *v.* rozun.
Halter, *n.* kamand, márúk, raj.
Ham, *n.* páz.
Ham (of leg), *n.* kúṭkáts.
Hammer, *n.* daukur.
Hand, to get the upper hand, *v.* póshun.
Handful, *n.* chrong, mŏṭh, gondur, lóv, gyiḍ, baud.
Handkerchief, *m.* daij.
Handle, *n.* dan.
Handle of plough, *n.* thap.
Handless, *adj.* raun.
Hang, *v.* álond tsunun, álont tsunun, álont karun, káṭhis ladun.
Hanged, to be, *v.* káṭhis pĕṭh ásun.
Happen, *v.* pyun.
Happy, to be, *v.* tsangun.
Harass, *v.* tulatál karinyi, talawúl karun.
Hard, *adj.* trakur, dur, durr.
Hardly, *adv.* kathinyisán.
Hare, *n.* khargosh, kharkan.
Harmony, *n.* maithri, militsár.
Harness, *n.* sámáná, sáz.
Harvest, *n.* khal, harúd.
Harvest-home, *n.* ankúṭ, jag.
Hash, to cause to, *v.* daganáwun.
Haste, *n.* tajíl, ṭakán.
Haste, to make, *v.* ṭakán karun.
Hasten, *v.* dorun, ṭakán karun.
Hastily, *adv.* ṭakán-ṭakán.
Hate, *v.* dushmani karinyi, shitrut karun.
Hatred, *n.* kínah, kín, dushmini, shitrut.
Haughtiness, *n.* kibar, takabúr.
Haunch bone, *n.* róṅk.
Have, *v.* tháwun.
Having pain, *adj.* dā̃dlad.
Having a bad smell, *adj.* phakalad.
Having a sore, *adj.* chhŏkalad.
Hawk, *n.* pā̃z.
Hay, *n. m.* gásuh.
He, *pron.* hú, sú, yih.
Head, *n.* kala, sher, hír, arbáb.
Head land, *n.* naih.
Headache, *n.* kalas-dód.
Head-dress, (woman's), *n.* zŏl, kasába.
Head-man, *n.* mokadam.
Heal, *v.* iláj karun.
Health, *n.* tandarusti, arir, sŏkhasán.
Healthiness, *n.* arir.

Healthy, *adj.* ur.
Heap, *n.* lam, ḍer, bana, ambár.
Hear, *v.* bozun.
Heart, *n.* dil, man, wãlinj, wálinj, wanda.
Hearth, *n.* tsol.
Heartless, *adj.* leḍ.
Heat, *n.* tatsar, sisar, nár.
Heat, *v.* tówarun, tatsaráwun táwun.
Heaven, *n.* ásmán, nab, ákásh, kham, súrug.
Heaviness, *n.* gŏbir.
Heavy, *adj.* gŏb, gaub.
Heavy, to be, *v.* gŏbun.
Hedge, *n.* paliyár, wár, wáḍ.
Heel, *n.* khúr.
Height, *n.* thazar.
Hell, *n.* naruk.
Help, *n.* chárah.
Helpless, *adj.* latsár.
Hem, *n.* dàúl.
Hen, *n.* kokir.
Hence, *adv.* yimi jáí nishi, yitih, yitih pĕṭhah.
Herd, *n.* gupun, khyul, jab.
Here, *adv.* yut, yutut, yiti, yitit, yiten.
Herein, *adv.* yat andar, yat manz.
Hermit, *n.* shúnt.
Heron, *n.* oṅkár, brág.
Herpes, *n.* harárat.
Hide, *v.* khaṭun, dubrun, tsipun.
Hideous, *adj.* yach.
High, *adj.* thaud, thŏd.
High, to be, *v.* thadun.
High-priced, *adj.* drŏg.
Highway, *n.* bádsháhí wat, maharáji wat.
Hill, *n.* koh, bál, pahár, sangur, parbat.
Himalayan Honeysuckle, *n.* títa baterí, pákhur (Lonicera quinquelocularis).
Himalayan Horse-chestnut, *n.* háne, hanúdún (Pavia Indica).
Himalayan Poplar, *n.* dúd phras, sulálí, bagnú, sufédar.
Hind, *n.* mínyimar.
Hindering, *n.* rŏk.
Hindu, *n.* Baṭah, Hyund.
Hindu female, *n.* Baṭaiṅ.
Hip, *n.* rónkh, mandul, tsakij.
Hither, *adv.* yutan, yúr, yutut (the final ut is equivalent to ko), yór, yúri.
Hitherto, *adv.* ungustaiṅ.
Hoar-frost, *n.* surah-dag, súr.
Hockey (on horse back), *n.* hálagogij.
Hold, *v.* raṭun.
Hold up, *v.* tulun.
Hole, *n.* gaud, gŏph, zud, khŏd, wál, gúd, tsiran.
Holla! *interj.* hatá, hato, haiyo, hatai, hata.
Hollow, *adj.* khókhur.
Honest, *adj.* rút, shónt.
Honey, *n.* máṅch.

Honey (in the comb), *n.* mánch-phar.
Honey bee, *n.* mánch-tilur.
Honour, *n.* óbré, izzat, aibro, yazat, mód.
Hoof, *n.* paḍur, nyúr.
Hook, *n.* náruts.
Hope, *n.* brãnt, ummed, ásha.
Hope, *v.* ummed tháwinyi, ásha tháwun.
Hopeful, *adj.* bránts, brãntwol.
Horn, *n.* hyáng, hyéng, heng.
Horse, *n.* gur.
Horse chestnut, *n.* hának dún.
Horseman, *n.* sawár.
Horse-shoe, *n.* nál.
Horse-shoer, *n.* nálband.
Horse-tail, *n.* matí (Equisetum debile).
Horse-whip, *n.* tázun.
Hostility, *n.* dushmaní, shitrut.
Hot, *adj.* tŏt, wushun, garm, zalawun.
Hot, to be, *v.* tatun.
Hot, to become, *v.* tatun.
Hot, to make red, *v.* tówarun, tatsaráwun, táwun.
Hot season, *n.* soṅt, Retakol.
Hour, *n.* gȧr.
House, *n.* lur, gar, larí, garah, lȧr, mar, nȧnz, lȧr-wȧr, garah-warah.
House, of the same, *adj.* ham-khánah.
House-carpenter, *n.* chhán.
Householder, *n.* garwol.
How? *adv.* kitha pãṭ, kyut?
How great, *adj.* kótah.
How many? *interrog. adj.* kátsah, kút.
How much, *adj.* kút.
Howl, *n.* banyul.
Howl, *v.* banyul karun.
Hump, *n.* lŏtur, kaub.
Hump-backed, *adj.* thar kaub.
Humped, to be, *v.* kŏbun.
Humility, *n.* hatsar.
Hundred, *adj.* hat.
Hundredth, *adj.* hȧtyum.
Hundred thousand, *adj.* lachh.
Hunger, *n.* bóchí, khyŏda, bŏchah, bŏchhar.
Hungry, *adj.* bochahut, khy-odaihut, bŏch.
Hunt, *v.* shikár karun.
Hunter, *n.* shikárí, sayyád.
Hunting, *n.* shikár.
Hurry, *n.* khalbali.
Hurt, *v.* zarar karun.
Husband, *n.* rún, kháwind, lára, rúm, rún, barthá.
Hut, *n.* mar.
Hyena, *n.* yachh, dimbashãj.
Hydrargyrum, *n. m.* párádu.
Hypochondrium, *n.* wacha-kányi.

I.

I, *pron.* bŏh.
Ibex, *n.* kail.
Ice, *n.* yakh, tȧla katur, kham-birri.

Icicle, *n.* shishirgánṭ.
Idiot, *n.* chór, chãr.
Idle, *adj.* bekár, kámirust.
Idol, *n.* pótul.
If, *conj.* ai, áí, yud, yudwanai, yudwai.
If not (nahin to), *adv.* nai.
Ignoble, *adj.* nyuk.
Ignorant, *adj.* bekal.
Ileum, *n.* rónk.
Ill, *adj.* bemár, dádlad.
Illuminate, *v.* prazaláwun.
Illumination, *n.* zúl.
Illustrious, *adj.* neknáo.
Ill-will, *n.* rish.
Image, *n.* súrat, shakl, rúp potul, ṭhókur.
Imagine, *v.* vetṣár karun.
Immediately, *adv.* wúin.
Immortal, *adj.* mótaveráí.
Impassable, *adj.* watirust.
Impostor, *n.* híla karanwol.
Impotant man, *n.* lánts.
Imprison, *v.* kaid tháwun, kaid karun.
Impropriety, *n.* nang.
Improve, *v.* zabar gatshun.
In, *prep.* manz, andar.
In the afternoon, *adv.* péshnas.
In the day time, *adv.* dŏhas.
In the evening, *adv.* shámas, shaman.
In the least, *adv.* yakrah.
In this manner, *adv.* yitai pãṭ, yithah pãṭ.
In that manner, *adv.* tithah pãṭ.
In the morning, *adv.* subhas, subhan.
In the presence of, *adj.* bronta kanyi.
Incendiary, *n.* nár tráwawun.
Increase, *n.* hurir, tsarir.
Increase, *v.* baḍun, hurun baḍráwun, hurávwun, nauráwun, veṭhun, hurrun, veṭharáwun, hurráwun.
Incurable, *adj.* ilájarust.
Indeclinable, *adj.* byun.
India, *n.* Hindustán.
Indian corn, *n.* makãi.
Indian hemp, *n.* bangí (Cannabis sativa).
Indigofera Heterantha, *n.* kuts.
Individual, *n.* mohanyú.
Industrious, *adj.* kámikár.
Infancy, *n.* lŏkatsar.
Infant, *n.* nechú, báluk, shur.
Infidel, *n.* káfir, bedín.
Inform, *v.* báwun.
Information, *n.* shich.
Informer, *n.* khabar karanwol, harkára, ḍúmb.
Ingenious, *adj.* truk.
Inhabitant, *n.* basawun, basanwol.
Injure, *v.* nuksán karun.
Injury, *n.* nuksán.
Ink, *n.* mil.
Ink-maker, *n.* miligur.
Inn, *n.* saráí, watalar, vatalur, dharamsál.
Inner, *adj.* andrum.

Inquire, *v.* pritsun, gárun.
Inquiry, *n.* prutsagár.
Insect, *n.* kyum, krel, kíth.
Insensible, *adj.* beján, zúrust.
Inside, *prep.* & *adv.* andar.
Instantly, *adv.* ṭakán.
Instead, *prep.* badal, adal badal.
Instep, *n.* chóp, khór.
Instruction, *n.* tãlím.
Insult, *v. t.* lánatána karun, leka dinyi.
Intelligent, *adj.* gáṭul, truk.
Intention, *n.* yetsa.
Interest, *n.* súd, bí,áz, láb, faida, súd.
Intercede, *v. i.* zárpár karun.
Intercession, *n.* zárpár.
Intercourse, *n.* hãl.
Interference, *n.* khalala.
Internal, *adj.* andrum.
Interpret, *v.* tarjuma karun.
Interpreter, *n.* tarjuma karanwol.
Interruption, *n.* gángal.
Interview, *n.* wasl.
Intestine, *n.* andram.
Intoxicated, *adj.* saniyás.
Intoxication, *n.* ṭĕṭ, mad.
Intricate, *adj.* hulhul.
Inundation, *n.* yúp, sailáb.
Invitation, *n.* duda, sál.
Inwards, *adv.* andar kun.
Ipomœa cœrulea, *n.* káládána, ishpecha.
Iris pseudacorus, *n.* ímarjol, marjal, kríshún.
Iris Florentina, *n.* ersa.
Iris Nepalensis, *n.* sosan.
Iron, *n.* shistar.
Iron (washerman's dressing-iron), *n.* kunḍh.
Is, *v.* chhu, chhih.
Island, *n.* ṭóp, dém.
Italian Poplar, *n.* phrast (Populus nigra).
Itch, *n.* kashan.
Itch, to have the, *v.* kashan yun.
Ivory, *n*, dáṅṭ.
Ivy, *n.* karmora, mandiá (Hedera Helix).

J.

Jackal, *n.* shál, sháj.
Jail, *n.* bándiván.
Jailer, *n.* tsról.
January, *n.* Mág.
Jar, *n.* lŏpun, naut.
Jasmine, *n.* hí, hí ásmán.
Jasminum grandiflorum, *n.* chamba.
Jasminum officinale and revolutum, *n.* chamba.
Jaw, *n.* tárkhanḍ, múganḍ.
Jealous, *adj.* wŏppar.
Jest, *n.* ṭhaṭha, gap, tasna.
Jest, *v.* gelun.
Jew, *n.* Jahúdí.
Jhelum water, *n.* Veṭhawóiṅ. (the wóin is manifestly for póiṅ).
Jhelum, *n. m.* Vyĕt.
John, *n.* Yahyá.

Join, *v.* miláwun.
Joint (of body), *n.* band.
Joke, *v.* gelun.
Jolting, *n.* yal, daka.
Journey, *n.* safar, wath, pethun.
Joy, *n.* prasandatáí.
Jug, *n.* naut.
Juglans regia, *n.* dún, akrot.
Juice, *n.* ras.
Jujube, *n.* brayí, brayikuj.
Jujube-tree, *n.* brayikul.
July, *n.* Shráwun or Sáwun.
June, *n.* Hár.
Jupiter (planet), *n.* Brahaspat, Góró.
Justice, *n.* insáf, ár.

K.

Kashmírí (the language of Kashmir), *n.* Kãshur, Káshir zeo.
Kashmírí (native of Kashmir), *n.* Kãshur, Kaushur, Káshir.
Kashmir, *n.* Kashmír, Kashír.
Keep silence, *v. i.* tshŏpah karinyi.
Keep together, *v.* lalawun.
Keeper of a brothel, *n.* gán.
Keeper of Hindu temple, *n.* resh.
Kennel, *n.* húiǹ tabela, hŏnyin hunz jáí, hŏnyiǹ hund gara.
Kernel, *n.* kod, mĕs, gúlyi.
Key, *n.* kúnz.
Khilta, *n.* kranda.
Kick, *n.* lath.
Kid, *n.* memna, memní, tsáwiji-mongúr, tsáwiji-mongir.
Kidney, *n.* bŏkawat.
Kill, *v.* márun.
Killed, *adj.* márah.
Kiln, *n.* kónda.
Kind, *adj.* narmdil, wandanarm, mana-kumul, mihrbán, diya karanwol.
Kindle, *v.* zálun.
Kindness, *n.* mihrbáni, daiya, yihsán, ratsar.
King, *n.* pádshah, ráza, shah.
Kingdom, *n.* rázasi, pádshãhí.
Kinsman, *n. m.* áshnáo.
Kiss, *n.* myút, monyi.
Kiss, *v.* myúth karun, monyi karun.
Kitchen, *n.* sulahar.
Kite, gáňth.
Knead, *v.* mándun, ádarun, adaráwun, mandun.
Knee, *n.* kuth, kóth.
Kneel, *v.* kóth tráwun.
Knee-pan, *n.* kútanyit.
Knife, *n.* shrák.
Knot, *n.* gand.
Know, *v.* zánun, parzun.
Known, *adj.* mólum.
Knowledge, *n.* khabar, zán.

L.

Labour, *n.* mihnat, kom, kót.
Labourer, *n.* mazúr.
Labourer's work, *n.* mazúri.
Lactuca Sativa, *n.* kahú.

Ladák merchant, *n.* boṭa-wányi.
Ladák-stone, *n.* lotakí.
Ladder, *n.* her.
Ladle, *n.* chonchih, kràts.
Lake, *n.* sar, már, dal.
Lake water, *n.* mãrwóin.
Lamb, *n.* chirrakat, chirr.
Lame, *adj.* laung.
Lamentation, *n.* wahwaila.
Lamenting, *adj.* wadawun.
Lamp, *n.* sóng, tsóng, díp, saiyat, set.
Lamp-stand, *n.* zúr.
Lancet, *n.* ṭŏp.
Land, *n.* zamin, butarát.
Landing, *n.* bránḍ.
Landing-place (on river or lake), *n.* yárbal, gáṭh.
Lantern, *n.* mashil.
Lapidary, *n.* manar.
Lapis Lazuli, *n.* lájavard.
Lapwing, *n.* satatút.
Larder, *n.* bánakuṭ.
Large, *adj.* bàuḍ.
Large, *v.* baḍun.
Largeness, *n.* bújir.
Lasso, *n.* maryuk.
Last, *adj.* patyum.
Last, at, *adv.* ákhir, pato-lákan.
Last year, *adv.* parus, and prãryus.
Last year's, *adj.* prór (a rural use of the word).
Lateness, *n.* tser.
Laugh, *v.* asun.
Laugh, to make to, *v.* asaná-wun.
Lawful, *adj.* ádal.
Lawsonia inermis, *n.* hená.
Lay hold of, *v.* raṭun.
Lay low, *v.* páwun.
Lazy, *adj.* áluts, dul, sút.
Lead, *n.* nág.
Leader, *n.* peshwá.
Leaf, *n.* pan, bãrag, páthar, wàthar, patar.
Lean, *adj.* nyuk, tun.
Lean, *v.* namun.
Leanness, *n.* nichar.
Leap, *n.* wŏth.
Leap, *v.* wŏṭ láyinyi.
Learn, *v.* hĕchhun, málum sa-panun.
Learn, to cause to, *v.* hechhi-náwun.
Learned, *adj.* gáṭul.
Learning, *n.* tãlim.
Leave, *v.* tráwun.
Leave off, *v.* tráwun.
Leave off, to make to, *v.* tráwa-náwun.
Leaven, *n.* ãtij.
Leech, *n.* drik, darak.
Leech-applier, *n.* dàrkawól, drikagur, gágar.
Leechman, *n.* gágar.
Leek, *n.* gauḍa prán.
Left, *adj.* khowur, kháwur.
Left, to be, *v.* rózun.
Leg, *n.* nal, groz, zang, gŏḍ.

Legal, *adj*. shrúts, halál.
Leisure, *n*. mokajár, sŏk, ánand.
Lend, *v*. wazun, wazum dyun.
Length, *n*. zĕchhar.
Lentil, *n*. masur.
Leo (zodiac sign), *n*. Sihim.
Leopard, *n*. techihór suh.
Leper, *n*. hittarilad.
Leprous, *adj*. myúnd.
Leprosy, *n*. myund, hittar.
Less, *adj*. kam.
Lesson, *n*. lúṭ.
Let fall, *v*. hárun.
Let go, *v*. tráwun.
Let go hold of, *v*. tráwun.
Let off, *v*. tráwun.
Let off, to make to, *v*. *t*. tráwanáwun.
Letter, *n*. harf, achhar, ruk.
Letter-carrier, *n*. dákawol, harkárá, kãsid.
Leucas cephalotis and aspera, *n*. phúman.
Level, *adj*. hyú, som, barobar, suttur.
Liar, *n*. apoziyòr, apoz wananwol.
Liber (of birch), *n*. Burza, Bojpatar.
Liberate, *v*. *t*. tráwun, mokaláwun.
Libra (zodiac sign), *n*. Trakur.
Lick (as a dog), *v*. lĕwun.
Lie, *n*. apoz, assat, durog.
Lie, to (tell lies), *v*. apoz wanun, apoz dapun.
Lie, *v*. shongun.
Lie down, *v*. shŏngun.
Lie with (a man with a woman), *v*. *i*. sombráwun.
Life, *n*. umr, wãñs, zindagi, hyátí, zú, ján.
Life time, *n*. umr, wens.
Lift, *v*. tulun.
Lift, to cause to, *v*. tulanáwun.
Light (flame), *n*. nár, agan, gãsh, prakásh, gásh, núr.
Light, *adj*. lot, lauts, láñṭ, gáshdár.
Light, to be, *v*. lŏtun.
Lighten, *v*. roshan karun.
Lightning, *n*. wúzmal, uzmal.
Ligularia, *n*. poshkar.
Like, *adj*. hyú, barobar.
Lilac, *n*. hí-ásmán.
Lily, *n*. sosan.
Lime, *n*. chúnah, gach.
Line, *n*. rik.
Linseed, *n*. alish, (Linum usitatissimum).
Linseed oil, *n*. alsi, katán ké,úm.
Linum usitatissimum, *n*. alish (linseed).
Lion, *n*. suh, pádir suh.
Lioness, *n*. síming, semin.
Lip, *n*. wuṭ, wuṭh.
Listen, *v*. bozun, kan dyun, káwah dyun.
Literally, *adv*. harfa pat harfa, achhra pat achhra.

Little, *adv.* kam kam, hana, han-wan.
Little, *adj.* tsút, tsauṭ.
Little, to be, *v.* lŏkun.
Little, very, *adv.* ratsah ratsah.
Littleness, *n.* lŏkachár, lŏkatsár.
Little finger, *n.* kis.
Little toe, *n.* kis.
Litter, *n.* dúl.
Live, *v.* lasun.
Liver, *n.* shishanor, khrenamáz, krehnamáz.
Liver stone, *n.* ratel.
Lizard, *n.* kekalaṭ.
Load, *n.* bór, bár.
Load, *v.* ladun, bor tulun.
Load a gun, *v.* top taiyár karun.
Loaf, *n.* tsŏṭ.
Loan, *n.* wazum.
Lock of hair, *m.* kokul, zulaf, ṭŏp, paṭyiní, kíhh, kúluph, tsog, shákhá.
Lock, *v.* kúluph karun, kúluph dyun.
Locust, *n.* hálau.
Log, *n.* múnd, kundá, gan.
Loin (of human body), *n.* haul, kamar, kányilar.
Long, *adj.* zyúṭ, zyúṭh, zuth.
Long, to be, *v.* zethun.
Long for, *v.* yatsun.
Longing, *n.* tamanná.
Lonicera quinquelocularis, *n.* títa baterí, pákhur, (Himalayan Honeysuckle).
Look, *n.* darshun.
Look, *v.* wuchhun.
Looking-glass, *n.* shíshí, áná.
Loose, *adj.* wusuṭ, kusháda.
Loose hair, *n.* kih, zaṭ.
Loranthus longiflorus, *n.* pand.
Lord, *n.* záza, pádshah, mālik, arbáb.
Lose, *v.* ráwarun, hárun.
Loss *n.* chhonyer, nuksán
Lost, to be, *v.* ráwun.
Lotus, *n.* pamposh.
Louse, *n.* zauv.
Louse's egg, *n.* lichh.
Love, *n.* lól, shank, ishk, mail, zauk, táchhar, sré, táchir, ashk.
Love, belonging to, *adj.* ishkun.
Loved, *adj.* ṭóṭ.
Lover, *n.* madanwár, áshak.
Low, *adj.* tshuṭ.
Low, to be, *v.* tshuṭun.
Lower, *adj.* talyum.
Lower extremity, *n.* lang, zang.
Lowing (of cattle), *n.* ṭáng.
Lucky, *adj.* bakhtáwár, ḍekabáuḍ.
Luggage, *n.* asbáb.
Luke warm, *adj.* sŏkhabŏl, sokhabaul, sokhawushun, ním garm.
Lumbricoidis, *n.* ám.
Luncheon, *n.* kój, mimuz.
Lung, *n.* shúshanor, shúsh, shushnór, shásh.

Lustre, *n.* tajallí.
Lycopus Europæus, *n.* gandamgúndú (Gipsywort).
Lying, *n.* shruk.

M.

Mad, *adj.* mŏt, dewánah, màúṭ.
Madder, *n.* manjit, majíth, rodang, dandú, phaharghás (Rubia cordifolia).
Made, *v.* banun.
Made, to cause to be, *v.* banáwanáwun.
Madman, *n.* maut, wanmat, matil, janún.
Magazine, *n.* ḍer.
Magistrate, *n. m.* peshkár, zyúṭ.
Magnificent, *adj.* ṭóṭ.
Mahalladár, *n.* tsról.
Maiden hair fern, *n.* dumtúlí (Adiantum capillus Veneris).
Maidservant, *n.* chúnz.
Maintain (as a family), *v.* rachhun.
Maintenance, *n.* rachhit.
Maize, *n.* makãí.
Majesty, *n.* hazrat.
Make, *v.* banáwun, karun, garun, párun.
Make, to cause to, *v.* karanáwun.
Make clean by sweeping, *v.* dúwun.
Make ready food, *v.* ranun.
Malacochæte pectinata, *n.* búd.
Male, *adj.* nar.
Malice, *n.* matbal.
Malleolus, *n.* gŏḍ, tsanun.
Mallows, *n.* sŏtsal.
Mamma, *n.* bab.
Man, *n.* mohanyụ, insán, zŏn.
Mango-bird, *n.* poshnúl.
Manifest, *adj.* drashṭánṭ.
Manly, *adj.* mardána, durr.
Manner, *n.* pãṭ.
Manufacturer, *n.* kárkhándár.
Manure, *n.* pah, guh.
Many, *adj.* seṭha.
Many times, *adv.* seṭhah laṭi, seṭhah phiri.
Map, *n.* naksha.
Maple, *n.* tílpatar, kílpatar, kanur (Acer).
Mar, *v.* ḍálun.
Marble, *n.* nílawaṭ.
March (month), *n.* Tsithar.
Mare, *n.* guir, guḍ.
Margin, *n.* bŏt.
Marigold, *n.* japhiri.
Mark, *n.* neb, nishán.
Mark on forehead of Hindu, *n.* ṭyuk.
Mark (small pox), *n.* ákh.
Market, *n.* bázar.
Marlea begonifolia, *n.* prót, siálú.
Marmot, *n.* drin.
Marriage, *n.* khándar, nyethar, veva, lagan, niká.
Married couple, *n.* bãts.
Marrow, *n.* was.
Marry, *v.* nyethar karun, veva karun, khándar karun.
Mars, *n.* Bóm, Mangal.
Marsilea quadrifolia, *n.* paphlú.

Mason, *n.* dosil.
Mason's wife, *n.* dosil-báí.
Master, *n.* ágah, garawol.
Masticate, *v.* tsápun.
Mastoid process (of ear), *n.* kanagogul.
Mat, *n.* wagú.
Mat (cover of a boat), *n.* shirwans, pash.
Matmaker *n.* wagívgur, wagívwonanwol.
Matter (purulent), *n.* pák.
Matting (chaṭáí), *n.* wagú, patij, trhas.
Matricaria chamomella, *n.* bábúnah?
Mat-weaver, *n.* wagívgur, wagívwonanwol.
May, *n. m.* zéṭh.
Meadow, *n.* nyúr.
Mean, *adj.* nyuk.
Meaning, *n.* mutlab, mání, arat.
Measure, *n.* wazan, tul, míṅts.
Measure, *v.* menun (nápná), myun.
Measuring chain, *n.* menanháṅkal.
Meat (flesh), *n.* máz, syun, ninyi, náṭa, mámas, pápadráo.
Meatus auditorious externus, *n.* kanagogul.
Medicine, *n.* dawa, shír, aushad.
Meditation, *n.* vetsár.
Meet, *v.* melun, samun, samakhun.
Meet together, *v.* samun.
Meeting, *n.* anjuman, wasl, mulákát.
Melissa nepeta, *n.* gandal, baibarang katai, banraihán.
Melon, *n.* kharbúz, hindavyend.
Melon-plant, *n.* kharbuzkul, hindavyendakul.
Melt, *v.* galun, gálun, kamalun.
Mend, *v.* sherun, sambálun.
Mender, *n.* róp-karanwol, rafúgar, róp-karawun.
Mending, *n.* róp.
Mentha incana and Royleano, *n.* vien, tarámusha.
Mentha viridis, *n.* púdína.
Merchandize, *n.* sauda.
Merchant, *n.* sódágar, bãpãrí.
Merciful, *adj.* áraburut.
Merciless, *adj.* beár.
Mercury (planet), *n.* Bŏd.
Mercury, *n.* párúd, símáb, párádu.
Mercy, *n.* ár, rahmat, shób.
Merry, *adj.* khush, shád, prasand.
Message, *n.* shĕch.
Messenger, *n.* kãsid, shĕch anawun.
Meteorite, *n.* traṭ.
Method, *n.* wat.
Midday, *n.* dopáhar, mandinyi.
Middle, *n.* aḍ.

Midnight, *n.* aḍ rát, ardah rát.
Midwife, *n.* wáryin.
Mihtar, *n. m.* wátúl.
Milk, *n.* dód.
Milk, *v.* dóyun.
Milkman, *n.* gúr.
Milk-seller, *n.* gúr.
Mill, *n.* graṭṭa.
Miller, *n.* kraṭṭawol.
Millet, *n.* shól (kangní), chinwa, píngí, shálí.
Millet-seed, *n.* pinga.
Mimosa rubicaulis, *n.* rál, riaul.
Minaret, *n.* kuṭhar, thong.
Mince, *v.* tseṭun.
Mine, *adj.* myon.
Mine, *n.* kán.
Minister, *n.* wazír.
Minstrel (wandering), *n.* bánḍ.
Mint, *n.* púdinah.
Mirror, *n.* ãna.
Miser, *n.* shúm, shúmir, lóbishṭ, lóbí.
Miserable, *adj.* dádalad, rógí.
Misfortune, *n.* baláe.
Mislead, *v.* watiráwarun, matsarawun, dalaráwun.
Mistletoe, *n.* wahal, ahalú (viscum album).
Mist, *n.* wunar, bahá, bakhár.
Mistake, *n.* mashrab, búl.
Mix, *v.* áḍráwun, áḍrun, milanáwun, melun.
Mode, *n.* pãṭ.
Model, *n.* rasm.
Modest, *adj.* sharminda.
Modesty, *n.* haiya, mandach.
Moist, *adj.* odurr, sirhúl, ŏdur.
Molasses, *n.* gór.
Mole (animal), *n.* anamur.
Moment, *n.* sát, viz.
Monday, *n.* Súmwár, Tsandrawár.
Money, *n.* pãṅsah, dayár, danna.
Monkey, *n.* ponz, wándur, pun.
Month, *n.* mah, rĕt, máṅs.
Months old (of so many), *adj.* móṅs.
Moon, *n.* zún, mahtáb, tsandar, sandramma.
Moonshine, *n.* prágásh.
Moor, *v.* bãli tháwun.
More, *adv.* yits, tsaur, yat, beyih.
Morel, *n.* kánakach, kangach (Morchella semilibera).
Moreover, *conj.* yúduwane.
Morning, *n.* subah, prabát, subhán.
Morsel, *n.* lŏkhar, myúnd, grás.
Mortar, *n.* wŏkhul, wokhij, káṅs, kúndí.
Mortgage, *n.* band.
Mosque, *n.* mashíd, masjid.
Moth, *n.* pŏpur, pómpur, panapómpur, parwána, pámpúr, patang.
Mother, *n.* mój, mãj, dĕd, máta.
Mother-in-law, *n.* hash.
Mount, *v.* khasun.

Mount, to cause to (charháná), *v. t.* khárun.
Mount a horse, *v.* guris khasun.
Mountainous region, *n.* kŏhistán.
Mounted, *adj.* jäür.
Mourn, *v.* wadun, réwun.
Mouse, *n.* khríñts, khráñts, gagur.
Moustache, *n.* góñts.
Mouth, *n.* ãs, chónṭ, dahan.
Mouthful, *n.* myúnd, lŏkhar.
Much, *adv.* seṭha, yats, tsaur.
Mucus (nasal), *n.* khain.
Mud, *n.* rab.
Mulberry, *n.* tút.
Mulberry-tree, *n.* tulakul.
Mule, *n.* káṭur, káṭir.
Murder, *n.* már.
Mushroom, *n.* mánskhel (agaricus campestris), kanaguch, heḍir.
Music, *n.* sóz, sor, gyauwun.
Musician, *n.* sázandar, gyauwanwol, bánṭ, bánḍ.
Musk, *n.* mushak.
Musk-deer, *n.* rus, ruskaṭ.
Musket, *n.* bandúk.
Musk-rat, *n.* anagagur.
Musquito, *n.* moh, múh.
Mussulman, *n.* Masalmán, Malíts.
Mustard, *n.* sandij, ásúr.
Mite, *adj.* kaul.
Mutton, *n.* kaṭamáz, madsnáṭa, ninyi, mámas, pápadráo.
My, *adj.* myón.
Myricaria Germanica, *n.* Shálakát.
Myriogyne minuta, *n.* nakchikni.
Myrsine Africana, *n.* baibarang, baring.
Mystery, *n.* sir.

N.

Nail, *n.* kyul, nam.
Naked, *adj.* nethanun, nanga.
Name, *n.* náo.
Name, *v.* náo karinyi.
Narcissus, *n.* yimbarzal.
Narcissus, *n.* tazetta, *n.* nargis.
Nardostachys jatamansi, *n.* bálchir, jatamásí.
Narrow, *adj.* tang.
Narthex Assafœtidiæ, *n.* híng, Angúza.
Native of Kashmir, *n.* kãshur, kãshir.
Navel, *n.* túñ, nabistán, tun, náfah.
Near, *prep.* nakha, nish.
Near, *adj.* nízík, nízik.
Near, *adv.* nishi, nyúr, lyúṭ.
Necessary, *adj.* zimah.
Necessity, *n.* wutsai.
Neck, *n.* kãr, gardan.
Necklace, *n.* tasbí, mál, ságalar, kãnṭh ṭruṭ, kauṭmál.
Needle, *n.* sitsan.
Negligent, *adj.* muḍah.

Negro, *n.* habshí.
Neigh, *n.* hin.
Neigh, *v.* hin dinyi, hin karinyi.
Neighbour, *n.* hamsáyih.
Neighbourhood, *n.* vehatir.
Neighing, *n.* hiṅg.
Neither, *conj.* nah.
Neither—nor, *conj.* nah—nah.
Nelumbium speciosum, *n.* pamposh (the Lotus).
Nepeta ruderalis, *n.* badranjboya.
Nephew, *n.* bápathir, benathir.
Nest, *n.* ól.
Net, *n.* zál.
Nettle (common), *n.* só,e.
Nettle-rash, *n.* thŏt.
Never, *adv.* mulai—nah, zohnah.
Nevertheless, *conj.* tilih tih, walí.
New, *adj.* nú.
New, to be, *v.* nauwun.
News, *n.* shĕch, khabar.
Newness, *n.* navir.
News-writer, *n.* harkára.
Next, *adj.* dúiyum.
Next year, *adv.* bonṭhus.
Nicotiana tabacum, *n.* tabákú.
Niece, *n.* báwazah, binzah, báwaz.
Night, *n.* rát. By night, rátas.
Night, at, *adv.* Rát kyut.
Night after night, *adv.* rãts pat rãts.
Nightingale, *n.* bulbul, bilbichhur, kastúr. These are different species.
Nightly, *adv.* rãts pat rãts.
Nimia quassides, *n.* baringí.
Nine, *adj.* nau, nauṅ.
Nineteen, *adj.* kunawuh.
Nineteenth, *adj.* kunawuhyum.
Ninetieth, *adj.* namatyum.
Ninety, *adj.* namat.
Ninety-eight, *adj.* aranamat.
Ninety-eighth, *adj.* aranamatyum.
Ninety-fifth, *adj.* pántsanamatyum.
Ninety-first, *adj.* akanamatyum.
Ninety-five, *adj.* pántsanamat.
Ninety-four, *adj.* tsunamat.
Ninety-fourth, *adj.* tsunamatyum.
Ninety-nine, *adj.* namanamat.
Ninety-ninth, *adj.* namanamatyum.
Ninety-one, *adj.* akanamat.
Ninety-second, *adj.* dunamatyum.
Ninety-seven, *adj.* satanamat.
Ninety-seventh, *adj.* satanamatyum.
Ninety-six, *adj.* shinamat.
Ninety-sixth, *adj.* shinamatyum.
Ninety-third, *adj.* trànamatyum.
Ninety-three, *adj.* trànamat.

Ninety-two, *adj.* donamat.
Ninth, *adj.* navyum and nauṅyum.
Nipple, *n.* pistán, bab, tana, babiṭunḍ.
No, *adv.* nah.
Noble, *adj.* buzurg, báuḍ, asíl.
Noble, *n.* wóiṅ.
Nod, *v.* namun.
Nod, to make to, *v. t.* numráwun.
Noise, *n.* krak, krek, nád, ṭhas, tútú.
Noise, to make a, *v.* krak túlinyi.
Noon, *n.* dopáhar, mandinyi, dopahar, mimiz.
North, *n.* wŏtur, shimál, dachun.
Nose, *n.* nast.
Nostril, *n.* nakawár.
Not, *adv.* nah, mah.
Not at all, *adv.* kihn nah.
Notice, *n.* shĕch, khabar.
Nourish, *v.* rachhun.
Now, *adv.* wúiṅ, wúinkin, wúiṅkinas, wunyi.
Now and then, *adv.* yili tili.
Nowhere, *adv.* kunyinah.
November, *n.* Monjhór, Magar, Ramzán.
Nuisance, *n.* yiza, dŏk, pída.
Number, *n.* grand.
Number, *v.* ganzarun, grand karinyi.
Nurse, *n.* dáe.
Nut, *n.* pír, gŏlúr, kand, pambach.
Nut-case, *n.* pambalokhir.
Nymphæa alba, *n.* brímposh (Water Lily).

O.

Oak, *n.* baráin (Quercus dilatata).
Oar, *n.* khúr.
Oath, *n.* drí, kasam, drayí.
Oats, *n.* wushka.
Obedient, *adj.* hukm tulanwol.
Obey, *v.* amal karun, mánun.
Oblique, *adj.* hul.
Obliterate, *v.* naháwun.
Obscure, *adj.* khaṭit.
Obtain, *v.* labun.
Occupied, *adj.* mushghúl.
October, *n.* Kártik, Katak.
Ocymum pilosum, *n.* raihán.
Of, *prep.* sund, etc.
Offend, *v.* malúl karun.
Oh! *interj.* afsos, vái, wosh.
Oil, *n.* tíl, til.
Oil-expresser, *n.* tilawóiṅ.
Oilman, *n.* wóiṅ.
Old, *adj.* prón, búḍ.
Old, *v.* buḍun, prón sapanun.
Old-age, *n.* bújar.
Old man, *n.* buḍa, vrad, zirin, búḍ, búḍa.
Olive, *n.* zaitun.
Omen, *n.* fál.
On, *prep.* peṭh.

Once, *adv.* aki laṭi, aki phiri.
One, *adj.* ak.
One-and-a-half, *adj.* ḍŏḍ.
One-and-a-quarter, *adj.* swád.
One even, ak tih.
One-eyed, *adj.* kón.
One o'clock, *adv.* peshan, peshnan.
One's self, *pron.* pán.
Onion, *n.* prán.
Only, *adv.* yót, ót.
Only, *adj.* kun, kunuí.
Onosma macrocephala, *n.* gáoza, bán.
Onyx, *n.* sulaimání.
Ooze, *v.* pashpun.
Opal, *n.* gursí.
Open, *adj.* khaul.
Open, *v.* mutsaráwun, wáharun, mutsarun.
Open, to cause to, *v.* mutsaranáwun.
Open to receive, *v.* dárun.
Opened, *v.* khulun.
Opening, *n.* khŏd, khajar.
Ophelia chireta, *n.* chiraita.
Ophthalmia, *n.* trŏsher, trápajár, trŏshur.
Opinion, *n.* mashwár, áphín, taryiák.
Opportunity, *n.* dáó, fursat, aginya, mokajár.
Oppose, *v.* shetaráz karinyi, dushmaní karinyi.
Oppress, *v. t.* zulm karun.
Or, *conj.* natah, ya, yátai.
Orange, *n.* nárang.
Order, *n.* yel.
Order, to set in, *v.* sherun, sambálun.
Ordure, *n.* gas, lĕd, guh, mengin, rĕkh.
Oreoseris lánuginosa, *n.* kho.
Origanum vulgare, *n.* marzanjosh.
Ornament, *v.* perun.
Ornaments, *n.* gehna, manárí.
Oryza sativa, *n.* dain, táni.
Ostensibly, *adv.* záhir pãṭ.
Ostentation, *n.* ṭeng, ṭimṭám.
Otherwise, *conj.* hargah nah (nahin to).
Otter, *n.* ndur.
Outer, *adj.* nebrum.
Outside, *adv.* nebar.
Outwards, *adv.* nebar kun.
Oven, *n.* dán, gaj.
Over, *prep.* ápor.
Overcoming, *adj.* zoráwar.
Owe, *v.* wazum tháwun.
Owl, *n.* rátamogul.
Own, *adj.* panun.
Ox, *n.* dánd, hakhúr.

P.

Pace, *n.* púr.
Paddle, *n.* khúr.
Padlock, *n. m.* kuluf.
Page, *n.* waruk.
Pain, *n.* dŏkh, dag, dód.
Painful, *v.* dód karun.

Paint, *v.* naksh karun.
Painter, *n.* nakkásh, muritsgar.
Pair, *n.* jórah.
Paise, *n.* pãüsah.
Palace, *n.* ḍab, dewán-khána, darshangah.
Palate, *n.* tál.
Palm-tree, *n.* khazir.
Palpitate, *v.* see 'Tremble.'
Pan, *n.* táo, kráí.
Panicum Italicum, *n.* shálí, píngí,
Panicum miliaceum, *n.* chínãü, arzán, rang-ghás, chinwa.
Panther, *n.* trúüts.
Pap, *n.* bab.
Paper, *n.* kágaz, shŏkshŏk.
Paper-maker, *n.* kágazgar.
Papier-maché, *n.* nakkãshí.
Papier-maché maker, *n.* nakkásh.
Papier-maché-work, *n.* nakkãshi.
Paradise, *n.* sorag.
Paralysis Agitans, *n.* Naṭh or Wenaṭh.
Pare, *v.* see 'Shave.'
Parents, *n.* mólmój.
Parmelia chamchadalis, *n.* chailchalíra.
Parrot, *n.* tota, shoga.
Part, *n.* chhal, tilyụn, ṭukar, hissa, bóg.
Partiality, *n.* wãnts.
Partition, *n.* parda, ṭhúr.
Partner, *n.* sharík.

Partridge, *n.* títar, rakú.
Pashmina-broker, *n.* makáim.
Pass (mountain), *n.* thúng, túng.
Pass (of time), *v.* gatshun, guzráwun.
Passing wind (backwards), *n.* sis.
Passionateness, *n.* tsak.
Pass over, *v.* tarun.
Path, *n.* wat.
Patella, *n.* kúṭanyiṭ.
Patience, *n.* sabr, santush, tséḍa, tsĕḍ.
Patient, *adj.* sabr karanwol, santushí.
Patient, *v.* tsĕḍ karinyi.
Paṭṭú, *n.* munul, pauṭ, loch.
Pavia Indica, *n.* háne, hanúdún (Himalayan horse-chesnut).
Pay, *n.* reta.
Pay, *v.* hórun, nakha wálun.
Peace, *n.* sala, sŏkh.
Peach, *n.* súnú, tsúnú, tsunun.
Peacock, *n.* mor.
Pear, *n.* ṭang, ṭánj, ṭang-wang.
Pearl, *n.* dúr, mokhtah.
Pearl ashes, *n.* ganahár.
Peasant, *n.* gróst.
Peg, *n.* kij, mekh, kíj.
Pellet, *n.* ryunz.
Pen, *n.* narkoñ, kalam.
Pen, to make a, *v.* kalam gárun.
Penis, *n.* álat, lúlí, mumar.
Pen-knife, *n.* shrákapúch.
Pension, *n.* rast, darmárt.

People, *n.* lúk, kaum.
Pepper, *n.* marits, martsa-wán-gun.
Peppermint, *n.* sóí.
Perceive, *v.* zánun.
Perfumer, *n.* búhur.
Perhaps, *adv.* má, dĕwah, baná.
Perjury, *n.* apozdrí.
Perish, *v.* marun.
Permission, *n.* rukhsat, ágnya.
Perplex, *v.* tambuláwun, paré-shán karun, hairán karun.
Perplexed, *adj.* hãrán, hairán, pareshán.
Perplexed, *v. i.* tambulun.
Persia, *n.* Irán, Fárs.
Persian, *adj.* Iráni, Fársí, Parvés.
Persian language, *n.* Phãrsí.
Person, *n.* zŏn, zaun.
Perspiration, *n.* gúma, wúsavás.
Pestle, *n.* muhil, ḍanḍa, káj-waṭ.
Petition, *n.* mángai.
Pharbites nil, see 'Ipomœa cœrulea.'
Pheasant, *n.* didur, zar kakú, rangatsur.
Phial, *n.* ábgínah.
Philosopher, *n.* gátúl, vidya-wán.
Phlegm, *n.* kaf, balgam.
Physician, *n.* waid, hakím.
Picea Webbiaña, *n.* birre, túng, ríyál, badar, búdar.
Pick, *v.* tsárun.
Pickaxe (small), *n.* tungarú.
Pick up, *v.* tsárun.
Picrorhiza kurrooa, *n.* haur.
Picture, *n.* murits.
Piece, *n.* myúnd, grás, lokama, hana, ṭukra, chhal, reza.
Pieces, in, *adj.* pára-pára.
Pierce, *v.* gaud karun, zúd karun.
Pigeon, *n.* kótur, kótir.
Piláo, *n.* puláo.
Pile (wooden), *n.* chil.
Piles, *n.* pŏṭ.
Pilgrim, *n.* hájí.
Pillar, *n.* tham, tsyún.
Pillow (for head), *n.* shánd, shándagunḍ, takiya.
Pimple, *n.* phĕphur.
Pin, *n.* phalsatsan.
Pincers, *n.* wauts.
Pine, *n.* yãr.
Pine-tree, *n.* chíl, yárí, tser, yero, káiar.
Pine-wood, *n.* káyúr.
Pinus excelsa, *n.* yero, yári, tser, káiar, chíl.
Pious, *adj.* shónt.
Pipe (smoking), *n.* jajir, guri-guri, jajír.
Pipe-bearer, *n.* jagír tulanwol.
Pipe-stalk-maker, *n.* nalchi-band.
Pisces (zodiac sign), *n.* Mín.
Pistacia integerrima, *n.* kakkar, drek, gurgú.
Pit, *n.* khŏd, gŏph.

Pitch a tent, *v.* khema dyun.
Pitcher, *n.* nauṭ, mallar.
Pitiful, *adj.* áraburut.
Pitiless, *adj.* beár, rahmrust.
Pity, *n.* ár.
Place, *n.* bal, jáí, sháí
Place, *v.* tháwun.
Placed, to cause to be, *v.* tháwanáwun.
Plain, *n.* wádí, maidán, wuḍar.
Plait, *n.* gut.
Plaited hair, *n.* wánk.
Plane, *n.* randah.
Plane tree (eastern), *n.* boíṅ, búiṅ, búna (Platanus orientalis).
Plank, *n.* paṭ, takhta.
Plant, *n.* kuj.
Plant, *v.* bihanáwun, wawun.
Plantago major, *n.* gúl, ísaphgol, bártang.
Plantain, *n.* kela.
Platanus orientalis, *n.* búin, búna (Plane tree).
Plate, *n.* bána.
Plateau, *n.* marg, wuḍar (karewah).
Platter, *n.* thál.
Play, *v.* wáyun, gindun.
Play music, *v.* sóz wáyun.
Pleased, to be, *v.* nanwun.
Pleasure, *n.* khushí.
Plectranthus rugosus, *n.* solei.
Pledge, *n.* band.
Pleiades, *n.* Suraiya.
Pliable, *adj.* sahulhul.
Plot, *v.* trakajár karun, wokhajár karun.
Plough, *n.* ála, álháṅ.
Ploughman, *n.* zamín khananwol, bútarát práṭanwol.
Ploughshare, *n.* phál.
Plough, *v.* wayun, lágun.
Plug, *n.* thaup.
Plum, *n.* olchí, er, ãr (álú Bokhára), álúch.
Plumbago Europea, *n.* chitra, chítah, shítraj.
Plum tree, *n.* áluchakul.
Pocket, *n.* chanda.
Pocket picking, *n.* chandatsúrí.
Podex, *n.* tsut.
Poetry, *n.* bait, shalúk, shrúk.
Point, *n.* phur, pyut, pyur.
Point out, *v.* ishára karun, háwun, tsínyaráwun, tsenawain dinyi.
Poison, *n. m.* zahar, vih.
Pole, *n.* hamtúl, lúr, lorihan.
Policeman, *n.* mókadam.
Polish, *v.* khái tulinyi.
Pollute, *v.* lárun.
Polygonum, *n. m.* kuwár, humáz.
Polygonum bistorta, *n.* maslún, anjabár.
Pomegranate, *n.* dãn, dáṅ.
Pomp, *n.* rít.
Pomum Adami, *n.* hírigogul.
Pond, *n.* sar.
Pony (mare), *n.* ṭaṭ.
Pony-herd, *n.* ṭohul.

Pool, *n.* ábakhŏd.
Poor, *adj.* miskín, gharíb, kangál, ájiz, adonáo, bekhak, nadeor dannarust, bechawun.
Poples, *n.* kúṭ-káts.
Poppy, *n.* gulál, guláła.
Poppy head, *n.* póstakhŏkhur.
Poppy oil, *n.* khash kásh.
Poplar, *n.* phras, phrast.
Populus nigra, *n.* phrast (Italian Poplar).
Populus alba, *n.* phras, phrast (White Poplar).
Populus ciliata, *n.* sufédar, bagnú, sulálí, dúd phras (Himalayan Poplar).
Populus fastigiata, *n.* safeda, phras.
Porter, *n.* kótsúl, bór tulanwol, ḍíḍwoin.
Portion, *n.* chhal, tilyim, bóg, hissa.
Portulacea oleracea, *n.* dhanní.
Possess, *v.* tháwun, see 'have.'
Possessor, *n.* arbáb.
Possibly, *adv.* dewa.
Postman, *n.* dákawol, harkárá, kãsit, kãsid.
Posture, *n.* nú,ar.
Pot, *n.* ṭikar.
Potato, *n.* álú.
Potter, *n.* král, krãj.
Potter's wife, *n.* krãj.
Poultice, *n.* lefa.
Pound, *v.* tseṭun, see 'Mince.'
Pound, to cause to, *v.* daganáwun.
Pour, *v.* hárun, tsunun, phirun, tráwun.
Pour out, *v.* tráwun.
Poverty, *n.* muhyum, láchárí, nádárí.
Powder (gun), *n.* shóra.
Power, *n.* tákat, kówat, yetsa, kuwat, hĕkit, bal, shakht, kudrat.
Powerful, *adj.* zoráwar, hekanwol.
Practise, *v.* vyendun.
Praise, *n.* shukr, hamad, táríf.
Praise, *v.* shukr karun, hamad karun, táríf karun.
Prangos Pabularia, *n.* fitrásályún.
Prayer, *n.* namáz, áhí.
Precious, *adj.* drug, ṭóṭ.
Precipice, *n.* nár.
Prefer, *v.* ṭóṭ tháwun.
Pregnant, *adj.* dúján, ásádivets, bárits, shikamdár, góbíkhora.
Prepare, *v.* sherun, sambálun.
Prepared, to cause to be, *v.* shubanáwun.
Presence, *n.* mukhátab.
Present, *n.* bakhsháish.
Present, *v.* dárun.
Present, *adj.* házir.
Preservation, *n.* rãchh.
Preserve, *v.* rãchh karun.
Pretence, *n.* híth.

Pretend, *v.* lágun.
Pretext, *n.* híth.
Pretty, *adj.* khúbrúí, núndbón, súndarmál.
Prevail, *v.* póshun.
Prey, *n.* sayad, shikár.
Price, *n.* mŏl.
Prick, *n.* trús.
Prick, *v.* trús dyun.
Pride, *n.* mad, kibar, takabúr.
Priest, *n.* yímám.
Prince, *n.* shah, shahzádah.
Prison, *n.* bãndiwán, kaid.
Prisoner, *n.* báñd, bandí.
Privacy, *n.* khalwat, kúṭ.
Probably, *adv.* dewa.
Probity, *n.* ratsar.
Proboscis (of elephant), *n.* karra.
Proclamation, *n.* ḍanḍora.
Prodigal, *n.* atráf.
Produce, *n.* hásil, láb.
Profession, *n.* kartút.
Proficiency, *n.* hurir.
Profit, *n.* zí, myuts, hásil, láb, mutsáí.
Profound, *adj.* saun.
Prolapsus ani, *n.* pŏṭ.
Promise, *n.* kol.
Prone, *adj.* namit.
Proof, *n.* nishánah.
Prop (wooden), *n.* ḍakh.
Proper, to be, *v.* shúbun.
Property, *n.* mál.
Prophet, *n.* wótár, shĕch-anawun.
Prophetess, *n.* shĕch-anamúin.
Propitious, *adj.* rut, wŏtam.
Prostitute, *n.* gányí.
Protect, *v.* rãchh karun, lalawun, rachhun.
Protection, *n.* rãchh, tsepan.
Proud, *adj.* madar.
Proverb, *n.* kat, wányí.
Provisions, *n.* khin.
Prow of boat, *n.* nam.
Prudence, *n.* gáṭajár.
Prudent, *adj.* gáṭul.
Prunella, *n.* ustukhudus.
Prunus Armeniaca, *n.* gurdálú, cherkúsh (Apricot).
Prunus domestica, *n.* olchí, er, ãr, (Plum).
Prunus Padus, *n.* zambchule (Bird cherry).
Pterygium, *n.* nókhun.
Publish, *v.* zahir karun.
Pudendum muliebre, *n.* tsot, khȧúḍ.
Pull, *v.* lamun.
Pulsation of an abscess, *n.* ṭŏp.
Pulse, *n.* dál, mong, sas, chana.
Pulverize, *v.* guhun, tseṭun.
Pulverize, to cause to, *v.* tséṭanáwun.
Pumpkin, *n.* al.
Pup, *n.* honyibokut, honyikutsur.
Pupil (of eye), *n.* lál, manyaphul.
Pupil, *n.* muríd, shágird.
Pure, *adj.* páwathar, shrúts, pák.

Purple, *n.* lájaward.
Purport, *n.* arth.
Purpose, *n.* mutlab.
Purse, *n.* chanda, ṭhela, gotsur.
Pus, *n.* pák.
Push, *n.* dakah.
Put on, *v.* tsunun, sunun.
Put, to cause to be, *v.* tháwan-áwun.
Put out, *v.* kaḍun.
Puzzle, *v.* pareshán karun, hairán karun.
Pyrus Kumaonensis, *n.* chitana, mail ṭang.
Pyrus variolosa, *n.* shindar.

Q.

Quadruped, *n.* ḍangur, gupun, hawán.
Quail, *n.* báṭúr, bátúrr.
Quantity, *n.* grand, kút.
Quarrel, *n.* har, nyáí, laṛáí.
Quarrel, *v.* harahar karinyi laṛáí karinyi.
Quarrelling, *n.* harahar, tsú-wán.
Quarrelsome, *adj.* ránḍa (from this word the Scotch word randy may have come).
Quarter, *adj.* páo.
Quay, *n.* yárbal, gáṭh.
Queen, *n.* rányí.
Quercus dilatata, *n.* baráin (oak).
Quercus incana, *n.* balút, síla-supárí.
Question, *n.* sawál, bikha.
Quick, to be, *v.* ṭakán karun.
Quick, *adj.* truk.
Quickly, *adv.* dó-aspah, ṭakán, jald, ṭakan-ṭakán, walwal, jàld pahan, jàld jald pahan.
Quickishly, *adv.* jald pahan.
Quickness, *n.* ṭakán.
Quicksilver, *n.* párúd, símáb.
Quietly, *adv.* sokhasán, ánanda-sán, sáwísán, ráhatsán.
Quilt, *n.* gaba.
Quince, *n.* bamtsúṅṭ.
Quince tree, *n.* bamtsúṅt kul.
Quit, *v.* tráwun.
Quiver, *n.* tíranor.

R.

Radish, *n.* múj.
Rag nail, *n.* mish.
Rage, *n.* tsak.
Rain, *n.* rúd, warshun.
Rain, *v.* rúd pyun, wálun.
Rainbow, *n.* rámabadrindúiṅ, or rámrambadrindúiṅ.
Rainy season, *n.* waiharát, wiharát, warshá.
Raise, *v.* túlun, thod túlun.
Raise dust, *v.* gard tulun.
Raise up, *v.* khárun.
Ram, *n.* kaṭ.
Randia dumetorum, *n.* main-phal, rárá.
Rank, *n.* martaba, kadr, izzat.
Raspberry, *n.* chhánch.

Rat, *n.* khrants, núl, gagur, gagir.
Ratify, *v.* mukarrar karun, mushakhas karun.
Raw, *adj.* óm, khám.
Ray, *n.* prakásh, ziza, prauwa, yitsah.
Razor, *n.* khúr.
Reach, *v.* wátun, pilun.
Read, *v.* parun.
Read, to teach to, *v.* parnáwun.
Ready, *adj.* taiyár.
Ready, to cause to be got, *v.* shubanáwun.
Reap, *v.* lónun.
Rear, *v.* rachhun.
Reason, *n.* sabab, wakána.
Rebellious, *adj.* kãrigarz.
Rebuke, *n.* pám.
Rebuke, *v.* pám dyinyi, malámat karinyi, lánatána karun, fazíhat karinyi, yihánat karinyi.
Receipt, *n.* kabuliyat, prai.
Receive, *v.* labun, mánun.
Recently, *adv.* nau, táza, kóra.
Recess (in a wall), *n.* ól.
Reckon, *v.* bozun.
Reckoning, *n.* grand.
Recline; *v.* shóngun.
Recognize, *v.* parzanun, parzanáwun, parzun, zánun.
Recollect, *v.* tsetas tháwinyi,—yinyi,—pyinyi.
Recollection, *n.* tsetas.
Reconcile, *v.* mashwara karun, maslahat karinyi.
Reconciliation, *n.* myul.
Recovered, *adj.* bàül.
Rectitude, *n.* pún, rátsar.
Rectum, *n.* pŏṭ, parmandij.
Red, *adj.* wŏzul, wazul.
Red pepper, *n.* matitsa wángrú (Capsicum annuum).
Reduplication. The Kashmírís are very fond of a species of reduplication in their nouns, *e. g.* phephar-wephar, hákwák, tresh-wésh.
Reed, *n.* nar, landৃ, péts, narkãnyí.
Reflect, *v.* vetsárun.
Refuge, *n.* tsalanshái, chhapanshái.
Refuge, to seek, *v.* chhapun.
Regard, *n. m.* parwa.
Regard, *v.* bozun.
Regard, to have a, *v.* mánun.
Reins, *n.* lákam, wag.
Rejoice, *v.* manprasand, sapadun, wandaprasand sapadun; dilkhosh sapadun; these same adjectives with karun.
Relate, *v.* báwun.
Relation, *n.* áshnáo, krón.
Release, *v.* athah tráwun, mokaláwun, khalás karun, atha tsunun, atha karun, tráwun.
Released, *adj.* atha-gatshawun.
Reliance, *n.* pats.
Relieve, *v.* yárí karinyi.

Religion, *n.* dín, milat, daram.
Remain, *v.* rózun.
Remain, to cause to, *v.* rozanáwun thaharanáwun.
Remainder, *n.* tshuṭ.
Remedy, *n.* iláj, wopáí, dawá, aushad.
Remember, *v.* yád karun, yád pyun, tsetas tháwun, yád tháwun, kanṭ tháwun.
Remembrance, *n.* tsetas.
Remorse, *n.* manuk dokh, wánduk dokh.
Remote, *adj.* dúr.
Remove, *v.* kásun.
Rend, *v.* tråt dyun, see 'Split.'
Renowned, *adj.* nun, námósdár.
Rent, *n.* tråt, trit, báúa, khŏd, kiráí.
Repair, *n.* róp, maramat.
Repair, *v. t.* sherun, sambálun, maramat karun.
Repairer, *n.* róp-karanwol, rafugar, róp-karawun.
Repay, *v.* horun, phirit dyun, naka wálun.
Repent, *v.* pashemán sapadun.
Report, *n.* shuhrat.
Reproach, *n.* pám.
Reproach, *v.*, see 'Rebuke.'
Repulse, *n.* dúr, dafá, badar.
Request, *n.* árz, zárpár, mángai.
Request, *v. t.* árz karun, mangun, tsádun.
Residence, *n.* jáí.
Resign, *v.* tráwun.
Resistance, *n.* dushmaní, shitrut.
Resolution, *n.* yetsha, níyat.
Respect, *n.* zár, militzár.
Respectfully, *adv.* zárah, zárahpárah.
Rest, *n.* sŏk, ánand, ráhat, pasár, warshun, árám, dáf.
Rest, *v.* dáf dyun.
Restless, *adj.* betáb.
Restrain, *v.* waṭun, band karun.
Result, *n.* natíja, phal.
Retinue, *n.* sawárí.
Retreat, *v.* paut phírit gatsun, phírit gatsun.
Return, *v.* paut phírit gatsun, phírit yun, phírit gatshun, pherun.
Revenge, *n.* zak, krúd.
Revenue, *n.* báj.
Reverence, *n.* yazat.
Revolt, *v.* fitna tráwun.
Revolution, *n.* gat, ghyúr.
Revolve, *v.* karun gat.
Reward, *n.* sawáb.
Rhamnus virgatus, *n.* nár, tadrú, dadúr.
Rheum Moorcroftianum, *n.* rewand, rewand-chíní, ribás.
Rhododendron anthopogon and lepidotum, *n.* tázak-tsun.
Rhododendron campanulatum, *n.* gagar yurmí, níkú.
Rhubarb, *n.* rewand, pamba hák.
Rhubarb-root, *n.* pamba-tsalan.

Rhus acuminata, *n.* arkhol.
Rhus buckiamela, *n.* tetar, títrí, chechar.
Rhus cotinus, *n.* phán, bhán, bana, manú.
Rib, *n.* larakaiṅ.
Rice, *n.* dányí, tumul, batah, arag.
Rice-bread, *n.* tomula-tsauṭ.
Rice-flour, *n.* tumla-óṭ.
Rice-gruel, *n.* ányimah.
Rice-water, *n.* kánz.
Rich, *adj.* dyór, dyãr, sov, málawol, ḍarawol, dánawol, sáó.
Riches, *n.* diyár, sŏn.
Rich man, *n.* diyárawol.
Rid of, *v.* kásun.
Ride, *v.* sawár sapadun.
Rider, *n.* sawár.
Ridicule, *v.* gelun.
Right (dahna), *adj.* dachun.
Right (proper), *adj.* lázim, mushahas, dachun (opposite to left).
Rind (of fruit), *n.* dyĕl.
Ring, *n.* nál. wáj, dáyira, wãj.
Ring, *v.* bajun, wajun, wayun, wazun.
Ringlet, *n.* zulf, kokul, mast, taup, kísh.
Ripe, *adj.* pop.
Ripe, *v.* papun (especially of fruit).
Rise, *v.* wŏthun, wótun.
Rise (as sun), *v.* nerun.
Rival, *n.* dushman, shithar.
River, *n.* daryá, kúl, lud, wit, kŏl.
Rivulet, *n.* kwŏl.
Rivulet-water, *n.* árawóin.
Road, *n.* wat.
Roar, *v.* grazun, krak karun.
Roast, *n.* átashín, kabáb.
Roast, *v.* buzun.
Roaster of grain, *n.* barbúz.
Rob, *v.* lúṭun, lúṭ karun.
Robbery, *n.* lúṭ.
Robust, *adj.* durr.
Rock, *n.* kaiṅ, shel, shela, pal.
Rod (long), *n.* lánz.
Roll, *v.* ḍula gatshun, ḍulan dyun, ḍulun.
Roll up in something, *v.* walun.
Roof, *n.* tálau, tál, pash.
Room, *n.* kúṭ, kúth.
Root, *n.* mól, múl, gŏḍ.
Rope, *n.* raz.
Rosa brumonis, *n.* phúlwárí, krùr (wild white rose).
Rosary, *n.* tasbíh.
Rose, *n.* guláb, pósh.
Rosin (of pine), *n.* yãri kilum.
Rot, *v.* dŏdarun, hótsun.
Rottenness, *n.* dŏdur.
Rottleria tinctoria, *n.* kamíla, rúlya.
Round, *adj.* dalom.
Rouse, *v.* wozanáwun.
Row, *v.* álawun.
Rub, *v.* malun, mathun, manḍun.
Rubbish, *n.* lats.

Rubia cordifolia, *n.* dandú, phaharghás (madder).
Rubus fruticosus, *n.* álish.
Rubus lasiocarpus, *n.* pakání, gurácha, kandiára, kharmach, surgauch.
Rubus rotundifolius? *n.* chench, kanáchí, pukána.
Rubus tiliaceus, *n.* púlla.
Ruby, *n.* rattan, lál, chauní.
Rug-maker, *n.* namdagur.
Ruined, *adj.* khwár, wairán, kharáb.
Ruler, *n.* hákim.
Rumex acutus, *n.* obúl.
Ruminating, *adj.* drámun.
Rump, *n.* mandul.
Run, *v.* dawun, tukun, dorun, lárun.
Run away, *v.* tsalun.
Run, to cause to, *v.* dóranáwun.
Run, to make to, *v. t.* dawanáwun, ṭukanáwun.
Runner, *n.* dorawun.
Running, *n.* ṭak, dór, tshál.
Rupee, *n.* rŏpai.
Rust, *n.* kháí, khai, zangár.

S.

Sack, *n.* guna, bastúr, gunah, ṭhelah, vĕtharan.
Sacrifice, *n.* khash, pā̃ri.
Sad, *adj.* dilgír, diltang.
Saddle, *n.* zín, kā̃ṭh, kā̃ṭhi, prayánand.
Saddle, *v.* zín ganḍun, zín ladun.
Saddle-cloth-maker, *n.* jálokhdóz.
Saddler, *n.* siráj.
Sad of heart, *adj.* dil-hazín.
Saffron, *n.* kongs (crocus sativus), kwong.
Saffron-flower, *n.* kóng-posh.
Sage, *n.* ríshí.
Sagittarius (zodiac sign), *n.* Dan.
Sail, *n.* wáwamál.
Saint, *n.* shúnt, ríshí, pír, sā̃d.
Sake of (for), *prep.* khā̃tra, bápat.
Salary, *n.* reta.
Saliva, *n.* thŏk.
Salix alba, *n.* vír (white willow).
Salix Babylonica, *n.* bisa, giur (weeping type of willow).
Salix Ægyptiaca, *n.* bed-mushk.
Salt, *n.* nun, núṅ, lawan tsáṅ.
Salute, *v.* salám karun, bandagí karinyi.
Salvia, *n.* kanaucha.
Salvia Moorcroftiana, *n.* farásium.
Same, *adj.* yaksán.
Sample, *n.* namúna.
Sand, *n.* sĕk, rĕt.
Sandals, *n.* khilahor.
Sandal-wood, *n.* tsandun.
Sapphire, *n.* nílam.
Saturday, *n.* Shanyiwár, Baṭawár.

Saturn (planet), *n.* Shanachar, Shanaschar.

Save, *v.* mokaláwun.

Saved, *v.* bachun.

Saw, *n.* litár, litur.

Sawyer, *n.* gótilyí.

Saxifraga ligulata, *n.* popal, wat-phúta.

Say, *v.* dapun, wanun, see 'Speak.'

Scab (of a sore), *n.* krór or król.

Scabbard, *n.* kómb, kumb.

Scabies, *n.* harárat, kashan.

Scald-head, *n.* khar.

Scald-headed, *adj.* khaur.

Scales (for weighing), *n.* trakur, kā̃nta, trakár, háyuk.

Scaling ladder, *n.* maryuk.

Scar, *n.* chŏk, zakham.

Scarce, *adj.* kam.

Scarcely, *adv.* kaṭhinyisán.

Scatter, *v.* chhikun, chhakun, pareshán karun, chakrun.

Scholar, *n.* hichara.

School, *n.* tsáṭahál.

Scissors, *n. m.* mikráz, dúkā̃r.

Scorpio (zodiac sign), *n.* Warchak.

Scorpion, *n.* puhur, bich, bích, búchh.

Scrape, *v.* kripun, zilun.

Scratch, *v.* kashun.

Screen, *n.* parda.

Screw, *n.* wuṭhan, péch.

Scrotum, *n.* pósh. There is no separate noun for this part of the male body. The name of the testes includes the scrotum.

Sea, *n.* samundar.

Seal, *n.* muhr.

Search, *v.* tsánḍun, tsáḍun, tshanḍun.

Search for, *v.* tsánḍun, tshanḍun.

Second, *adj.* dŏyum.

Secret, *n.* gambur, sir.

Sedan chair, *n.* dúl.

Sediment, *n.* lum, lamb.

See, *v.* wuchhun, deshun.

Seed, *n.* byól, bíz, byol, khol.

Seek for, *v.* tsánḍun, tshanḍun.

Seek, to cause to, *v. t.* tsáḍanáwun, manganáwun.

Segeretia Brandrethiana, *n.* bhándí-bajan, ganger.

Segeretia oppositifolia, *n.* kanak, gídardák.

Seize, *v.* raṭun, see 'Take hold of.'

Seize, to cause to, *v.* raṭanáwun.

Select, *v.* tsárun.

Self, *pron.* pána, pánah, pánai.

Selfish, *adj.* pánas yitzawun, ahambáví.

Seller of dyes, *n.* phalgur.

Seller of Singhara nuts, *n.* golikutsur.

Sell, *v.* kánun, kunun, banzarun.

Send for, *v.* manganáwun.

Send, *v.* ladun, sozun.

Senecio, *n.* sadbag, sadbarg.
Seniority, *n.* zichhar.
Senseless, *adj.* sádah.
Sentence, *v.* hukm karun.
Sentry, *n.* rátarãch.
Sent, to cause to be, *v.* sozanáwun.
Separate, *adj.* byun.
Separate, *v.* byun karun, juda karun, tsárun.
Separation, *n.* hijar, firák, durir.
Sepoy, *n.* Sipah.
September, *n.* Ãshid, Asuh.
Serpent, *n.* sŏruph, nág, sarruph, serriping, gunas, shahmár.
Serratula anthelmintica, *n.* kálí ziri, kála zíra, bukoki, kakshama, malwa bakchí.
Serum, *n.* ras.
Servant, *n.* parzun, nókar, naukar, dás.
Service, *n.* naukarí, khidmat, bandagi, dásabáo.
Sesame, *n.* tél (the Persian kunjid and the Arabic simsim).
Sesamum, *n.* tíl.
Sesamum Orientale, *n.* til, kunjad.
Set down, *v.* bihanáwun.
Set free, *v.* mokaláwun.
Set free, to be, *v.* mŏkalun.
Settlement (of taxes, &c.), *n.* bandobast.
Seven, *adj.* sat.
Seventeen, *adj.* sadah.
Seventeenth, *adj.* sadãhyum.
Seventh, *adj.* satyum.
Seventieth, *adj.* satatyum.
Seventy, *adj.* satat.
Seventy-eight, *adj.* arasatat.
Seventy-eighth, *adj.* arasatatyum.
Seventy-fifth, *adj.* pántsasatatyum.
Seventy-first, *adj.* akasatatyum.
Seventy-five, *adj.* pántsasatat, dúnhat, dúnyihatih.
Seventy-four, *adj.* tsŭsatat.
Seventy-fourth, *adj.* tsŭsatatyum.
Seventy-nine, *adj.* kunashít.
Seventy-ninth, *adj.* kunashítyum.
Seventy-one, *adj.* akasatat.
Seventy-second, *adj.* dŭsatatyum.
Seventy-seven, *adj.* satasatat.
Seventy-seventh, *adj.* satasatatyum.
Seventy-six, *adj.* shisatat.
Seventy-sixth, *adj.* shisatatyum.
Seventy-third, *adj.* trasatatyum.
Seventy-three, *adj.* trasatat.
Seventy-two, *adj.* dŭsatat.
Sew, *v.* síwun, suwun.
Shade, *n.* shuhul, tsáí, shihul.
Shade of a lamp, *n.* kandíl.

Shadow, *n.* tshá,e, pauttsháe, sáyi, shuhul, tsáya, shihul.
Shake, *v.* harakat karinyi, alun, alanáwun.
Shaking, *n.* naṭh, gráe, láran, naṭ.
Shaking palsy, *n.* naṭ, we, wenaṭ.
Shallow, *adj.* wógun.
Shame, *n.* haiya, mandach, mandachh, ár.
Shampooing, *n.* tsĕl.
Shape, *n.* shakl, súrat.
Shape, *v.* thurun.
Share, *n.* bóg, hissa, bagir.
Share, *v.* bagrun.
Sharp, *adj.* téz.
Sharp-witted, *adj.* truk.
Shave, *v.* kásun, zulun, tachhun, zilun.
Shawl, *n.* tsádar, shál, tsádir.
Shawl-maker, *n.* rafugur, shálbáf, khándawáo.
Shawl-manufacturer, *n.* kárkhándár.
Shawl-mender, *n.* rafugur, rufúgar.
Shawl-pattern, *n.* siyahtara, Tálím.
Shawl-thread seller, *n.* púíwányí.
Shawl-weaver, *n.* shálbáf, khándawáo, shálpút.
Shawl-wool, *n.* kíliphamb.
She, *pron.* suh.
Sheaf, *n.* lov, tsap.
Shear, *v.* nyetun.
Shears, *n.* mikráz.
Sheath, *n.* kómb, kabza.
Shed, *v.* hárun.
Sheep, *n.* ter, gŏb, kaṭ.
Sheet, *n.* tsádar.
Shelf, *n.* ól, paṭ.
Shell, *n.* hãngin.
Shell (of worship), *n.* shenk.
Shepherd, *n.* púhul, pohol, dúm.
Shepherdess, *n.* pahaj.
Shepherd's functions, *n.* shubání.
Shew *v.* báwun, háwun.
Shew, to cause to, *v.* háwanáwun.
Shi,a, *n.* ráfiz, ráfizbá,í.
Shield, *n.* ḍál, sipar.
Shift, *n.* jatan.
Shine, *v.* prazalun, rakhshun, zótun.
Shine, to make to, *v.* prazaláwun.
Ship, *n.* náo.
Shiver, *v.* kamun, see 'Tremble.'
Shivering, *n.* láran, naṭ.
Shoe, *n.* pãzár, kúńsh.
Shoe-maker, *n.* tsamar, moch.
Shoes, *n.* paizár.
Shoot, *v.* tráwun.
Shop, *n.* wán.
Shop keeper, *n. m.* wánawol. wányí, wóiń, dukándár.
Shop keeper's wife, *n.* wányain.
Shopman, *n.* wánawol, wóiń, dukandár.

Shore, *n*. hauṭ, hauṭh.
Short, *adj*. tshauṭ, tsauṭ.
Short, in, *adv*. patolákin, patolákan.
Shorten, *v*. tsauṭ karun.
Shortness, *n*. tsŏchar.
Shoulder, *n*. pyuk, phyuk, phúk, shána.
Shoulder blade, *n*. kangú.
Shove, *n*. dakah.
Shrewd, *adj*. gáṭúl.
Shrub, *n*. kuj.
Shut, *v*. band karun.
Sick, *adj*. bemár, dádlad.
Sickle, *n*. drót.
Sickness, *n*. dód, manzar, bemárí, marz, rúg.
Sickness (squeamishness), *n*. drŏk.
Side (of human body), *n*. laṛa kányi, kányilaṛ.
Side (direction), *n*. pór.
Side, other, *adv*. ápor.
Side, this, *adv*. yipor.
Sieve, *n*. paryun, shíp, shup, shyúp.
Sift, *v*. chhánun.
Sigh, *n*. áh, wŏsh.
Sigh, *v*. áh kaḍun, áh tráwun, wŏsh kaḍun.
Sight (impaired), *n*. tsámp.
Sight (faculty of seeing), *n*. gásh, drenṭ, drashṭ, ḍenṭh, wuch, nazar.
Sign, *n*. nishán, zír.
Signal, n. ishára, achnánṭ.
Signature, *n*. álabda, sahí.
Silence, *n*. tsŏpa, tsŏpah.
Silence, to keep, *v*. tsŏpa karinyi, tsŏpah karinyi.
Silent, *adj*. moń.
Silk, *n*. póṭ.
Silk, *adj*. póṭ.
Silk braid-maker, *n*. pãtigur.
Sílk cloth, *n*. pãṭ thán.
Silk cocoon, *n*. pãt-guts.
Silk thread, *n*. pãṭ-pandáo.
Silk worm, *n*. pãṭ kyum.
Silly, *adj*. mutwál.
Silver, *n*. rŏp, chãndi.
Silversmith, *n*. sŏnar (literally goldsmith).
Sin, *n*. páp, aprád, gonah, taksír, gunah.
Since, *adv*. yimih pata.
Sincere, *adj*. poziyor, sádik.
Sind water, *n*. Sindawóiń.
Singhára, *n*. gór (water chesnut).
Singhara collector, *n*. gãrihánz,
Singhara nut, *n*. gólí, gãri.
Single, *adj*. kunuí.
Sing, *v*. gyauwun, gyewun.
Sink, *v*. bŏḍun, phaṭun.
Sink, to cause to, *v*. phátáwun.
Sir, *n*. Sa, sah.
Sister, *n*. benyi.
Sister-in-law, *n*. sál, bái kákin.
Sisymbrium irio, *n*. khákshí.
Sit, *v*. bihun.
Sit, to cause to, *v*. bĕhanáwun.
Six, *adj*. shih.

Sixteen, *adj.* shurah.
Sixteenth, *adj.* shurãhyum.
Sixth, *adj.* shihyum, sháyum.
Sixtieth, *adj.* shéṭhyum.
Sixty, *adj.* shéṭh.
Sixty-eight, *adj.* arahéṭh.
Sixty-eighth, *adj.* arahaiṭhyum.
Sixty-first, *adj.* akahaiṭhyum.
Sixty-five, *adj.* pántsahéṭh.
Sixty-fifth, *adj.* pántsahaiṭhyum.
Sixty-four, *adj.* tsŏhéth.
Sixty-fourth, *adj.* tsŏhaiṭhyum.
Sixty-nine, *adj.* kunasátat.
Sixty-ninth, *adj.* kunasatatyum.
Sixty-one, *adj.* akahéṭh.
Sixty-second, *adj.* dŏhaiṭhyum.
Sixty-seven, *adj.* satahéṭh.
Sixty-seventh, *adj.* satahaiṭhyum.
Sixty-six, *adj.* shihéṭh.
Sixty-sixth, *adj.* shihaiṭhyum.
Sixty-third, *adj.* trahaiṭhyum.
Sixty-three, *adj.* trahéṭh.
Sixty-two, *adj.* dŏhéṭh.
Size, *n.* thazar, kad.
Skewer, *n.* tuj.
Skewer-maker, *n.* tujigur.
Skilful, *adj.* wosta.
Skilfully, *adv.* wárah.
Skill, *n.* honar.
Skin, *n.* tsam, drúl, dyĕl, dĕl, músla, post.
Skirt, *n.* daul.
Skull-cap, *n.* tópi.
Sky, *n.* ásmán, nab, ákásh, kham.
Slain, *adj.* kushta.
Slander, *n.* gãbat, ghaibat, paut-kat.
Slap, *n.* thápir, chapát, kil.
Slaughter, *n.* khash.
Slave, *n.* ghulám, kaníz, tsúns, tsŏns.
Sleep, *n.* nindar, nindará, ḍáp.
Sleepless, *adj.* bedár.
Sleep, *v.* shongun, nindar karinyi, ḍáp tráwinyi.
Sleep, to put to, *v.* sáwun.
Sleeve, *n.* múr, nur, nâür.
Slender, *adj.* áyul, názuk, tun.
Slipper, *n.* paizár.
Slip, *v.* khúũt lagun.
Slit, *n.* trit.
Slow, *adj.* sust, laut, lot-lot.
Slowly, *adv.* warawara.
Slowness, *n.* tãr.
Slow of understanding, *adj.* muḍah.
Small, *adj.* lúk, lŏkuṭ, kam, lŏk, tshauṭ.
Smallness, *n.* lokachár.
Small-pox, *n.* shitil, shililyí, shittil.
Small, to be, *v.* lŏkun.
Smarting (of a wound), *n.* tatur.
Smell, *n.* mushik, mushk, phak.
Smell, *v.* mushik hyun.
Smile, *n.* ním-khanda, asun.

Smoke, *n*. dàh, duh.
Smooth, *adj*. sáf, sum, sutur.
Snake, *n*. duh, saruf.
Snake-catcher, *n*. saruf raṭanwol.
Snare, *n*. kamand.
Snatching, *n*. thapul.
Sneezing, *n*. pónd.
Snoring, *n*. khrŏk.
Snow, *n*. shín.
Snow water, *n*. shínawóiṅ.
Snuff, *n*. nást.
Snuff-seller, *n*. nástigur.
So, *adv*. tyuth, yuth, tithúí, tithanhyú.
Soap, *n*. sában.
Soap maker, *n*. sábinyigur, sã-bunsáz.
Sob, *n*. *m*. ṭúnga.
Sob, *v*. wadun.
Society, *n*. milatsár.
Socks, *n*. jaráb, mass.
Soda, *n*. phul.
Soft, *adj*. pishul, pishól, sahal, narm, kumul, nazuk, záyul.
Soft, to become, *v*. *i*. kamalun.
Solanum melongena, *n*. baingan, buntakí.
Solanum nigrum. *n*. mako, kámbeí.
Solanum tuberosum, *n*. álú.
Soldier, *n*. sipah, sipáhí.
Sole of foot, *n*. tálpód, talpud, paud.
Sole, *adj*. kunuí.
Solitary, *adj*. tanha, kunúí, akúí.
So long as, *conj*. yutámat.
So many, *adj*. yút, tyút.
Some, *pron*. kám, káṅ.
Some one, *pron*. kuhn, ḳahn.
Sometimes, *adv*. kensih phirih, kunyi, kunyi-kunyi.
So much, *adj*. yút, tyút, yúth, yutuí.
Some where, *adv*. kunyi.
Son, *n*. gŏbur, santán, walád, nechú, pharzand, farzand, puthar.
Song, *n*. samah, naghma.
Son-in-law, *n*. zámatur.
Sore, *n*. chhŏk.
Sorghum halepense, *n*. brahám.
Sorrow, *n*. gam, waswás, wodás.
Sorrowful, *adj*. daiyiwun.
So to speak, *adv*. zan.
Sound, *n*. sada, nád, áwáz, wányi.
Sound, *v*. bajun, wajun, wayun, wazun.
Soup, *n*. ras.
Sour, *adj*. tsauk.
Source, *n*. kán.
Sourness, *n*. techhar.
South, *n*. dakhin, dàchhun, dachun, dakhun.
South, *adj*. dachun.
Sow, *n*. súṛin.
Sow (seed), *v*. wawun.
Space, *n*. kál.

Spade, *n.* bel, liwan, tongur, bílchí.
Span, *n.* git.
Spare time, *n.* sul.
Spark, *n.* tembir.
Sparrow, *n.* kánṭur, tsar.
Speak, *v.* báwun, dapun, wanun, see 'Say.'
Speak a language, *v.* zeo karinyi, waninyi, dapinyi.
Spear, *n.* bála, néz, nyeza.
Spectacle, *n.* tamáshá, tsareṭ.
Species, *n.* kism, prakár.
Speechless, *adj.* kaul.
Spell, *v.* achar kaḍun.
Spendthrift, *n.* atráf.
Spend, *v.* kharch karun.
Spend (time), *v.* guzráwun.
Sphere, *n.* gera.
Sphœranthus mollis, *n.* mundí, mundí butí, guruk mundí.
Spider, *n.* zalur, wówur.
Spike, *n.* túj, prats.
Spikenard, *n.* sambul.
Spill, *v.* mandun, mandanáwun, tráwun.
Spinal column, *n.* tharkúnḍ.
Spine (thorn), *n.* kúnḍ.
Spinach, *n.* pálak.
Spinning-wheel, *n.* yandar.
Spin, *v.* katun.
Spiræa Kamtschatika, *n.* angrásha.
Spiræa Lindleyana, *n.* dor, batpís.
Spirit, *n.* zú.
Spite, *n.* rish.
Spiteful, *adj.* vār, mánir.
Spleen, *n.* pauh, poh.
Splendid, *adj.* ṭoṭ.
Splinter (of wood), *n.* mish.
Split, *v.* pháṭawun, pháṭanáwun, phaṭun.
Spoil, *v.* nashun, nashráwun.
Spoon, *n.* chóṅchih, shoncha, krats, káshawah, káshawahhan.
Sport, *v.* gindun.
Spot, *n.* dág, khál, khal, tyuk, shámaṭ.
Spotted, *adj.* techihor.
Spotted-veil, *n.* ṭikipúts.
Spray, *n.* dù.
Spread, *v.* watharun, waharáwun.
Spring (season), *n.* sóṅṭ, phulai, bahár.
Spring (of water), *n.* nág, nágarád.
Spring water, *n.* nágawóiṅ.
Spruce, Himalayan, *n.* súngal, pústúl (Abies Smithiana).
Spurious, *adj.* khŏṭ, khuṭ.
Spy, *n.* harkára, shakhdar.
Squash, *n.* al (Cucurbita maxima).
Squeamishness, *n.* drŏk.
Squeeze, *v.* chírun, see 'Wring.'
Stable, *n.* tabéla.
Stack, *n.* gúiṅ.
Staff, *n.* lór, lorihin, ása.
Stag, *n.* harnah, rús.

Stage, *n.* hangul, mazhar.
Stain, *v.* lárun, dághadár karun.
Stair, *n.* her.
Stairs, *n.* hyer.
Staircase, *n.* hér.
Stalk (of grain), *n.* gúiṅ.
Stalk (of apple or pear), *n.* lauṭ, dan.
Stand, *v.* wathun.
Stand up, *v.* thŏd wathun.
Staphylea Emodi, *n.* chitra, kúrkní (Serpent Stick).
Star, *n.* táruk.
Starling, *n.* gãr.
Starling (a species of), *n.* hãr.
Starving, *adj.* bochahut, gúshna, chhŏda, khyoda.
State, *n.* hál.
Stature, *n.* kámat, zechhar, kad.
Stay, *v.* rozun.
Steal, *v.* tsúri ninyi, tsúri karinyi.
Steam, *n.* báha.
Stealthily, *adv.* tsúrih.
Steel, *n.* fólád, pólád, fauládd, polád, dána.
Stem, *n.* múnḍ, kuṭ, gŏḍ.
Stench, *n.* phak.
Step, *n.* púr, kadam, paud, pu,úr, pád.
Step by step, *adv.* páda pat páda, kadama pat kadam, padi pat padi, pairi pat pairi.
Step-daughter, *n.* warakúr.
Stern, *n.* nam.

Stick, *n.* lúr, lorihan, trushi.
Still, *adv.* wunyi.
Sting, *n.* ṭŏp.
Sting, *v.* buchhun, ṭŏp dinyi, ṭŏp láyinyi.
Stingy, *adj.* kánjús.
Stink, *n.* phak.
Stinking, *adj.* phakalad.
Stirrup, *n.* páyir.
Stitch, *n.* ṭĕb.
Stockings, *n.* moza.
Stocking-maker, *n.* jarábagar.
Stocking-weaver, *n.* jarábsáz.
Stomach, *n.* bós, ḍamiṅ, yaḍ, wŏdur, myáda.
Stone, *n.* kain, kainyi, shela, pal.
Stone (of fruit), *n.* ãṅṭ, ánt, ánṭh.
Stone-engraver, *n.* moharkand.
Stony country, *n.* kanyal.
Stool (baráz) *n.* mal.
Stool, to go to, *v.* chharun.
Stoop, *v.* namun.
Stop, *v.* rozun, prárun, rozanáwun.
Store, *n.* der.
Storm, *n.* ãndhí, wáo, túfãn, zalamai, sailáb yúp.
Story, *n.* kissah, kath.
Straight, to be, *v.* sidun.
Straight, *adj.* syud.
Strange, *adj.* parud.
Stranger, *n.* wŏpar.
Stratagem, *n.* jatan.
Straw, *n.* prej, práj, hauk gás.
Strawberry *n.* ingrách yangtash.

Stream, *n.* nála, jwí.
Streamlet, *n.* kŏl.
Street, *n,* dúr, kóchik, bázar.
Strength, *n.* kówat, samrut, hĕkat.
Strew, *v.* tráwun, wáwun.
Strike, *v.* láyun, see 'Beat.'
String, *n.* ezárḍúr, raz.
String (a bow), *v.* ladun.
Strip off, *v.* wálun.
Strive, *v.* see 'Endeavour.'
Stroke, *n.* dŏg.
Stroke, *v.* phash dyun.
Strongly, *adv.* zórah.
Strong, *adj.* dur, durr, zórwár.
Strong, to be, *v.* ganun.
Stumble, *v.* see 'Slip.'
Stupid, *adj.* zauḍ, maunḍ, bekal, shók.
Substitute, *n.* badla, adilabadal, wakíl.
Success, *n.* tále, ḍeka, karam, bakht.
Such, *adj.* yut, yuth, tyuth, tithanhyú, yithanhyú, ithúi.
Such a person (name unknown) *pron.* falán.
Such as this, *adj.* yút.
Suck, *v.* tsihun.
Sudden, *adj.* hangamanga.
Suddenly, *adv.* nágah, hangatah-manga.
Suffer pain, *v.* dód ésun, sapadun, lagun.
Sugar, *n.* nábad, shakar, gór, kand.
Sugar-candy, *n.* gand, nábad.
Sugar-cane, *n.* naishakar.
Suit (law) *n.* dáwa.
Suit, *v.* shúbun, samakhun.
Summer, *n.* rĕtakól.
Summit (of mountain) *n.* tentol.
Summons, *n.* nád.
Sun, *n.* áftáb, sirí, áyút, siriyi.
Sunrise, *n.* prabát.
Sunset, *n.* sáyam.
Sunshine, *n.* táp, prau, prauwah.
Superfluous, *adj.* hurr, tsur.
Superannuate, *v.* zyút karun.
Superindendent, *n.* darogha, gumáshta.
Supine, *adj.* wútín.
Supper, *n.* kál.
Suppliant, *n.* bekhek, bechawun, gada, fakír.
Support, *v.* tulun, nyun.
Surface, *n.* but.
Surname, *n.* krám.
Surprise, *v.* hairat tráwun, waswa tráwun.
Surrender, *v.* pushirun, pushiráwun, hawála karun.
Surround, *v.* phiranáwun.
Suspend, *v.* lamkáwun.
Suspicion, *n.* shenk, shakk.
Sustain, *v.* tulun.
Swallow, *n.* kâtij, kotiz.
Swallowing, *n.* grŏk, nyingal.
Swallow, *v.* ningalun.
Swear, *v.* drí khinyi, drí háwinyi, drayí khinyi, drayí há-

winyi, drayi karinyi, kasam karun, kasam khyun, kasam háwun.

Swear by, *v.* sinz drí ásinyi, with dative of person swearing.

Sweat, *n.* guma, gumah, arak.

Sweep, *v.* dúnun, ḍuwun, dúwun.

Sweeper, *n.* wátul, dúnawol.

Swelling, *n.* hunyir, hunyar, lantsar, warm.

Swell, *v.* hunun.

Sweet, *adj.* myúth, mŏdur, mạdúr, shírín, myúṭ.

Sweet-basil, *n.* babar. It is abundant in the valley of Kashmir.

Sweeten, *v.* meṭhráwun, mudráwun.

Sweetheart, *n.* dildár.

Sweetness, *n.* mŏdarir.

Sweet, to be, *v.* meṭhun, mudrun.

Swift, *adj.* vyuṭ.

Swiftly, *adv.* téz.

Swiftness, *n.* ṭakán.

Swim, *v.* tsánṭ láyinyi, tsánṭ wáyinyi.

Swimmer, *n.* tsáṅṭal, tsáṅtul.

Swimming, *n.* tsáṅṭ.

Sword, *n.* shamsher, kartal, khaḍak.

Syphilis, *n.* bád.

Syria, *n.* Shám.

Syringa persica, *n.* híásmín.

T.

Table, *n.* mez, pír, khánchí, khán.

Tack, *n.* kíj.

Tagetes erecta, *n.* sadbargí.

Tail, *n.* phúd, lauṭ, lŏṭ, lat, dumah.

Tail (yaks), *n.* gajga.

Tailor, *n.* súts.

Take, *v.* raṭun, hyun.

Take away, *v.* nyun.

Take back, *v.* phírit hyun.

Take, to cause to, *v.* nyáwun.

Take hold of, *v.* raṭun.

Take off, *v.* wálun, kaḍun.

Tall, *adj.* thod, zyút, wanut.

Tallow, *n.* charab.

Talon, *n.* panjí.

Tamarisk, *n.* swoi.

Tank, *n.* kŏnḍ, taláo.

Tanner, *n.* ganz.

Taraxacum officinale, *n.* dúdal, (Dandelion).

Tardiness, *n.* raṭ, tãr.

Target, *n.* mánṭ.

Taste, *n.* sád, swád, maza, mazah, mechhar.

Taste, *v.* tsáhun, tsuhun.

Tasteless, *adj.* lazatarust, mazarust.

Taurus (zodiac sign) *n.* Warísh,

Tax, *n.* báj.

Tax-gatherer, *n.* guzurbán.

Taxus baccata, *n.* túng, postil, sungal, bráhmí.

Tea, *n.* chái.
Teach, *v.* hechhun, gáṭa dyun, hechhináwun, hechhanáwun.
Teacher, *n.* ustád, wŏsta, ókhun, ãkhun.
Tea pot, *n.* patila, bhógun, paitila.
Tear, *v.* tsaṭun, pháṭáwun, tràt dyun, tsaṭun, phalnáwun, phaṭun.
Tears, *n.* ush.
Teaze, *v.* satáwun.
Tease out, *v.* vetsanun.
Tell, *v.* báwun, dapun, wanun.
Temper, *n.* mizáj, khó.
Temperate, *adj.* shont, pársá.
Temple, *n.* mandar, shawálah, mashíd.
Temple (of head), *n.* myĕng, menga.
Tempt, *v.* ázmáwun.
Temptation, *n.* saragí, ázmáísh, tshalarawan, ázmãish.
Ten, *adj.* dah.
Tenant, *n.* grost.
Tender, *adj.* narm, kumul.
Ten millions, *adj.* karór.
Tendo Achillis, *n.* grŏz, takanár.
Tendon, *n.* nãr.
Tent, *n.* khema, khemah.
Tent-peg, *n.* kyul.
Tenth, *adj.* dahyum.
Terrible, *adj.* khotsawun.
Terrify, *v.* see 'Fear.'
Terror, *n.* bím.
Test, *v.* sara karun.
Testes, *n.* posh, pyúl.
Testicle, *n.* pyul.
Testimony, *n.* shahidí, giwáhí.
Tether, *n.* gudóm, wag.
Than, *conj.* khota, nishi.
Thankful, *adj.* shukrkarawun, shukrguzár.
That, *pron.* hú, sú.
That (in order that), *conj.* yuth, yut.
That is to say, *adv.* yáne, zan.
That very, *pron.* suí.
The, *def. art.* su.
Theatre, *n.* mazhar.
The day after to-morrow, *adv.* kãl kyĕt (parsoṅ).
Theft, *n.* tsúri.
Then, *adv.* & *conj.* tili, tilih, adah, tawí, tawai, tutám (tab tak).
Thence, *adv.* hutih, tatih.
There, *adv.* hut, hutut, huti, hutit, tut, tutut, tati, tatit, hutih.
Therefore, *adv.* & *conj.* yimi khátra, tawai, yawai.
These, *pron.* yim.
They, *pron.* yim.
Thick, *adj.* mauṭ.
Thick, to be, *v.* ganun.
Thick, to become, *v.* ganun.
Thief, *n.* tsúr.
Thigh, *n.* rán, lang, mandul, mandij.
Thigh, posterior aspect of, *n.* bóv.

Thin, *adj.* tan, nyuk, taun, tŏn.
Thin, to be, *v.* tanun, nyikun.
Thin, to make, *v.* nikráwun.
Thine, *adj.* chón.
Thing, *n.* chíz.
Think, *v.* sor karun, fikrr karinyi, hosh karun.
Thinness, *n.* tanyar, nichar.
Third, *adj.* trihyum.
Thirst, *n.* tresh, pepás, treshwésh.
Thirsty, *adj.* treshahut.
Thirteen, *adj.* truwah.
Thirteenth, *adj.* truwãhyum.
Thirtieth, *adj.* tráhyum.
Thirty, *adj.* tràh.
Thirty-eight, *adj.* aratràh.
Thirty-eighth, *adj.* aratràhyum.
Thirty-fifth, *adj.* pántsatràhyum.
Thirty-first, *adj.* akatràhyum.
Thirty-five, *adj.* pántsatràh, paintri.
Thirty-four, *adj.* tsŏyitràh.
Thirty-fourth, *adj.* tsŏyitràhyum.
Thirty-nine, *adj.* kunatájih.
Thirty-ninth, *adj.* kunatájihyum.
Thirty-one, *adj.* akatràh.
Thirty-second, *adj.* dŏyitràhyum, dótràhyum.
Thirty-seven, *adj.* satatràh.
Thirty-seventh, *adj.* satatràhyum.
Thirty-six, *adj.* shayitràh.
Thirty-sixth, *adj.* shayitràhyum.
Thirty-third, *adj.* títràhyum.
Thirty-three, *adj.* títràh, treyitràh.
Thirty-two, *adj.* dŏyitràh, dotràh.
This, *pron.* yih.
This very, *pron.* yihoi, yihuí.
This year, *adv.* yuhus.
Thither, *adv.* hór, tór, hutut, hutan.
Thorn, *n.* kŏnḍ, kúnḍ.
Thoroughly, *adv.* wárah.
Thou, *pron.* tsuh.
Thought, *n.* vetsár, ráe.
Thoughtless, *adj.* bekhabar, khabarirust, ázányi.
Thousand, *adj.* sás.
Thread, *n.* pan, phamb, sathir.
Thread (woollen), *n.* púí.
Thread (Brahminical), *n.* yónyí.
Thread-merchant, *n.* púíwóiṅ.
Thread-winder, *n.* nakáthí, nakót.
Threat, *n.* khrang.
Threaten, *v.* dabáwun, khrang karun.
Three, *adj.* trih.
Three-fourths, *adj.* dún.
Three-quarters, *adj.* dún.
Threshing floor, *n.* khal.
Threshold, *n.* bránd, ástánah.
Thrice, *adv.* trayi laṭi, trayi phiri, treyih phirih.

Throat, *n.* huṭ, kãĩṭ, hauṭ, hyur, kanṭh.
Throne, *n.* takht.
Throw, *v.* tshunuṇ, tráwun.
Throw away, *v.* trawit tsunun.
Thumb, *n.* nyeṭ, nyaṭ, nyuṭ, noṭh.
Thump, *n.* thápur.
Thunder, *n.* gargarí, gagaráí, gagarárai.
Thunder bolt, *n.* traṭ, nártraṭ.
Thursday, *n.* Braswár, Górawár.
Thus, *adv.* yuthyu, ithinyu, yuthuí hyu, yiṭhah pãṭ.
Thy, *adj.* chón, tuhund.
Ticket, *n.* chhiṭhí.
Tickle, *v.* kuta-kuta karun.
Tie, *v.* gánḍun, shruk karun.
Tiger, *n.* suh, sah, seham.
Tight, *adj.* tang, tsut.
Tigress, *n.* sihmin, símiṅ.
Till, *prep.* támat.
Till when, *conj.* yutámat.
Time, *n.* velah, wakt, vil, viz, samáí, án, anwár, laṭ, kál, phiri, laṭi.
Timid, *adj.* khotsawun.
Tin, *n.* kaláí.
Tinner of pots, *n.* kaláígur.
Tired, to be, *v.* lósun, thakun.
To, *prep.* nish, nishi.
Tobacco, *n.* tamók.
Tobacco-pipe, *n.* jajír, guriguri.
To-day, *adv.* az.
Toe, *n.* anguj, ungaj.
Toe (big), *n.* nyaut.
Toe (little), *n.* kis.
Together, *adv.* pánawuiṅ.
Toil, *n.* mihnat.
Token, *n.* neb.
Tomb, *n.* mazár.
To-morrow, *adv.* pagaṅ. The day after to-morrow, kãl, kãl kyĕt.
Tongue, *n.* zeo.
Toon, *n.* drawí, ḍrab, túní (Cedrela Toona).
Tooth, *n.* dánt, aram.
Tooth-pick, *n.* dandakhilál, dainditnj.
Topaz, *n.* pokhráj.
Topmost floor of a house, *n.* kányi.
Torment, *v.* íza dyun, dokh dyun.
Torn, *adj.* tsauṭ, chák.
Torn, to be, *v.* tshenun.
Tomato, *n.* bóṭawángan.
Torrent, *n.* yúp, sailáb.
Touch, *n.* sárun.
Towards, *prep.* kun.
Towel, *n.* daiṅj, daj, angocha.
Tower, *n.* kuṭhar, thong.
To wit, *adv.* yáne.
Town, *n.* nagar, shahr.
Trace, *n.* neb.
Trade, *n.* kasab, honar, shalpa, sódágarí, bápár.
Tradesman, *n.* saudágar, bápárí.
Traffic, *n.* sódá (saudá).
Traitor, *n.* daghabáz.

Trample down, *v.* manḍun.
Translate, *v.* nakal karun, tarjuma karun, ṭíka karinyi, ádrish karinyi.
Translation, *n.* nakal, turjuma, ṭíka, ádrish.
Translator, *n.* tarjuma karanwol.
Trapa bispinosa, *n.* gaunri (Water caltrops).
Travel, *v.* manzila tsaṭun, safar karun.
Traveller, *n.* musáfar, pardeshí.
Travelling expense, *n.* watasámána.
Tray, *n.* majma.
Treacle, *n.* gór.
Tread, *v.* manḍun.
Treasury, *n.* khazána.
Treaty, *n.* shart, báí.
Tree, *n.* kul, kuj.
Tree-gardener, *n.* bágbán.
Trellis work, *n.* panjara.
Tremble, *v. i.* naṭun, kamun, kampun.
Trembling, *n.* naṭh, tsrát.
Trench, *n.* kháí, khanduk.
Tribe, *n.* kaum, kwŏl, krón.
Trichodesma indica, *n.* nílakrai.
Trick, *n.* bram.
Trident, *n.* trashúl.
Tried, *adj.* ázmomut.
Trifolium pratense, *n.* chit-bato.
Triturate, *v.* pyuhun.
Trochanter (great of femur), *n.* zur.
Trouble, *n.* hol, dŏkh.
Troubled, *adj.* khuts.
Trough (stone), *n.* wŏkhul.
Trousers, *n.* paijám, paijámá, yezár.
Trowel, *n.* karin.
True, *adj.* poz, hakk, sath, poziyor.
Trunk (of the) *n.* gŏḍ.
Trust, *n.* báwar, pats.
Trust, *v.* báwar karun, pats karinyi, pats nyinyi.
Trustworthy, *adj.* wafádár, sór.
Truth, *n.* poz, pazir, pazar, pazpáth.
Truth, in, *adj.* paz pãṭ.
Try, *v.* sarakarun, ágmáwun, see 'Endeavour.'
Tuesday, *n.* Bomwár (Bóm) Mangalwár, Mangalworwár, Bauiiwár.
Tulip, *n.* gulála, lál.
Tumbler, *n.* glás.
Tumnet, *n.* kaziyih, máraka, har, nyáí.
Tumour, *n.* ses, gãnṭ.
Turban, *n.* dastár, pagir, tón.
Turban (female), *n.* taranga, kasába, sarpéch.
Turbid, *adj.* gauṭ.
Turk, *n.* Truk.
Turkish Empire, *n.* Rúm.
Turmeric (curcuma longa), *n.* lidir, lidar.
Turn, *n.* anwár.
Turn, *v.* pherun, pheranáwun.

Turning round, *n.* gat.

Turnip, *n.* gunglú, gugchí, gogij.

Turn round, *v.* pherun, phernáwun.

Twelfth, *adj.* bâhyum.

Twelve, *adj.* bah.

Twentieth, *adj.* wuhyum.

Twenty, *adj.* wuh.

Twenty-eight, *adj.* ãṭhãwuh, ãṭhówuh (2d form).

Twenty-eight, *adj.* ãṭhãwuhyum, ãṭhówuhyum (2nd form).

Twenty-fifth, *adj.* paintsahyum.

Twenty-first, *adj.* akawŏhyum.

Twenty-five, *adj.* pántsawuh, paintsah.

Twenty-four, *adj.* tsŏwuh.

Twenty-fourth, *adj.* tsŏwuhyum.

Twenty-nine, *adj.* kunatrâh.

Twenty-ninth, *adj.* kunatrâhyum.

Twenty-one, *adj.* akawuh.

Twenty-second, *adj.* zatãwuhyum, zatówuhyum (2nd.).

Twenty-seven, *adj.* satáwuh, satówuh.

Twenty-seventh, *adj.* satówuhyum, satáwuhyum.

Twenty-six, *adj.* shiwuh.

Twenty-sixth, *adj.* shiwŏh-

Twenty-third, *adj.* trŏwuhyum.

Twenty-three, *adj.* trŏwuh, trewuh.

Twenty-two, *adj.* zitáwuh, zatãwuh, zatówuh.

Twice, *adv.* dúbárah, dŏyi laṭi, dŏyi phiri.

Twilight, *n.* shafak, nabuknár, digar.

Twilight, at the evening, *adv.* dígaras.

Twist, *n.* táo, wuṭhin.

Two, *adj.* zâh.

Two and a half, *adv.* dún zah, ḍáí.

Two and a quarter, *adj.* swádzah.

Two and three quarters, *adj.* dún trih.

Typha angustifolia, *n.* pits, yira, dab, luk (bulrush).

Typha latifolia, *n.* pits, yira (bulrush).

Tyranny, *n.* sitam, zulum.

Tyrant, *n.* jafâkár, zâlim.

U.

Udder, *n.* than, babah, mamah.

Ugly, *adj.* yach.

Ugly-faced, *adj.* yach-but.

Ulmus campestris, *n.* brárí, brerí, brankul (elm).

Ulmus erosa and pumila, *n.* brén, bran, amráí, (species of Elm).

Umbrella, *n.* tápdán, tápadán.

Unable, *adj.* nahekanwol, kuwatrust, tákatrust, nyerbal, balarust.

Unawares, *adv.* nágah.
Unclean, *adj.* mókur.
Uncle, *n.* pitár, mám.
Uncle's wife, *n.* pihchain.
Uncooked, *adj.* óm.
Under, *prep.* tal.
Under ground floor, *n.* gán,
Understand, *v.* bozun, zánun.
Understanding, *n.* bŏd.
Uneasy, *adj.* dokhalad, dokhí,
Unexpectedly, *adv.* hanga-tah-manga.
Unfortunate, *adj.* badbakht, dályedir dralid, kamnasíb, shikaslad.
Unhealthy, *adj.* bemár.
Unjust, *adj.* nahakk, ánalarust, pristinarust, bedád.
Unless, *conj.* nai, magar.
Unlucky, *adj.* shikaslad.
Unmanly, *adj.* lánts.
Unmanliness, *n.* hánṭ.
Until, *conj.* yutám, yutámat, yŏtányi.
Up, *prep. adv.* hyúr.
Up to, *prep.* támut.
Upper, *adj.* peṭhyum.
Upper floor of a kouse, *n.* kuṭ.
Upon, *prep.* peṭh.
Upwards, *adv.* hyur kun.
Urine, *n.* muthar, pesháb, muthir, labashankhá, idrár.
Usage, *n.* ádat.
Use, *v.* kámi manz anun.
Use, *n.* kóm.
Useful, *adj.* muts, nafadár, faidamand.
Useless, *adj.* faidarust, nafarust, lábavenna, nyerláb.
Utensil, *n.* chhanin.
Utility, *n.* mutsái.
Utter (cry) *v.* láyun.

V.

Vacation, *n.* mokajár, mokal.
Valeriana Wallichiana, *n.* dálá, wálá, bálá, char, bálámuskh, chargodar.
Valley, *n.* páthul, duru.
Valuable, *adj.* mŏlul, drŏg.
Value, *n.* mŏl.
Vanish, *v.* ádrisht sapadun.
Various, *adj.* byun.
Vast, *adj.* baùḍ.
Vault, *n.* ḍumuṭ.
Vegetable-gardener, *n.* árum.
Vegetables, *n.* syun, tarkárí hák, ság.
Vegetate, *v.* bŏwun.
Veil, *n.* zúj, púts, tsádar, wóḍín.
Vein, *n.* rag, nãr, naur, nádí.
Velvet, *n.* makhmal.
Venerable, *adj.* ṭóṭ.
Venom, *n.* vih, zahr, zahar.
Venus, (planet) *n.* Shŏkhur.
Verandah, *n.* rawak.
Verbascum thapsus, *n.* vúlr, phúl.
Verbatim, *adv.* harafa pat harafa, achhira pat achhira, pada pat pada.

Verbena officinalis, *n.* pámúkh, chiraita.

Verily, *adv.* paz pãṭ.

Verse, *n.* nazm, bait, shrúk, shalúk.

Vertigo, *n.* gyúr, ghyúr.

Very, *adv.* tsŏr, tsŏruí sĕṭhah, yits, seṭha.

Very, *adv.* yȧts.

Vessel, *n.* thál, túr, rikib, dígchi. bhogun, glás, gaḍawa ábkhor bána.

Vetch, *n.* móng.

Vexation, *n.* dokh.

Viburnum cotinifolium, *n.* rích-hábí kílmich, gúch.

Viburnum fœtens, *n.* gúch kulára, jamára, kílmich, kwíl-lim.

Viburnum stellulatum, *n.* amli-ácha, phulsel.

Vice, *n.* pap, aprád, gŏnah, taksír.

Victorious, to be, *v.* see 'prevail.'

Victorious, *adj.* fatahmand.

Victory, *n.* fatah, jít.

Vigilance, *n.* gáṭajár.

Vigilant, *adj.* hoshiyár, bedár.

Vile, *adj.*ránḍa, harámzod, katál.

Village, *n.* gám.

Villarsia nymphoides, *n.* kúrú, khair posh.

Vine, *n.* dach, dach-kul, dacha-ránt, tanaur, talor dach, ne-wala (vitis).

Vinegar, *n.* sirka, káṅz.

Víneyard, *n.* dacharaṅṭ.

Violence, *n.* zulm.

Violet, *n.* kósam.

Virgin, *n.* anhirsh, kúr, dakhlar, kanya.

Virgo (zodiac sign) *n.* Kin.

Viscum album, *n.* wahal, ahalú (misleṭoe).

Visible, *adj.* drashṭáṅt, záhir, namúd.

Visit, *n.* mulákát.

Vitis, *n.* tanaur, talor dach, neẉala.

Voice, *n.* shabid, áwáz, nád, krak, álau.

Volume, *n.* tsam, jild, makawa.

Vomiting, *n.* kasiyana, drŏk.

Vulture, *n.* ghánṭ, gánṭ, gred.

Vulva, *n.* bag, gúd. khauḍ, wajúd.

W.

Wage, *n.* mazúrí, talab.

Wager, *n.* dáo.

Wages, *n.* talab, mazúrí.

Waist, *n.* haul, kamar.

Waistband, *n.* ḍenṭoṅ, hiláṭ, kamarband, haliganḍun.

Wait, *v.* prárun.

Waken, *v.* wozanáwun.

Walk, *n.* pethun, sair.

Walk, *v.* pakun, see 'Go.'

Walk about, *v.* ḍalun, see 'To turn.'

Walking, *n.* gasht, pherun.
Wall, *n.* dŏs, dewár, lab.
Wallet, *n.* bastah, kisht.
Walnut, *n.* dúṅ.
Walnut-tree, *n.* dúnyikul.
Wan, *adj.* ledur.
Wander, *v.* pherun, óryór pakun.
Wanderer, *n.* ámárah.
War, *n.* yŏd, laḍáí, jang, har, harahar.
War, to make, *v.* har karinyi (har being feminine, the feminine form of the infinitive is used).
Warm, *adj.* garm, tut, wushun, zalawun.
Warm, *v.* tapun, wushnáwun, wushnun.
Warm, to become, *v.* wushnun.
Warm-bath, *n.* hamám.
Warp, *n.* yain, yĕn.
Warp, to prepare the, *v.* yain yerinyi.
Warp-preparer, *n.* nakót.
Warrant, *n.* parwána.
Was, *v.* ásus (I), os (he), ás (she).
Wash, *v.* chhalun, manḍun, manḍanáwun.
Washed, *perf. p.* chhúlmut.
Washer of woollen cloth, *n.* málidagar.
Washerman, *n.* daub, daubi.
Washerwoman, *n.* daubibáí.
Wasp, *n.* tular.
Waste, *v.* nyikun.
Water, *n.* áb, poiṅ, zal, guláb, sag, muthar.
Water, to make, *v.* muthar karun.
Watch, *n.* gàir.
Watchfulness, *n.* sŏr.
Watch-house, *n.* guzar.
Watchman, *n.* rãch, ḍhúmb, rátarãch, guzarbán, ḍúmb, mahalladár.
Water-carrier, *n.* saka, pányúr, sakah.
Water chesnut, *n.* gaunrí (Trapa bispinosa), gór, górú.
Water chesnut (dried kernel), *n.* gãr.
Water chestnut (unripe), *n.* mĕs.
Waterfall, *n.* pántsádar.
Water-fowl, *n.* pachhin, pind, hárawat, tech.
Water lily, *n.* brímposh (Nymphæa alba).
Water melon, *n.* hindavyend.
Water spout, *n.* pántraṭ.
Water vessel, *n.* nuṭ, malir, wãr, tsuḍ (ghaṛa).
Wax, *n.* kúsh, syut, móm.
Way, *n.* wat, wath.
We, *pron.* àis.
Weak, *adj.* lyaḍ, kamzor, nyerbal.
Wealth, *n.* diyár, máyih.
Wealthy, *adj.* sov.
Weary, to be, *v.* losun, thakun.

Wearied, *adj.* thukmut.
Weave, *v.* wonun.
Weaver, *n.* wówúr, khándawáo, shálbáf, wãwur, wáúr, wáwúr.
Weazel, *n.* núl.
Web (spider's), *n.* zál.
Wedge, *n.* tsorats.
Wednesday, *n.* Bŏdwár.
Weed, *n. m.* lats.
Week, *n.* hafta.
Weep, *v.* ush tráwun, wadun, ryiwun.
Weep aloud, *v.* faryád dyun.
Weep, to make to, *v.* wadanáwun.
Weeping, *adj.* wadawun.
Weigh, *v.* tólun.
Weight, *n.* gober, tól, túl, wazn, parmán.
Welcome! *interj.* prasandákha, khoshákha, mubárak.
Well, *n.* cháh, krúr, kyúr, khuh, bóbalí, arhaṭ.
Well, *adv.* ján, zabar.
Well, to be, *v.* balun.
Well, to become, *v.* balun.
Well done! *interj.* shábash.
Well water, *n.* krír-wóiṅ.
West, *n.* maghrib, pachhum.
Wet, *adj.* ŏdur, adur.
Wet, *v.* udaráwun, wazanáwun.
Wet, to cause to, *v.* adráwun.
What? *interrog.* kya?
What? *pron.* kus?
What like? *adj.* kyut? kyuth?
Wheat, *n.* kanak.
Wheel, *n.* charkh, pinj, tsruṭ, tsrauṭ, arhaṭ.
When? *adv.* kar, kámi wakt?
When, *adv.* yilih.
When, *conj.* yányi, yám, yámat, yányit.
Whence, *adv.* katih.
Where? *adv.* kut, kati, katih?
Wherefore? *adv.* kámi khátra?
Whetstone, *n.* bilau.
Which? *pron.* kus?
Whiff, *n.* hawáwah.
While, *conj.* yutám, yutámat, yŏtányi.
Whilst, *adv.* yutámut, yutám (jab-tak).
Whip, *n.* tázun, chobuk, kamchi, kurra.
Whirlpool, *n.* áwalún.
White, *adj.* chhaut, safed, chhut, prun.
Whither, *adv.* kór, kŏt.
Whisper, *v.* lút wanun.
Who, *pron.* yus.
Who? *pron.* kus?
Whole, *adj.* tsorúí.
Whore, *n.* gányi.
Why? *adv.* kyázi, kámi kátra?
Why not? *adv.* kóná?
Wick, *n.* soyet.
Wicked, *adj.* yach.
Wide *adj.* kusháda, khol.
Wideness, *n.* khajar.
Widow, *n. m.* monḍ, vediva, bekháwind.

Width, *n.* panah, khajar.
Wife, *n.* tré,í, áshain, kolai, zenána, báriya, lárí, báriá, áshainyi, bãts.
Wife (rival), *n.* sŏn.
Wife's brother, *n.* hahar.
Wife's father, *n.* hyihur.
Wife's mother, *n.* hash.
Wife's sister, *n.* sál.
Will, *n.* yatshá, khúshí.
Willing, *adj.* prasand, khosh.
White willow, *n.* vír (Salix alba).
Willow (weeping type), *n.* vír (Salix Babylonica).
Win, *v.* zénun, hárun.
Wind, *n.* hawá, páwan, wáo, wáyí.
Window, *n.* wŏga, dãr, dári-pauṭ, panjara.
Wine, *n.* sharáb, madapán, mas.
Wine shop, *n.* mekhánah.
Ving, *n.* pakh, par, tihir, pakha.
Wink, *v.* ach títun.
Winter, *n.* wandah.
Wipe out, *v.* bójáwun.
Wisdom, *n.* gáṭajár.
Wise, *adj.* gátúl.
Wish, *n.* yetsa, khwá,ish.
Wish, *v.* yatsun.
With, *prep.* seth, sán, nishih.
Wither, *v.* see 'decay,' 'to be dry,' tsamaṭhun.
Withered, *adj.* hauk.
Within, *adv.* & *prep.* aṅdar.
Withinwards, andar kin.
Without, *prep.* siwáí, veráí, rust, venna.
Without, *adv.* nĕbar.
Witness, *n.* giwáhí dinawol shahiḍí-dinawol, gawá, shá-hid, sákhí.
Witnessing, *n.* shahidí, giwáhí.
Wolf, *n.* rámahún, rámahúiṅ.
Woman, *n.* zenána, zanána, trai.
Womb, *n.* hal, garba thela, gabiṅ.
Wonderful, *adj.* nãdir.
Wood, *n.* haṭ, zyun, hàṭ, zún.
Woodman, *n.* tabardár.
Wood-seller, *n.* menzúr.
Woof, *n.* sáz, wónun.
Wool, *n.* yer, wonun, phaṁb, kílphamb, lena.
Woollen cloth, *n.* pauṭ.
Woollen thread, *n.* yerakón.
Word, *n.* kat, kalám.
Word, in a, *adv.* patolákan.
Work, *n.* kóm.
Workshop, *n.* wán.
World, *n.* zagat, samsár, duṅya, jahán, 'álam.
World-illuminating, *adj.* sam-sáras-prazaláwanwol.
Worm, *n.* kyúm, kíṭh, ám.
Worn, to be, *v.* dódarun.
Worship, *n.* púz, púza, shrád, pãṭ.
Worship, *v.* puza karinyi.

Worship, to perform, for the dead, *v.* shrád karun.
Worthless, *adj.* nyuk, kharáb.
Worthy, *adj.* shubawun.
Worthy, to be, *v.* shúbun.
Wound, *n.* chhŏk, zakhm.
Wound, *v.* khasta karun.
Wounded, *adj.* khasta.
Wrap up, *v.* walun.
Wreath (of flowers), *n.* poshagund.
Wrightea antidysenterica, *n.* andusurun.
Wring (as wet clothes), *v.* chírun.
Wrinkle, *n.* geṅ, phuṭ.
Wrist, *n.* hauts, biní, gul.
Write, *v.* lĕkhun.
Write (to make to), *v.* lekhanáwun.
Writer, *n.* lekhanwol.
Wych hazel, *n.* páhú, po. (Parrotia Jacquemontiana).

X.

Xanthium strumarium, *n.* tsúr, láne tsúrú.
Xanthoxylon hostile, *n.* tímbrú, tímbar.

Y.

Year, *n.* weri.
Year, last, *n.* parur.
Yellow, *adj.* zard, lidur, pítámbar.
Yemen, *n.* Yaman.
Yes, *adv.* auwah, áṅs.
Yesterday, *adv.* yauwa, yawai, yihwah, yáo, yauwah, rát.
Yew tree, *n.* postil, túng, sungal.
Yoke, *n.* ípuṭ, panjālí.
Yoke, *v.* ganḍun.
You, *pron.* tohi.
Young (of any animal), *n.* latúrih.
Younger, *adj.* lúk, lokut.
Young gentleman, *n.* khánamól.
Young man, *n.* chŏbur, jawán.

Z.

Zinziber officinale, *n.* adrak.
Zinziber zerumbet, *n.* kachúr nar kachúr.
Zizyphus flexuosa, *n.* sínjlí, símlí, bárj, bán.
Zizyphus vulgaris, *n.* phitni, kokan ber.

KASHMÍRÍ-ENGLISH.

A.

A is pronounced like u in but.

Ã is pronounced a little like au in cause.

Á is pronounced like a in ark.

Ȧ has no corresponding sound in the English Language.

Á, sign of a question, and sometimes of the vocative case.

Ãb, *n. m.* blame, defect.

Áb, *n. m.* water. This is the word used by the Mussulman inhabitants of the valley. No water at the bottom of the valley is good for drinking. It is all brackish, except that of the river itself.

Ábádat, *n. m.* devotion.

Ábakhŏd, *n. m.* pool.

Abar, *n. m.* cloud.

Abdul Ģofár, *n. m.* a proper name.

Abdullah, *n. m.* a proper name.

Abdu Samad, *n. m.* a proper name.

Ábgínah, *n. m.* bottle, phial.

Abíd, *n. f.* compliment.

Abíd Karinyi, *v. t.* to compliment.

Abirahám, *n. m.* a proper name.

Ábkhor, *n. m.* a brazen drinking-vessel, of a larger size than the 'glás.'

Abr, *n. m.* cloud.

Achabal, *n. m.* a delicious fountain to the south-east of Islámabad. This word is derived from Ach or Yech, the Satyr of heathen mythology, and bal, a place. The spring of Achabal is the largest in Kashmir. The bath, the reservoir, and the garden were constructed by the Emperor Shah Jehán, after whom the place to this day is called by the Mussulmans, Sahib Ábád.

Achaposh, *n. m.* a white flower, growing on the mountains of Kashmir.

Achawal, *n. m.* a village of the Kúṭahár, pargana.

Ȧchh, *n. f.* eye, eye-ball.
Achhar, *n. m.* letter of alphabet.
Achharwál, *n. m.* eye-lashes.
Achhira pat achhira, *adv.* verbatim.
Achhar kaḍun, *v. t.* to spell.
Achh ghul, *n. m.* eye-ball.
Achnánṭ, *n. m.* signal.
Achhra pat achhra, *adv.* literally.
Achh títun, *v. t.* to wink.
Achhur, *n. m.* letter of alphabet.
Aḍ, *n. m.* middle.
Adah, *conj.* then.
Adal, *adj.* lawful.
Adalabadal, *n. m.* change, substitute.
Adalabadal karun, *v.t.* to change.
Adalbadal, *prep.* instead.
Aḍalyuk, *adj.* deficient.
Adanáo, *adj.* poor.
Ádar karun, *v. t.* to forgive.
Áḍarun and aḍaráwun, *v. t.* to knead, oḍarówun, áḍarán, aḍaráwán, oḍarómut, áḍarih.
Ádat, *n. f.* custom, usage, habit.
Áḍavĕn, *n. m.* a pargana of Maráz.
Ȧḍij, *n. f.* bone.
Adna, *n. m.* a proper name.
Adrak, *n. m.* Zinziber officinale (ginger).
Ad-rát, *n. m.* midnight.
Ȧdráwun, *v. t.* to cause to wet or be made wet; ȧdróv, ȧdráwán, ȧdromut, ȧḍráwih.
Áḍráwun, *v. t.* to mix; oḍrowun, oḍráwán, oḍromut, oḍráwih.
Ádrish, *n. f.* translation.
Ádrish karinyi, *v. t.* to translate.
Ȧdrisht sapadun, *v. i.* to vanish, see 'Sapadun.'
Ẵḍrun (miláná), *v. t.* to mix; oḍur, ã̄ḍrán, oḍurmut. This verb is said to be used only in reference to flour (áṭá).
Áḍrun, *v. i.* to mix, oḍro, áḍrán, oḍromut, áḍrih.
Ȧḍur (ὕδωρ), *adj.* wet, damp.
Adyul, *n. m.* rounded head of bone.
Adz, *interj.* good!
Afsantín, *n. m.* Artemisia indica.
Afsos! *interj.* oh!
Afsús, *interj.* alas!
Aftáb, *n. m.* sun.
Afzal, *n. m.* a proper name.
Ágah, *adj.* compassionate, aware, acquainted.
Ágah, *n. m.* master.
Agan, *n. m.* fire, light, flame.
Ágáz, *n. m.* beginning.
Agház, *n. m.* beginning.
Aginya, *n. f.* opportunity, permission.
Ágnya karinyi, *v. t.* to decide.
Áh, *n. m.* a sigh.

Ah, sometimes the sign of the vocative case, and also the sign of the ablative case.

Ah, an affix signifying one. It is equivalent to the Persian affix é.

Ahad, *n. m.* a proper name.

Ahadí, *n. f.* a proper name.

Ahad Jú, *n. m.* a proper name.

Ahadú, *n. m.* a proper name.

Ahalú, *n. m.* mistletoe (Viscum album).

Áham is made up of ák and mih.

Áhambávi, *adj.* selfish.

Ãharanḍ, *n. f.* clavicle, or collar bone.

Áhí, *n. f.* prayer.

Áh kaḍun, *v. i.* to sigh.

Ahmad, *n. m.* a proper name.

Ahmad Khán, *n. m.* a proper name.

Ahmad Shah, *n. m.* a proper name.

Áho, *n. m.* deer.

Áh tráwun, *v. t.* to sigh.

Ai, *conj.* if. It never stands first in a sentence.

Aibro, *n. m.* honour.

Ail, *n. f.* Cardamom.

Ȧis, *pron.* we.

Á,istán, *n. m.* crown of head.

Ajá,ib, *adj.* extraordinary.

Ájdá, *n. m.* boa constrictor, said to be known in the valley, which I very much doubt.

Ajiz, *adj.* poor.

Ak, *adj.* one.

Akahéṭh, *adj.* sixty-one.

Akahaiṭhyum, *adj.* sixty-first.

Akanamat, *adj.* ninety-one.

Akanamatyum, *adj.* ninety-first.

Akasatat, *adj.* seventy-one.

Akasatatyum, *adj.* seventy-first.

Akásbil, *n. m.* Cuscuta reflexa.

Ákásh, *n. m.* air, sky, heaven.

Ákãshi Ganga, *n. m.* the name of the river into which the ashes of departed Hindus are thrown by their relatives.

Akashít, *adj.* eighty-one.

Akashítyum, *adj.* eighty-first.

Akatãjih, *adj.* forty-one.

Akatãjihyum, *adj.* forty-first.

Akȧtrȧh, *adj.* thirty-one.

Akatrãhyum, *adj.* thirty-first.

Akawanzah, *adj.* fifty-one.

Akawanzãhyum, *adj.* fifty-first.

Akawuh, *adj.* twenty-one.

Akawŏhyum, *adj.* twenty-first.

Akbar, *n. m.* a proper name.

Ákh, *n. m.* mark (of small pox).

Ãkhir, *adv.* at last.

Ãkhun, *n. m.* Mussulman religious teacher.

Ȧki laṭi, *adv.* once.

Ȧki pheri, *adv.* once.

Akl, *n. m.* a proper name.

Akram, *n. m.* a proper name.

Akrót, *n. m.* Juglans regia (walnut).

Akuí, *adj.* solitary.

Al, *n. m.* Cucurbita maxima (squash).

Al, *n. f.* pumpkin. Three varieties grow in Kashmír; viz. kãshir al, pãryim al, and mashãd al. The Hindus do not eat the last variety, the Mussulmans, on the contrary, are very fond of it.

Alabányi, *n. f.* goad.

Álabda, *n. m.* signature.

Alabel, *n. m.* goad.

Álah, *n. m.* plough.

Aláka, *n. m.* estate.

Alákadár, *n. m.* owner of an estate.

Alam, *n. m.* flag.

Álam, *n. m.* world.

Alanáwun, *v. t.* to shake; álanowun, alanáwán, alanomut, alanáwih.

Alaphál, *n. m.* goad.

Álau, *n. m.* voice, cry, call.

Álau dyun, *v. t.* to call, to cry aloud.

Álawun, *v. i.* to row.

Álháṅ, *n. m.* plough.

Alí, *n. m.* a proper name.

Alí Baṭ, *n. m.* a proper name.

Alí Kadal, *n. m.* a bridge over the Jhelum in Srínagar.

Alí Muhamdí, *n. m.* a proper name.

Alípalí, *n. f.* asparagus (Asparagus filicinus).

Álish, *n. m.* rubus fruticosus.

Àlish, *n. f.* linseed.

Álit, *n. m.* penis.

Almás, *n. m.* diamond.

Álond tsumun, *v. t.* to hang; álond tsunun; tsunán; tsunmut; tsunih.

Álont tsunun (barawekhtan), *v. t.* to hang.

Alsí, *n. f.* linseed oil.

Álú, *n. m.* solanum tuberosum, potato.

Álúch, *n. m.* plum.

Álucha kul, *n. m.* plum-tree.

Álulí, *n. m.* a proper name.

Alun (hilná), *v. i.* to shake; aleo, alán, aleomut, alih.

Áluts, *adj.* lazy.

Ám, *n. m.* human entozoon, lumbricus. The lumbricus is extremely common in Kashmir.

Ama (ammá), *n. f.* grandmother. This word is said to be common among the prostitute families of Srínagar.

Amá, *conj.* but.

Amal karun, *v. t.* to obey.

Amal karanwol, *n. m.* collector.

Ámárah, *n. m.* wanderer.

Amarnáth, *n. m.* a cave very sacred in the estimation of Hindus. It is away up among the sources of the

Sind river, at an elevation of about 17,000 feet. The cave is of gypsum. The Hindus of Kashmir, and many from the most distant parts of Hindustan, may be seen trooping to this sacred spot in the beginning of July. It is a journey of great fatigue. The god worshipped at Amarnáth is Sadashau, or Mahadeo. The 16th of July is the great day of the feast.

Amb, *n. m.* bramble.

Ámba haldí, *n. f.* Curcuma zedoaria.

Ambár, *n. m.* heap.

Ambir tsúnt, see 'Tsúnt.'

Amdí, *n. m.* a proper name.

Amíri kadal, *n. m.* the uppermost bridge over the Jhelum in Srínagar.

Amír Jú, *n. m.* a proper name.

Amír Malak, *n. m.* a proper name.

Amliácha, *n. m.* Viburnum stellulatum.

Ámób, *adv.* extremely, exceedingly.

Amráí, *n. f.* species of elm (Ulmus erosa and pumila).

Án, *n. m.* time.

Áná, *n. m.* looking-glass.

Ãna, *n. m.* mirror.

Anagagur, *n. m.* musk-rat.

Anamur, *n. m.* mole (animal).

Ánand, *n. m.* rest, leisure.

Ánanda sán, *adv.* quietly.

Anapán, *n. m.* bread.

Anású, *n. m.* anagallis cœrulea.

Anatnág, *n. m.* a pargana of Maráz. It is also called Islámabád, after the chief town of the division. Anatnág means innumerable fountains.

Ánchár sar, *n. m.* a large lake about two kos distant from the city. The reeds alone of this lake are said to bring to the Government a revenue of 4,000 chilkies.

And, *n. m.* egg.

Andar, *prep.* & *adv.* in, within, inside.

Andar atsun, *v. i.* to enter.

Andar gatshun, *v. i.* to enter.

Andar kin, withinwards.

Andar yun, *v. i.* to enter, to come in.

Ãndhí, *n. f.* a dust storm.

Andram, *n. m.* intestine (roda).

Andrum, *adj. n. m.* bowels.

Andrum, *adj.* inner, internal.

Andrun, *n. m.* gut.

Andusurun, *n. m.* Wrightea antidysenterica.

Ang (Fr. angúr), *n. m.* granulations of a wound.

Angocha, *n. m.* towel.

Angrásha, *n. m.* Spiræa Kamtschatika.

Angrezi, *adj*. English.

Anguj, *n. f.* toe, finger.

Angun, *n. m.* the court of a house, enclosure.

Angúza, *n. m.* Narthex assafœtida.

Anhirish, *n. f.* virgin.

Anjabár, *n. m.* Polygonum bistorta.

Anjám, *n. m.* end.

Anjámavenna, *adj*. endless.

Anjámavaráí, *adj*. endless.

Anjámrust, *adj*. endless.

Anjír, *n. m.* Ficus carica, and Ficus caricoides. It is small and wild.

Anjuman, *n. m.* assembly, meeting.

Ankár, *n. m.* denial.

Ankár karun (íkrár kardan), *v. t.* to confess.

Ankúṭ (jag), *n. m.* a feast given by His Highness the Maharaja to the inhabitants of Kashmir at the close of the rice harvest. The feast corresponds to our harvest home. See 'Cunningham's Ladak.'

Áṅs, *adv*. yes.

Ãṅṭ, *n. f.* stone of fruit.

Anun (láná), *v. t.* to bring; un, anán, unmut, anih.

Anwar, *n. m.* a proper name.

Anwár, *n. f*, time or turn.

Anyigaṭih, *n. f.* darkness.

Ányimah, *n. m.* rice-gruel.

Apaimán dach, see 'Dach.'

Áphín, *n. f.* opium. The poppy grows in the valley.

Aphsós, *interj*. alas!

Ápor (pár), *prep*. & *adv*. over, across, on that side, the other side.

Ápor tarun, *v. i.* to cross: ápor tur, ápor tarán, ápor turmut, ápor tàrih.

Apoz, *n. m.* lie.

Apoz, *adj*. false, untrue.

Apoz dapun, *v. t.* to speak falsely, to lie, to tell lies.

Apoz drí, *n. m.* perjury (literally, a false oath).

Apoziyor, *n. m.* liar.

Apoziyor, *adj*. false, untrue.

Apozyor, *adj*. false, untrue.

Apoz wananwol, *n. m.* liar.

Apoz wanun, *v. t.* to tell lies, to lie.

Aprád, *n. m.* sin, vice.

Aputr, *adj*. childless.

Apuz, *n. m.* lie.

Ãr, *n. m.* shoe-maker's awl, a plum (Álú-i-Bokhára, Prunus domestica).

Ár, *n. m.* justice, mercy, pity, shame?

Áraburut, *adj*. pitiful, merciful.

Arag, *n. m.* rice in husk.

Arahéṭh, *adj*. sixty-eight.

Arahaiṭhyum, *adj*. sixty-eighth.

Arak, *n. m.* sweat.

Arám, *n. m.* ease, rest.

Aram, *n. m.* a double tooth.

Aranamat, *adj.* ninety-eight.

Aranamatyum, *adj.* ninety-eighth.

Arandotí, *n. f.* the star Canopus.

Arasatat, *adj.* seventy-eight.

Arasatatyum, *adj.* seventy-eighth.

Arashít, *adj.* eighty-eight.

Arashítyum, *adj.* eight-eighth.

Arat, *n. f.* meaning.

Aratã̃jih, *adj.* forty-eight.

Aratã̃jihyum, *adj.* forty-eighth.

Araträh, *adj.* thirty-eight.

Araträhyum, *adj.* thirty-eighth.

Árawal, see 'Guláb.'

Arawanzah, *adj.* fifty-eight.

Arawanzãhyum, *adj.* fifty-eighth.

Árawóin, *n. m.* rivulet water.

Arbáb, *n. m.* a chief or head, lord, possessor.

Ardah, *adj.* eighteen.

Ardah rát, *n. m.* midnight.

Ardãhyum, *adj.* eighteenth.

Arer, *n. m.* health.

Argon, *n. m.* a person whose father is a Kashmírí, but whose mother is not. These hybrids between the Kashmírís and the surrounding native races are pretty numerous in Ladak, Kashgar, Yarkand, and other neighbouring cities and states.

Arhaṭ, *n. m.* Persian, well, Persian wheel for raising water.

Aripánṭin, *n. m.* a village in the Bírú pargana.

Arir, *n. m.* health, healthiness.

Arkhol, *n. m.* Rhus acuminata.

Arkóla, *n. m.* a poisonous kind of wood which, when green, blisters the hand that holds it. The branches of this tree droop like those of the weeping ash.

Ãr kul, *n. m.* plum-tree?

Arnah, *n. m.* Clerodendron siphonanthus.

Arth, *n. m.* explanation, purport.

Árum, *n. m.* vegetable-gardener, greengrocer, kitchen-gardener.

Arz, *n. m.* request.

Arzán, *n. m.* Panicum miliaceum.

Arz karun, *v. t.* to request.

Ãs, *n. m.* mouth.

Ás (she), *v.* was.

Ása, *n. m.* staff of office.

Asad, *n. m.* a proper name.

Ásádivets (*f.*), *adj.* pregnant.

Ásan, *n. m.* anus.

Ásán, *adj.* easy.

Asanáwun, *v. t.* to make to laugh.

Asbáb, *n. m.* furniture, goods, luggage.

Asbarg, *n. m.* the flowers of the Delphinium saniculæfolium.

Ásha, *n. m.f.* hope.

Asháí, *n. m.* hope.

Áshain, *n.f.* wife.

Áshainyi, *n.f.* wife.

Ásháírúst, *adj.* desperate.

Áshak, *n, m.* lover.

Ashan, *n.f.* a proper name.

Ásha tháwun, *v. i.* to hope.

Ásha thávinyi (ummed dáshtan), *v. i.* to expect.

Ashgul, *n. m.* a tax levied on the Mussulmans of the valley for the support of the Hindu priests.

Ãshid (Ramazán), *n. f.* September, or ninth month of the Mussulman year.

Ashim, *n.f.* a proper name.

Ashk, *n. m.* love.

Ashkapechán, *n. m.* a Kashmir plant.

Ashmí, *n.f.* a proper name.

Áshnáo, *n. m.* blood relation, kinsman.

Áshtsarí, *adj.* extraordinary.

Ashud, *n. m.* a collyrium.

Asih, *pron.* to us.

Asíl, *adj.* noble.

Ásmán, *n. m.* sky, heaven.

Asnáwun, *v. t.* to make to laugh.

Assat, *n. m.* lie.

Ástánah, *n. m.* threshold.

Asuh, *n. m.* see 'Ãshid.'

Ásun, *v. i.* to be, to dwell, os, ásán, osmut, ásih.

Asun, *v. i.* to smile, to laugh, us, asán, usmut, asih.

Ásur, *u. m.* mustard, which ripens about September.

Ásus (I), *v.* was.

Átashín, *n. m.* roast.

Ãṭh, *adj.* eight.

Athagatshawun, *adj.* released.

Athah tráwun, *v. t.* to release.

Athah karun, *v. t.* to release.

Athakur, *n. m.* a large kind of bracelet, either of gold or silver.

Atha tsunun, *v. t.* to release.

Aṭhãwuh, *adj.* twenty-eight.

Ãṭhãwuhyum, *adj.* twenty-eighth.

Ãṭhówuh, *adj.* twenty-eight.

Ãṭhówuhyum, *adj.* twenty-eighth.

Ãṭhyum, *adj.* eighth.

Ãtij, *n.f.* leaven.

Átij, *n.f.* glue.

Ãtiraz, *n. m.* the name given to the cooked water chesnut by the people living on the shores of the Wulur Lake.

Aṭkal, *n. m.* anxiety.

Atráf, *n.m.* spendthrift, prodigal.

Átsárí Brahman, *n. m.* a Brahman who is very strict and punctilious in religious matters. Such Brahmans form a small company in Kashmir.

There are said to be only five houses of such in the valley.

Atsun (andar áná) *v. i.* to come in, to enter, tsáo, atsán, tsámut, atsih.

Áualarust, *adj.* unjust.

Aubur, *n. m.* cloud.

Auktsor, *n. m.* fire-place.

Aul, *n. f.* a proper name.

Aurhel, *n. m.* the chief village of the Suprúsaman pargana. Goitre is said to be very common among the women of this village.

Aushad, *n. m.* remedy, medicine.

Aushra, *n. m.* a proper name.

Auwah, *adv.* yes.

Auwal, *n. m.* beginning.

Auz, *n. m.* a bird of Kashmir.

Ãvyil, *adj.* delicate, thin.

Awãh is the enclitic of the plural objective case of the second personal pronoun.

Áwalún, *n. m.* whirlpool, gulf.

Áwántipúr, *n. m.* a wretched village between Pámpur and Bij Behára on the right bank of the Jhelum. It was the ancient capital of Kashmir, and derived its name from King Ávante Verma. There are some beautiful remains to be seen here, which Bishops Cotton and Cowie took great pains in unearthing in 1865.

Áwarain, *n. f.* funeral pile.

Áwarĕn, *n. m.* place of burning, see 'Shumshán.'

Áwáz, *n. f.* voice, sound.

Áyistan, *n. m.* anterior fontanelle.

Ãyul, *adj.* delicate, thin, slender.

Áyút, *n. m.* sun.

Az, *adv.* to-day.

Ázád, *adj.* free.

Azãnyi, *n. m.* foreigner.

Ázányi, *adj.* thoughtless.

Azím, *n. m.* a proper name.

Azíz, *n. m.* a proper name.

Azízi, *n. f.* a proper name.

Ázmáísh, *n. f.* temptation.

Ázmãish, *n. f.* temptation.

Ázmáwun, *v. t.* to try, to tempt.

Azmí, *n. f.* a proper name.

Ázmomut, *adj.* tried.

Azmomuth, *adj.* clever.

Azrá, *n. f.* a proper name.

Azumarát, *n. m.* a proper name.

B.

B: this letter is pronounced as in English.

Báb, *n. m.* chapter.

Bab, (pistán) *n. f.* pap, nipple, breast (mamma).

Báb, *n. m.* father.

Bab, *n. m.* father.

Babah, *n. m.* udder.

Babar, *n. f.* the sweet basil (ríhán).

Babiṭunḍ, *n. m.* nipple.

Bábúnah, *n. m.* matricaria chamomella.

Báchibaṭ, *n. m.* brahman.

Bachhih, *n. m.* dancing boy.

Bachun, *v. i.* to be saved.

Bád, *n. m.* syphilis.

Badal, *prep.* & *adv.* instead.

Badal dyun, *v. t.* to exchange.

Bádám, *n. m.* almond, two species grown in Kashmir; Khar bádám, and Mŏdur bádám. The almond is mature in September.

Bádám Kul, *n. m.* almond tree, which is numerous in the valley.

Badar, *n. m.* repulse.

Badar, *n. m.* Picea Webbiana.

Baḍáwun (nashándan) *v. t.* to extinguish.

Badbakht, *adj.* unfortunate.

Baḍgám, *n. m.* a village of the Dúns pargana.

Badí, *n. f.* evil.

Bádirpet, *n. f.* August. It corresponds to Shábán the eighth month of the Mussulman year,

Bãdirú, *n. m.* the sixth month of the Hindu year, and corresponding to our month of August.

Bãdiyána, *n. m.* sweet fennel.

Bad Karun, *v. t.* to disable.

Badla *n. m.* substitute.

Badranjboya, *n. m.* Nepeta ruderalis.

Baḍráwun, *v. t.* to increase.

Badrigul, *n. m.* a village in the Machipor pargana where are the ruins of a temple called Badrikálí.

Bádsháhí wat. *n. m.* highway.

Baḍun, (fr. baúḍ) *v. i.* to be great, to be big, to increase, to be large; baḍiyo, baḍán, baḍiyomut, baḍih.

Bag, *n. f.* the vulva.

Bág, *n. m.* garden.

Bágbán, *n. m.* tree-gardener.

Bághbán, *n. m.* (tree) gardener.

Bagí, *n. f.* a long barge with a hood like that of a buggy which covers the passenger.

Bagir, *n. f.* share.

Bãgla, *n. m.* beaṇ.

Bágnai, *n. f.* fate, fortune.

Bagnú, *n. m.* Himalayan poplar (Populus ciliata).

Bágráwun, *v. t.* to divide.

Bágrun, *v. t.* to divide, to distribute.

Bagrun, *v. t.* to share.

Bágwán, *n. m.* tree and shrub-gardener.

Bagwán, *n. m.* God.

Bah, *adj.* twelve.

Bahá, *n. m.* mist.

Báha, *n. m.* steam.

Bahanáwun, *v. t.* to fix.

Bahár, *n. m.* spring time.

Baháts, *n. m.* the largest boat with mat or straw covering used for the carriage of goods.

Bahikat, *n. m.* adhatoda vasica.

Bahs, *n. m* dispute.

Bahum, *adj.* twelfth.

Báhyum, *adj.* twelfth.

Báí, *n. m.* treaty.

Báí, *n. m.* brother.

Baibarang, *n. m.* Myrsine Africana.

Baibarang, Katai, *n. m.* Melissa nepeta.

Báíkákin, *n. f.* brother's wife, sister-in-law.

Baingan, *n. m.* solanum melongena.

Bàir, *n. f.* a crack or fissure in stone, wood or wall.

Baisáka, *n. m.* one of the names of the second month of the Hindu year. It corresponds to our month of April.

Bait, *n. m.* poetry, verse.

Baiya, *n. m.* fear.

Baiya khyun, *v. i.* to fear.

Báj, *n. m.* tax, revenue.

Bajar, *n. m.* greatness.

Bajir, *n. m.* degree (rank).

Bajun, *v. i.* to ring, to sound.

Bák, *n. f.* cry.

Bakhár, *n. m.* mist.

Bakhsháísh, *n.* gift, present, gratuity.

Bakhshanwol, *adj.* generous.

Bakhshawun, *adi.* forgiving.

Bakht, *n. m.* success.

Bakhtáwár, *adj.* lucky.

Bakhwun, compassionate, forgiving.

Bákrun, *v. t.* to divide.

Bál, *n. f.* bank of river.

Bál, *n. m.* hill.

Bal, *n. m.* a place, power, ability, energy.

Bálá, *n. m.* see 'Dálá.'

Bála, *n. m.* spear.

Baláe, *n.* misfortune, calamity.

Bálahom, *n. m.* a village in the Véhí pargana.

Baláí, *n. f.* misfortune.

Bálak, *n. m.* boy, male child.

Bálak, Rám, *n. m.* a proper name.

Bálá muskh, *n. m.* 'Dala.'

Balarust, *adj.* unable.

Bálchir, *n. m.* Nardostachys jatamansi? This is probably the 'spikenard' of the ancients.

Balel, *n. m.* Coriaria Nepalensis.

Balgam, *n. m.* phlegm.

Balmúj. *n. f.* carrot (Daucus Carota).

Bál tang, *n. m.* belly-band.

Báluk, *n. m.* infant, boy, a male child.

Balun, *v. i.* to be convalescent, to become well, to get better from some sickness; to be well, bŏl and baleo, balán, bŏlmut and baleomut, balih. He has become well. Su baleomut chhu.

Balút, *n.* acorn of the Quercus incana.

Bamazú, *n. m.* a village of the Kháwurpor pargana.

Bamtsúnṭ, *n. m.* quince. There are two varieties of quince growing in Kashmir: Tsŏk bamtsúnṭ and Moḍur bamtsúnṭ, the sour quince and the sweet quince. The quince is ripe in the month of October, and is of superior quality.

Bamtsúnṭ Kul, *n. m.* quince tree.

Bán, *n.m.* arrow, onosma macrocephala, zizyphus flexuosa.

Baná, *adv.* perhaps.

Bána, *n. m.* vessel, basin, plate.

Bana, *n. m.* heap, Rhus Cotinus.

Bána Kándur, *n. m.* china merchant.

Bánakuṭ. *n. m.* larder.

Banáwanáwun, *v. t.* to cause to be made.

Banáwun, *v. t.* to make, to form.

Band, *n. m.* mortgage, pledge, joint of body.

Bánḍ, *n. m.* musician, wandering minstrel, dancing man.

Báṅd, *n. m.* prisoner.

Bandagí, *n. f.* service, farewell, compliment.

Bandagi Karinyi, *v. t.* to compliment, to salute, to bid farewell.

Bandapúr, *n. m.* a village in the Khwíháma pargana.

Bandí, *n. m.* prisoner.

Bándiván, *n. m.* jail.

Bãndiwán, *n. m.* prison.

Band karun, *v. t.* to shut, close.

Bandobast, *n. m.* settlement.

Bandúk, *n. m.* gun, musket. That manufactured in Kashmir is remarkably good.

Báng, *n. m.* call to mussulman prayers in the morning.

Banga, *n. m.* Indian hemp. An intoxicating beverage is manufactured from it by the Hindus. The hemp of Kákapúr is said to be the best in the valley. See 'Bangí.'

Bangarí, *n. f.* armlets or bracelets, worn by the mussulman women.

Bangí, *n. f.* Indian hemp, (Cannabis sativa). The fibre is used in rope and papermaking.

Bángil, *n. m.* the largest pargana of the Kamráz.

Banihal, *n. m.* a pass 9200 feet high, in the south-east end of the valley. The Maharaja has reserved this Pass for his own exclusive use.

Banjírú, *n. m.* Artemisia Indica and vestita.

Bankeintí, *n. m.* Edwardsia mollis.

Banlás, *n. m.* a cloud.

Banraihán, *n.m.* Melissa Nepeta.

Báùs, *n. m.* buffalo.

Báùsa, *n. m.* Adhatoda vasica.

Bánṭ, *n. m.* musicians. See 'Bánḍ.'

Bantil, *n. m.* Balsam (Balsamina impatiens).

Banun, *v. i.* to be, to be made, to become.

Banyul, *n. m.* howl.

Banyul karun, *v. i.* to howl.

Banzarun (old), *v. t.* to sell.

Bápár, *n. m.* trade.

Bápárí, *n. m.* tradesman, merchant.

Bápat (liye) *prep.* for, for the sake of. For the sake of seeing Wuchhana bápat.

Bápathir, *n. m.* nephew on brother's side.

Bar, *n. m.* door.

Bár, *n. m.* burden.

Barábar, also barobar (muáfiq) *prep.* according to.

Barábar, *adj.* flat, equal, even, level.

Bárag, *n. m.* leaf.

Baráin, *n. m.* oak (Quercus dilatata).

Báramúla, *n. m.* a town at the north-west end of the valley in the Hamal pargana. The population is about 8000. The Mussulmans call it Waramúl.

Bárau, *n. m.* complaint.

Barbúz, *n. m.* a roaster of grain, chiefly maize.

Bar dyun, *v. t.* to shut the door.

Barg, *n. m.* leaf.

Barí, *n. f.* Acorus calamus.

Báriá, *n. f.* wife.

Baring, *n. m.* Myrsine Africana.

Baringí, *n. m.* nimia quassides.

Baringur, *n. f.* the person, generally a woman, who arranges the warp in the weaver's comb.

Bárits (*f.*), *adj.* pregnant.

Báriya, *n. f.* wife.

Bárj, *n. f.* zizyphus flexuosa.

Barkat, *n. m.* blessing, one. You often hear a Kashmírí when counting money or anything else call one "barkat" instead of ak, by way of asking God's blessing on the whole transaction.

Baróbar, *adj.* like, level, flat, equal.

Barrun (pur Kardan), *v. t.* to fill.

Bártang, *n. m.* Plantago major.

Barthá, *n. m.* husband.

Barun, *v. t.* to collect, to fill; bŭr, barán, bŭrmut, barih.

Basanwin (ahl), *n. m.* family.

Basanwol, *n. m.* inhabitant.

Basawun, *n. m.* inhabitant.

Basmagúl, *n. m.* the rent in the earth, to the north-west end of the Wulur Lake, by which the waters of the Valley escaped. See 'Kashmír.'

Basmat Dányí, see 'Danyí.'

Basta, *n. m.* wallet.

Basta, *adj.* bound.

Bastah, *n. f.* blister.

Bastah, *n. m.* beggar's wallet, made either of cow's skin, sheep's skin, or goat's skin.

Basta Karun, *v. t.* to bind.

Bas tháo, *interj.* enough.

Bastúr, *n. m.* a leather sack, or bag.

Basun, *v. i.* to dwell.

Baṭ, *n. m.* a frequent portion of Mussulman names. It is probably derived from the word Baṭa or Baṭah, which signifies Panḍit, who is always a Hindu of course. Probably when this word Baṭ is used by a person, it points to the fact that originally his family was Hindu; for we know from history that when the Mussulmans conquered the valley of Kashmir in the fourteenth century they compelled many of the inhabitants, who at that time were Hindus, to become Mussulmans.

Baṭa, *n. m.* Hindu. The Hindus of Kashmir are divided into (1.) The Brahman Hindus, whose only work is to perform the Hindu worship. In short, they are exclusively priestly, and number about 500 houses; (2.) The Jótish Hindus, who study the stars for the purpose of predicting future events. They number from 100 to 150 houses; (3.) The Kárkun Hindus, who are writers, merchants, and farmers, but never soldiers. Relatively, this is a very numerous class.

Bata, *n. m.* food, cooked rice, varieties of which are Wurbata, Wugrabata, Khetsirbata.

Batah (Bhát) *n. m.* cooked rice.

Bata dyun, *v. t.* to feed.

Baṭain, *n. f.* Hindu female.

Báṭa wángún, *n. m.* tomáto, of which the Mussulmans of the valley are very fond. They dry it in the season for use in winter. The Hindus of the valley do not eat it.

Baṭawár, *n. m.* Saturday.

Batawol, *n. m.* one possessed of food.

Baṭh, *n. f.* fire-place.

Bãtí, *n. f.* chilimchí or washing basin.

Batij, *n. f.* goose.

Bátirgám, *n. m.* a village in the Wutar pargana. Here there is a numerous colony of monkeys.

Batŏk, *n. m.* duck.
Batpís, *n. f.* Spiræa Lindleyana.
Báts (qabíla), *n. m.* the part of a house occupied by the females.
Báts, *n. f.* the female portion of a house.
Bãts, *n. f.* wife.
Bãts, *n. m.* a married couple.
Batuk, *n. m.* duck.
Bátúr, *n. m.* quail.
Bátúrr, *n. m.* quail.
Báú, *n. m.* fore-arm.
Baud (not bàúḍ), *n. m.* a handful.
Bàúḍ, *adj.* great, big, vast, noble.
Bàúḍ Karun, *v. t.* to increase, to augment.
Bâúḍ máz, *n. m.* beef.
Bàül, *adj.* recovered in health.
Baun, *n. m.* chisel for cleaving wood.
Baunwár, *n. m.* Tuesday.
Bàúr, *n. m.* a large crack or rent.
Bauṭ, *n. m.* dried dung.
Baut, *n. m.* rivers bank.
Bauṭh, *n. m.* bank of a river, shore.
Báv, *n. m.* forgiveness.
Báv Karun, *v. t.* to forgive.
Báwar, *n. m.* faith, trust, belief.
Báwar Karun, *v. t.* to believe, to trust.
Báwaz, *n. f.* brother's daughter, niece.
Báwazah, *n. f.* niece on brother's side.
Báwun, *v. t.* to shew, to tell, to inform, to relate.
Bayán, *n. m.* explanation.
Bayán karun, (bayan kardan), *v. t.* to explain.
Báyi, *n. f.* danger,
Báz, *adv.* again.
Bázar, *n. m.* a street with shops in it, market.
Bazzáz, *n. m.* cloth merchant.
Be,ák, *adj.* another.
Be,ár, *adj.* pitiless, merciless.
Bĕb, *n. f.* bosom (gŏd).
Bechanwol, *n. m.* beggar.
Bechawun, *n. m.* suppliant.
Bechawun, *adj.* poor.
Bechun, *v. i.* to ask alms.
Bedád, *adj.* unjust.
Bedána túl, see 'Túl.'
Bedána tulakul, see 'Tulakul.'
Bedár, *adj.* vigilant, sleepless.
Bedín, *n. m.* infidel.
Bed-mushk, *n. m.* Salix Ægyptiaca.
Begãri, *n. f.* working against one's will and without wages.
Begána, *n. m.* foreigner.
Behadráo zamín, *n. f.* fallow land.
Bĕhanáwun, *v. t.* to cause to sit, bĕhanov, bĕhanáwán, bĕhanómut, behanáwih.

Be,ih, *conj*. and.

Beiya, *n. m.* fear.

Be,izzaté, *n. f.* disgrace.

Beján, *adj.* insensible.

Bekal, *n. m.* fool.

Bekal, *adj.* stupid, ignorant.

Bekalí, *n. f.* foolishness.

Bekár, *adj.* idle.

Bekarárí karun, *v. t.* to disturb.

Bekár karun, *v. t.* to dismiss, discharge, to degrade.

Bekhabar, *adj.* thoughtless.

Bekhák, *adj.* poor.

Bekháwind, *n. f.* widow.

Bekhek, *n. m.* suppliant.

Bekh sumbul, *n. m.* convallaria.

Bekh záfrán, *n. m.* Aristotochia rotunda.

Bekh-zambak, *n. m.* convallari.

Bel, *n. m,* spade.

emár, *adj.* ill, sick.

Bemárí, *n. f.* sickness, illness.

Benathir, *n. m.* nephew on sister's side.

Bend, *n. m.* drop.

Benyi, *n. f.* sister.

Bera, *n. f.* edge, border.

Bàrrit, *adj.* full.

Bárrit karun, *v. t.* to fill.

Beshna, *n. m.* a proper name.

Betáb, *adj.* restless.

Bewafá, *adv.* faithless.

Beyák, *adj.* another.

Beyih, *adv.* & *conj.* more, again, and.

Beyih, *adj.* else.

Beyih yun, *v. i.* to come again, to return.

Bhagit, *n. f.* a proper name.

Bhán, *n. m.* Rhus Cotinus.

Bhándí bajan, *n. m.* Segeretia Brandrethiana.

Bhang, *n. m.* Cannabis sativa. See 'Banga' and 'Bangí.'

Bhógun, *n. m.* tea-pot, a brazen vessel, small, with wide mouth.

Bhojpatr, *n. m.* Betula tartarica, the birch. The bark of this tree, which grows abundantly on the mountains of Kashmir, is easily separated into thin sheets or leaves, which are largely used by the natives of the valley as paper for rolling up different kinds of goods in. It keeps out damp most thoroughly.

Bhoyí, *n. m.* brother.

Bhútrát, *n. m.* the earth.

Bí,ák Bíbí, *n. f.* a proper name.

Bí,áz, *n. m.* interest on money.

Bich, *n. m.* a small scorpion.

Biga, *n. m.* a square measure. The Kachba Biga contains forty square gaz. The Pakka Biga contains sixty square gaz.

Biha, *n. m.* the parts of the wooden stand of the spinning-wheel in contact with the ground.

Bihanáwun, *v. t.* to set down, to plant, to make to sit.

Bihun, *v.* to sit.

Bíj Bihára, *n. m.* a town of some 400 houses, on the left bank of the Jhelum, a few miles below Islamabad. It is famous for its trellis-work, and the manufacture of blankets.

Bíkabata, *n. m.* a dish consisting of rice, goat's fat, and water.

Bikha, *n. f.* question.

Bilau, *n. m.* whetstone.

Bilbichhur, *n. m.* nightingale.

Bilbichur, *n. m.* nightingale. The Bulbul corresponds to the Bilbichur,

Bílchí, *n. m.* a small spade.

Bím, *n. m.* fear, terror, dread.

Bimyun, *n. m.* village situate in the Dúns pargana. Here there is a great plain.

Bindak, *n. m.* see 'Findak.'

Biní, *n. f.* wrist.

Binzah, *n. f.* niece on sister's side.

Birre, *n. m.* Picea Webbiana (the Silver fir).

Birú, *n. m.* a pargana in the Kamráz division of the valley.

Bisa, *n. m.* Salix Babylonica.

Bishan Dás, *n. m.* a proper name.

Bishtah! *exclam.* used to drive away a cat.

Biṭh, *n. f.* assembly.

Biṭhchod, *n. m.* one guilty of incest with his own daughter. Biṭhchod is derived from beṭí, daughter, and chodua, to copulate.

Bít-zamín, *n. f.* fallow land. Formerly there used to be as much fallow land in Kashmir as there was cultivated. Now three fourths of the valley are said to be under cultivation, and two millions of kharwárs of grain are said to be produced annually.

Bújir, *n. f.* greatness.

Bíz, *n. m.* seed.

Bó, a poetical form of bŏh.

Bó, *n. m.* habit.

Bóbalí, *n. f.* a well.

Bŏch, *adj.* hungry.

Bŏchah, *n. f.* hunger.

Bochahut, *adj.* hungry, starving.

Bŏchhar, *n. m.* hunger.

Bŏchí, *n. f.* hunger, famine, appetite.

Bŏd, *n. m.* the planet Mercury, understanding.

Bŏḍun, *v. i.* to sink; bauḍ, bŏḍán, bauḍmut, bŏḍih.

Bŏdwár, *n. m.* Wednesday.

Bóg, *n. m.* share, portion, part.

Boh, *pron.* I.
Bóí, *n. m.* brother.
Bó,iṅ, *n.* oriental plane-tree, or chunár, see 'Búiṅ.'
Bójáwun, *v. t.* to wipe out.
Bojpatar, *n. m.* see 'Búrza.'
Bók, *n. m.* claw.
Bokawaṭ, *n. f.* kidney.
Bóm, *n. m.* the planet Mars.
Bombur, *n. m.* drone bee.
Bómwár (Bóm), *n. m.* Tuesday.
Bŏn, *prep.* & *adv.* down, below.
Bŏn anun, *v. t.* to bring down.
Bŏn gatshun, *v. i.* to go down, to descend.
Boniṅ, *n. m.* see 'Búiṅ.'
Bŏn-kun, *adv.* downwards.
Boṅt, *n. m.* bank (of river).
Bonṭ, *prep.* & *adv.* before.
Bónṭh, *prep.* & *adv.* before.
Bonṭhum, *adj.* future.
Bónṭhus, *adv.* next year.
Bŏn wasun, *v. i.* to descend; bŏn wut, bŏn wasán, bŏn wutmut, bon wasih. Bŏn is here pleonastic.
Bonyi-kul, see 'Búiṅ.'
Bór or bár, *n. m.* load, burden.
Bór tulanwol, *n. m.* porter (of burdens).
Bór tulun, *v. t.* to load, to carry.
Bós, *n. m.* stomach.
Bŏt, *n. m.* margin, brink.
Bóṭ, *n. m.* a pargana of Maráz.
Boṭarát, *n. f.* the earth.
Boṭa-tsera, *n. m.* a species of apricot.
Boṭa túl, see 'Túl.'
Boṭa tulakul, see 'Tulakul.'
Boṭawángan, *n. m.* tomato; eaten by Mussulmans, but not by Hindus.
Boṭawányi, *n. m.* a Ladák merchant, who imports into Kashmir the shawl-wool from Ladák.
Bóṭawóin, *n. m.* a Ladák merchant. A brisk trade is carried on between Kashmir and Ladak, from which the wool of which the Kashmir shawls are made is imported.
Bóv, *n. m.* posterior aspect of thigh.
Bówala, *adj.* furious.
Bŏwun, *v. i.* to grow, to vegetate.
Bozan, *n. m.* feast.
Bozanáwun, *v. t.* to make to understand, to explain, to make to hear.
Bozun (sunná, samajhná), *v. t.* to hear, to understand, to regard, to consider, to reckon, to listen; búzun, bozán, búzmut, bozih.
Brag, *n. m.* heron, crane.
Brág, *n. m.* heron. There are two or three heronries in the valley very carefully watched over by the Maharaja's

officials. The Pandits on marriage days, and the soldiers when visiting the Maharája, adorn themselves with the feathers of the heron.

Close to the village of Kuligám, in the south-east end of the valley, is a heronry upon two huge chunar-trees. There is another in the village of Paṭun in the east side of the valley; another heronry exists behind the Shálimár gardens. The herons are said to be of the same species as is common in England. Plumes of herons' feathers are worn by the Panjab chiefs.

Brahám, *n. m.* Sorghum halepense.

Brahamiṅ, *n. f.* a woman belonging to the Brahmin caste.

Brahaspat, *n. m.* the planet Jupiter.

Bráhmí, *n. f.* Taxus baccata.

Brahmun, *n. m.* Brahmin, see 'Baṭa.'

Brám, *n. m.* deception, deceit, fraud, trick.

Brám dinawol, *adj.* false, deceptive, deceitful.

Brám dyun, *v. t.* to cheat, to deceive, to defraud, to forge.

Bramráwun (fareftan), *v. t.* to deceive, to cheat, to defraud.

Bran, *n. m.* species of elm (Ulmus erosa and pumila).

Branakul, *n. m.* elm-tree.

Bránd, *n. m.* threshold, the landing outside the door of a house.

Brang *n. m.* a pargana of Maráz.

Brankul, *n. m.* elm-tree (Ulnus campestris).

Brãnt, *n. m.* hope.

Bránt, *n. m.* hope, faith.

Bránts, *adj.* hopeful.

Brãntwol, *adj.* hopeful.

Brãr, *n. f.* a cat.

Brárí, *n. f.* elm (Ulmus campestris).

Braswár, *n. m.* Thursday.

Brayí, *n. f.* jujube (fruit).

Brayí kuj, *n. f.* jujube (tree).

Brayi kul, *n. m.* jujube-tree.

Braz Dányí, see 'Dányí.'

Bren, *n. m.* a species of elm (Ulmus erosa and pumila).

Brerí, *n. f.* elm (Ulmus campestris).

Brestí, *n. m.* a proper name.

Brímdú, *n. m.* Celtis Caucasica.

Brimla, *n. m.* Celtis Caucasica.

Brímposh, *n. m.* Water-lily (Nymphæa alba).

Brimráwun, *v. t.* to cheat, deceive.

Brinjakul, *n. m.* a tree of Kashmir.

Bronṭ, *prep.* & *adv.* before, forward.

Before me (as to time), mih bronṭ.

Before me (as to position), mih bronṭah kanyih.

I have come before, bŏh chhus bronṭ ámut.

Bronṭa kanyih, *prep.* in the presence of, face to face, before.

Bronṭ kun, *adv.* forwards, in a forward direction.

Brór, *n. m.* a he-cat.

Brúmíj, *n. f.* Celtis caucasica.

Bú, a lengthened form of buh, I, which is poetical.

Búchh, *n. m.* scorpion.

Buchhun, *v. t.* to bite, to sting.

Búd, *adj.* old.

Búd, *n. m.* Malacochæte pectinata.

Búḍ, *n. m.* old man.

Búḍa, *n. m.* old man.

Budal (Hindee, tung?), *n. m.* fir-tree.

Búdar, *n. m.* Picea Webbiana.

Buḍun, *v. i.* to be old.

Buḍun, *n. m.* a bird which is said to emigrate to Ladak in the hot season, and to return to Kashmir in the cold season.

Buhir, *n. m.* the royal white falcon.

Buhir, *n. m.* perfumer and seller of drugs.

Buhur, *n. m.* druggist.

Búí, *n. f.* a species of gentian.

Búiṅ, *n. f.* the Chunár or oriental plane-tree (Platanus orientalis), a tree of great beauty in the valley. It was introduced by the Mussulman conquerors, and is now very abundant. It is the finest tree I have seen. The wood is said to be good for building purposes, but there is a prohibition against cutting it. It is used for papier maché boxes. It is rather soft, but well suited for furniture, doors, and turnery. This tree is not indigenous to the valley, but was introduced by the Mussulmans from the west. It never bears seeds in Kashmir, in which it is always propagated by cuttings. Its bark is sometimes subject to a morbid hypertrophy, which has many, if not all the properties of cork.

Vigne, the English traveller, saw a Chunar tree at Thana, and believes that it is no where found nearer the plains of India. The same traveller says, 'near Avin in

Persia, is the largest chenar, or platanus orientalis tree I ever saw, measuring about sixty-four feet in circumference, and having a copious stream flowing from beneath its roots.' I have not seen one with a greater girth than thirty-seven feet.

Bújar, *n. m.* old age.

Bújir, *n. f.* largeness.

Bukhãrí, *n. f.* a fire place built in the winter time for a fire to warm the house, not for cooking purposes at all. Wood alone is used in the bukhãri, whereas in the other fire-places wood and prepared dung are burned.

Búkirdúr (shokh) *adj.* dissolute.

Bukokí, *n. f.* see 'Kálí zírí.'

Bul, *n. f.* proper name of woman, forgetfulness.

Búl, *n. m.* mistake.

Bulbul, *n. m.* nightingale.

Bulgar janglí, *n. m.* Boletus igniarius.

Bum, *n. m.* eyebrow.

Búma, *n. f.* eyebrow.

Búmai, *n. m.* a village in the Zainager pargana.

Búmb, *n. f.* eyebrow.

Búmba, *n. f.* eyebrow.

Búmbh, *n. m.* a vegetable like a cord growing in the several Kashmir lakes. On account of heating qualities it is eaten by the natives in winter.

Bumbur, *n. m.* bee.

Búmika, *n. f.* the earth.

Bumposh, *n. m.* a flower of Kashmir.

Búna, *n. m.* Eastern Plane tree (Platanus Orientalis).

Búná, *n. m.* see 'Búiṅ.'

Bunapúr *n. m.* a village in the Brang pargana. Many Pandits reside here.

Bungarigur, *n. m.* bracelet-maker.

Bungir, *n. f.* bracelet. Bracelets are made of different shapes and materials. They are made of gold, silver, brass, copper, tin, and a fine kind of clay. The following are the names of the chief varieties: Katsakar, Kãnkan, Gunus, Kur, Kátsabungir, Phalibungir, Karelabungir.

Bungiriwóiṅ, *n. m.* bracelet-seller.

Buntakí, *n. f.* Solanum Melongena.

Búnyi, *n. f.* chunar.

Bunyúl, *n. m.* earthquake.

Earthquakes are by no means rare in the valley. It is said that in 1828, more than 1000 persons were killed from buildings falling upon them. It is noticeable that a most destructive epidemic of Cholera began its ravages soon after the occurrence of the earthquakes of 1828.

Búrj. *n. m.* the inner bark of the Betula Tartarica, which see. It keeps out damp admirably, and so is used as an under covering of the roofs of houses. It is used as paper for rolling up fruit, tea, sugar, and such like things.

Búrjrí, *n. f.* birch (Betula Bhojputra).

Burka, *n. m.* a long white garment worn by the respectable Mussulman women in Kashmir. It covers the whole body, head, face, and all. For the eyes there are sometimes two small openings, at other times there are two small pieces of mesh work in front of the eyes.

Burut, *adj.* full.

Búrza, *n. m.* the liber of a species of birch called in the valley búrzakul. Búrza is extensively used in the valley as paper for rolling up goods in. See Bhójpatr.

Burzali dún, see 'Dúṅ.'

Bushkába, *n. m.* the vessel out of which the poorer Mussulmans eat. It is of clay.

Bushkám, *n. m.* a portion of the boat called Dungá, situated in front of the stern Mahtábí.

Bustán, afroz, *n. m.* amaranthus cruentus.

Bustúr, *n. m.* the bag in which coolies or porters carry their supply of provisions.

But, *n. m.* bank of a river.

Buṭ, *n. m.* face, countenance, cheek, surface.

Bútarát, *n. f.* the earth, land, country.

Bútarát práṭanwol, *n. m.* ploughman.

Buṭh, *n.* bank of a river.

Búṭh, *n. m.* cheek.

Bútrát, *n. f.* the earth.

But tsokráwun, *v. i.* to frown.

Búzdil, *adj.* cowardly.

Buzmut, *adj.* baked, fried.

Búzun (bhúnná), *v. t.* to roast, to bake, to fry, búzun, búzán, búzmut, búzih.

Buzurg, *adj.* noble.

Buzurgí, *n. f.* glory, nobility.

Byól, *n. m.* seed.

Byól-kuk, *n. m.* cuckoo, so called from its cry being heard at seed time in spring.

Byun, *adj.* apart, separate, different, various, indeclinable, distinct.

Byun karun, *v. t.* to separate.

Ch.

Ch: is to be regarded as one letter, and to be pronounced as in English.

Cháh, *n. m.* a well.

Cháhi, *n. f.* tea.

Cháí, *n. f.* tea.

Two kinds of tea find their way into the market of Kashmir. These are called Suratí and Sabz. The Suratí tea is like English tea. The Sabz tea, on the other hand, is the famous brick tea which reaches Kashmir by way of Ladak. The Suratí tea reaches Kashmir from Ladak and the Panjab.

There are two ways of preparing tea in Kashmir. The first is called Mogul Cháí. For every tola of tea five cups of water are poured upon it in the Bhogun or tea pot. It is then boiled for half an hour, when more cold water is added, along with condiments and sugar, after which it is boiled for half an hour more. Milk is then added. It is now ready for drinking. The colour is reddish.

The second mode of preparing tea is called Shiri Cháí. The tea is placed in the tea pot with a little soda and water and boiled for half an hour. Milk, salt, and butter are then added, after which it is boiled for another half hour, when it is ready for drinking. Tea imported from China via L'hassa is a state monopoly.

Cháí karinyi, *v. i.* to make tea.

Chailchalíra, *n. m.* Parmelia chamchadalis.

Cháínãr, *n. m*, the vessel in which tea is placed after it has been made.

Chák, *n. m.* a crack.

Chák, *adj.* broken, torn.

Chakrun, *v. t.* to scatter.

Chamba, *n. m.* jasminum grandiflorum.

Chamba, *n. m.* jasminum officinale and revolutum.

Chamkát, *n. m.* Desmodum tiliæfolium.

Chán, *n. m.* house carpenter.

Chana (nukhúd, Cicer Arietinum) *n. m.* a kind of pulse.

Chánch, *n. m.* bramble.

Chanda, *n. m.* pocket, purse.

Chandatsúrí, *n. f.* pocket-picking.

Chãndi, *n. f.* silver.

Cháng, *n. m.* cone of fir-tree.

Changus, *n. m.* a village famous for its singing and dancing girls. These performers are generally, if not always, women of bad character.

Chapa, *n. m.* a crumb of bread.

Chapát, *n. f.* slap.

Chãr, *n. f.* an idiot.

Char, *n. m.* see 'Dálá.'

Chára, *n. m.* help.

Charab, *n. m.* tallow, grease.

Chárah, *n. m.* help.

Charba-bagaira, *n. m.* a dish composed of suet and vegetables.

Charbadár, *n. m.* groom.

Char godar, *n. m.* see 'Dálá.'

Charkh, *n. m.* wheel.

Chasham, *n. m.* eye.

Chashma Sháhí, *n. m.* a fountain on the northern shore of the city lake. Its waters are very delicious.

Chasma Sahibí, *n. m.* see previous word.

Chasht, *n. m.* see 'Koj.'

Chaṭi, *n. f.* fine.

Chatsakŏl, *n. m.* the white river. It gets its name from the circumstance that it takes its rise near a white stone, called Chats Kanyi. in the pargana of Nágám. For a large part of its course, it flows parallel to the road going to Rámú and Shupiyan. It joins the Jhelum near the Safah Kadal in Srínagur.

Chatsa trela, see 'Trela.'

Chauní, *n. m.* ruby.

Cháwun, *v. t.* to give to drink, to cause to drink, chov, cháwán, chomut, cháwíh.

Chechar, *n. m.* Rhus Buckiamela.

Chĕhit (mánsúkh), *adj.* abolished.

Chench, *n. m.* Rubus rotundifolius.

Cherkúsh, *n. m.* Prunus Armeniaca (Apricot).

Cheṭ labinyi, *v. t.* to forfeit.

Cheṭ hinyi, *v. t.* to forfeit.

Chhá is made of chhíh and á.

Chhak, *v.* 2nd *p. s. f.* art.

Chhakaráwanwol, *adj.* dispersing.

Chhakarawun, *adj.* dispersing.

Chhakun (titar bitar karná) *v. t.* to scatter (as seed); chhuk, chhakán, chhukmut, chhakih.

Chhal, *n. m.* a bit, part, portion, fragment, piece.

Chhalun, *v.* t. to clean, to wash, chhúl, chhalán, chhúlmut, chhalih.

When cotton cloth is referred to, 'chhalun' is used. When the reference is to woollen cloth, 'manḍun,' or 'manḍanáwun,' is the word employed.

Chhán, *n. m.* carpenter, house-carpenter.

Chhánabáí, *n. f.* carpenter's wife.

Chhánch, *n. m.* bramble, raspberry.

Chhanin, *n. m.* utensil.

Chhánun, (chhánná) *v. t.* to sift, chhónun, chhánán, chhónmut, chhánih.

Chháo, *n. f.* boiling.

Chhapan, *v. i.* to seek refuge.

Chhapanshái. *n. f.* a place of refuge.

Chharú gáḍ, *n. m.* a species of fish found in the valley from 8 to 15 seers in weight.

Chharun, *v. i.* to go to stool, chhurun, chharán, chhurmut, chharih.

Chhas, *v.* 1st *p. s. f.* am.

Chhata túl, see 'Túl.'

Chhata tulakul, see 'Tula kul.'

Chhaut, *adj.* white.

Chhena, *n. m.* cymbal.

Chhih (*f.*), *v.* is.

Chhih, *v.* 3rd *p. pl.* are.

Chhihná is made up of chhih, nah, and á.

Chhikun, *v. t.* to scatter (páshídan).

Chhira, *n. m.* lamb.

Chhiṭhí, *n. f.* ticket.

Chhiṭi dutai, *n. f.* a chintz garment with very wide sleeves, worn by the Mussulman women. It is sometimes simply called dutai.

Chhiṭigar, *n. m.* chintz-maker. There are some fifteen houses in Srínagar and Islamabad engaged in this trade.

Chhŏda, *adj.* starving.

Chhŏk, *n. m.* wound, sore, blow with effusion of blood.

Chhokalad, *adj.* having a sore.

Chhŏnói, *adj.* empty.

Chhonyer, *n. f.* loss.

Chhorun, *v. t.* to dismiss; chhúr, chhorán, chhúrmut, chhorih.

Chhu (*m.*), *v.* is.

Chhuk, *v.* 2nd *p. s. m.* art.

Chhúlmut, *perf. p.* washed.

Chhun, *n. m.* a draught.

Chhun, *v. t.* to drink; chhón, chhĕwán, chhónmut, chheyih.

Chhunyer. *n. m.* detriment.

Chhus, *v.* 1st *p. s. m.* am.

Chhuṭ, *adj.* white.

Chich, *n. f.* event.

Chíjlá, *n. m.* ash (Fraximus xanthoxylloides).

Chikan, *n. m.* embroidery with silk thread.

Chikandór, *n. m.* an embroiderer.

Chil, *n. m.* a wooden pile for support.

Chíl, *n. m.* Pinus excelsa.

Chin, *n. f.* a large dish.

Chín, *n. m.* China.

Chínáṅ, *n. m.* Panicum miliaceum.

Chinwa, *n. m.* Panicum miliaceum.

Chiraita, *n. m.* Verbena, Ophelia chireta.

Chirr, *n. m. f.* lamb.

Chirrakat, *n. m.* lamb.

Chírun (nichoṛná), *v. t.* to squeeze, to wring (as wet clothes); chúrun, chírán, chúrmut, chírih.

Chítah, *n. m.* Plumbago Europea.

Chitana, *n. m.* Pyrus kumaonensis.

Chik-bato, *n. m.* Trifolium pratense.

Chitra, *n. m.* Serpent-stick (Staphylea emodi).

Chitra, *n. m.* Plumbago Europea.

Chíz, *n. f.* thing.

Chób, *n. f.* beating.

Chób dinyi, *v. t.* to beat.

Chobuk, *n. m.* whip.

Chŏbur, *n. m.* young man.

Chogul dányí, see 'Danyí.'

Chŏk, *n. m.* scar.

Chŏka, *n. m.* a cooking range. In the houses of the common people it is placed either in the small hall of the house, or in the topmost floor.

Chon, *adj.* thy.

Chóṅchih, *n. m.* spoon, a wooden cooking-ladle.

Chónṭ, *n. m.* mouth.

Chóp, *n. m.* instep.

Chopándíga, *n. m.* Achillea millefolium.

Chór, *n. m.* an idiot.

Chráṭ, *n. m.* a pargana of Maráz, the rice of which is esteemed excellent.

Chrong, *n. m.* handful (of grain).

Chúál, *n. m.* Enonymus fimbriata and Hamiltonii.

Chúj, *n. f.* ash (Fraximus xanthoxylloides).

Chun (pína), *v. t.* to drink; chau, chĕwán, chomut, cheyih.

Chúna, *n. m.* lime. It is supplied from Safapór, near to Mánasbal.

Chúnah, *n. m.* lime, see 'Chúna.'

Chunyer, *n. m.* loss, defeat, detriment.

Chúnz, *n. f.* maid-servant.

Chyun, *v. t.* to drink.

D.

D: this letter is pronounced as in English.

Ḍ, with a dot under it, is pronounced by rolling the tongue back upon itself.

Ḍab, *n. m.* a villiage in the Sáirí pargana. Near to it is a lake called Ḍabsar.

Ḍab, *n. m.* palace.

Dab, *n. m.* Typha angustifolia.

Dabáwun, *v. t.* to threaten.

Ḍabsar, *n. m.* a lake near to the village of Ḍab.

Ḍabsar, *n. m.* a lake near to Shádapór. The Lotus or Nelumbium grows in it.

Dach, *n. m.* grape. There are said to be at least six varieties of grape growing in Kashmir. These varieties are: Kishmishi dach, Krihun dach, or Káwir dach, Apaimán dach, Dún dach or Pán dach, Hasain dach, Káwa dach. The last variety is so named from its being as black as a crow. The first, third, and fifth varieties are said to be the finest. Grapes are in season in Kashmir in the month of September. Unripe grapes are called Kur.

The vine may be seen in some parts of the valley hanging in beautiful festoons about the trees of the forests in a wild state. The Hindus express the juice of the grape, strain it, place it in the sun for four or five days, and then drink it. It is said to be a good drink.

Dachanpór, *n. m.* a pargana of Maráz.

The pargana of Dachanpára is famous for its horses. A native pays for a good Kashmírí horse from twenty-five to forty rupees double, or from 2*l.* 10*s.* to 4*l.*

Dacharáñṭ, *n. m. f.* vineyard, vine.

Dáchhul, *n. m.* bruised grain, either wheat or barley.

Dáchhun, *n. m.* south.

Dachhun, *adj.* right.

Dachun, *n. m.* south.

Dachun, *adj.* right (dahna).

Dádalad, *adj.* miserable.

Dadarinág, *n. m.* a fountain in the Vehi pargana, near to the village of Khrú.

Dadir, *n. m.* the edible part of a cucumber.

Dãdkóṭ, *adj.* grieved, afflicted.

Dãdlad, *adj.* having pain, grieved, afflicted.

Dádlad, *adj.* ill, sick, pained, grieved.

Dadúr, *n. m.* Rhamnus virgatus.

Dadyun, *n. m.* an extensive karewah or plateau in the Dachanpór pargana.

Dáe, *n. f.* nurse.

Dáf, *n. m.* rest.

Dafá, *n. m.* repulse.

Dáf dyun (árám kardan), *v. t.* to rest.

Dag, *n. m.* the smarting pain of a wound.

Dág, *n. m.* spot.
Daga, *n. m.* fraud.
Dágal, *n. m.* agate.
Daganáwun, *v. t.* to cause to hash or pound; daganov, daganáwán, daganómut, daganáwih.
Dága-shálwol, *n. m.* the chief of the shawl department.
Dágdár sapadun, *v. i.* to become defiled.
Daghabáz, *n. m.* traitor.
Dághadár karun, *v. t.* to stain.
Ḍagun (kuftan), *v. t.* to crush.
Dàh, *n. m.* smoke.
Dah, *adj.* ten.
Dahan, *n. m.* mouth.
Dàhyum, *adj.* tenth.
Dai, *n. m.* God.
Dáí, *n. m.* God.
Dai, *adj.* two and a half.
Ḍáí, *adj.* two and a half.
Daij, *n. f.* handkerchief, bandage.
Dain, *n. m.* Oryza sativa. Sandals are made of the straw.
Dainditu̧j, *n. f.* toothpick.
Daiya, *n. f.* favour, kindness.
Daiyiwun, *adj.* sorrowful.
Daj, *n. f.* towel.
Dàj, *n. f.* a bandage.
Dajiryel, *n. m.* bandage.
Dajitur, *n. m.* bandage.
Daka, *n. m.* jolting
Dakah, *n. m.* push, shove.
Ḍãkar, *n. m.* eructation, belch, belching.
Dákawol, *n. m.* postman.
Ḍakh, *n. m.* a prop (wooden), a lock of hair behind the ears of Hindu children.
Dakhin, *n. m.* South.
Dakhlar, *n. f.* virgin.
Dakhun, *n. m.* South.
Ḍákir, *n. f.* basket for holding fruit.
Ḍãkur, *n. m.* belch, belching, eructation.
Ḍákur, *n. m.* belch, belching, eructation.
Ḍãkur karun, *v. i.* to belch, to eructate.
Ḍãkur khasun, *v. i.* to belch, to break wind upwards, to eructate.
Ḍãkur, tráwun, *v. i.* to belch, to eructate.
Ḍãkur yun, *v. i.* to belch, to eructate.
Ḍal, *n. m.* lake. Dal is also a Tibetan word, meaning "still." The Ḍal is a large lake close to the city of Srínagar. It is said to have been at one time an extensive plain, called Vitálamarg, and to have been converted into a lake by a Hindu Rájá. This lake is a source of large revenue to the Government, who let it to the highest bidder. It was let in 1869 for 30,000 chilkies a-year. The

farmers of it are said to make out of it 40,000 chilkie rupees annually.

Ḍál, *n. f.* shield.

Dál, *n. m.* a kind of pulse. The dál of Khampur is considered the best in Kashmir.

Dálá, *n.* Valeriana Wallichiana?

Dalaráwun, *v. t.* to mislead, to delude.

Dalom, *adj.* round.

Ḍálun, *v. t.* to mar.

Ḍalun, (bigaṛná) *v. i* to go wrong.

Ḍalun, *v. i.* to walk about.

Dályedir, *adj.* unfortunate.

Dam, *n. m.* breath.

Damanbasta, *n. f.* bellows.

Dámbur, *n. m.* fire-place (rural name).

Ḍamiṅ, *n. f.* stomach.

Damjádá, *adj.* breathless.

Dan, *n. m.* handle.

Dan (zodiac sign), *n. m.* Sagittarius.

Dan, *n. m.* stalk of apple or pear.

Dãn, *n. m.* pomegranate.

Dáṅ, *n. m.* pomegranate. Three species grow in Kashmir; tsŏk dáṅ, mŏdur dáṅ, and jigari dáṅ. The pomegranate ripens in September. It is of inferior quality.

Dán, *n. m.* fire-place, oven.

Dána, *n. m.* drop, steel, grain.

Dánawol, *adj.* rich.

Dand, *n. m.* tooth.

Dánd, *n. m.* ox, bull, bullock. This is the name current in the city for bull, in the country, hakhur is the word used.

Ḍanḍa, *n. m.* pestle.

Ḍanda-khilál, *n. m.* toothpick.

Dandása, *n. m.* the bark of the walnut-tree.

Dandir, *n. f.* the edge of every thing except that of cutting instruments.

Dándir, *n. m.* kitchen-gardener.

Dándirain, *n. f.* female kitchen-gardener, or gardener's wife.

Ḍanḍora, *n. m.* proclamation.

Dandú, *n. m.* madder (Rubia cordifolia).

Ḍáng, *n. m.* a club. This word is used out of Sirinagar.

Ḍangur, *n. m.* quadruped, also a term of abuse.

Daṅj, *n. f.* towel.

Dán-kul, *n. m.* pomegranate-tree. The fruit is mature in the month of September.

Danna, *n. m.* fortune.

Danna (naqd), *n. m.* cash, money.

Dannarust, *adj.* poor.

Ḍánṭún, *n. m.* envy.

Dânt, *n. m.* ivory.

Danun, *v. t.* to disperse; dun, danán, dunmut, danyih.

Dányí (shãlí), *n. f.* rice in the husks, rice-growing. There are the following varieties: Safed dányi, Zag dányi, Lãr-byol dányi, Reban dányi, Káthachhán danyi, Púthi-brár dányi, Mushkabudij dányi, Sokhdás dányi, Wú-lag dányi, Braz dányi, Yim-birzal dányi, Kunyi dányi, Basmati dányi, Chogul dányi. The last three varieties named are the best. The Kunyi dányi grows near a village called Goḍasut, in the pargana of Yich The Basmati dányi grows near to Nathipor, in the same pargana. And Chogul dányi, the finest of all, grows in Telbal, in the pargana of Phák.

Rice is the staple grain of Kashmir. The inhabitants live chiefly upon it. Rice-land is regarded as the most valuable, the saffron-fields alone excepted. Rice is sown in April, and reaped in September and October. The rice of Nepúr is considered by some as the best in the valley.

Before the present Rájá began to reign, twelve years ago, the kharwar of rice was procurable for eight annas, and the trak of oil, *i.e.* six seers, was then seven annas.

Dányih, *n. f.* growing-rice, rice in husks.

Dányiwal, *n. f.* coriander-seed.

Dáo, *n. m.* (favourable) opportunity, wager.

Ḍáp, *n. f.* sleep.

Ḍáp-tráwinyi, *v. i.* to sleep.

Dapun, *v. t.* to tell, to explain, to say, to speak; du̇p, dapán, dúpmut, dapih.

Dãr, *n. f.* beard.

Dãr, *n. m.* window. Small windows in the houses of the rich are sometimes filled with glass in Kashmir. The glass is imported from the Panjab. Mica, too, is used for the same purpose.

Dãr, *n. m.* cornfield, beam.

Ḍar, *n. m.* fear.

Dára, *n. f.* the edge of cutting instruments.

Darak, *n. m.* leech, dispute.

Daram, *n. m.* religion.

Ḍaranáwun, *v. t.* to frighten.

Ḍarawol, *adj.* rich.

Darengrí, *n. f.* the astringent leaves of Rhus cotinus, or allied species used in dying.

Dáripauṭ, *n. m.* a window which is closed by a board.

Dárkawól, *n. m.* leech-applier.

Darm (dharm), *n. m.* charity.

Darmárt, *n. m.* pension.

Darogha, *n. m.* superintendent.

Darshun, *n. m.* look, meeting, interview.

Darshangah, *n. m.* palace.

Darthí, *n. f.* the earth.

Dárun, *v. t.* to present for the purpose of receiving something, as when a beggar presents his hand or his wallet, to open (the hand or wallet), to receive something.

Ḍárun, *v. i.* to fear.

Darwáza, *n. m.* door.

Daryá, *n. m.* river.

Dás, *n. m.* desolation, servant.

Dásabáo, *n. m.* service.

Dastár, *n. m.* turbán (man's).

Dattur, *n. m.* Datura Stramonium. It grows wild in Kashmir.

Dáturr, *n. m.* Datura fastuosa.

Dáturr chhat, *n. m.* Datura alba.

Daub, *n. m.* washerman, who is generally a Mussulman.

Daubi, *n. m.* washerman.

Daubibáí, *n. f.* washerwoman, or washerman's wife.

Daug, *n. m.* fist, a blow.

Dauker, *n. m.* hammer.

Ḍâúl. *n. m.* border, hem.

Daul, *n. m.* skirt of a garment.

Daulat, *n. f.* fortune.

Dawa, *n. f.* medicine, remedy.

Dáwá, *n. m.* claim, law-suit.

Dawanáwun, *v. t.* to make to run; dawanowun, dawanáwán, dawanomut, dawanáwih.

Dawun, *v. i.* to run; dau, also dúv, dawán, daumut, dawih.

Dayár (naqd), *n. m.* cash, money, fortune.

Dáyira, *n. m.* a stoneless ring, worn chiefly by women.

Dazawun, *adj.* burning.

Dazun, *v. i.* to burn; daud, dazán, daudmut, dazih, also dúd, dúdmut.

Dĕd, *n. f.* mother.

Dejihor, *n. f.* ear-ring.

Ḍeka, *n. m.* success.

Ḍekabáuḍ, *adj.* lucky.

Dekah, *n. m.* the forehead.

Deko, *n. m.* the forehead.

Dĕl, *n. m.* skin of fruit, bark of tree.

Ḍel, *n. f.* a thong made of straw.

Dela, *n. m.* clod.

Dém, *n. m.* island.

Ḍemb (guzargah), *n. m.* ferry, ford.

Ḍenṭh, *n. m.* sight.

Ḍenṭon, *n. m.* girdle, waistband.

Deo, *n. m.* demon.

Deodár, *n. m.* Himalayan cedar (Cedrus deodara).

Ḍer, *n. m.* a heap of rupees or grain, store, granary, magazine.

Deshun, *v. t.* to see.

Deví, *n. f.* a proper name.

Dewa, *adv.* perhaps, possibly, probably.

Dĕwah, *adv.* perhaps.

Déwána, *adj.* mad.

Dewánah, *adj.* mad.

Dewán-khána, *n. m.* palace.

Dewár, *n. f.* wall.

Dharam Chand, *n. m.* a proper name.

Dharamsál, *n. m.* inn.

Dhanní, *n. m.* Portulacea aleracea ?

Dhehra, *n. m.* a musical instrument consisting of an iron rod about a foot and a-half long, on which are placed several iron rings ; the rings are shaken to keep time with the music.

Ḍhúmb, *n. m.* the watchman of a village.

Dhúp, *n. m.* Dolomiæa Macrocephala.

Diár, *n. m.* Himalayan cedar (Cedrus deodara). The wood of this magnificent tree is the most valuable to be found on the Panjab Himalayas. It reaches a height of from 100 to 200 feet, and has a girth ranging from 20 to 40 feet. The Deodar forests are very extensive, and of great value. The Cedrus deodara is supposed to be identical with the cedar of Lebanon.

Didarí, *n. f.* a proper name.

Didur, *n. f.* pheasant. Its gait is so much thought of that the natives of the valley, when praising the gait of a woman, say she walks like a pheasant.

Díḍwoin, *n. m.* watchman, door-keeper, porter, gate-keeper.

Dígar, *n. m.* five o'clock, twilight, a part of the fourth division of the day, lasting for about an hour before sunset.

Digaran, *n. m.* five o'clock.

Dígaras, *adv.* at the evening twilight.

Dígchí, *n. m.* a cooking-vessel, large, round, brazen, with narrow mouth.

Dijahur, *n. m.* earrings.

Dikh, thou shalt or wilt give.

Dil, *n. m.* heart.

Dilása karun, *v. t.* to console.

Dilas-praywun, *adj.* cheering.

Dilas tasalli dinyi, *v. t.* to comfort.

Dilband, *adj.* beloved.

Dildár, *n. m.* & *f.* sweetheart.

Dilerí, *n. f.* courage.

Dilgír, *adj.* sad.

Dil hazín, *adj.* sad of heart.

Dil-khosh, *adj*. comfortable.

Dil-khosh karun, *v. t.* to rejoice, to gladden.

Dil-khosh sapadun, *v. i.* to rejoice.

Dil-o-jánah set, *adv*. cordially.

Diltang, *adj*. sad, distressed.

Dimah, I will, or shall give.

Dimai is made up of dimah and í.

Dimau, we shall or will give.

Dimb, *n. m.* a kind of vegetable found only in the Dal and in the Anchár lake. This vegetable is said to be found only in Kashmir.

Dimbashãj, *n. m.* hyena. It is said to be very rare in the valley.

Dín, *n. m.* religion.

Din, *n. m.* day.

Din, they shall, or will give.

Dinawol, *n. m.* giver.

Dinawol, *adj*. generous.

Díp, *n. m.* lamp.

Dísh, *n. f.* native country.

Divadár, *n. m.* cedar. This is the word in use in Srínagar. The best houses in the valley, as well as the long bridges spanning the river Jhelum, are built of this wood, which is remarkable for its strength and durability.

Divagŏn, *n. m.* the name of the ceremonies which take place on the third day after the boy has been invested with the Brahminical thread (yónyí).

Divasar, *n. m.* a pargana of Maráz.

Divasaribála, *n. m.* a village in the Divasar pargana.

Díwána, *adj*. furious.

Diyah, he shall, or will give.

Diya karanwol, *adj*. friendly, kind.

Diyár, *n. m.* wealth, riches.

Diyárawol, *n. m.* rich man, Dives.

Diyu, you shall, or will give.

Ḍiyung, *n. m.* a ball of thread.

Dizah! *exclam*. used to drive away a dog.

Dó-aspah, *adv*. quickly.

Dŏbarun, *v. t.* to bury.

Dód (dard), *n. m.* pain, sickness, ailment, disease, agony.

Dŏd, *n. m.* milk.

Ḍŏḍ, *adj*. one-and-a-half.

Dodabungir, *n. m.* a kind of bracelet.

Dŏdarnu, *v. i.* to rot, to be worn; dodareo, dodarán, dodareomut, dodariḥ.

Dód ásun, *v. i.* to suffer pain, to be pained.

Dód lagun, *v. i.* to suffer pain, to be pained.

Dód sapadun, *v. i.* to suffer pain, to be pained.

Dódur, *n. m.* rottenness.

Dŏg, *n. m.* stroke.

Dŏg dyun, *v.* to beat.

Doh, *n. m.* day. By day, dohas. To-day, az.

Dohai, *adv.* continually, always, eternally, ever.

Dŏhaiṭhyum, *adj.* sixty-second.

Dohas, *adv.* in the day-time, by day.

Dohéṭh, *adj.* sixty-two.

Dó,íkhár, *n. m.* a kind of charm.

Doilití, *n. f.* a proper name.

Dŏk, *n. m.* nuisance, trouble.

Dŏkh, *n. m.* trouble, annoyance, affliction, vexation, pain.

Dŏkhalad, *adj.* uneasy, pained, afflicted, vexed, troubled, annoyed.

Dŏkh dyun, *v. t.* to torment.

Dŏkhí, *adj.* uneasy.

Dólnah, *n. m.* the small tin or silver case in which charms are worn by the Mussulmans.

Dŏn, *adj.* both.

Dŏn, *obj.* of zah, two.

Donamat, *adj.* ninety-two.

Dónun, *v. t.* to card or clean cotton ; dún, dónan, dunmut, dónih.

Dopáhar, *n. m.* midday, noon.

Dór, *n. f.* running.

Dór, *n. m.* Spiræa Lindleyana.

Dór, *n. m.* field, little garden.

Dŏr, *adj.* hard.

Dóranáwun, *v. t.* to cause to run ; dóranov, dóranáwán, dóranómut, dóranáwih.

Dorawun, *n. m.* runner.

Dorgat (shikast), *n. m.* defeat.

Dorun, *v. i.* to hasten, to run ; doreo, dorán, doreomut, dorih, doreyo, doreyomut.

Dŏs, *n. f.* a wall of earth or brick, surrounding a garden or house.

Dóshawa, *adj.* both (donoṅ).

Dosil, *n. m.* mason, builder.

Dosil báí, *n. f.* builder's wife, mason's wife.

Dost, *n. m.* male friend.

Dostdãri, *n. f.* friendship.

Dost sapadun, *v. i.* to befriend.

Ḍóṭ, *n. m.* hailstones.

Dótãjih, *adj.* forty-two.

Dótãjihyum, *adj.* forty-second.

Ḍoṭh, *n. m.* hail.

Dótrãh, *adj.* thirty-two.

Dótrãhyum, *adj.* thirty-second.

Dowanzah, *adj.* fifty-two.

Doyshít, *adj.* eighty-two.

Dŏyi laṭi, *adv.* twice.

Dŏyi phiri, *adv.* twice.

Dŏyitãjih, *adj.* forty-two.

Dŏyitãjihyum, *adj.* forty-second.

Dŏyitrãh, *adj.* thirty-two.

Dŏyitrāhyum, *adj.* thirty-second.

Dŏyum, *adj.* second, another.

Dóyun, *v. t.* to milk; dóyun, dóyán, dóimut, dóyih.

Drab, *n. m.* the Toon tree (Cedrela Toona).

Drág, *n. m.* famine.

Drál, *n. m.* an agent.

Drálid, *adj.* unfortunate.

Dramun, *n. m.* the short grass of the field, green grass.

Drashṭ, *n. m.* faculty of sight.

Drashṭánṭ, *adj.* manifest, visible, evident.

Draug, *adj.* dear.

Drawí, *n. m.* the toon (Cedrela Toona).

Drayí, *n. f.* oath.

Drayí háwinyi, *v. i.* to swear.

Drayi karinyi, *v. t.* to swear.

Drayí khinyi, *v. i.* to swear.

Drek, *n. m.* Pistacia integerrima.

Drenṭ, *n. m.* eye-sight.

I have no eye-sight at night, Rát kyut drenṭ iwán chhumnah.

Drí, *n. f.* oath.

Drí ásinyi, *v. i.* to swear.

Drí háwinyi, to swear.

Drik, *n. m.* leech; much used in Kashmir by the native hakíms.

Drikagur, *n. m.* leech-applier.

Drí khinyi, *v. i.* to swear.

Drin, *n. m.* marmot.

Drŏg, *adj.* dear, high-priced, valuable.

Drŏk, *n. f.* vomiting, sickness, squeamishness.

Drót, *n. m.* sickle.

Drug, *adj.* dear, expensive, costly, precious.

Drugamul, *n. m.* a village in the Wutar pargana.

Drúl, *n. m.* skin.

Dü, *n. m.* spray.

Dúbárah, *adv.* again, twice.

Dubrun, *v. i.* to hide.

Duda, *n. m.* invitation.

Dúdal, *n. m.* dandelion (Taraxacum officinale).

Dúd-phras, *n. m.* Himalayan poplar (Populus ciliata).

Dug, *n. m.* box with the closed fist, blow.

Duh, *n. m.* smoke.

Duh, *n. f.* snake.

Dúiyum, *adj.* next.

Dúján, *adj.* pregnant.

Ḍúk, *n. m.* the reed covering of a boat.

Dukándár, *n. m.* shop-keeper.

Dúkăr, *n. f.* scissors.

Ḍúl, *n. m.* a large earthenware vessel in which one can bathe.

Dul (dáman), *n. m.* hem.

Dúl, *n. m.* a kind of litter or sedan.

Dúl, *adj.* lazy.

Ḍula gatshun, *v. i.* to roll.

Ḍulan dyun, *v. t.* to roll.

Ḍulun, *v. i.* to roll; ḍul, ḍulán, ḍulmut, ḍulih.

Dúm, *n. m.* cow herd, shepherd, cotton-carder.

Dumah, *n. m.* tail of a horse.

Ḍúmb, *n. m.* informer, policeman, night watchman of a village.

Ḍum-ḍum, *n. m.* a drum.

Ḍum-ḍum wayanwol, *n. m.* a drummer.

Dúmij, *n. f.* crupper.

Dumtúlí, *n. f.* maiden-hair fern (Adiantum capillus Veneris).

Ḍumuṭ, *n. m.* dome, vault.

Dún, *n. m.* juglans regia, walnut. The walnut-tree flourishes in a remarkable manner in Kashmir. The fruit is good and cheap, and is largely eaten by the natives. The oil which is expressed from the nut is eaten and burnt. The old wood is hard and dark. It is used for cabinet-work, papier-maché boxes, and gun stocks. Flies are greatly attracted by the fragrance of the leaves. The walnut of Kashmir ripens in September. One thousand walnuts may be bought for sixpence. There are three species; Burzali dún, Wónṭ dún, and Tsuts dún.

Dún, *n. m.* a cotton carder.

Dún, *adj.* three quarters, a quarter less. Dúnhat, a quarter less a hundred, *i. e.* seventy-five.

Dŭnamat, *adj.* ninety-two.

Dŭnamatyum, *adj.* ninety-second.

Dúnawol, *n. m.* sweeper.

Dún dach, see 'Dach.'

Dunga, *n. m.* a covered boat for passengers with their baggage and servants. The names of the different parts of the 'Dunga' are, nam, tram, mahtábtí, gálo, khaut, bushkám, which see.

Dúnhat, *adj.* seventy-five.

Dúns, *n. m.* a pargana in the Kamráz division of the valley.

Dún tríh, *adj.* two and three quarters.

Dúnun, *v. t.* to sweep.

Dunya, *n. m.* world.

Dúnyí, *n. f.* bow.

Dúnyikul, *n. m.* walnut-tree.

Dún zah, *adj.* one-and-three-quarters.

Dúpaṭṭa, *n. m.* a cotton shawl.

Dúr, *n. m.* pearl. This word is generally used of pearls adorning female ears.

Dúr, *n. m.* repulse.

Dúr, *n. f.* a street without shops.

Dúr, *n. f.* a border round the bottom of the pheran.

Dúr, *adj.* & *adv.* far, distant, remote.

Dur, *adj.* hard, firm, strong.

Dúré, *adv.* at a distance.

Dúrih, *adv.* at a distance.

Dúri pĕṭ, *adv.* at a distance.

Dúrir, *n. f.* separation, distance.

Dúr karun (dafā sákhtan), *v. i.* to expel.

Dúrma, *n. m.* a woollen blanket.

Duróg, *n. m.* lie.

Durr, *adj.* strong, robust, earnest, manly, hard, durable.

Duru, *n. m.* valley.

Dúryir, *n. f.* distance.

Ḍus, *n. m.* a club. This is the word used in Srínagar.

Dúsatat, *adj.* seventy-two.

Dusatatyuṃ, *adj.* seventy-second.

Dushít, *adj.* eighty-two.

Dushítyum, *adj.* eighty-second.

Dushman, *n. m.* enemy, rival.

Dushmaní, *n. f.* enmity, hostility, resistance, discord.

Dushmaní karinyi, *v. t.* to oppose, to hate, to resist.

Dúwanzah, *adj.* fifty-two.

Dúwanzāhyum, *adj.* fifty-second.

Dúwun (jháṛná), *v. t.* to sweep, to make clean by sweeping: ḍúwun, ḍúwán, dúmut ḍúwih.

Dyáwun, *v. t.* to cause to give, dyov, dyáwán, dyómut, dyáwih.

Dyãr, *n. f*, a rich woman.

Dyĕl, *n. m.* skin of fruit.

Dyón, *n. m.* foundation.

Dyór, *n. m.* a rich man.

Dyul, *n m.* a soft kind of grass with which merchants tie up their goods.

Dyun (dená) *v. t.* to give, to deliver, dyutun, diwán, dyutmut, diyih.

E.

E: There are two varieties of this letter, viz. e or é, and ĕ; é is pronounced as *a* in the English word mate; ĕ is pronounced as *e* in the English word pet.

Eikangom, *n. m.* a village in the Bráng pargana.

Eish Makám, *n. m.* a village of the Kháwurpor pargana, where a large Mussulman mela, or fair, is held.

Ekbáldár, *n. m.* a proper name.

Enkasing, *n. m.* the Berberis, (Barberry).

Er, *n. m.* Prunus domestica (Plum).

Ering, *n. m.* a flower of Kashmir.

Ersa, *n. m.* Iris florentina.

Ezárdúr, *n. m.* the string with which drawers are tied.

F.

F: this letter is pronounced as in English. The Kashmíris have a habit of pronouncing *f.* in most cases as if it were *ph*.

Faida, *n. m.* interest, profit.

Faidamand, *adj.* useful, profitable.

Faidarust, *adj.* useless.

Fáka, *n. m.* fast.

Fakír, *n. m.* suppliant, beggar, who in Kashmir is generally, if not always, a Mussulman. The Hindu beggars met with in the valley are, I believe, from the plains of Inda.

Fál, *n. m.* a good omen.

Falán, *pron.* such a person.

Falãnyi, *pron.* certain one.

Farásíum, *n. m.* Salvia Moorcroftiana.

Faréb, *n. m.* deception, deceit.

Fark tháwun, *v. t.* to differ.

Fárs, *n. m.* Persia.

Fársí *adj.* Persian.

Faryád, *n. f.* complaint.

Faryád dunyi, *v. t.* to weep aloud, to complain.

Faryád karinyi, *v. t.* to complain.

Faryádí, *n. m.* defendant.

Farzand, *n. m.* son.

Fatah, *n. m.* victory.

Fatahkadal, *n. m.* a bridge over the Jhelum, in Srínagar.

Fatahmand, *adj.* victorious.

Fath, *n. m.* a proper name.

Fauj, *n. m.* army.

Faulád, *n. m.* steel.

Fazíhat karinyi, *v. t.* to rebuke.

Feringistán, *n. m.* Europe.

Fikr, *n. m.* consideration.

Fikr karinyi, *v. t.* to think.

Findak, *n. m.* nut of the Corylus avellana.

Firák, *n. m.* separation.

Fitna, *n. m.* revolt, revolution.

Fitna tráwun, *v. t.* to revolt.

Fitrásályún, *n. m.* prangos pabularia.

Rot in sheep is said to be cured by the shepherds of Kashmir by their making the sheep eat the Prangus leaf. It is also said that they successfully cure the foot rot by the application of a decoction of peach-leaves. Cattle too are fattened on the Prangos Pabularia. It is said to be abundant in the Drás valley to the north of Kashmir.

Fój, *n. m.* detachment, army.

Fólád, *n. m.* steel.

Forhat, *n.* gladness.

Fretsar, *n. m.* good fortune.

Fursat, *n. f.* opportunity.

G.

G: this letter is always pronounced hard.

Gaba, *n. m.* a kind of quilt.

Gãbat, *n. m.* slander.

Gabin, *n. f.* womb.

Gach, *n. m* lime.

Gaḍ, *n. m.* fortress.

Gáḍ, *n. m.* fish. There are several varieties of fish found in Kashmir. viz., chharú gáḍ, gurau gáḍ, and ropiṭh gáḍ. There is also the háj gáḍ, the scales of which are large and silvery and spotless. The shoulders are broad, the body gradually tapering towards the tail. Next is the Soj Gád, which is covered with small golden coloured scales. It is rather a shapeless fish: there is little difference in size between the shoulders and the tail. Lastly, there is the Ḳhrunt Gáḍ, which is very like the last named species, only that the scales are silvery and spotless.

In 1868 the prohibition to catch fish, which had existed for twelve years prior to that date, was removed by the native government. This proved a great boon to the poor Kashmíris, who are afflicted with most abject poverty.

Both Hindus and Mussulmans eat fish.

Gada, *n. m.* suppliant.

Gáḍahánz, *n. m.* fisherman.

Gáḍahánzain, *n. f.* fisherwoman.

Gaḍawa, *n. m.* a brazen drinking vessel, shaped like a bowl.

Gáḍ raṭanwol, *n. m.* fisherman.

Gáḍ raṭinyi, *v. t.* to fish.

Gaḍur, *n. m.* goitre, bronchocele. In the adjacent valley of Chambah this affection is called gilaṛ.

The inhabitants of a great many villages in Kashmir suffer from goitre. The idea prevalent in the valley as to its cause is, that the water drunk by the patients has produced it. The waters of Kashmir are largely impregnated with lime. Burnt seaweed is used by the natives in the western Himalayas as a cure for goitre.

Gafãr, *n. m.* a proper name.

Gafãra, *n. m.* a proper name.

Gafúr, *n. m.* a proper name.

Gágar, *n. m.* leechman, leech-applier.

Gagarái, *n. f.* thunder.

Gagarárai, *n. f.* thunder.

Gagaryurmí, *n. f.* Rhododendron Campanulatum.

Gagir, *n. f.* rat.

Gagur, *n. m.* rat, mouse.

Gãij, *n. f.* fireplace.

Gãir, *n. f.* clock, watch, also

native instrument or vessel for measuring time. In the bottom of the vessel there is a small aperture which allows the water filling the vessel to escape in a fixed and known time.

Gairat, *n. m.* courage.

Gaj, *n. f.* furnace, oven.

Gajga, *n. m.* tail of the ox of Ladak (yák). In India it is used for driving away flies.

Galah (ghalla), *n. m.* grain.

Galba karanwol, *n. m.* conqueror.

Galba karun, *v. t.* to conquer.

Galla, *n. m.* corn.

Gálo, *n. m.* the space in the centre of a boat occupied by the passenger.

Galun, *v. i.* to abate, to decrease, to dissolve to melt, gúl, galán, gúlmut, galih.

Gálun (galáná) *v. t.* to melt, gol, gálán, golmut, gálih.

Gam, *n. m.* sorrow, grief.

Gám, *n. m.* village.

Gambur, *n. m.* secret.

Gam kásun, *v. t.* to remove grief (literally to shove off grief).

Gán, *n. m.* keeper of a brothel. There are said to be about 30 such houses in Srínagar, buṭ none in Islamabad, Bij Bihara, Pámpur, Sopur, Báramúla, and Shupiyon. Shángas, a village in the Kútahár pargana is notorious for its prostitutes.

Gán, *n. m.* the under ground floor of a house.

Gan, *n. m.* log, bee-hive.

Ganahár, *n. m.* pearl ashes of burnt wood. The washermen use it for cleaning linen.

Ganai, the class name of the butchers.

Ganas, *n. m.* said to be a very poisonous kind of snake, about a yard long and very thick.

Ganḍ, *n. m.* knot, bandage.

Gand, *n. m.* sugar-candy.

Gandal, *n. m.* Melissa nepeta.

Gandamgúndú, *n. m.* Gipsywort (Lycopus Europæus).

Ganḍanwol, *n. m.* the framer of the Tálím which see.

Ganḍapan, *n. m.* a tassel attached to the lower ends of the silken cords which eke out the hair of the head behind, and extend down to the loins.

Ganḍun, *n. m.* betrothal, the ceremony of betrothal. This word literally means to bind.

Ganḍun, *v. t.* to entangle, to yoke, to bind.

Ganḍun, *v. t.* to bind; gonḍ, ganḍán, gonḍmut, ganḍih.

Gánḍun, (bándhná) *v. t.* to bind, to tie, gúnḍ, gánḍán, gúnḍmut, gánḍih.

Gangabal, *n. m.* a stream tributary to the Sind river. Hither go those Pandits who have had relations die during the past year, bearing their ashes, which they throw into this sacred stream with great ceremony.

Gangain, *n. m.* the large brush with which the warp is arranged. It is made of a reed called nar-kãnyi, found chiefly in the Anchár lake.

Gangajaṭan, *n. m.* a village in the Dúns pargana, highly thought of by the Pandits.

Gángal, *n. m.* interruption.

Gángal (nádurustí), *n. f.* the state of being not right.

Ganger, *n. m.* Segeretia Brandrethiana.

Ganhár, *n. m.* Amaranthus Anardana and Gangeticus.

Gãnṭ, *n. f.* a tumour behind the ear.

Gánṭ, *n. m.* vulture.

Gáith, *n. f.* kite.

Ganun, *v. i.* to become thick (of liquids), to be strong.

Gányi, *n. f.* whore, prostitute. There are said to be 150 prostitutes in Srínagar. No Panditání is among the number. The Mihtar caste and the most degraded of the Mussulmans are said to sell their daughters for this abominable trade. A heavy tax is said to be levied by the native government on these unfortunate wretches.

Ganyipora, *n. m.* a village in the Machipor pargana.

Ganz, *n. m.* tanner.

Ganzaráwun, *v. t.* to make to count.

Ganzarun, *v. t.* to number, to count; gunzur, ganzarán, gunzurmut, ganzarih.

Gáo, *n. f.* cow. Formerly, any one killing a cow was punished with death, now he is imprisoned for life. The punishment is said to be the same for killing a bull or a calf. The prisoners for killing kine are said to undergo very great hardships.

Gáoza, *n. m.* see 'Bán.'

Gap, *n. m.* jest.

Gar, *n. m.* dwelling, house.

Gar, *n. f.* hour.

Gãr, *n. m.* a species of starling.

Gãṛ, *n. m.* the Singhara or water-chesnut, without the enveloping skin. See 'Gáṛi.'

Gãṛ, *n. f.* the dried kernel of the water-chesnut.

Garah, *n. m.* house.

Garah-warah, *n. m.* house.

Garanáwai, *n. m.* the name of the first day of the Mekhla,

when the young Hindu child is invested with the Brahminical thread.

Garbathela, *n. m.* womb.

Garawol, *n. m.* master of the house.

Gard, *n. m.* dust.

Gardan, *n. f.* neck.

Gardi, *n. f.* circle.

Gáṛí, *n. f.* the Singhara, or water-chesnut, as found in the lakes of Kashmir. It ripens in the month of October. During that and the succeeding months the people extract it in enormous quantities. The nut is dried and then formed into a flour or meal, of which cakes are made. These the Kashmíris eat with salt, ghee, and flesh. The Pandits, or Hindu portion of the native population of the valley, are in the habit of fasting two days in every month, and during these two days they eat nothing but a little flour made out of the gáṛí, or water-chesnut, which flour, when cooked, is called gáṛyiwugara or phalhár, which latter word is the term applied to this simple dish by the Pandits themselves. To the people living round the Wulur Lake, by far the most extensive of the Kashmir lakes, the gáṛí, or water-chesnut, is a substitute for rice. The nut is stored away in the people's houses, and when cooked, gets the name of ã̄ṭiraz.

Gãriházn, *n. m.* collector of the Singhara nut on the lakes.

Gariyál, *n. m.* a small bell.

Garm, *adj.* warm, hot.

Gárun, *v. t.* to inquire.

Garun, *v. t.* to cut, to make, as a carpenter or blacksmith.

Garwol, *n. m.* householder.

Gaṛyiwugara, *n. m.* the name of cooked water-chesnut, see 'Gáṛí.'

Gas, *n. m.* human ordure.

Gása, *n. m.* grass.

Gásah, *n. m.* tall grass.

Gása khyun (charídan), *v. i.* to graze.

Gãsh, *n. m.* light.

Gásh, *n. m.* eyesight, light,

Gásh, *n. f.* a proper name.

Gáshdár, *adj.* light (not dark).

Gasht, *n. m.* walking.

Gásuh, *n. m.* hay.

Gaṭ, *n. m.* ferry.

Gat, *n. m.* turning round, revolution.

Gáṭa dyun, *v. t.* to teach.

Gaṭah, *n. f.* darkness.

Gáṭajár, *n. m.* prudence.
Gáṭajár, *n. m.* vigilance, wisdom.
Gáṭh, *n. m.* quay, landing-place. Washermen usually ply their work here.
Gaṭih, *n. f.* darkness.
Gat karun, *v. t.* to revolve.
Gatshun, *v. i.* to go, to become, to blow (of the wind), to depart, pass (of time); gau, gatshán, gomut, gatshih.
Gáṭúl, *n. m.* philosopher.
Gáṭul (*m.*) gáṭij (*f.*), *adj.* wise, shrewd, conscious, complete, learned, intelligent, eloquent, clever, prudent.
Gaub, *n. f.* ewe.
Gaub, *adj.* heavy.
Gaud, *n. m.* hole.
Gauḍaprán, *n. m.* leek. The Hindus of the valley do not eat it.
Gaud karun, *v. t.* to pierce.
Gaunrí, *n. m.* water chesnut (Trapa bispinosa).
Gau-roch, *n. m.* cowherd.
Gauṭ, *adj.* turbid, dark.
Gawá, *n. m.* witness.
Gawáhi, *n. f.* evidence.
Gawá,í, *n. m.* eye-witness.
Gaz, *n. m.* a measure equal to four páo.
Gazah, *n. m.* elephant.
Gázar, *n. f.* carrot eaten by the Mussulman inhabitants, but not by the Hindus.

Gehna, *n. m.* woman's ornaments.
Gelun, *v. t.* to ridicule.
Gelun, *v. i.* to joke, to jest.
Geṅ, *n. f.* wrinkle.
Gera, *n. m.* sphere, circle.
Ghabghab, *n. m.* dewlap, double chin.
Gháfiz, *n. m.* the flowers of the Delphinium saniculæfolium.
Ghaibat, *n. m.* slander.
Gham barun, *v. i.* to grieve.
Gham khyun, *v. i.* to grieve.
Ghanísha, *n. m.* a proper name.
Ghánṭ, *n. m.* vulture.
Gharíb, *adj.* poor.
Ghãs, *n, m.* a grass cutter.
Gháso, *n. m.* grass.
Ghulám, *n. m.* slave.
Ghusal, *n. m.* bath.
Ghusal karun, *v. t.* to bathe, see 'Karun.'
Ghyau, *n. m.* ghee.
Ghyúr, *n. m.* vertigo, revolution.
Gídardák, *n. m.* Segeretia opposititifolia.
Gil, *n. m.* earth.
Giláf, *n. m.* cover.
Gilás, *n. m.* Cerasus vulgaris (cherry).
Gindun, *v. i.* to sport, to gambol (as children), to play; gyund, gindán, gyundmut, gindih.

Gira, *n m.* forefinger's length.

Git. *n. m.* a span about nine inches in length.

Giur, *n. m.* Salix Babylonica.

Giwáhi, *n. f.* testimony, witnessing.

Gíwáin, *n. m.* a species of Elæagnus.

Glás, *n. m.* a drinking vessel, shaped like an English tumbler. It is made either of iron, brass, or silver; Cerasus vulgaris (cherry).

Glás-kul, *n. m.* cherry tree.

Gŏb, *n. f.* ewe.

Gŏb, *adj.* heavy.

Gobar, *n. m.* deafness.

Gŏber, *n. m.* weight, heaviness, deafness.

Góbikhora, *adj.* pregnant.

Gŏbir, *n. m.* heaviness, deafness, weight.

Gŏbur, *n. m.* son.

Gŏbun, *v. i.* to be heavy.

Gŏḍ, *n. m.* malleolus, external malleolus, ankle, leg (the part being put for the whole), root, stem, trunk of tree.

Gŏḍ, *n. f.* fish, commencement, beginning. In (or at) the beginning, gŏdanyi.

Gŏḍain, *n. f.* beginning, commencement.

Gŏḍain, *adv.* especially.

Goḍakur, *m.* an anklet.

Goḍanyí (awalan), *adv.* at first, in the beginning.

Goḍanyuk (*m.*), goḍanyich (*f.*), *adj.* first, elder. Elder brother, Goḍanyuk boi.

Goḍasut, *n. m.* a village of the Yach Pargana, near to which the best rice in the valley is said to grow.

Goḍuk (*m.*), goḍich (*f.*), *adj.* first.

Gofár Sháh, *n. m.* a proper name.

Gogij, *n. f.* turnip. In the winter time both Hindus and Mussulmans consume large numbers of turnips. The turnips of Haripúṛ are said to be the best in the valley.

Gogul, *n. m.* ball, sphere.

Goh, *n. m.* fæces.

Gohistán, *n. m.* anus.

Gólí, *n. f.* the Singhara nut free of its shell and skin.

Góli kutsur, *n. m.* seller of the Singhara nuts, stripped of their shells and skins.

Gŏlúr, *n. m.* nut.

Gón, *n. m.* bow-string.

Gona, *n. m.* bow for projecting pellets.

Gŏnah, *n. m.* sin, vice.

Gonḍal, *n. m.* the earthenware vessel of the Kángrí.

Gondur, *n. m.* handful of anything except grain and grass.

Góńts, *n. f.* moustache.

Gontsa, *n. m.* moustache.

Gŏnyi, *n. f.* granary.

Gŏp (ghár), *n. m.* den.

Gŏpan-gúr, *n. m.* cow-herd. The cow-herds are not Kashmírís. They are not numerous. In the spring time they collect large herds of cattle belonging to others, and drive them away to the mountains to graze. They take their wives and families with them.

Gŏph, *n. m.* pit, hole, cavern.

Gór, *n. m.* a Brahman, a grave, the Singhárá nut, a kind of sugar, water-chesnut (Singhárá), treacle, molasses.

Goramal, *n. m.* gravedigger.

Góramala, *n. m.* gravedigger.

Górawár, *n. m.* Thursday.

Gordol, *n. m.* a small apricot.

Góró, *n. m.* the planet Jupiter.

Górú, or Gór (Singhárá) *n. m.* the water-chesnut, which abounds in the large Kashmir lakes.

Gọshabab Tangakul, see 'Tangakul.'

Gosha Rám, *n. m.* a proper name.

Goshibeigi ṭang, see 'Tang.'

Goshú, *n. m.* a proper name.

Gŏta, *n. m.* dip, dive.

Gotilyí, *n. m.* sawyer.

Gótsh, *n. f.* moustache.

Gotsur, *n. f.* small purse, bag.

Grad, *n. m.* eagle. Eagles are said to be numerous towards the south-east end of the valley.

Gráe, *n. f.* shaking.

Grahan (gruhun), *n. f.* eclipse.

Grakun, *v. i.* to boil; grĕkeo, grakán, grekeomut, grakih.

Grand, *n. f.* number, reckoning, quantity, counting, computation.

Grand karinyi, *v. t.* to number, to reckon, to compute, to count.

Gráo, *n. m.* complaint, accusation, blame.

Gráo karun, *v. t.* to accuse, to complain, to blame.

Grás, *n. m.* piece, morsel.

Gratij kain, *n. f.* grindstone.

Graṭṭa, *n. m.* mill.

Graz, *n. m.* calf of the leg.

Grazun, *v. i.* to roar; grozun, grazán, grozmut, grazih.

Gred, *n. m.* vulture.

Grĕkanáwun, *v. t.* to cook.

Grestil, *n. f.* agriculture, cultivation of the soil.

Grŏk, *n. m.* swallowing.

Gróst, *n. m.* tenant farmer, peasant, cultivator of the soil. The farmers in Kashmir are nearly all Mussulmans.

Grotsun, *v. i.* to be agitated (of water).

Grŏz, *n.f.* calf of leg, leg, (technically) Tendo Achillis.

Grúst, *n. m.* cultivator of soil. Form in use in Srínagar.

Gubur, *n. m.* son.

Gúch, *n. m.* Viburnum cotinifolium, Viburnum fœtens.

Guḍ, *n.f.* mare. The word in use towards Islamabad.

Gúd, *n.f.* vulva, hole,

Gudóm, *n. m.* tether.

Gufta Ganga, *n. m.* a spring of water near to the famous Shalimár gardens and a village called Ishabar, where a Hindu festival is held in April.

Gugchí, *n. m.* turnip (Brassica rapa).

Guh, *n. m.* manure. The Kashmírí farmers have several ways of manuring their ground. At times the manure is all put in one place, and water is then poured on it; and this water is made to cover the whole field by means of small channels: at other times the manure is spread over the fields, as is the way with British farmers; and at other times, the manure is first dried and then burned, and then the ashes are scattered over the fields. The ordure if oxen is used for manuring the cereals, while human ordure is employed for manuring vegetables.

Guhun (surma karná), *v. t.* to pulverize, to powder, to grind, guhun, guhán, guhmut, guhih.

Gúiṅ, *n. m.* stack of grain.

Gúiṅ, *n. f.* a stalk of grain.

Guir, *n. f.* mare.

Gújar, *n. m.* cow-herd, see 'Gŏpan-gúr.'

Gul, *n. m.* Cichorium intybus.

Gúl, *n. m.* Plantago major.

Gúl, *n.* the forearm, the arm from the elbow to the wrist.

Gúl, *n. m.* wrist.

Gul, *n. m.* a species of bracelet, massive and open.

Guláb, *n. m.* rose water, rose. There are two great varieties of rose in Kashmir. Lál guláb, or the red rose, and Arawal, or the yellow rose.

Guláb-bág. *n. m.* a village of the Phák pargana.

Gulábi ṭang, see 'Tang.'

Gulábí Tangakul, see 'Tangakul.'

Gulál, *n. m.* field poppy.

Gulála, *n. m.* tulip,

Gul-lála, *n. m.* the field poppy, the young leaves of which the Kashmírís eat.

Gulitálím, *n. m.* the pattern of a Kashmir shawl intended for the manufacturer that he may see the design of the shawl.

Gulmarg, *n. m.* a beautiful little valley nestling among the mountains, at an elevation of 3000 ft. above the valley of Kashmir. Gulmarg is a favourite resort of the English visitors during the months of June and July, to escape the disagreeable heat of the valley. Gulmarg is derived from gul, a rose, or flower and Marg, a valley or plain among the mountains. This little valley is carpeted with flowers of different varieties.

Gulubán, *n. m.* one who takes care of a herd of horses during the pasturage season.

Gúlyí, *n. f.* ripe kernel of the water-chesnut, the unripe water-chesnut, see gárí.

Gúma, *n. m.* perspiration, sweat.

Gumah, *n. m.* sweat, perspiration.

Gumáshta, *n. m.* agent, superintendent.

Gumbaz, *n. m.* arch.

Guna, *n. m.* sack.

Gunafsh, *n. m.* amethyst.

Gunah, *n. m.* a sack made of goat's hair,

Gunah, *n. m.* sin, crime, fault.

Gunas, *n. f.* a poisonous, round-headed, short, thick serpent, found on the mountains of Kashmir. It is said to be black on the back, and yellowish on the belly. It is a foot and a half long, and ash coloured according to some natives. Its bite is often fatal. When a person is stung, on the arm, or leg, a ligature is applied between the heart and the wound, which is besmeared with foam. The patient has arak and conserve of roses given him to eat, while music is played to cheer him up. This is the native treatment of serpent-bites. The Gunas is said to be numerous in the Lãr pargana.

Serpents are seldom seen on the southern side of the valley.

Gunaz, *n. f.* scorpion.

Gúnḍ, *n. m.* a crown, a diadem.

Gunglú, *n. m.* turnip (Brassica rapa).

Gunús, *n. m.* a small band adorned with beads, etc. and worn by the Mussulman women.

Gunus, *n. m.* a kind of bracelet.

Gunzarun, *v. t.* to count.

Gopangúr, *n. m.* cow-herd.

Gupan rachhanwol, *n. m.* cow-herd.

Gupun, *n. m.* quadruped.

Gur, *n. m.* horse, see 'gurr.'

Gúr, *n. m.* milk-seller.

Gúr, *n. m.* cow-herd. One of the four classes into which the Mihtar or Wátul caste is divided is the cow-herd class.

Gur. *n. f.* a clock, a watch.

Gurácha, *n. m.* Rubus lasiocarpus.

Gurál, *n. m.* Himalaya chamois.

Guran, *n. m.* a bunch of grapes.

Gurau gád, *n. m.* a small species of fish.

Gurdálú, *n. m.* Prunus Armeniaca (Apricot).

Gurgú, *n. m.* Pistacia integerrima.

Guriguri, *n. f.* a smoking pipe of brass or copper.

Gúrit mits, *n. f.* clay.

Gurr, *n. m.* horse. The horses of Kashmir are small, tough, and swift.

Gursí, *n. f.* opal.

Gúruk mundí, *n. m.* Sphœranthus mollis.

Gúrun, *n. m.* bunch.

Gurus, *n. m.* butter-milk of which the Kashmíris are very fond.

Gurus-wurus, *n. m.* butter-milk. Observe the reduplication.

Guzah, *n.* food.

Guzar, *n. m.* watchhouse.

Guzárban, *n. m.* watchman.

Guzráwun, *v. t.* to pass, to spend(one's time), to forward.

Guzurbán, *n. m.* tax gatherer who is placed at an entrance or avenue of some town or city.

Gut, *n. m.* a plait.

Gútul, *adj.* deep.

Gusánaji Teng. *n. m.* a village in the Hamal pargana, where are three sacred wells or springs, Ráma kŏnd, Síta kŏnḍ, and Lachman kŏnḍ.

Gush, *n. m.* a village in the Wutar pargana.

Gúshna, *adj.* starving.

Gyau, *n. m.* clarified butter.

Gyau, *n. m.* ghee.

The ghee of Pámpúr is considered the best in the valley.

Gyanabagaira, *n. m.* a dish composed of clarified butter and vegetables.

Gyauanwol, *n. m.* musician.

Gyauwun, *n. m.* music.

Gyauwun, (gáná), *v. t.* to sing gyau, gyauwán, gyaumut, gyauwih, also gyúwun, gyewán, gyúmut, gyauwih.

Gyeg, *n. m.* fauces.

Gyewun, *v. t.* to sing.

Gyiḍ, *n. f.* handful.

Gyúr, *n. m.* vertigo.

H.

H : this letter is pronounced exactly as in English.

H is the enclitic form of the case of the agent of the third personal pronoun, plural number, when it is coupled with *m*, the enclitic form of the dative of the first personal pronoun.

Há, a prefix to the vocative case.

Habba Kadal, *n. m.* a bridge over the Jhelum in Srínagar.

Habíb, *n. m.* a proper name.

Habíba, *n. m.* a proper name.

Habíb Shah, *n. m.* a proper name.

Habshí *n. m.* negro.

Habush, *n. m.* Abyssinian.

Hada nishi nebar, *adv.* enormously.

Háe ! *exclam.* alas.

Háe karun, *v. i.* to groan.

Hafta, *n. m.* week.

Hágar, *n. m.* a Kashmírí bird.

Hahar, *n. m.* wife's brother, brother-in-law.

Haibat, *n. f.* example.

Haidir Khán, *n. m.* a proper name.

Haihar, *n. m.* a pargana of the Kamráz division of the valley.

Hailah, *n. m.* artifice.

Hairán, *adj.* confounded, perplexed.

Hairání, *n. f.* confusion, perplexity.

Hairán karun, *v. t.* to perplex, to puzzle.

Hairat tráwun, *v. t.* to surprise.

Haiya, *n. m.* bashfulness, modesty, shame.

Haiyát, *n. m.* a proper name.

Haiyo, *interj.* holloa, sing. mas. also plur. mas.

Hájí, *n. m.* pilgrim.

Hájin, *n. m.* a village in the Sáírí Mawazih Páin pargana. The sheep of this village and district are the finest in the valley, or perhaps any where on the Himalayas. In fat and flavour they vie with the South Downs' sheep.

Hák, *n. m.* vegetables.

Hakhúr, *n. m.* ox.

Hakhur or hakhuḍ, *n. m.* bull. These words are in use towards Islamabád.

Hakím *n. m.* physician, doctor. There are said to be fifteen hakíms, or native doctors, in receipt of pay from his Highness. These live in Srínagar. There are besides 130 other hakíms.

Hákim, *n. m.* ruler.

Hakk, *n. m.* duty.

Hakk, *adj.* true.

Hák-wák, *n. m.* cabbage.

Hál, *n. m.* state, condition, circumstance.

Hál, *n. f.* a ball, a sphere.

Hãl, *n. f.* custom, habit, intercourse.

Hal, *n. m.* womb.

Hálagogij, *n. f.* hockey on horseback.

Halál, *adj.* legal.

Hálau, *n. m.* locust.

Halawói, *n. m.* confectioner.

Haligandun, *n. m.* waistband.

Hálú, *n. m.* locust. Small numbers of locusts visit Kashmír nearly every year. Sometimes great swarms invade the valley and do immense damage to the crops. The Mussulmans regard them as 'halál,' and a great delicacy. They dry them in the sun, grind them to powder, and make cakes of them.

Halwáí, *n. m.* confectioner.

Ham, *n. m.* the long pole with which the Dungá boat is propelled: see 'Hamtúl.'

Hamad, *n. m.* praise.

Hamad karun, *v. t.* to praise.

Hamal, *n. m.* a pargana in the Kamráz division of the valley.

Hamaryár, *n. m.* a village in the Lóláb pargana.

Hamatúl, *n. m.* the long pole with which the Dungá is propelled.

Hamdí, *n. f.* a proper name.

Hamdú, *n. m.* a proper name.

Hamesha, *adv.* always, eternally, ever.

Hamid, *n. m.* a proper name.

Hamkhánah, *adj.* of the same house.

Hammám, *n. m.* a hot bath, warm bath.

Hammámí, *n. m.* bath man.

Hamsáyih, *n. m.* a neighbour.

Hamtí, *n. f.* a proper name.

Hamtúl, *n. m.* the long pole by means of which boats are propelled.

Hamú, *n. m.* ash (Traxinus floribunda).

Han, an affix of diminution and endearment; as, Káshawahhan, a small spoon; Lórihan, a small stick; Korihan, a little girl.

Hana, *n. m.* bit, fragment, piece, a little.

Hánakdún, *n. m.* horse-chesnut.

Hand, *n. m.* Cichorium intybus

Háne, *n. m.* Himalayan horse-chesnut (Pavia Indica).

Hangamanga, *adj.* sudden.

Hanga-tah-manga, *adv.* suddenly, unexpectedly, by chance, accidentally.

Hãngin, *n. m.* a shell.

Hangkal, *n. f* bar.

Hangkuṭ, *n. m.* the small centre chamber on the second floor, which is often used as a dormitory.

Hánglu, *n. m.* the stag of Kashmír. A very noble animal, of great size, and often with twelve-pointed antlers. Both Hindus and Mussulmans eat the flesh of the stag.

Hangul, *n. m.* the stag, or barah-singh. The following parganas are famous for the stag: Bráng, Lãr, Kotahár, Dachanpára, and Khúíhóm.

Haṅharáí, *n. f.* breathlessness.

Hánj, *n. m.* boatman, see 'Hanz.'

Hánjí, *n. f.* boatman's work.

Háṅkal, *n. f.* a chain. The Kashmíris measure their ground by means of a chain, which they call Menan-háṅkal.

Hansuráj, *n. m.* Adiantum caudatum, venustum.

Hãnṭ, *n. f.* a barren woman.

Hánṭ, *adj.* barren (of woman).

Hanúdún, *n. m.* the Himalayan horse-chesnut (Pavia Indica)

Hánz, *n. m.* boatman. The boatmen of Kashmir are, physically, a very fine class, but morally, they are a very bad portion of the population.

Hap, *n. m.* corpse.

Hápat ṭang, see 'Tang.'

Haph, *n. m.* corpse, dead body.

Hápits, *n. f.* she-bear.

Hápút, *n. m.* bear. The bear is very common in Kashmir, or, rather, on the mountains and slopes of the valley. There are two species, the brown and the black. The brown bear is often of great size. In the fruit season, the bears do much injury to the fruit. The black bear is smaller and fiercer than the brown bear.

Háput-Nág, *n. m.* the bears' spring, in the valley of the Lidur. Near to it is a copper-mine, which was worked in former days.

Hápúts, *n. f.* she-bear.

Hár, *n. f.* June (=Jamádá-s-Sání, or Jamádá-l-ákhir), the sixth month of the Mussulman year, and corresponding to the fourth month of the Hindu year.

Hár, *n. f.* a cowrie—a small shell used as current money. It is of very small value.

Har, *n. m.* branch.

Hãr, *n. f.* a species of starling.

Har, *n. f.* a proper name.

Hár, *n. f.* defeat.

Har(laṛáí), *n. f.* fighting,

tumult, contention, quarrel, war. This word, however, more properly denotes private wrangling where there is no effusion of blood.

Harafa pat harafa, *adv.* verbatim.

Harahar, *n. f.* fight, fighting, contention, war.

Harahar karinyi, *v. i.* to dispute, to fight.

Harakat karinyi, *v. t.* to shake.

Harám, *n. m.* adultery, fornication.

Harámkárí, *n.f.* adultery, fornication.

Harámzod, *adj.* vile.

Hãrán, *adj.* astonished, disturbed, perplexed.

Harárat, herpes, scabies.

Hárawaṭ, *n. f.* a species of water-fowl in Kashmir.

Hardas, *n. m.* a proper name.

Hardam, *adv.* always.

Hár dinyi, *v. t.* to defeat.

Harf, *n. m.* letter of alphabet.

Harfa pat harfa, *adv.* literally.

Hargahnah, *conj.* otherwise.

Hárí, *n. f.* a proper name, corn.

Hárij, *n. f.* a bow.

Hárinj, *n. f.* bow (for shooting).

Harí Parbat, *n. m.* a hill in Srínagar, on which stands the fort protecting the city. The present fort is said to have been built some sixty years ago by Ata Muhammad Khán. In the month of March there is a Hindu festival in honour of Shárika held on this hill. The fort was originally built by Akbar the Great, at a cost of 1,100,000*l.*, in 1597, A.D. Geologically, the Harí Parbat is composed of a beautiful amygdaloidal trap.

Haripúr, *n. m.* a small village about five miles from Shupiyon. The word is composed of Harí, Vishnu, and púr, a city; the city of Vishnu.

Harkára, *n. m.* informer, spy, postman, letter-carrier, a police constable. The Dúmb's superior. In every village there is one. In the towns and capital, the mahalladárs do the Harkáras work.

Har karinyi, *v. t.* to make war, see 'Karun'

Harmuka Ganga, *n. m.* name of a river, see 'Ákãsh Ganga.'

Harna, *n. m.* antelope.

Harnah, *n. m. f.* a deer.

Hãrpúr, *n. m.* a village in the Brang pargana.

Hár sapadinyi, *v. i.* to be checkmated.

Harúd, *n. m.* autumn, cold season, harvest.

Hárun, *n. m.* detriment.

Harun, *v. i.* to fall (especially of leaves and petals); hur, harán, hurmut, harih.

Hárun, *v. t.* to cause to fall, to let fall, to pour, to win, to defeat, to shed (as blood), to lose in gambling; horun, hárán, hórmut, hárih.

Hasad, *n. m.* envy.

Hasain dach, see 'Dach.'

Hasan, *n. m.* a proper name.

Hash, *n. f.* wife's mother, mother-in-law.

Hashmat, *n. m.* degree.

Hásil, *n. m.* produce, profit.

Haṭ, *n. f.* wood, faggot.

Hat, *adj.* hundred.

Hata, *interj.* holloa (*s. f.*).

Hatá, *interj.* holloa (*s. m.*).

Hatai, *interj.* holloa (*s.* & *p. f.*)

Hátam, *n. m.* a proper name.

Hato, *interj.* holloa (*s. m.* & *p. m.*).

Háts, *n. f.* accusation, conviction.

Hatsar, *n. m.* humility.

Háts karinyi, *v. t.* to accuse.

Hatú, *n. m.* a proper name.

Hátyum, *adj.* hundredth.

Haud, *n. m.* endive. There are said to be three varieties, viz. rubu haud, arim haud, wan haud. This last variety is given along with rice and other articles of diet to the parturient patient for ten days after the birth of the child.

Hauk, *adj.* withered, dry.

Hauk-gás, *n. m.* straw.

Haul, *n. m.* loin of human body, waist.

Haul, *adj.* crooked.

Haur, *n. m.* Picrorhiza kurrooa.

Haust, *n. m.* elephant.

Hauṭ, *n. m.* shore, throat.

Hauts, *n. m.* wrist, forearm.

Hawá, *n. m.* wind.

Hawála, *n. m.* deposit, custody.

Hawála karun, *v. t.* to surrender, to deposit, to entrust, to commit to the care of, to commit to the custody of.

Hawán, *n. m.* quadruped.

Hawánáwun, *v. t.* to cause to show or be shown; háwanov, háwanáwán, háwanomut, háwanáwih.

Hawáwah, *n. m.* a whiff, puff.

Háwun, *v. t.* to point out, to show; howun, háwán, homut, háwih.

Háyuk, *n. m.* large scales for weighing grain.

Hazímat, *n. m.* defeat.

Hazímat khyun, *v. i.* to be defeated.

Házir, *adj.* present.

Hazmí, *n. f.* a proper name.

Hazrat, *n. f.* majesty.

Hazratbal, *n. m.* a village of the Phák pargana. It is so named from there being here, according to Mussulman accounts, a veritable hair of Muhammad's beard! This village is the most sacred spot in the valley, in the estimation of Muhammadans.

Hĕchhináwun, *v. t.* to teach, to cause to learn; hechhinov, hechhináwán, hĕchhinómut, hechhináwih.

Hĕchhun, *v. t.* to learn; hechhun, hechhán, hechhmut, hechhih.

Heḍir, *n. m.* a species of edible mushroom, growing upon trees.

Hĕḍur, *n. m.* mushroom, eaten largely both by Hindus and Mussulmans, who cook it with ghee and condiments. The people in the district preserve them by drying. Large quantities are said to be annually exported to the Punjab.

Hĕkanwol, *adj.* powerful.

Hĕkat, *n. f.* strength.

Hĕkit, *n. f.* power, ability.

Hĕkun (tawánistan), *v. i.* to be able; hyuk, hĕkán, hyukmut, hĕkih.

Hená, *n. m.* the Lawsonia inermis. It is with this tree that the Indians stain the nails of their hands and feet.

Hendawand, *n. m.* water-melon.

Heng, *n. m.* a horn.

Hĕnur, *n. m.* drain.

Her, *n. f.* ladder, stair, staircase.

Hí, *n. f.* jasmine.

Híásmín, *n. m.* Syringa Persica.

Hí-ásmán, *n. m.* lilac, jasmine.

Hichara, *n. m.* scholar.

Hijar, *n. m.* separation.

Hil, *n. f.* an aquatic weed. It is placed over the region of the bladder by the native Hakíms, when there is strangury. It grows abundantly in the city lake.

Hil, *n. m.* cluster of grapes.

Híla, *n. m.* fraud, imposition.

Híla karanwol, *n. m.* impostor.

Hílah, *n. m.* fraud.

Hiláṭ, *n. m.* waistband.

Hilau, *n. m.* a crane (bird), both Hindus and Mussulmans eat it.

Hilyi, *n. f.* ear of corn.

Hin, *n. f.* neighing of horse.

Hindavyend, *n. m.* water-melon, which is mature in August.

Hindavyendakul, *n. m.* the water-melon plant.

Hin dinyi, *v. i.* to neigh.

Hindur, *n. m.* drain.

Hindustán, *n. m.* India.

Hiṅg, *n. f.* neighing.

Híng, *n. m.* Narthex assafœtida. It does not grow in the valley.

Hin karinyi, *v. i.* to neigh.

Himayit karinyi, *v. t.* to entrust.

Hír, *n. f.* the head of any animal used for food, therefore never applied to the human head.

Hírigogul, *n. m.* apple of the throat (pomum Adami).

Hiritsundar, *n. m.* said to have been one of the ancient kings of Kashmir.

Hisáb, *n. m.* account.

Hish! an exclamation to drive away fowls.

Hishir, *adj.* convenient.

Hishir karun (tashbíh kardan), *v. t.* to compare.

Hissa, *n. m.* part, share, portion.

Hít, *n. m.* pretence.

Híth *n. m.* pretence, pretext, excuse, apology.

Hittar, *n. m.* leprosy.

Hittarilad, *n. m.* leper.

Hŏchir, *n. m.* drought.

Hŏḍ, *n. f.* disobedience.

Hŏk, *adj.* dry.

Hŏkh, *adj.* dry.

Hŏkun, *v. i.* to be dry, húk, hŏkán, húkmut, hŏkih.

Hól, *n. m.* trouble.

Honar, *n. m.* trade, skill.

Hoṅgaiṅ, *n. f.* chin.

Hŏngainyi, *n. f.* chin.

Honyibokut, *n. m.* pup.

Honyikutsur, *n. m.* pup.

Hŏnying-hund-gara, *n. m.* kennel.

Hŏnyin-hunz-jái, *n. f.* kennel.

Hór, *adv.* thither.

Hórun, *v. t.* to pay, (a loan), to repay.

Hoshiyár, *adj.* awake, vigilant.

Hoshíyár gatshun, *v. i.* to be or to become awake.

Hosh karun, *v. t.* to think.

Hotsun, *v. i.* to rot.

Hó,ú, *adj.* evident, clear.

Hú, *pron.* he, (when present but not near) that, (when object present.

Húiṅ, *n. f.* bitch.

Huiṅ-tabela, *n. m.* kennel.

Huk, *adj.* dry.

Hukhanáwun, *v. t.* to dry.

Hukhun, *v. i.* to dry.

Hukm, *n. m.* decree, command.

Hukm dyun, *v. t.* to command.

Hukm karun, *v. t.* to convict, to sentence, to condemn, to decide, to command.

Hukm-tulanwol, *adj*. obedient.
Hukmut, *adj*. dry.
Hul, *n. m.* girdle.
Hul, *n. m.* flank.
Hul, *adj*. flexible, oblique.
Hulhul, *adj*. intricate.
Humáz, *n. m.* Polygonum.
Húm, *n. m.* the ash. The wood of the ash is considered the best for paddles.
Hún, *n. m.* a dog.
Hunar, *n. m.* skill.
Hunun (sojná), *v. i.* to swell; hunyeo. hunán, hunyeomut, hunih.
Hunur, *n. m.* art.
Hunyar, *n. m.* swelling.
Hunyir, *n. m.* swelling.
Hunzura, *n. f.* collar.
Hur, an affix signifying couple or pair, as a couple of legs, zangahur.
Hur, *adj*. abundant.
Hurawun, *v. t.* to increase.
Hurír, *n. m.* increase, abundance, proficiency.
Hurr, *adj*. superfluous.
Hurráwun, *v. i.* to increase; hurrowun, hurráwán, hurromut, hurráwih.
Hurrun, *v. i.* to increase; hurreo,hurrán,hurreomut,hurrih.
Hurun, *v. i.* to become greater, (ziyáda hona), to increase, hureo, hurán, hureomut, hurih.
Hust, also hast, *n. m.* elephant.
Huṭ *n. m.* throat.
Hut, *adv.* there.
Huti, *adv.* there.
Hutih, *adv.* thence, there.
Hutit, *adv.* there.
Hutut, *adv.* there.
Hyáng, *n. m.* horn.
Hyátí, *n. f.* life.
Hyéng, *n. m.* horn.
Hyer, *n. f.* stairs of a house.
Hyĕt, *conj*. pl. of hyun.
Hyihur, *n. m.* wife's father. father-in-law.
Hyú (manind), *prep*. like, according to.
Hyú, *adj*. equal, even, level, flat.
Hyuhur, *n. m.* father-in-law.
Hyuk (*m.*) hish (*f.*) *adj*. equal.
Hyun, *v. t.* to take, hyutun, hewán, hyutmut, heyih.
Hyund, *n. m.* Hindu.
Hyur, *n. m.* throat.
Hyúr, *prep*. up.
Hyur-kun, *adv*. upwards.

I.

I: this letter is pronounced like the letter *i* in the English word it, but when *i* has an acute accent over it, it is then pronounced like *ee* in the word reed.

I, the affix of emphasis. It is very often preceded by a short *u*, or zabar, as baḍí ḍer, a great heap, kunuí, solitary.

Iblí, *n. m.* a proper name.

Ibrahím, *n. m.* a proper name.

Ichagám, *n. m.* a village of the Yach Pargana, inhabited chiefly by Mussulmans.

Ichakúṭ, *n. m.* the chief village of the Yach Pargana, many Pandits or Hindus live here.

Íd, *n. f.* a festival, (Mussulman).

Idabár, *n. m.* defeat.

Ídgá, *n. m.* an extensive common, near the Mar canal.

Idrár, *n. m.* urine.

Ikhbál, *n. m.* a proper name.

Iláj, *n. m.* remedy.

Ilájarust, *adj.* incurable.

Iláj karun, *v. t.* to heal, to cure.

Imán, *n. m.* faith, belief.

Imán anun, *v. t.* to believe.

Imarjal, *n. m.* iris (Iris pseudacorus).

Indar-muhul, *n. m.* bruiser of grain.

Ingrách, *n. m.* Fragaria vesca (Strawberry).

Injíl, *n. f.* the gospel.

Injír, *n. m.* fig.

Insáf, *n. m.* justice.

Insán, *n. m.* man, creature.

Îput, *n. m.* yoke of plough.

Irán, *n. m.* Persia.

Iráni, *adj.* Persian.

Isa, *n. m.* a proper name.

Isaphgol, *n. m.* Plantago major.

Ishára *n. m.* signal.

Ishára karun, *v. t.* to point out, to shew, to signal.

Ishk, *n. m.* love.

Ishpecha, *n. m.* Ipomæa cœrulea or Pharbites nil.

Ishwai, *n. m.* a proper name.

Islámabád, *n. m.* a pargana of Maráz, also the chief town of the pargana, in the south-east end of the valley. Like the other towns of Kashmir, it is in a most dilapidated state. Near to the town is a hill, which rises to the height of about 350 feet above the level of the plain. It is composed of strata of fine grey mountain limestone, with a quantity of shingly conglomerate. Out from the foot of this hill flows the fountain of Anat Nág. The town itself gets the name of Anat Nág from the Kashmíris. There are two sulphur springs in Islamabad. It is a Kasábah, or market town, has a few shawl weavers, and is still famous for its manufacture of rugs.

Ismael, Baṭ, *n. m.* a proper name.

Ismál, *n. m.* a proper name.
Ithai, *adv.* gratis.
Ittifák, *n. m.* accident.
Ithinyu, *adv.* thus.
Ithúí, *adj.* such.
Iza dyun, *v. t.* to torment.
Iztaráb karun, *v. t.* to disturb.
Izzat, *n. f.* rank, honour.

J.

J: this letter is pronounced as in English.
Jab, a herd.
Jabajáma, *n. m.* armour. It is composed of small rings manufactured in Kashmír.
Jabajáwa, *n. m.* a coat of mail.
Jabín, *n. m.* forehead.
Jafákár, *n. m.* tyrant.
Jag, *n. m.* harvest-home. See Cunningham's "Ladak."
Jahán, *n. m.* world.
Jáí, *n. f.* residence, place.
Jaipál phal, *n.* Croton tiglium.
Jáí pěṭh anun, *v. t.* to execute.
Jajir, *n. f.* a clay smoking-pipe.
Jajír tulanwol, *n. m.* pipe-bearer.
Jal, *n. m* a bird of Kashmír.
Jálakhdóz, *n. m.* a maker of saddle-cloths and rugs.
Jalál-ud-dín, *n. m.* a proper name.
Jald, *adv.* quickly.
Jald-jald pahan, *adv.* quickly.
Jald pahan, *adv.* quickly.
Jám, *n. m.* cup.
Jáma khós, *n. m.* a large bowl.
Jamál, *n. m.* a proper name.
Jamála, *n. m.* a proper name.
Jamál Baṭ, *n. m.* a proper name.
Jamal gotah, *n.* Croton tiglium.
Jama Masjid, *n. m.* the main Mussulman Masjid in Srínagar. Over the gate is a Persian inscription telling us that the Jama Masjid was built by Shah Jehán.
Jamára, *n. m.* Viburnum fœtens.
Jamát, *n. m.* Friday.
Jámbáz trela. See 'Trela.'
Ján, *n. m.* life.
Ján, *adj.* good; also *adv.* well.
Ján-but, *adj.* good-looking.
Jang, *n. m.* fight, war.
Jang Karun, *v. t.* to fight.
Jangal, *n. m.* forest.
Janglí Kits, *n. f.* Edwardsia mollis.
Janún, *n. m.* madness.
Jánwar, *n. m.* bird, animal.
Japhiri, *n. m.* the marigold. There are two varieties; Shashbarg japhiri, and Makhmal japhiri, which is small and fragrant.
Jaráb, *n. m.* very short socks, reaching only to the ankles.
Jarába, *n. m.* socks reaching the ankles only and made of wool.

Jarábagar, *n. m.* stocking maker.
Jarábsáz, *n. m.* stocking weaver.
Jatamásí, *n. m.* Nardostachys jatamansí. This is probably the 'spikenard' of the ancients.
Jatan, *n. m.* shift, stratagem.
Jaubrãr, *n. m.* a village situated near Wantipór, in the Wular pargana. Here are to be seen some temple ruins.
Jàúr, *adj.* mounted (as jewels).
Jawáb, *n. m.* answer.
Jawán, *n. m.* a young man.
Jẹga, *n. m.* a crown.
Jewar, *n. m.* the Euryale ferox, an aquatic plant, the seeds of which are eaten by the natives of the valley.
Jhan, *n. m.* Artemisia elegans.
Jhan, *n. m.* clang.
Jigari dáṅ, see 'Dáṅ.'
Jild, *n. m.* volume.
Jildagur, *n. m.* bookbinder.
Jilí, *n. m.* a proper name.
Jím, *n. m.* the letter J.
Jin, *n. m.* demon.
Jintyána, *n. m.* Gentiana.
Jishna, *n. m.* male dance.
Jít, *n. m.* victory.
Join, *n. f.* a proper name.
Jóra, *n. m.* pair, couple, accomplice.
Jorah, *n. m.* couple, pair, accomplice.
Jorah, *adj.* common.
Joshan, *n. m.* armour.
Jótish, *n. m.* astrology, astronomy, see 'Baṭa.'
Juda karun, *v. t.* to separate.
Juma, *n. m.* a proper name.
Juma Khán, *n. m.* a proper name.
Júra, *n. m.* a proper name.
Jutipúr, *n. m.* the place where was fought the successful battle which gave Kashmir to the Sikhs, in 1819. Jutipur is not far distant from Shupiyon.
Jwí, *n. f.* stream.

K.

K : this letter is pronounced as in English.
K is the enclitic form of the dative, the accusative, and the case of the agent of the third personal pronoun, plural number. It is also the enclitic form of the nominative case of the second personal pronoun, singular number.
Kabáb, *n. m.* roast.
Kabar-wabar, *n. f.* grave.
Kabílah, *n. m.* family.
Kabíra, *n. m.* a proper name.
Kabúl, *n. m.* choice.
Kabuliyat, *n. f.* receipt.
Kabúl karun *v. t.* to choose,

(pasandídan),to accept (qabul namúdan).

Kabza, *n. m.* sheath.

Kabzbandí, *n. f.* constipation.

Kách, *n. m.* carrot (Daucus carota).

Kach, *n. m.* the short grass of the field, green grass.

Kachharí, *n. m.* court of justice.

Kachhírí, *n. f.* court of justice.

Kachúr, *n. m.* zinziber zerumbet.

Kã̄ḍ, *n. m.* brain.

Kad, *n. m.* size, stature.

Kadal, *n. m.* bridge. The bridges spanning the Jhelum in Kashmir are of a peculiar construction. Piles formed of the deodar, or Himalayan cedar, are driven into the bed of the river, enclosing an oblong space, but wedge-shaped, to the current of water, and truncated at the lower end. The wedge-shaped portion is then filled with huge stones, which serve as a sort of breakwater. On the oblong spaces are laid layers of deodar trunks, which are placed alternately at right angles to one another, and gradually increase in length towards the top of the wood pile or pier, so that the space between two adjacent piers is greatly diminished at the top. Trunks of deodar are then made to span the spaces between the wooden piers, and thus the bridge is formed. Even the broad Jhelum is spanned in this fashion. And although the frequent floods of the valley greatly test these wooden bridges, they are remarkably strong, and stand the repeated severe tests well.

Kadam, *n. m.* step.

Kaddus, *n. m.* a proper name.

Káḍhí, *n. m.* cotton carder.

Kádir, *n. m.* a proper name.

Kádir Bakhash, *n. m.* a proper name.

Kádir Baṭ, *n. m.* a proper name.

Kadr, *n. m.* rank.

Kã̄dra, *n. m.* a proper name.

Kaḍun (utárna), *v. t.* to take off, to strip.

Kaḍun (kashídan), *v. t.* to drag out, to put out, to drive out, to expel, to extract, to draw out; kúḍ, kaḍán, kuḍmut, kaḍih.

Kaḍun kamán, *v. t.* to draw a bow.

Kaf, *n. m.* phlegm.

Kafan, *m. m.* grave-clothes.

Káfir, *n. m.* infidel.

Kágaz, *n. m.* paper. The

manufacture of paper in the valley is said to have begun in the time of Akbar the Great. Before that time, the liber or inner bark of a species of birch was used instead. This substitute for paper was called Búrzá or Bojpatar, which see. The great paper works of Kashmir are situated at Naushá-har, near to Srínagar. A great many varieties are manufactured.

Kágazgar, *n. m.* paper-maker.

Kágazgur, *n. m.* paper-maker.

Kágaz-kyum, *n. m.* an insect very destructive of paper; literally, the paper insect.

Kah, *adj.* eleven.

Kahn, *pron.* some one.

Kahú, *n. m.* Lactuca Sativa.

Kàhyum, *adj.* eleventh.

Káiar, *n. m.* Pinus excelsa.

Kaid, *n. m.* prison.

Kaid karun, *v. t.* to confine, to imprison.

Kaid tháwun, *v. t.* to imprison.

Kail, *n. m.* the ibex. It is found on the higher mountains of Kashmir.

Kailas, *n. m.* a proper name.

Kàilí, *n. f.* a proper name.

Kain, *n. f.* chalk, stone, rock.

Kainsaring kuṭhar, *n. m.* a double-peaked mountain in the Pír Pantsál range.

Kainyi, *n. f.* a stone.

Kàir, *n. f.* a barren woman.

Kā̃jis, *adv.* at breakfast-time.

Kájiwat, *n. m.* pestle.

Kájwaṭ, *n. m.* pestle.

Kák, *n. m.* the eldest son of a family is so called by his brothers and sisters.

Kák, *n. m.* father.

Kákain, *n. f.* the wife of the eldest son in a Hindu family.

Kakkar, *n. m.* Pistacia integerrima.

Kakkú, *n. m.* a species of partridge?

Kakshama, *n. m.* see 'Káli zirí.'

Kakú, *n. m.* partridge, met with in the valley.

Kákur, *n. m.* barking deer.

Kā̃l, *n. m.* the day after tomorrow.

Come the day after tomorrow. Pagah do karit ísí, or kā̃lyi kyet ísí.

Kál, *n. m.* space of time, death, supper.

Kàl, *adj.* dumb. Kaj (*f.*).

Kalà, *n. m.* head.

Kalachan, *n. m.* evening.

Káladána, *n. m.* Ipomœa Cœrulea, or Pharbites nil.

Kalái, *n. f.* tin which is exported from the Punjáb, fort, fortress, castle.

Kaláígur, *n. m.* a tinner of pots.

Kalám, *n. m.* word.

Kalam, *n. m.* pen.

Kalam gárun, *v. t.* to make a pen.

Kalamtsakalur, *n. m.* a village in the Machipor pargana.

Kalapósh, *n. m.* a close-fitting skull-cap, worn by male and female Kashmírís.

Kalar, *n. m.* fallow ground.

Kalas-dód, *n. m.* headache.

Kála zíra, *n. m.* see 'Kálí zírí.'

Kálbáf, *n. m.* a carpet-maker.

Káldach, *n. m.* bramble.

Kali, *n. f.* a proper name.

Kálízewar, *n. m.* Bupleurum marginatum.

Kálí zírí, *n. f.* Serratula anthelmintica.

Kãl kyĕt, *adv.* the day after to-morrow.

Kalposh, *n. m.* cap, generally worn by the Kashmírís, and fits close to the head.

Kalush, *n. m.* a religious cup.

Kám, *pron.* some.

Kam, *adj.* scarce, deficient, less, small, few.

Kámadayan, *n. f.* a cow.

Kámadín, *n. m.* cow.

Kamál, *n. m.* a proper name.

Kamála, *n. m.* a proper name.

Kamalun, *v. i.* to melt (as ice or snow), to become soft.

Kamán, *n. m.* bow.

Kamand, *n. m.* a halter, a snare.

Kamar, *n. m.* flank, loins, waist.

Kamarband, *n. m.* waistband, girdle.

Kámat, *n. m.* stature.

Kámbeí, *n. f.* Solanum migrum.

Kamcha, *n. m.* whip.

Kamcha láyun, *v. t.* to flog, to whip.

Kamchí, *n. m.* whip.

Kámikár, *adj.* clever, industrious.

Kámi khátra, *adv.* wherefore? why?

Kamíla, *n. m.* Rottleria tinctoria.

Kámi manz anun, *v. t.* to use, (lit. to bring into use) see 'Anun.'

Kámirust, *adj.* idle.

Kámirust karun, *v. t.* to dismiss, to discharge.

Kámi wakt? *adv.* when?

Kam kam, *adv.* little.

Kam karun, *v. t.* to diminish to lessen.

Kamnasíb, *adj.* unfortunate.

Kampanáwun, *v. t.* to frighten.

Kampun, *v. i.* to tremble.

Kamráz, *n. m.* one of the three

great divisions of the valley comprehending the north, west end and the water shed of the Jhelum as far as its junction with the Krishan Ganga.

Kam sápadun, *v. i.* to diminish, to grow less, to lessen.

Kamun, *v. i.* to tremble, to shiver.

Kamzor, *adj.* weak.

Kán, *n. m.* arrow.

Kan, *n. m.* ear.

Kán, *n. f.* source.

Kán, *n. m.* mine.

Kán, *n. m.* foundation of a house.

Kan, *n. m.* foundation.

Kanáchí, *n. m.* Rubus rotundifolius.

Kanadúr, *n. m.* ear-ring.

Kanagich, *n. m.* a large and very savoury species of mushroom, which is said to grow on the mountains surrounding the valley of Kashmir.

Kanagogul, *n. m.* meatus auditorius externus, mastoid process (of ear).

Kanaguch, *n. m.* mushroom. The Kashmíris are fond of mushrooms, and export large quantities dried to the Panjáb.

Kanahaiping, *n. f.* a centipede.

Kának, *n. m.* wheat. Eaten both by Hindus and Mussulmans.

Kanak, *n. m.* Segeretia oppositifolia.

Kána kach, *n. m.* morel (morchella semilibera). It is very common in Kashmir. Large quantities are dried and exported from the valley to the plains.

Kanar, *n. m.* is that on which the little wheel of the spinning wheel rests.

Kanasdód, *n. m.* ear-ache.

Kanaucha, *n. m.* salvia.

Kanawáj, *n. f.* a small ear-ring.

Kanawãj, *n. f.* ear-ring. Ear-rings are of different shapes and materials. The Kashmírí women are very fond of ornaments.

Kanawol, *n. m.* large ear-rings.

Kand, *n. m.* sugar.

Kanḍ, *n. m.* nut.

Kándar, *n. m.* baker.

Kándarain, *n. f.* female baker, or baker's wife.

Kándaryain, *n. f.* baker's wife.

Kandiára, *n. m.* Rubus lasiocarpus.

Kanḍikhás, *n. m.* a pargana in the Kamráz division of the valley.

Kandíl, *n. m.* shade of a lamp.

Kando, *n. m.* cæsalpinia sepiaria.

Kandú, *n. m.* Eryngium planum.

Kándur, *n. m.* baker.

Kangach, *n. m.* morel (morchella semilibera).

Kangain, *n. f.* a comb for the hair, a weaver's comb.

Kangál, *adj.* poor.

Kangan, *n. m.* Crocus sativus.

Kanganyigur, *n. m.* brushmaker.

Kangar, *n. m.* large portable brazier, see 'Kángrí.'

Kángri, *n. f.* a portable brazier, very extensively in use in the valley. It generally consists of two parts: an earthenware vessel (Kónḍal) and an encasement of wicker work. Sometimes, however, it is destitute of the wicker work, and then it is called Manan. As the dress of the Kashmírí is of a loose fashion, the Kángrí can be placed in immediate contact with the skin of the abdomen and thighs, where in many cases cancer (Epithelioma) is in process of time generated. Probably the Kashmírís learned the use of the Kángrí from the Italians in the retinue of the Mogul Emperors who were in the habit of visiting Kashmir.

Kangú, *n. m.* shoulder blade, scapula.

Kangú, *n. m.* a comb.

Kangu dyun, *v. t.* to comb.

Kangun, *n. m.* a kind of bracelet.

Kaníz, *n. m.* slave.

Kanj, *n. m.* breakfast.

Kanjis, *adv.* at breakfast (time).

Kánjús, *adj.* stingy.

Kánkaiṅ, *n. f.* a kind of bracelet.

Kãnkan, *n. m.* a kind of bracelet.

Kankol, *n. m.* a species of Elæagnus.

Kankol mirich, *n. m.* Eleagnus orientalis.

Káṅs, *n. m.* the large wooden mortar in which grain is bruised.

Kãṅṭ, *n. m.* throat.

Kãnta, *n. m.* small scales for weighing gold, &c.

Kanṭh, *n. m.* throat.

Kãnṭhmál, *n. m.* a necklace composed of brass or gold beads.

Kanṭ tháwun, *v. t.* to remember.

Kánṭur, *n. m.* cock-sparrow.

Kȧnun (bechná). *v. t.* to sell, kunun, kȧnán, kunmut, kȧnih.

Kanur, *n. m.* the maple (acer).

Kanya, *n. f.* girl, virgin, daughter.

Kanyal, *n. m.* stony country.

Kányi, *n. f.* the topmost floor

of a house where the tenants live during the summer time.

Kányíhom n. m. a village of the Máchihom pargana.

Kányilar̤, n. m. loin, side of human body where the ribs are.

Kanyinol, n. m. the broad strap at the end of the rope with which the Dúngá is dragged along.

Kanyiphalyi, n. m. gravel of bladder.

Kányúl, n. m. basket maker.

Kánz, n. m. gruel, rice water.

Káňz, n. m. vinegar made from rice.

Káo, n. m. crow.

There are two species of the genus crow to bemet with in Kashmir. One species is wholly black, the other has a dirty white neck.

Kapas, n. m. cotton, seeds and all, cotton plant.

Kapur, n. m. cloth.

Kapur-tsádar, n. m. a cotton shawl.

Kár, n. m. action, deed.

Kár, n. f. neck, both of animals and men.

Kãr, n. f. neck.

Kar, adv. when?

Karam, n. m. success.

Karam shekh, n. m. a proper name.

Karanáv, n. m. ferry man.

Karanáwun, v. t. to cause to make, karanóv, karanáwán, karanómut, karanáwih.

Kárdár, n. m. the Hindu overseer of a village, a government official whose duty is to collect theMaharajá's share of the grain.

Karela, n. m. one of the cureurbitaceæ.

Karelabungir, n. f. a kind of bracelet.

Karewah, n. m. a plateau or raised plain.

There are six karewahs in Kashmir, the largest of which is that of Islamabad. The other karewahs are those of Zainapúr, No Nagar, Khámpur, Damudur Udur.

The karewahs of Kashmir are formed of lacustrine clay, and when watered and cultivated, yield abundant crops of wheat and barley. In all probability, the karewahs, or raised plains, owe their formation to the fact that the alluvium of which they are formed was deposited at the bottom of the waters of a still lake.

Kãrigarz, adj. rebellious.

Karím, n. m. a proper name.

Karin, n. m. trowel.

L

Kár khándár, *n. m.* proprietor of a shawl manufactory, a shawl manufacturer.

Kárkun, see 'Baṭa.'

Karmí, *n. f.* a proper name.

Karmora, *n. m.* ivy (Hedera Helix).

Karór, *adj.* ten millions.

Karra, *n. m.* proboscis of elephant.

Kartal, *n. m.* sword.

Kártik, *n. m.* the eighth month of the Hindu year, and corresponding to our month of October. It corresponds to Shawál, the tenth month of the Mussulman year.

Kartúl, *n. m.* business, profession.

Karun, *v. t.* to make, to do, to compose, commit; kụr, karán, kürmut, karih. It is worthy of notice that when this verb is joined to a national adjective it means to speak the language of the country referred to, as Káushar karun, to do the Kashmírí, that is, to speak Kashmírí. Ángrezí karun, to play the Englishman, that is, to speak English.

Karwánah, *n. m.* caravan.

Karz, *n. m.* debt.

Karzdár, *n. m.* debtor.

Kasab, *n. m.* trade.

Kasába, *n. m.* a small red cap worn by the Mussulman women.

Kasam, *n. m.* oath.

Kasam háwun, *v. i.* to swear.

Kasam karun, *v. i.* to swear.

Kasam khyun, *v. i.* to swear.

Kasar, *n. m.* defect.

Kashaf, *n. m.* a tortoise.

Káshawah, *n. m.* table or dessert spoon.

Káshawahhan, *n. m.* a teaspoon.

Kashí, *n. m.* a proper name.

Káshir, *n. f.* a female native of Kashmir.

Kãshir, *n. f.* a female native of Kashmir.

Kashír, *n. f.* the country of Kashmir.

Kãshírí múj, *n. f.* a species of radish.

Káshir zeo, *n. f.* the Kashmírí language.

Kashmír, *n. f.* Kashmír, which is both the name of the valley, and of Srínagar the capital. This name, Kashmír, is derived from Kashaf, the drainer of the valley, and mar, a place.

Kashmir is called by the inhabitants of Little Tibet Khacheyul, and the natives are called Khachepa. The people of Gulghit call Kashmír Kashír. It has been roughly calculated that the plains of Kashmir, including the Karewas, comprise an area of at least 650 square miles, while on the surrounding mountains there is another area of 150 of pasture land.

The following story respecting the desiccation of the valley of Kashmir is now current in the country:—

Long, long ago, the country called Kashmir was an extensive lake, whose name was Sahtísar. A numerous population dwelt on the surrounding mountains. In process of time the beautiful waters of lake Sahtísar became infested by a terrible monster, called Zaldeo, which first destroyed all the fish in the lake, and then emerging from its placid waters, began to attack and devour the inhabitants of the mountains. In great consternation, they fled from their happy homes, and sought safety among the fastnesses of the mountains. In their retreat they came upon the abode of a Ríshí, or holy man, whose name was Kashaf. They told him their sad story. He heard their doleful account about the awful monster and his murderous doings. So great was the sanctity of this Ríshí, that God had given him power to work miracles. Accompanied by a great crowd of fugitives, the Ríshí directed his steps to the north-west end of the Wulur lake, and here he struck the ground violently with his trident. The earth opened, and in course of time, the whole waters of the Lake Sahtísar disappeared, and again reappeared near to the Krishan Ganga. In consequence of the draining of the lake, the monster, Zaldeo, perished, to the great joy and safety of the previously terrified mountaineers, and the valley was called Kashafmar, the place or country of Kashaf, in honour of the Ríshí.

A line drawn from Bandipúr through the Wulur lake to Baramula divides the valley into two portions. The part to the north of the line is called Kamraj, or Kamráz, and the portion to the south of the line is named Miráj, or Miráz. It has been conjectured that Kamráj is derived from Kama Ráj, the territory of Kama, the god of love, and Miráj from Maya Ráj, the territory of his mother Maya, or Lakshmí, the wife of Vishnu.

The southern aspect of the range of mountains bounding Kashmir to the north, is bare when compared with the northern face of the southern range, which is richly wooded. The fruit grown on the southern side of the valley is superior to that grown on the north. In the months of April and May, spring weather prevails. The wind is pleasant, the sky is clear, and the leaves come out. The land is prepared for rice. The months of June and July are the hottest of the year. In July, the temperature outside in the shade is sometimes as high as 94°, Farenheit. In the months of June and July, mulberries, cherries, plums, and cucumbers are in their season. Wheat, barley, oats, and the different kinds of pulse ripen, and are reaped. In the months of August and September, rice ripens, and is reaped. Apples, pears, peaches, grapes, and quinces come to maturity in these months. The leaves now get seared. In the months of October and November the climate is pleasant and bracing. Saffron is gathered in October. Wheat, barley, and oats are sown in October and November. The cold is severe in the months of December and January. Snow sometimes falls in the valley, and the river Jhelum and shallow parts of the lakes are frozen. Vigne knows of no granite in the valley. The trade of Kashmir is falling off greatly, and this is caused mainly by the tyranny and exhorbitant exactions of the Diwáns, who, besides being officials, are the chief traders or merchants of the valley. To those parts of Kashmir to which there is no water communication, goods are carried on the backs either of men or donkeys. In the valley there are several very fine temple-ruins.

The peculiarities of the architecture of these ruins are the following: gable with pediment of high pitch, arch trefoil, roof pyramidal. Probably Hindu or Asiatic architects had copied the Roman style of architecture, which they had seen in Syria and Egypt, modifying it of course, to please the Eastern taste. The chief temple-ruins are to be seen at Mártand, Wentipúr, Pa-yech, Pándretton, Takht-i-Sulimán, Zojibal, Paṭan, Baramula, and in the Baramula Pass.

Kashmírí, *n. m.* a proper name.

Kashun (kujhláná), *v. t.* to scratch; kúsh, kashán, kushmut, kashih.

Kãshur, *n. m.* the Kashmírí language. The Kashmírí language differs considerably in different parts of the valley.

Kashmírí is a pracrit or derivative of the Sanscrit language. It has been said that out of 100 Kashmírí words, 25 will be found to be Sanscrit, 40 Persian, 15 Hindustání, 10 Arabic, and 10 Tibetan, Turki, &c. The original letters of the Kashmírí alphabet are called Shâradah Achhar, and the following is the story given in Kashmir as to their introduction into the valley. There lived about two thousand years ago, in the city of Ujjain, in the province of the same name, a person whose name was Bikramájít, or Vikramadat, whose brother was king in that city and province. This brother's wife was a woman of bad character. She wished Bikramájít to cohabit with her; and because he stoutly and persistently refused, she fabricated a story against him, and prevailed upon her husband to expel his own brother from his territories. Bikramájít, thus driven from house and home, and accompanied by a few companions, began his travels. The exiles at last reached Kashmir. One of the little company was called Shâradah Nandan, who taught the inhabitants of Kashmir how to write the letters, which have ever since been called after him. There is a remarkable similarity between the Sanscrit and the ancient Kashmírí letters. The books written in the ancient character and language are unintelligible to the Hindus of the valley, except to a very few of the sacerdotal class among them. It is said that Thumí Sambhota, in the first half of the 7th century of our era, introduced the Kashmírí characters into Tibet. These characters remain unchanged to this day. See "Cunningham's Ladak."

Kãshur, *n. m.* a Kashmírí, or a male native of Kashmir. The Kashmírí has been called the Neapolitan of the East. The features of the Kashmíris are Jewish in character. And, apropos of this, it is very remarkable that the old temples of Kashmir bear a strong resemblance in plan to the Temple of Jerusalem. The chief features of the Kashmírí character are timidity, cowardice, laziness, gaity, mendacity, faithlessness, dexterity, inventiveness, and good mental powers.

Kãsid, *n. m.* messenger, letter-carrier, postman who carries the letter bags from one stage to another.

Kásid, *n. m.* courier.

Kásim, *n. m.* a proper name.

Kasír, *n. m.* Cornus macrophylla.

Kãsit, *n. m.* postman, see 'Kãsid.'

Kasiyána, *n. m.* vomiting.

Kásní, *n. m.* Cichorium intybus.

Kastúr, *n. m.* blackbird? nightingale. The shah-bulbul and hazár-dastán correspond to the kastúr.

Kásun, *v. t.* to shave, to rid of, to remove; kósun, kásán, kósmut, kásih.

Kasúr, *n. m.* defect.

Kat, *n. f.* word, fable, proverb.

Kaṭ, *n. m.* ram.

Káṭ, *n. m.* fetter.

Katak, *n. m.* see 'Kártik.'

Katál, *adj.* vile.

Kaṭamáz, *n. m.* mutton. The mutton of Hájin is the best in the valley.

Katán keúm. *n. m.* linseed oil.

Kat-bát, *n. f.* conversation.

Kat-bát karinyi, *v. i.* to converse.

Kath, *n. f.* story.

Kãṭh, *n. m.* saddle.

Katha pátha, *n. m.* conversation.

Káṭhachhán dányi, see 'Dányi.'

Kathah, *n. m.* conversation.

Kãṭhí, *n. f.* saddle. This is the name of the old Kashmírí wooden saddle, which I am told was similar to the one now in use in the neighbouring country of Ladak.

Kaṭhenyisán, *adv.* hardly, scarcely,

Káṭhis ladun (phánsí kardan), *v. t.* to hang.

Káṭhis pĕṭh ásun, *v. i.* to be hanged.

Kaṭhun, *adj.* ferocious.

Kati, *adv.* where?

Katih, *adv.* whence.

Kãtij, *n. m.* swallow.

Káṭir, *n. f.* mule.

Katir, *n. f.* baked clay.

Katra, *n. m.* drop.

Kats, *n. m.* arm-pit, groin.

Kaṭsabror, *n. m.* bubo.

Kátsabungir, *n. f.* a very common kind of bracelet made of a species of pottery.

Kátsagur, *n. m.* bracelet-maker, bottle-maker.

Kátsah, *interrog. adj.* how many?

Kátsakur, *n. m.* a bracelet made of a fine kind of earthenware.

Katsawádir, *n. m.* bubo.

Katun, *v. t.* to spin; kótun, katán, kótmut, katih.

Kaṭun (káṭná), *v. t.* to cut kuṭ, kaṭán, kuṭmut, kaṭih.

Káṭur, *n. m.* mule.

Katurun, *v. t.* to cut in slices.

Kaub, *n. m.* hump.

Kàüb, *adj.* hump-backed.

Kauḍhi, *n. f.* brain.

Kãiún, *n. m.* Faba vulgaris.

Kaul, *adj.* mute, dumb, speechless.

Kaum, *n. m.* people, tribe.

Kaur, *n. m.* a species of bracelet, massive and open.

Kausar, *n. m.* name of a celebrated fountain in heaven.

Kaushar, *n. m.* a Kashmírí, a native of Kashmir.

Kaushur, *n. m.* a male native of Kashmir.

Kauṭ, *n. m.* the front of the neck.

Kauṭmal, *n. m.* necklacc; or, rather, an ornament for the front of the neck.

Kauts, *n. m.* a bribe.

Kauts khyun, *v. i.* to take bribes.

Kauwul, *n. m.* large cup.

Kávin, *n. f.* crow.

Káwa dach, see 'Dach.'

Káwah, *n. m.* ear. The word in use towards Báramula.

Káwah dyun, *v. t.* to listen. This is the phrase in use towards Báramula.

Káwin, *n. f.* crow.

Káwir dach, see 'Dach.'

Káwúj, *n. m.* a burner of dead bodies (Hindus'). The Káwúj is always a Mussulman in Kashmir.

Káyiri tsínyi, *n. f.* gunpowder charcoal. It is made from pine-wood, or fir-wood.

Káyúr, *n. m.* the wood of the pine or fir.

Kaziyih, *n. m.* tumult.

Kekalat, *n. f.* lizard.

Kela, *n. m.* plantain. The plantain does not grow in the valley.

Kelam, *n. m.* a village in the Divasar pargana.

Kensih phiri, *adv.* sometimes.

Kensti phiri (chand bár), *adv.* frequently.

Keüz, *n. f.* a cup with a foot to it. The Mussulman women eat their rice out of it. It is either of clay or copper.

Kháb, *n. m.* dream.

Khabar, *n. m.* knowledge, fame, news, notice.

Khabardár, *adj.* conscious.

Khabarirust, *adj.* thoughtless.

Khabar karanwol, *n. m.* informer.

Khad, *n. m.* ass. This is the word in use towards Islamábád.

Khadak, *n. m.* sword.

Khádmí, *n. f.* a proper name.

Khahád, *n. m.* a place where wine is made and deposited.

Khai, *n. f.* rust.

Kháí, *n. f.* rust, trench.

Khain, *n. f.* nasal mucus.

Kháir, *n. f.* a she-ass.

Khaira, *n. m.* a proper name.

Khair posh, *n. m.* Villarsia nymphoides.

Khair shah, *n. m.* a proper name.

Kháí tulinyi, *v. t.* to polish; kháí tujin, kháí tulán, kháí tujmits, kháí tulih.

Khajar, *n. f.* opening, aperture.

Khajar, *n. m.* width, extension, wideness, finger's breadth.

Khajal, *adj.* ashamed.

Khákshí, *n. m.* Sisymbrium irio.

Khal, *v. m.* harvest, crop, granary, threshing-floor, usually a carefully prepared piece of ground in some field.

Khál, *n. m.* an artificial spot painted on the face to increase beauty.

Khal, *n. m.* beauty spot.

Khalalá, *n. m.* interference.

Khalás, *adj.* free.

Khalásí, *n. f.* freedom.

Khalásí dinyi, *v. t.* to discharge.

Khalás karun, *v. t.* to release.

Khalbali, *n. f.* hurry.

Khálí, *adj.* empty.

Khálik, *n. m.* a proper name.

Khálká, *n. m.* a proper name.

Khalkat, *n. m.* creature.

Khalur, *n. m.* skin of animals.

Khalwat, *n. m.* privacy.

Khám, *adj.* raw.

Kham, *n. m.* sky, heaven.

Khambirri, *n. f.* a large piece of ice from the heavens. Those pieces of ice are said to be so large as to kill people.

Khamun, *v. i.* to be breathless, to breathe with difficulty; khom, khamán, khommut, khamih.

Khán, *n. m.* table. The Hindus have no tables.

Khanabal, *n. m.* a bridge near to Islamabad.

Khánamól, *n. m.* young gentleman.

Khanchí, *n. m.* table.

Khand, *n. m.* the Hindustaní Chíní, a kind of sugar.

Khándar, *n. m.* marriage.

Khándar karun, *v. t.* to marry.

Khándawáo, *n. m.* shawl-maker, shawl-weaver. The shawl-weavers of Kashmir are Mussulmans, and the most miserable portion of the population, both physically and morally. There are 23,013 shawl-weavers in the valley of Kashmir. The number has greatly diminished of late years. Many have made their escape to the Punjab with their wives and families. They followed unfrequented and dangerous paths to escape the soldiery, who guard all the common outlets of the valley. A first rate shawl-weaver will earn from fourpence to fivepence of our money a-day. The generality earn about threepence a-day.

Khanduk, *n. m.* trench.

Khání, *n. f.* a proper name.

Khanjar, *n. m.* dagger.

Khanjari, *n. f.* a dagger.

Kháṅkur, *n. m.* the osseous rim of the orbital cavity.

Khanun, *v. t.* to engrave, to dig.

Khanun (khodná), *v. t.* to dig; khún, khanán, khúnmut, khanih.

Kháo, *n. m.* eater, glutton.

Khap-khap, *n. m.* adultery.

Khapun, *v. i.* to commit adultery.

Khár (lohár), *n. m.* blacksmith, farrier.

Khar, *n. m.* donkey, ass, scald-head, a proper name.

Khar, *adj.* bitter.

Khár and kharwár, *n. f.* a dry measure containing sixteen

traks. The literal meaning of the word khár, or kharwár, is ass-load. When the cultivators of the soil sell or pay grain to the government, they have to give sixteen traks in every khár or kharwár; but when the government sells grain to the people, but fourteen traks are given in the khár.

Kharáb, *adj.* ruined, desolate, worthless.

Khárabáí, *n. f.* blacksmith's wife.

Kharáb karun, *v. t.* to corrupt.

Khárah, *n. m.* desire.

Kharaj, *n. m.* a proper name.

Khar bádám, see 'Bádám.'

Kharbúz, *n. m.* musk melon. It is mature in August.

Kharbúz-kul, *n. m.* the musk melon plant.

Kharch karun, *v. t.* to spend.

Khargosh, *n. m.* hare. The hare is said not to be found in the valley.

Kharij, *n. f.* a proper name.

Kharin, *n. f.* she-ass.

Khárinyigar, *n. m.* cutler.

Kháriz, *n. m.* Cotoneaster obtusa and rotundifolia.

Kharj, *n. m.* expense, cost.

Kharjí, *n. m.* expense.

Kharkan, *n. m.* hare, see 'Khargosh.'

Kharmaeh, *n. m.* Rubus lasiocarpus.

Khar ṭánj, see 'Tánj.'

Khárun, *v. t.* to raise up, to cause to ascend, to cause to mount.

Kháryuk, *n. m.* foal.

Khasawun, *n. m.* an ascender.

Khash (gatl), *n. m.* execution, slaughter, killing, sacrifice.

Khásir, *n. f.* crown of head.

Khashkásh, *n. m.* poppy oil.

Khasra, *n. m.* a proper name.

Khasta, *adj.* wounded.

Khasta karun, *v. t.* to wound.

Khas-tsera, *n. m.* a species of apricot.

Khasun (chaṛhná), *v. i.* to ascend, to go up, to mount, to climb, to grow; khŏt, khut, khasán, khŏtmut, khutmut, and khasih. The primary meaning of khasun is to ascend; and from this, its primary meaning, its secondary meaning—to grow, comes.

Khásun, *v. t.* to make to ascend, to make to mount, to make to climb, and to make to grow.

Khat, *n. m.* letter, epistle.

Khâṭit, *adj.* concealed, obscured.

Khâtit sapadun, *v. i.* to disappear.

Khâṭit tháwun, *v. t.* to conceal.

Khat ninawol, courier.

Khatra, *n. m.* danger.

Khãtra, *prep.* for the sake of.

For the sake of seeing. Wuchana khãtra.

Khaṭun, *v. t.* to conceal, to hide; khuṭ, khaṭán, khuṭmut, khaṭih.

Khâuḍ, *n. f.* pudendum, vulva.

Khaul, *adj.* open.

Khaur, *adj.* having a scald head.

Khá,úr kun, *adv.* towards the left.

Khauṭ, *adj.* counterfeit.

Khaut, *n. m.* portions of the boat called dungá, situated immediately before and behind the gálo.

Kháwind, *n. m.* husband.

Kháwur, *adj.* left (opposite of right), south.

Kháwurpor, *n. m.* a pargana of Maráz.

Khayál, *n. m.* fancy.

Khazána, *n. m.* treasury.

Khazir, *n. m.* date (fruit).

Khazir-kul, *n. m.* the date palm.

Khazir, *n. m.* palm tree. No species of palm grows in Kashmir. Therefore, when Moore, in "Lalah Rookh," s̄peaks of the "Palms of Baramúl," he is egregiously wrong.

Khazra, *n. m.* a proper name.

Khema, *n. m.* tent.

Khema dyun, *n. i.* to encamp, to pitch a tent.

Khemah, *n. m.* tent.

Khĕn, *n. m.* food.

Khen dyun, *v. t.* to feed.

Kherun, *v. i.* to bloom, blossom.

Khidmat, *n. m.* service.

Khilahor, *n. m.* sandals.

Khin, *n. f.* provisions.

Khírah, *adj.* astonished.

Khislat, *n. m.* habit.

Khít, *n. f.* cultivated field.

Khó, *n. m.* temper, Oreoseris lanuginosa.

Khŏd, *n. m.* opening, pit, hole, cavity, rent.

Khoḍaven, *n. m.* a village in the Áḍaven pargana.

Khoḍatsar, *n. m.* back of head.

Khóf, *n. m.* fear.

Khoitij, *n. f.* a proper name.

Khojah, *n. m.* a title of honour.

Khokhur, *adj.* hollow.

Khol, *n. m.* seed.

Khŏl, *adj.* wide, clear.

Khólah, *n. m.* ascaridis.

Khŏn, *n. m.* elbow.

Khŏnawaṭ, *n. m.* elbow.

Khŏnḍ, *adj.* broken (only of pottery).

Khómah, *n.f.* the familiar and endearing form of the female name Khorim. The vocative is Khómo.

Khór, *n. m.* instep, foot. This word properly means instep, but it is generally used for foot.

Khŏr, *n. m.* foot.

Khorim, *n.f.* a proper name.

Khŏs, *n. m.* a cup.

Khós, *n. m.* glass vessel, small metal cup. The khós of the Mussulmans is much larger than that of the Hindus. It is either of copper, iron, or brass. The Mussulmans eat rice out of it, which the Hindus do not do. It is shaped like a bowl.

Khosh, *adj.* willing, gay, glad, cheerful, happy, contented.

Khoshák, *n. m.* compliment.

Khoshákha, *interj.* welcome!

Khosrau, *n. m.* Cyrus.

Khosh sapadun, *v. i.* to exult.

Khŏṭ, *adj.* false, spurious.

Khŏta, *prep.* than (=nisbat).

Khotij, *n.f.* a proper name.

Khótin, *n.f.* a proper name.

Khóts, *n. m.* alarm.

Khotsanáwun (ḍaráná), *v. t.* to cause to fear, to make to fear, to frighten; khotsanowun, khotsanáwán, khotsanomut, khotsanávih.

Khotsawun, *adj.* terrible, timid.

Khotsun (ḍarná), *v. i.* to fear; khúts, khotsán, khútsmut, khotsih.

Khotunyi trela: see 'Trela.'

Khówur, *adj.* left (opposite of right).

Khrang, *n. m.* threat.

Khrang karun, *v. t.* to threaten.

Khránts, *n.f.* rat, mouse.

Khráo, *n. m.* patten, or wooden soles, worn by the Kashmírís in winter.

Khrúṅts, *n.f.* mouse.

Khrŏk, *n. m.* snoring.

Khrú, *n. m.* a village in the Véhí pargana.

Khubání. *n. m.* apricot.

Khúbrúí, *adj.* pretty.

Khúch, *n. m.* a very large boat, coverless, and used for the carriage of goods.

Khuda, *n. m.* God.

Khudáí, *n. m.* God.

Khúdashih, *n. m.* danger.

Khuh, *n. m.* the Persian well.

Khulun, *v. i.* to be opened.

Khúṅt lagun, *v.i.* to slip; khúnt laug, lagán, laugmut, lagih.

Khuprah, *n. m.* chesnut.

Khúr, *n. m.* heel, oar, paddle, razor.

Khurák, *n. m.* food.

Khurmí. *n. f.* a proper name.

Khúsh, *adj.* merry.

Khushámud, *n. m.* flattery.

Khushámud karun, *v. t.* to flatter.

Khúshbú, *adj.* fragrant.

Khush-dil, *adj.* delighted, happy.

Khush-dil karun, *v. t.* to delight.

Khushí, *n. f.* pleasure, will.

Khushí karinyi, *v. t.* to exult.

Khut, *n. m.* a small cupboard, part of a boat answering the same purpose.

Khut, *adj.* false, spurious.

Khuts, *adj.* troubled, distressed.

Khwãbi, *adv.* in a dream.

Khwáb, *n. m.* a dream.

Khwáb wuchhun, *v. i.* to dream.

Khwábas manz, *adv.* in a dream.

Khwahishmand, *adj.* eager.

Khwáish, *n. f.* wish.

Khwár, *adj.* ruined, desolate.

Khwí, *n. m.* a pargana in the Kamráz division of the valley.

Khwíháma, *n. m.* a pargana in the Kamráz division of the valley.

Khwíjih, *n. m.* a village in the Kruhin pargana.

Khwŏd, *n. m.* ditch.

Khwunamut, *n. m.* ditch.

Khyáwaham, is made up of Khyáwak and mih.

Khyáwun, *v. t.* to give to eat, to feed, to cause to eat; khyov, khyáwán, khyómut, khyáwih.

Khyewun, *n. m.* eater.

Khyŏda, *n. m.* hunger.

Khyoda, *adj.* starving.

Khyodaihut, *adj.* hungry.

Khyul, *n. m.* flock, herd.

Khyun (kháná), *v. t.* to eat; khyau, khyĕwán, khyomut.

Kí, *n. m.* the cord bending the spokes of the large wheel together in the spinning-wheel.

Kibar, *n. m.* pride, haughtiness.

Kih, *n. f.* the loose hair found in the hand or comb when dressing the hair.

Kihn (koi), *pron.* anyone.

Kihnnah, *adv.* not at all.

Kíj, *n. f.* tack, wooden peg.

Kil, *n. f.* a slap with the edge of the open hand.

Kílmich, *n. m.* Viburnum fœtens.

Kíl-phamb, *n. m.* shawl wool. The shawl wool is imported intô Kashmír from Ladak by the Ladak merchants. It is then bought by the women of Kashmir, who are best acquainted with it. The respectable Mussulman women go to market dressed in the garment called the Búrka; which see at p. 102. The Hindu women go to market with their chadars drawn over their heads and faces. The wool is taken home by the women who have bought it. They do not buy much at a time. They clean it. The hair and the rough and coloured wool are separated from the white fine wool. The cleaned wool is then spread on a board and a paste, composed of pounded rice and water, is rubbed into it, after which it is dried, teased out and spun into thread by the women, which they then take and sell to the thread merchants. This wool is superior to all other wools, and finds it way with great difficulty to the Indian market. Quantities, however, do percolate down to India. The name of the wool in Ladák is 'lena.'

Kílpatar, *n. m.* the maple (acer).

Kin, *n. m.* virgo (zodiac sign).

Kín, *n. m.* hatred.

Kínah, *n. m.* hatred.

Kirái, *n. f.* rent.

Kirái hinyi, *v. t.* to borrow.

Kirmri, *n. f.* fig (Ficus caricordes).

Kis, *n. f.* little finger, little toe.

Kisar, *n. m.* head of barley.

Kísh, *n. m.* hair, ringlet.

Kishmishi-dach, see 'Dach.'

Kisht, *n. f.* a beggar's wallet or cup.

Kism, *n. m.* species.

Kisr, *n. f.* rice chaff.

Kissah, *n. m.* story.

Kitáb, *n. f.* book.

Kitába-lĕkhanwol, *n. m.* clerk, writer.

Kíṭh, *n. m.* worm, insect.

Kitha pãṭ, *adv.* how?

Kiṭha póṭh, *adv.* how

Knís, *n. m.* Dioscorea deltoidea. The shawl pashim is washed with the root of this plant.

Kó (for kós), *n. m.* a distance of about a mile and three quarters.

Kŏb, *adj.* crooked.

Kŏbun, *v. i.* to be humped; kŏbeo, kŏbán, kŏbeomut, kŏbih.

Kóchih, *n. m.* a shopless street.

Kod (maghaz), *n. m.* brain.

Koḍ, *n. m.* kernel.

Koh, *n. m.* hill.

Kŏhistán, *n. m.* a mountainous region.

Koilí, *n. f.* a proper name.

Koj, *n. f.* forenoon, second division of day, extending from 9 o'clock till noon, breakfast.

Koj, *n. m.* (chást), dinner, luncheon.

Kokanber, *n. m.* Zizyphus vulgaris.

Kokur-báng, *n.m.* cock-crowing in the morning.

Kŏkar-bángi, *adv.* at day-dawn.

Kŏkir, *n. f.* hen, fowl.

Kŏkirpút, *n. m.* chicken.

Kokul, *n. m.* ringlet, lock of hair.

Kŏkur, *n. m.* cock.

Kokur-mur, *n. m.* fowl-house.

Kokur-pút, *n. m.* chicken.

Kol, *n. m.* promise.

Kŏl, *n. f.* small river, streamlet.

Kolagom, *n. m.* a village in the Divasar pargana, the workmen of which are said to be very skilful.

Kŏlai, *n. f.* wife.

Kóm, *n. f.* business, use, action. deed, labour, work. What work do you do? kya kóm chhuk, (*m.*) or chhak, (*f.*) karán?

Komárí, *n. f.* girl, daughter.

Kómb, *n. f.* sheath, scabbard.

Kom karinyi, *v. t.* to execute.

Kón (kánà), *adj.* one-eyed.

Koṅ, *n. m.* branch of tree.

Kóná, *adv.* why not.

Kŏnḍ, *n. m.* thorn, ḍeep still spring.

Kónda (áwá), *n. m.* kiln.

Konḍal, *n. m.* the tail feathers of the nílŭj.

Kóng, *n. m.* saffron. The famous saffron fields of Kashmir are situated in the vicinity of Pampur. Last year 1380 traks of saffron were produced, and of this quantity 690 traks were taken by the government. When the season is dry and warm, as many as 2000 traks are produced. From six to eight annas, or from nine pence to a shilling is given for a tóla weight, or 180 grains of saffron. Saffron is used as a frequent condiment and medicine. The Mussulmans of the valley are generally unable to buy it. The mark on the forehead of a Hindu Pandit is partially formed of saffron. Saffron is composed of the stigmata of the flowers of the Crocus Sativus. The saffron of Kashmir is grown on the famous Pampur plain, the soil of which is said to be composed of a light ferruginous clay, and to have been dug up near the Jhelum and conveyed at great labour to the Pampur fields. The bulbs are planted out in June, and the Stigmata are collected in October.

Some 1600 lbs. of saffron

are exported yearly from Kashmir to Ladak.

Kóng-pósh (Crocus Sativus), *n. m.* saffron flower.

Kongs, *n. m.* saffron, (Crocus Sativus). See 'Kóng.'

Kóṅth, *n. m.* a high-heeled wooden shoe worn by the Pandits.

Kór, *adv.* whither.

Kóra, *adv.* recently.

Kórihan, *n. f.* a little girl.

Korr, *n. m.* glove.

Kósam, *n. m.* violet.

Kŏsh, *n. m.* chaff of wheat, barley, and maize.

Kostúr, *n. m.* nightingale.

Kŏt, *n. m.* Aucklandia Costus. Kŏṭ grows on the mountains around Kashmir at a minimum elevation of 7000 feet above the sea. It is mature in September. It belongs to the Cynaracephalæ, a suborder of the Asteraceæ, of the family Compositæ. It is a perennial plant, the stem and leaves dying yearly down to the root stock. It is supposed to be the same as the ancient Costus. It is a fragrant root. The native government monopolizes it, and compels each Kashmiree living near to the habitats of this root to collect about 200 lbs. of it. It is all brought to Srínagar, whence it is exported to the Punjab. It thereafter finds it way to Bombay, and after that to China, where it is said the Chinese burn it in their temples for its fragrant odour. The people receive from the Government two rupees chilkí, for every Kharwár weight which they collect. It grows abundantly on the hills of Kashmir. It is very abundant on the hill of Gangabal, and on the hill behind the Shálimár gardens. Under Guláb Singh, each village had to dig up eight Kharwárs weight of Kŏṭ, in return for which they received as much rice. This arrangement is said to have given satisfaction to the people. Kŏṭ is used in Kashmir as an application to ulcers, a hair-wash, a remedy in Cholera, a preserver of cloth against the ravages of moths and other vermin, a fumigatory, and by the native hakíms, as an expectorant. There are said to be four varieties: (1) Kŏṭ, (2) Drankhar, (3) Poshkar, (4) Kór.

Kóṭ, *n. f.* labour.

Kóṭ (súlí), *n. m.* gallows.
Kŏt, *adv.* whither.
Kótah, *adj.* how great.
Kótar, *n. m.* pigeon.
Kotarnal ṭang, see 'Tang.'
Kotarnal ṭanga kul, see 'Tanga kul.'
Koṭh *n. m* knee.
Kóṭh tráwun, *v. t.* to kneel.
Kotib Shah, *n. m.* a proper name.
Kótir, *n. f.* pigeon.
Kotiz, *n. m.* swallow.
Kŏtsúl, *n. m.* porter (of burdens).
Kótur, *n. m.* pigeon.
Kówat, *n. m.* strength, power, energy.
Krai, *n. f.* alms, especially in connection with the dead.
Kráí, *n. f.* a large pan.
Krãj, *n. f.* female potter, potter's wife.
Krak, *n. f.* noise, a cry (in Sírnagar), exclamation, complaint.
Krak dinyi, *v. t.* to cry aloud.
Krak karinyi, *v. t.* to complain.
Krak-karinyi *v. i.* to roar.
Krak-túlinyi, *v. i.* to make a noise; krak tujin, krak túlán, krak tujmits, krak túlih.
Král, *n. m.* potter, always a Mussulman.
Krám, *n. f.* caste.
Krám, *n. m.* surname.
Kranḍa, *n. m.* khilta. The natives of the valley have their khiltas made a little larger than those used by English travellers, and they are not covered with leather.
Kranjul, *n. m.* basket.
Krãr, *n. f.* cake made of the milk of the buffalo.
Krás, *n. m.* the Taihr of the Chur mountain near Simla.
Kraṭawol, *n. m.* miller.
Krats, *n. f.* a metal spoon.
Kràts, *n. f.* a brazen or iron cooking ladle.
Krehnamáz, *n. m.* liver.
Krĕhun, *adj.* black.
Krek, *n. f.* noise, a cry (out of Srínagar.)
Krel, *n. m.* insect.
Krihun dach, see 'Dach.'
Krihun túl, see 'Túl.'
Krím, *n. m.* crocodile.
Krim, *n. m.* a kind of vegetable.
Kripun, *v. t.* to scrape.
Krír-wóiṅ, *n. m.* well water.
Krís, *n. m.* Dioscorea deltoidea.
Kríshún, *n. m.* iris (Iris pseudacorus).
Krits, *n. f.* species of Cousinia.
Król, *n. m.* scab of an ulcer.
Krŏn, *n. m.* a relation.
Krón, *n. m.* tribe (a word of Hindu women).
Krór, *n. m.* the scab or crust that forms over a sore.
Krúd, *n. m.* revenge,

Kruhin, *n. m.* a pargana of the Kamráz division of the valley.

Kruhun, *adj.* black.

Krúr, *n. m.* a well, out of which the water is raised by a vessel, which is attached by means of a rope to one end of a pole, almost balanced on another pole fixed perpendicularly in the ground.

Krür, *n. m.* wild white rose (Rosa Brunonis).

Kúch, *n. m.* departure.

Kuchh, *n. f.* bosom.

Kúḍ, *n. f.* daughter. This is the form of the word in use towards Báramulá, where there is a great tendency to change r into ḍ.

Kuddú, *n. m.* a proper name.

Kudrat, *n. f.* power (God's).

Kuḍur, *adj.* coarse.

Kuduseri tsúnṭ, see 'Tsúnṭ.'

Kuhn, *pron.* some one.

Kuj, *n. f.* plant, bush, shrub.

Kúkil, *n. f.* cuckoo, dove.

Kukir Nág, *n. m.* a fountain in the Brang pargana.

Kúl, *n. m.* river.

Kul, *n. m.* tree.

Kulára, *n. m.* Viburnum fœtens.

Kulúf, *n. m.* padlock.

Kúluph, *n. m.* lock.

Kúluph karun, *v. t.* to lock.

Kum, *n. m.* chaff.

Kumb, *n. f.* scabbard.

Kumbak, *n. m.* assistance.

Kumul, *adj.* tender (as to flesh), soft.

Kun, *prep.* in the direction of, towards.

Towards the East. Purabus kun.

Towards the other side. Ápor kun.

Kún, *n. m.* corner.

Kun, *adj.* only, bare.

Kunahaiṭhyum, *adj.* fifty-ninth.

Kunaheṭh, *adj.* fifty-nine.

Kunanamat, *adj.* eighty-nine.

Kunanamatyum, *adj.* eighty-ninth.

Kunashít, *adj.* seventy-nine.

Kunashítyum, *adj.* seventy-ninth.

Kunasatat, *adj.* sixty-nine.

Kunasatatyum, *adj.* sixty-ninth.

Kunatájih, *adj.* thirty-nine.

Kunatájihyum, *adj.* thirty-ninth.

Kunatráh, *adj.* twenty-nine.

Kunatráhyum, *adj.* twenty-ninth.

Kunawanzah, *adj.* forty-nine.

Kunawanzãhyum, *adj.* forty-ninth.

Kunawuh, *adj.* nineteen.

Kunawuhyum, *adj.* nineteenth.

Kúnch, *n. f.* corner.

Kúnḍ, *n. m.* spine, thorn.

Kundá, *n. m.* log.

Kunḍh, *n. m.* washerman's dressing iron.

Kúnḍí, *n. f.* mortar.

Kungí, *n. m.* a proper name.

Kúnj, *n. f.* corner.

Kunjad, *n. m.* Sesamum orientale.

Kúñsh, *n. f.* a kind of shoe worn by the Hindu and Mussulman women, having high iron heels, and the uppers lessening towards the heels.

Kuntihin, *n. m.* a place on the face of the hill situated towards the Chashma Sháhí, where the Ákhun Malásha built a large house.

Kunuí, *adj.* sole, single, solitary, alone, only.

Kunun, *v. t.* to sell.

Kunyi, *adv.* sometimes, any where, somewhere.

Kúnyib, *n. m.* the sign Aquarius.

Kúnyí Dányí, see 'Dányí.'

Kunyinah, *adv.* nowhere.

Kunz, *n. f.* key.

Kúr, *n. f.* virgin, daughter, girl, damsel.

Kúr, *n. m.* a kind of bracelet.

Kur, *n, m.* unripe grapes, of which the Kashmíris make excellent vinegar.

Kúris, *n. f.* chair, foundation.

Kúrkní, *n. m.* serpent stick (Staphylea emodi).

Kurra, *n. m.* a long whip made of pliant branches of the vine, with which gardeners frighten away the birds during the vintage. Its crack is very loud.

Kúrta, *n. m.* six gaz.

Kurtin, *n. f.* inner garment worn by Hindus.

Kúrú, *n. m.* Villarsia nymphoides. It is very abundant in the lakes, and is used for fodder.

Kurukauṭ, *n. m.* Cancer (sign).

Kus? *pron.* who, which, what? What city? Kus shahr.

Kúsh, *n. m.* chaff, wax (bee's).

Kusháda, *adj.* loose, wide.

Kushta, *adj.* slain.

Kút, *n. m.* quantity.

Kuṭ, *n. m.* knee, room, chamber, the floor or floors between the ground-floor and the topmost floor of a house.

Kúṭ, *n. m.* privacy, long slender stem of a tree.

Kút, *adv.* where?

Kút, *adj.* how many, how much?

Kúṭahár, *n. m.* a pargana of Maráz. There is said to be a very extensive forest of deodars in this pargana.

Kuta-kuta karun, *v. t.* to tickle.

Kútanyíṭ, *n. f.* patella, knee-pan.

Kutawál, *n. m.* chief of city police.

Kúth, *n. m.* a room, knee, chamber.

Kuthàr, *n. m.* a tower, minaret.

Kúṭher, *n. m.* a mountain in the Kúṭahár pargana, where an iron mine is said to exist, which has been worked for the last two years.

Kuṭhun, *v. i.* to be distressed, to be in distress.

Kúṭkáts, *n. f.* poples, ham (of leg).

Kùts, *n. f.* Indigofera heterantha. The twigs are used in basket-making.

Kutuba, *n. m.* a proper name.

Kuwár, *n. m.* Polygonum.

Kuwat, *n. m.* power, ability.

Kuwatrust, *adj.* unable.

Kwíklapot, *n. m.* Cuscuta pedicellata.

Kwíllim, *n. m.* Viburnum fœtens.

Kwŏl, *n. m.* tube.

Kwŏl, *n. f.* rivulet.

Kwong, *n. m.* saffron.

Kya? *interrog. adj.* what?

Kyází, *adv.* & *conj.* why, because.

Kyul, *n. m.* flock, tent peg, iron nail.

Kyúm, *n. m.* insect, worm.

Kyúr, *n. m.* well.

Kyut, *prep.* for.

Kyut? *adv.* how?

Kyut, *adj.* what like (kaisá?).

Kyuth, *adj.* what like?

L.

L: this letter is pronounced exactly as in English.

Láb, *n. m.* interest on money, produce, profit.

Lab, *n. f.* the wall of a house.

Labashankhá, *n. m.* urine.

Lábavenna, *adj.* useless.

Labrez, *adj.* full.

Labun (yáftan), *v. t.* to find, to get, to receive, to obtain; lùb, labán, lùbmut, labih.

Labur, *n. m.* a rising ground, eminence (this is the name used in Srínagar), see 'Lábur.'

Lábur, *n. m.* the name used by the country-people for an eminence or rising ground, see 'Labur.'

Lach, *adj.* hundred thousand.

Lachakah, *n. m.* a head-dress consisting of a skull cap, with a long appendage behind.

Láchárí, *n. f.* poverty.

Lachh, *adj.* hundred thousand.

Lachiká, *n. m.* a piece of woollen cloth that hangs

down on the neck, from the back of the head of a Mussulman woman.

Laḍáí, *n. f.* war, fight.

Laḍáí karinyi, *v. t.* to fight.

Ládana, *n. f.* abuse.

Ládana karinyi, *v. t.* to abuse.

Ladun (banáná), *v. t.* to build, to load, to send, to string (a bow).

Láf, *n. m.* boasting, bragging.

Lagan, *n. m.* marriage.

Láganai, *n. f.* crop, cultivated ground.

Láganai karinyi, *v. t.* to cultivate.

Lagun, *v. i.* to be applied, to apply one's self, to fit, to be, to be bound.

Lágun, *v. t.* to plough, to pretend, to apply, to attach; log, lágán, logmut, lágih.

Láhan Tar, *n. m.* Hill of Shupiyon. It it about 350ft. in height, and a mile and a-half from the town. The hill is composed of amygdaloid trap. A most extensive view of the valley is obtained from its summit.

Lá,ik, *adj.* expedient.

Lá,ik sapadun, *v. i.* to be worthy, to deserve.

Lailyitádat, *n. m.* said to have been one of the ancient kings of Kashmir.

Lájavard, *n. m.* lapis lazuli.

Lájaward, *n. m.* a beautiful purple.

Lákam, *n. m.* rein, bridle.

Lakij, *n. f.* a proper name.

Lál, *n. m.* tulip, ruby, pupil of eye.

Lála, *n. m.* a proper name.

Lála Baṭ, *n. m.* a proper name.

Lálach, *n. m.* avarice.

Lálachí, *adj.* covetous, greedy, avaricious.

Lalawun, *v. t.* to keep together (of a fire), to protect.

Lál guláb, see 'Guláb.'

Lálpór, *n. m.* the principal village in the Bírú pargana, the chief village of the Laláb pargana.

Lam, *n. m.* a heap of stones or earth.

Lamb, *n. m.* sediment, dregs.

Lamkáwun, *v. t.* to suspend.

Lamun (khenchná), *v. t.* to draw, to pull, to drag; lŏm, lamán, lŏmmut, lamih.

Lánatána, *n. f.* abuse, insult, rebuke.

Lánatána karinyi, *v. t.* to insult, to rebuke, to abuse.

Lanḍ, *n. f.* reed, branch of tree.

Lãnḍ, *n. f.* a large branch.

Láne tsúrú, *n. m.* Xanthium strumarium.

Lang, *n. m.* lower extremity, thigh.

Pain of the thigh. Langas dód.

Lang, *n. m.* branch.

Lang, *n. f.* a small branch.

Langiyat, *n. m.* a village in the Machípor pargana.

Lãnk, *n. f.* a stride. This is the word used out of Srínagar.

Lãnk, *n. m.* a house built upon an island, island.

Lánts, *n. m.* eunuch, an impotent man. The eunuchs live chiefly in Táshawán, in Srínagar. They are all Mussulmans. They dance and sing at marriages, and are hired to make loud lamentations at burials of the rich.

Lánts, *adj.* unmanly, cowardly.

Lantsar, *n. m.* swelling.

Lánz, *n. m.* a long rod with which people knock down leaves and fruit from off trees.

Láp, *n. m.* Gymnosporia spinosa.

Lar, *n. m.* house.

Lãr, *n. m.* cucumber (khíra).

Lár, *n. m.* a pargana of the Kamráz division of the valley.

Lára, *n. m.* husband.

Láran, *n. f.* shaking, shivering.

Larakain, *n. f.* rib.

Laṛakányi, *n. f.* side of human body where are the ribs.

Lãrbyol Dányí, see 'Dányí.'

Lárí, *n. f.* wife.

Larináo, *n. m.* a state barge with the boatmen seated both before and behind the portion occupied by the passenger. This barge is used on long journeys only.

Lãrkul, *n. m.* cucumber plant.

Lárun, *v. i.* to run, to run after, to stain, to defile, to pollute.

Lár-wár, *n. m.* house.

Lasaj, *n. f.* Artemisia elegans.

Lasam, *n. m.* Allium sativum.

Lasan, *n. m.* cat's eye stone.

Lásh, *n. m.* dead body, corpse.

Lãsh, *n. f.* a black cat.

Lashkar, *n. m.* army.

Lashkari-hinz-jái karinyi, *v. t.* to encamp.

Lassí, *n. f.* a proper name.

Lassú, *n. m.* a proper name.

Lassu Khán, *n. m.* a proper name.

Lasun (jíná), *v. i.* to live; lüs, lasán, lüsmut, lasih.

Laṭ, *n. f.* tail, see 'Lŏṭ.'

Laṭ, *n. m.* time.

Three times. Tren laṭan.

Laṭ, *n. f.* kick.

Laṭh, *n. f.* epilepsy.

Laṭh, *n. m.* kick.

Latí, *n. f.* a proper name.

Laṭi, *n. f.* time (dafa). Three times (trih laṭih).

Latíf, *n. f.* a proper name.

Latifi, *n. f.* a proper name.

Laṭitáruk, *n. m.* comet. The inhabitants of Kashmir think that when a comet appears in the heavens it betokens a famine, a pestilence, or some other dire calamity. In the laṭitáruk, the tail points downwards.

Lats, *n. f.* rubbish, dust. Do not raise the dust, lats mah tul, or gard mah tul.

Latsar, *n. m.* ease, facility.

Latsár (láchár). *adj.* helpless.

Latúrih, *n. f.* the young (of any animal).

Lau, *n. m.* said to have been one of the ancient kings of Kashmir.

Lau, *n. f.* ewe.

Laung, *adj.* lame.

Lauṭ, *n. m.* the tail of a quadruped, stalk of apple or pear.

Laut, *adj.* easy, slow.

Laut, *adj.* light (not heavy).

Lauts, *adj.* light (not heavy).

Lautsar, *n. m.* facility, easiness.

Lauwa, *n. f.* dew.

Lawa, *n. f.* dew.

Láwa, *adj.* damp.

Lawan, *n. m.* salt.

Láyinah, *n. m.* beating.

Láyun (márná), *v. t.* to beat, to strike, to discharge (a pellet), to utter (cry); loe, láyán, loemut, láyih.

Lazarust, *adj.* tasteless.

Lázim, *adj.* right, proper.

Lĕḍ, *n. f.* dung, ordure of horses, camels, elephants, and donkeys.

Lĕḍ, *adj.* cowardly, heartless.

Ledur, *adj.* yellow, wan.

Lefa, *n. m.* poultice.

Lehan, *n. m.* Cotoneaster obtusa and rotundifolia. The twigs are used in basket-making, and for twig bridges.

Lej, *n. f.* a small cooking-vessel.

Lejí, *n. f.* an earthenware pot, smaller than the Lul. The Lejí is used in cooking.

Lĕk (gálí), *n. f.* abuse, insult.

To abuse. Lĕk kaḍinyi, lĕk tsárinyi.

Lĕk dinyi, *v. t.* to insult, to abuse.

Lekhanwol, *n. m.* writer, moonshee. The writers of the valley are chiefly Pandits.

Lekhanáwun, *v. t.* to make to write; lekhanowun, lekhanáwán, lekhanomut, lekhanáwih.

Lekin, *conj.* but.

Lĕkhun (likhná), *v. t.* to write, lyukh, lĕkhán, lyukhmut, lĕkhih.

Lena, *n. m.* shawl-wool. The word is Ladákí.

Letapór, *n. m.* a village in the Wular pargana. Here in ancient times reigned Lailyitádat, after whom, no doubt, the city was called Lailyitádatpúr, which, in process of time, became Letapór.

Lĕwun (Lesná), *v. t.* to lick (as a dog); lyú, lĕwán, lyúmut, lĕwih.

Lichh, *n. f.* the egg of the body louse.

Lidir (zard-i-chob), *n. m.* turmeric.

Lidar, *n. f.* turmeric (haldí) imported from the Punjab. The word Lidar properly means yellow.

Lidur, *n. m.* the third river of Kashmir for size. It rises away to the north-east of the valley among the mountains and glaciers of that region; and, after a south-westerly course, joins the Jhelum between Islamabad and Bíj Bihára. The word Lidur means, in Kashmírí, yellow.

Lidur, *adj.* yellow.

Lij, *n. f.* an earthenware dish (deghchí), a small earthenware cooking-vessel.

Lín, *n. m.* Cotoneaster obtusa and rotundifolia.

Litâr, *n. f.* saw.

Litur, *n. f.* saw.

Líwan, *n. f.* spade.

Liwan, *n. f.* spade.

Lobí, *n. m.* miser.

Lóbisht, *n. m.* miser.

Loch(pheran), *n. m.* a woollen garment, paṭṭú, or coarse woollen cloth.

Lodhú, *n. m.* a village in the Vehí pargana. Here are to be seen the ruins of a temple in the midst of a spring.

Loganai, *n. f.* sown field.

Loh, *n. m.* fox.

Lóí, *n. f.* brass.

Lok, *adj.* small.

Lokachár, *n. m.* smallness.

Lokama, *n. m.* piece.

Lŏkatsár, *n. m.* littleness, infancy, smallness.

Lŏkhar, *n. f.* morsel, mouthful.

Lokhit Paraspór, *n. m.* a village in the Paraspór pargana.

Lŏkochár, *n. f.* littleness.

Lŏkun (Fr. lŏk), *v. i.* to be small, to be little.

Lokuṭ, *n. m.* a boy till his beard appears.

Lŏkuṭ, *adj.* small, younger.

Lokut tháwun, *v. t.* to despise.

Lŏl, *n. m.* love, desire, compassion.

Loláb, *n. m.* a pargana of the Kamráz division of the valley.

Lolabrut, *adj.* desirous.

Lólapór, *n. m.* a village in the Bángil pargana.

Lolau, *n. m.* the popular name of the Loláb pargana. It is said to have got this name from Lau, one of its ancient kings.

Lón, an affix to the name of an inhabitant of the village of Lán, which is situated in the direction of Islamabad.

Long, *adj.* crippled.

Lonun (káṭná), *v. t.* to reap; lún, lonán, lúnmut, lonih.

Lŏpun, *n. m.* a large earthenware jar, shaped like a khilta, and capable of containing from fifty to sixty seers, or one hundredweight of grain.

Lor, *n. m.* staff (láṭhí).

Lórihan, *n. f.* little pole, small stick, small staff.

Loriwol (chóbdár), *n. m.* club-bearer.

Losh, *n. m.* fox.

Losun, *n. m.* fatigue.

Lósun (mánda honá), *v. i.* to be weary, tired (from walking); lús, lósán, lúsmut, lósih.

Lŏṭ, *n. m.* the tail of a dog, sheep, fox, jackal, lion, tiger, cat, cow, or camel.

Lot (halká), *adj.* light.

Lotakí, *n. m.* Ladak stone.

Lot-lot, *adj.* slow.

Lotun, *v. i.* to be light (not heavy).

Lŏtur, *n. m.* hump on the back of one species of bullock.

Lóv, *n. m.* handful of grass, sheaf of grain.

Lúb, *n. m.* bank of a river, covetousness.

Lúb karun, *v. t.* to covet.

Lud, *n. m.* river.

Ludir, *n. m.* coral. A necklace of coral is ludirimál, *m.*

Luhf, *n. m.* fox.

Luhv, *n. m.* fox.

The fox is very common in Kashmir.

Lúk, *n. m.* people.

Luk, *n. m.* Typha Angustifolia.

Lúk, *adj.* younger, small.

Lul, *n. m.* a large earthenware pot used in cooking.

Lúlí, *n. f.* penis.

Lum, *n. m.* sediment, dregs.

Lun, *n. m.* salt.

Salt is a state monopoly.

Lung, *adj.* lame.

Lúngi, *n.f.* a cotton shawl, a long piece of cotton stuff worn round the waist over the pheran. A Panditanee never goes abroad without her lúngí, female girdle.

Lur, *n. m.* house.

The general plan of a Kashmir house is as follows. First there is a ground floor, in which are two chambers, with the small hall of the house. The second floor contains three rooms, and the floor under the roof usually consists of one long chamber, where the household spend the summer months.

Kine are often housed in the ground floor.

The wood of which houses are built are deodar, káyur, and songul. The woods of the poplar and plane are used by the poor, but they are far from being durable. No one is allowed to cut down a mulberry tree, or a plane tree, without permission from the native Government. The materials of which houses in Kashmir are built are, stones for a foundation, wood for the frame work, bricks and mortar to fill up the divisions of the frame work, and earth and the liber of the birch tree, called Bójpathar, for the roof, which is slanting. At times, however, instead of the fine inner bark or liber of the birch, a reed called tshai is used. In Baramula, Shupujon and Tsrár, the roofs are made simply of thick boards of wood nailed firmly, on account of the very strong winds to which these places are exposed. The reed called Tshai is found on the roofs of the houses in Srínagar, Sopór, and the adjacent villages, because they are near to the Ḍal, Wulur, and Anchár Lakes, where the reed grows abundantly. In some villages, the houses are thatched with straw.

In some of the houses there are fire-places, but generally they are without. The smoke finds its way out by the doors and windows. Fires are used only for cooking purposes. Wood is the fuel generally burned, sometimes cow dung, baked into cakes with straw, is also burned.

Lúr, *n. f.* pole, club, stick.

Lúṭ, *n. m.* lesson, robbery, plunder.

Lúṭkarun, *v. t.* to rob, to plunder.

Lúṭun, *v. t.* to rob, ravage; lúṭun, lúṭán, lúṭmut, lúṭih.

Lút wanun, *v. i.* to whisper.

Lyad, *adj.* weak.

Lyĕk, *n. f.* abuse.

Lying, *n. m.* a bush or shrub, the branches of which are used for making baskets.

Lyul, *n.* an earthenware cooking vessel.

Lyúṭ, *adv.* near.

M.

M: this letter is pronounced exactly as it is in English.

M is the enclitic form of the singular objective case of the first personal pronoun. There is no enclitic for the plural. This letter is also the enclitic form of the dative and of the case of the agent of the first personal pronoun, singular number.

Má, *conj.* perhaps, never the first word in a sentence.

Mach, *n. m.* fly.

Machh, *n. f.* fly.

Machhámá, *n. m.* a dish eaten by the Kashmiris consisting of rice, vegetables, raisins, colouring matter, and sugar.

Máchihóm, *n. m.* a pargana in the Kamráz division of the valley.

Machipór, *n. m.* a pargana in the Kamráz division of the valley.

Mad, *n. m.* pride, intoxication.

Madad, *n. m.* assistance, help.

Madanwár, *n. m.* lover.

Madapán, *n. m.* wine, made out of pears, apples, mulberries, or grapes.

Madar, *adj.* proud.

Maḍáṛá, *adj.* encouraged, comforted.

Maḍí, *n. f.* a proper name.

Madir, *adj.* proud.

Mads-náṭa, *n. m.* mutton.

Mádúr, *adj.* sweet.

Máe, *n. f.* deceit, deception.

Mág, *n. f.* first month of Mussulman year (Muharram), and the eleventh month of the Hindu year, and corresponding to our month of January.

Magar, *n. m.* November.

Magar, *conj.* except, unless.

Maghrib, *n. m.* west.

Mah, *n. m.* mouth.

Mah, *adv.* not (prohibitive).

Mahadí, *n. m.* a proper name.

Mahallodár, *n. m.* an officer in charge of a division of a city. His chief duty seems to be to act as a spy over the people. Sometimes women fill this post. Mahalladars are generally heartily hated by the people, which is not to be wondered at.

Mahalladarinyi, *n. f.* a woman who has charge of a district of the city; the wife of the Mahalladar.

Maharájí wat, *n. m.* highway.

Mahdú, Jú, *n. m.* a proper name.

Mahesh, *n.* buffalo.

Mahmándárí Karinyi, *v. t.* to entertain.

Mahora, *n. m.* Bassia latifolia.

Mahtáb, *n. m.* moon.

Mahtábí, *n. f.* a portion of a boat, situated behind the prow or in front of the stern.

Mahwa-mowa, *n. m.* Bassia latifolia.

Maidán, *n. m.* field, plain.

Maikhambiri tsúnṭ, see 'Tsúnṭ.'

Mail, *n. m.* love.

Mail-tang, *n. m.* Pyrus Kumaonensis.

Mainah, *n. m.* frog. This word is used out of Srínagar.

Mainphal, *n. m.* Randia dumetorum.

Mait, *n. m.* corpse.

Maith, *n. m.* corpse, dead body.

Maithri, *n. f.* harmony.

Máj, *n. f.* mother.

Majíth, *n. m.* madder.

Majlis, *n. m.* council, assembly.

Majma, *n. m.* tray.

Májú, *n. m.* the fruit or nuts of Cupressus sempervirens or allied species.

Makahom, *n. m.* a village in the Máchihóm pargana, where chadars of great fineness are manufactured.

Makãí, *n. f.* maize, Indian corn.

Makáim, *n. m.* pashmina-broker.

Makal, *n. m.* a proper name.

Makarrar karun, *v. t.* establish, to ratify.

Makawa, *n. m.* volume.

Makaz, *n.* a large axe.

Makhmal, *n. m.* velvet, imported from Kábul and India.

Makhmal japhiri, see 'Japhiri.'

Makím, *n. m.* an agent who sells pashmina for another.

Makir, *n. m.* forgery.

Mako, *n. m.* Solanum Nigrum.

Makol, *n. m.* gypsum.

Makur, *n. m.* Capricorn (sign).

Makuts, *n. f.* axe.

Mal, *n. m.* stool, dirt.

Mál, *n. m.* necklace, garland, property.

Mãl, *n. m.* desire, desire for food.

Mãl, *n. f.* a proper name.

Mãl, *adj.* dirty.

Malabángi, *adv*. at day dawn.

Malah, *n. m.* a Mussulman priest, a grave-digger.

Malah-báng, *n. m.* call to Mussulman matins.

Malakhosh, *n. m.* grave digger.

Malámat karinyi, *v. t.* to rebuke.

Málawol, *adj*. rich.

Malbúrut, *adj*. foul, dirty.

Malguzár, *n. m.* grave-yard.

Málidagar, *n. m.* a washer of woollen cloth.

Mãlik, *n. m.* lord.

Malir, *n. f.* a large water pot of earthenware.

Malíts, *n. m.* Mussulman. A name conferred by the Hindus. It properly means 'unclean.'

Mallar, *n. f.* pitcher.

Malúl karun, *v. t.* to offend.

Málum karun, *v. t.* to ascerain.

Málum sapanun, *v. i.* to learn.

Malun, *v. t.* to rub, to anoint.

Malwa bakchí, *n. f.* see 'Kálí zírí.

Mám, *n. m.* uncle on mother's side.

Mamah, *n. m.* udder.

Mámain, *n. f.* aunt, mother's brother's wife.

Mámas, *n. m.* mutton, flesh.

Mámatir, binyi, *n. f.* cousin, mother's brother's daughter.

Mámaturboí, *n. m.* cousin, mother's brother's son.

Mammú, *n. m.* a proper name.

Man, *n. m.* heart.

Manah set, *adv*. cordially.

Manai, *adj*. few.

Mána karun, *v. t.* to forbid.

Manakumal, *adj*. kind.

Manan, *n. m.* a kángrí without wicker work.

Manar, *n. m.* lapidary.

Manárí, *n. f.* ornaments for women, consisting of bracelets, rings for the nose, ears, and neck, made of earthenware, tin, iron, brass, and copper.

Mánasbal, *n. m.* a lake near to Safapór. It is sometimes called Mánasnág.

Máńch, *n. m.* honey.

Manchh, *n. m.* honey.

Mánchphar, *n. m.* honey in the comb.

Mánch-tular, *n. m.* bee.

Mánch-tulir, *n. f.* honey bee.

Mánch tilar, *n. f.* honey bee.

Mandach, *n. m.* bashfulness, modesty, shame.

Mandachh, *n. f.* shame.

Mandachháwun, *v. t.* to confuse, to make ashamed.

Mandichháwun, *v. t.* to make ashamed, to confuse.

Mandachhomut, *p. p.* disgraced,

made ashamed, confused, confounded.

Mandachun, *v.i.* to feel ashamed, to be ashamed; mandachhov, mandachhán, mandachhomut, mandachih.

Mandain, *n. m.* noon.

Mandanáwun, *v. t.* to spill.

Mandanáwun, *v. t.* to cause to knead, especially with the feet. This word is applied to the kneading of large quantities of dough, and to the washing of thich coarse wollen cloth (Paṭṭú.)

Mandar, *n. m.* temple.

Manḍan, *n. m.* chamber. This is the word in use towards Báramula.

Mandiá, *n. m.* ivy, (Hedera Helix).

Mandij, *n. f.* the inner fleshy part of the thigh.

Mandinyi, *n. f.* noon, mid-day.

Mandir, *n. m.* temple.

Manḍul, *n. m.* rump, buttock, hip, thigh.

Mandun, *v. i.* to spill.

Manḍun, *v. t.* to knead, to clean (as cloth), to rub, to anoint, to tread, trample down; munḍun, manḍán, munḍmut, mánḍih.

Mánḍun, *v. t.* to knead; monḍun, manḍán, mónḍmut, mánḍih.

Máne karun, *v. t.* to diminish, to lessen.

Máne sapadun, *v. i.* to diminish, to grow less.

Mángai, *n. f.* a request, petition.

Mangal, *n. m.* planet Mars.

Mangalwár, *n. m.* Tuesday.

Manganáwun, *v. t.* to send for, to claim (talab namúdan), to cause to seek.

Mangata, *adj.* adopted (as a child).

Mangatah, *adj.* adopted (of a child).

Mangun, *v. t.* to beg, to request, to ask, to demand, to desire; móng, mangán, móngmut, mangih.

Máni, *n. f.* meaning.

Mánir, *adj.* spiteful, envious.

Manjagur, *n. m.* a maker of manjih, which is composed of rice and oil.

Manjít, *n. m.* madder.

Man-prasand, *adj.* comfortable.

Man-prasand karun, *v. t.* to rejoice, to gladden.

Man-prasand sapadun, *v. i.* to rejoice.

Máṅs, *n. m.* month.

Mãnsh, *n. f.* buffalo cow.

Mánsha kauṭ, *n. m.* buffalo bull. The buffalo is numerous on the Kashmir hills. It is not indigenous.

Mánskhel, *n. m.* common mushroom (Agaricus campestris).

Mánṭ, *n. m.* target.

Mãnthár, *n. f.* charm. The Mussulmans have great faith in the power and efficacy of charms. The native government of the valley, during the severe epidemic of cholera of 1867, derived no inconsiderable revenue from the sale of charms to the pestilence-stricken inhabitants of Srínagar.

Manṭun, *n. m.* three pounds of any thing.

Manú, *n. m.* Rhus Cotinus.

Manukdokh, *n. m.* remorse.

Mánun, *v. t.* to agree, to have a regard, to esteem highly, to obey, to accept, to approve, to receive; mon, mánán, monmut, mánih.

Manuṭ, *n. m.* the weight (usually a stone) of three pounds.

Manyaphul, *n. m.* pupil of eye.

Manyiphul, *n. m.* the image of a man in the eye. The word in Persian is Mardumak.

Manz, *prep.* among, in.

Mánz, *n. m.* the Lawsonia inermis. This is the Indian Hinna, with which the Indians stain their hands and feet.

Manzar, *n. f.* sickness.

Manzila tsatun, *v. i.* to travel.

Manzimyãriii, *n. f.* a go-between in love matters.

Manzimyor, *n. m.* a go-between in love matters.

Mánzirát, *n. m.* the name of the day and the ceremonies that take place on the second day after the investment of the boy with the Brahminical thread. The word is derived from Mánz (the Lawsonia inermis), with which the women and children stain their hands and feet, and Rát, night.

Manzur (*m.*), manzir (*f.*), *adj.* cripple.

Máo, *n. m.* a cutting from a plant.

Máo, *n. f.* back of hand.

Mar, *n. f.* fort, castle.

Mar, *n. m.* house, hut.

Már, *n. m.* a lake.

Már, *n. m.* murder, beating.

Marah, numerical affix, signifying "about."

Márah, *adj.* killed, beaten.

Máraka, *n. m.* tumult.

Maramat, *n. m.* repair.

Maramat karun, *v. t.* to repair.

Máranwol, *adj.* deadly.

Marára, *n. m.* Desmodium tiliæfolium.

Márawátul (jallád), *n. m.* executioner.

Maráz, *n. m.* one of the three great divisions of the valley, of which it comprehended the whole south-east end.

Mardána, *adj.* manly.

Már dyun, *v. t.* to beat.

Marg, *n. m.* plateau, valley up among the mountains.

Marhom, *n. m.* a large village in the Dachanpór pargana.

Marits, *n. m.* pepper, black pepper.

Marjal, *n. m.* iris (Iris pseudacorus).

Márkhor, *n. m.* wild goat of Ladak, where the animal is called rapho-chhe, great goat. Márkhor means the snake-eater.

Mãrmund, *adj.* beautiful.

Martaba, *n. m.* rank.

Mártand, *n. m.* a village some four or five miles to the north-east of Islamabad. The spring of Mártand, or Bówan, is considered by the Hindus as the most sacred in the valley. The reservoir is full of Himalayan trout, which are very tame. The Hindu priests of Bowán keep a roll containing the names of most of the visitors to this holy spot for many years past. The object of the roll is to obtain money from the visitors. The word Mártaṇd is the Sanscrit for sun, see 'Matan.'

Marts, *n. m.* black pepper.

Marts-wángun, *n. m.* red pepper.

Martsa-wángun, *n. m.* long pepper. It is said to grow in Kashmir.

Márúk, *n. m.* horse's halter.

Marun, *n. m.* death.

Marun, *v. i.* to perish, to die; múd marán, múdmut, marih.

Márun, *v. t.* to kill, to destroy, to beat; mor, márán, mormut, márih.

Mãrwóin, *n. m.* lake-water.

Maryuk, *n. m.* lasso, scaling-ladder used by thieves.

Marz, *n. m.* sickness.

Marzan josh, *n. m.* Origanum vulgare.

Más, *n. f.* aunt, mother's sister.

Mas, *n. m.* wine. It is made out of the juice of the grape, which grows luxuriantly in Kashmir.

Mas, *n. f.* boot.

Masalman, *n. m.* a Mussulman.

Másatir-binyi, *n. f.* cousin, mother's sister's daughter.

Másatur-bói, *n. m.* cousin, mother's sister's son.

Mashíd, *n. f.* mosque, temple.

Mashil, *n. f.* lantern.

Mashrab, *n. m.* mistake.

Mashrah karun, *v. t.* to forget.

Mashrak, *adj.* common.

Mashráwun, *n. t.* to forget.

Mashrik, *n. m.* east.

Mashun, *v. i.* to be forgotten; muṭh, mashán, muṭhmut, mashih; also mush, mashán, mushmut, mashih.

Mashwar, *n. m.* opinion.

Mashwara, *n. m.* counsel.

Mashwara karun, *v. t.* to consult, to reconcile.

Mashín, *n. m.* Polygonum bistorta.

Masjid, *n. f.* mosque.

Maskhahád, *n. m.* a place in the south-east end of the valley. This word is derived from mas, new wine, and khahád, a place where wine is made and deposited.

Mas-khós, *n. m.* wine-cup.

Maslahat karinyi, *v. t.* to reconcile.

Mass, *n. m.* socks reaching to the calves of the legs.

Mast, *n. m.* hair of head, a curl of hair, ringlet.

Mast, *adj.* drunk.

Mastárú, *n. m.* Artemisia indica.

Masur, *n. m.* lentil.

Maswal, *n. m.* a flower of Kashmir.

Mãt, *adj.* dead.

Máṭa, *n. f.* flesh.

Maṭan, *n. m.* a celebrated spring of water in the village of Maṭan, or Bauwan.

Maṭan, *n. m.* a pargana of Maráz consisting of a karewah or plateau, upon which are the grand old ruins of the Temple of Mártand, or the Sun.

Matbal, *n. m.* malice.

Mát dyun, *v. t.* to checkmate.

Maṭhun (álúdan), *v. t.* to defile.

Mathun, *v. t.* to rub, to anoint; muth, mathán, muthmut, mathih.

Maṭi, *n. f.* a very large earthenware vessel, about three feet in height, for containing grain and beverages.

Matí, *n. f.* horse tail (Equisetum debile).

Matil, *n. f.* madness.

Matitsa wángrú, *n. m.* red pepper (Capsicum annuum).

Mát karun, *v. t.* to checkmate.

Màts, *n. f.* clay.

Máts, *n. f.* the arm, from the shoulder to the elbow.

Mats, *n. f.* arm (anatomice).

Matsaband, *n. m.* a kind of charm.

Matsh, *n. f.* arm (anatom.), properly the region of the biceps and triceps.

Mát sapadun, *v. i.* to be checkmated.

Matsaráwun, *v. t.* to delude, to mislead, to deceive; matsróv, matsráwán, matsromut, matsráwih.

Matun, *v. i.* to become foolish; mateo, matán, mateomut, matih.

Maunḍ, *adj.* stupid.

Maunjhór, *n. f.* November (Zika'da, the eleventh month of the Mussulman year).

Maur, *n. m.* body.

Maut, *n. m.* madman.

Maüt, *adj.* mad.

Mauṭ, *adj.* fat, coarse, thick.

Mauṭ-kóḍ, *n. m.* cerebrum.

Máwal, *n. m.* cockscomb (Celosia cristata).

Mawur, *n. m.* the plant known as the cock's comb (Amaranthus cruentus). Bread-cakes made from the seed are a common food with the peasants of the Himalayas.

Mayazál, *n. m.* a figure drawn on the ground by the Brahmans at the burning of a Hindu corpse.

Máyí, *n. f.* glue.

Máyih, *n. m.* wealth.

Máz, *n. m.* flesh, meat, butcher meat, the fleshy part of fruit.

Maza, *n. m.* taste, flavour.

Mazah, *n. m.* taste.

Mazár, *n. m.* tomb, graveyard.

Mazarust, *adj.* tasteless.

Mazeṭ, *n. m.* a root used in the almond-coloured dye. It is said to be found at Pámpúr and at Nágóm, a village lying between Srínagar and Rámú. Most of the root, however, comes from Ladak, where it is called Tsŏt.

Mazhar, *n. m.* stage, theatre.

Mazúr, *n. m.* a labourer, who is always a Mussulman.

Mazúrí, *n. f.* labourer's wages, labourer's work.

Mechhar, *n. m.* taste.

Meg, *n. m.* cloud.

Mekad, *n. m.* anus.

Mekh, *n. f.* iron peg.

Mekhánah, *n. m.* wine-house, wine-shop.

Mékhla, *n. m.* the name of the occasion on which the young Hindu child is invested with the Brahminical thread (yónyí).

Melun (milná), *v. i.* to meet, to mix; myúl, melán, myúlmut, melih.

Memna, *n. m.* kid.

Memní, *n. f.* kid.

Menga, *n. m.* temple (of head).

Mengin, *n. m.* ordure of sheep and goats.

Menun (nápná), *v. t.* to measure, to guess; myúnun, menán, myúnmut, menih.
Menzúr, *n. m.* wood-seller.
Mĕs, *n. f.* unripe kernel of the water chesnut.
Mĕṭ, *n. m.* corpse.
Meṭhráwun, *v. t.* to sweeten.
Methrí, *n. f.* friendship.
Methum, *n. m.* Gemini (zodiac sign).
Meṭhun, *v. i.* to be sweet.
Mets, *n. f.* dust.
Mewa, *n. m.* fruit.
Mewadár, *n. m.* fertile.
Mewah, *n. m.* fruit.
Méz, *n. f.* table. Such an article of furniture is not in use in Kashmir.
Midasat, *n. m.* Cuscuta reflexa.
Míg, *n. m.* cloud.
Mih, *pron.* to me.
Mihnat, *n. m.* toil, labour.
Mihráb, *n. m.* the pulpit in a Mussulman temple.
Mihrbán, *adj.* friendly, kind.
Mihrbaní, *n. f.* favour, kindness.
Mikráz, *n. m.* shears, scissors.
Mihrí, *n. f.* a proper name.
Míl, *n. m.* ink.
Milanáwun, *v. t.* to mix; milanowun, milanáwán, milanomut, milanáwih.
Milasár, *n. m.* confederate.
Milasár sapadun, *v. i.* to connive at, to share, to be a party to.
Milat, *n. m.* religion.
Milatsár, *n. m.* accident, society.
Miláwun, *v. t.* to join.
Miligur, *n. m.* inkmaker.
Militsár, *n. m.* concord, harmony.
Militzár, *n. m.* respect.
Mím, *n. m.* the letter m.
Mimiz, *n. f.* noon, the midday meal of children, luncheon.
Mimyamar, *n. f.* doe—the female of the bárah sing.
Mín, *n. m.* Pisces (zodiac sign).
Míṅts, *n. f.* measure.
Minyamar, *n. f.* doe.
Mínyimar, *n. f.* hind.
Mírakhor, *n. m.* groom. Probably this word is derived from mír, chief, and ákhúr, stable.
Misgur, *n. m.* coppersmith.
Mish, *n. f.* edge of eyelid.
Mísh, *n. m.* the sign Aries.
Mish, *n. f.* a rag-nail, a splinter of wood, the Caruncula lachrymalis.
Mishkín, *adj.* black.
Miskín, *adj.* poor.
Miṭ, *n. f.* clay.
Mithar, *n. m.* male friend.
Mithar sapadun, *v. i.* to con-

nive at, to share, to be a party to, to befriend.

Mitharain, *n.f.* a female friend.

Mithir, *n. m.* companion.

Mithrachárí, *n.f.* friendship.

Mitrut, *n. m.* friendship.

Mits, *n.f.* earth.

Mizáj, *n. m.* temper, disposition.

Moch, *n. m.* shoemaker. One of the four divisions of the Mihtar or Wátul caste is the shoemaker class.

Mód, *n. m.* character, honour, dignity.

Mŏdarir, *n. m.* sweetness.

Modari-tsera, *n. m.* a species of apricot.

Mŏdir ṭánj, see 'Ṭánj.'

Moḍir zeo, *adj.* eloquent.

Mŏḍur bádám, see 'Bádám.'

Moḍur bamtsúnt, see 'Bamtsunṭ.'

Mŏdur dáṅ, see 'Dáṅ.'

Moḍur tsúnṭ, see 'Tsúnṭ.'

Mŏdur, *adj.* sweet.

Mogul Cháí, see 'Cháí.'

Mogil Cháí, *n.f.* coffee.

Moh, *n. m.* gnat, musquito. Musquitoes are very troublesome in some parts of Kashmir at certain seasons.

Mohanyú, *n. m.* individual, man.

Mohar-kand, *n. m.* stone-engraver.

Mŏhnyu, *n. m.* man.

Mŏhur, *n. m.* a gold coin valued at 12 chilkí rupees.

Mój, *n. f.* mother.

Mŏk, *n. m.* cheek.

Mokaddam, *n. m.* a policeman, headman of an office, the chief man of a village.

Mokajár, *n. m.* leisure, opportunity, vacation, freedom.

Mokajár dyun, *v. t.* to discharge.

Mokal, *n. m.* vacation.

Mŏkaláwun, *v. t.* to deliver, to save, to liberate, to release, to free, to finish, to set free; mokalowun, mokaláwán, mokalomut, mokalomut, mokaláwih.

Mŏkalun, *v. i.* to be free, to be set free, to be liberated, to be freed, to escape, mŏkaleo, mŏkalán, mŏkaleomut, mokalih.

Mŏkaṭ, *n. m.* a crown.

Mŏkh, *n. m.* face, cheek.

Mokhta, *n. m.* pearl.

Mokhtah, *n. m.* pearl. The Mussulman women are often called by this name, which they often pronounce Mokhit.

Mokhit, *n.f.* a proper name.

Mokhtí, *n.f.* a proper name.

Mŏkul, *adj.* free, emancipated.

Mŏkur, *adj.* unclean, dirty (of food).

Mŏl, *n. m.* price, value.

Mól, *n. m.* root.

Mól, *n. m.* father.

Mólmój (mábáp) *n. m.* parents, father and mother.

Mŏlul, *adj.* valuable.

Mólum, *adj.* known.

Molut, *n. m.* dung.

Molyi-hyun, *v. t.* to buy; hyĕt, hĕwán, hyĕtmut, hĕyih.

Móm, *n. m.* wax.

Momádrú, *n. m* Achillea millefolium.

Mŏn, *n. m.* breast (mamma).

Moṅ, *adj.* silent.

Monál, *n. m.* the Impeyan pheasant, which is said to be found in Kashmir.

Monḍ, *n. f.* widow.

Mŏnḍ, *adj.* blunt.

Móng (Phaseolus Max or Radiatus), *n. m.* a vetch or kind of kidney bean.

Monjhór, *n. m.* the ninth month of the Hindu year, and corresponding to our month of November.

Móṅs, (*m.*) mã̃ṅs, (*f.*) *adj.* of so many months old.

Monul (pheran), *n. m.* a woollen garment.

Monyi karun, *v. t.* to kiss.

Mór, *n. m.* peacock, not indigenous to the valley.

Mŏrda, *adj.* dead.

Mordár, *adj.* dirty,

Mormúj, *n. f.* carrot (Daucus Carota).

Mót, *n. m.* death.

Mŏt, *adj.* mad.

Motaverái, *adj.* immortal.

Mŏṭh, *n. m.* handful (of grain).

Moth, *n. m.* fist.

Móth, *n. m.* death.

Moza, *n. m.* stockings reaching above the knees.

Mṛag, *n. m.* deer.

Mubárak, *interj.* welcome.

Mubárak karun, *v. t.* to congratulate.

Muḍah, *adj.* negligent, slow of understanding.

Múdmut, *adj.* dead.

Mudráwun, *v. t.* to sweeten.

Mudrun, *v. i.* to be sweet.

Mudur, *adj.* sweet.

Muft, *adv.* gratis, gratuitously.

Múgnnḍ, *n. m.* cheek, upper jaw.

Múh, *n. m.* musquito.

Muhad, *n. m.* a proper name.

Muhammad Jú, *n. m.* a proper name.

Muhammad Rã̃thar, *n. m.* a proper name.

Muhammad Woin, *n. m.* a proper name.

Muhil, *n. m.* the long heavy wooden pestle with which grain is bruised.

Muhr, *n. m.* seal.

Muhyum, *n. m.* poverty.

Múj, *n. f.* radish. There are two varieties of radish in the valley, Wáṭa múj, and Kāshírí muj.

Mukál, *n. m.* fist.

Mukarrar, *adj.* decided, fixed.

Mukhta, *n. m.* pearl.

Muikhátab, *n. m.* presence.

Mukht, *n. f.* a proper name.

Mukht Amír, *n. m.* a proper name.

Mukhti, *n. f.* a proper name.

Múl, *n. m.* root.

Mulai, *adv.* ever.

Mulai-nah, *adv.* never.

Mulákát, *n. m.* visit, meeting.

Múlat, *n. m.* filth.

Mumar, *n. m.* penis.

Múnd, *n. m.* log, block of wood, short thick stem of a tree.

Mundí, *n. m.* Sphœranthus mollis.

Mundí butí, *n. m.* Sphœranthus mollis.

Munul, *n. m.* paṭṭú or coarse woollen cloth.

Mur, *n. m.* fowl-house.

Múr, *n. f.* a sleeve.

Murda, *n. m.* corpse, dead body.

Murdah, *adj.* dead.

Muríd, *n. m.* pupil.

Murits, *n. f.* picture.

Muritsgar, *n. m.* painter.

Murr sapadun, *v. i.* to exist.

Musáfar, *n. m.* traveller.

Musalah, *n. m.* a small skin used as a mat, on which the Mussulman says his prayers. It is derived from the Arabic

Musallá, *m.* a carpet to pray on.

Musalmán, *n. m.* Mussulman.

Musalmanain, *n. f.* Mussulmání, or a woman who holds the Mohammedan religion.

Mushahas, *adj.* right, proper.

Mushak, *n. m.* musk.

Mushakhas, *adj.* decided, fixed.

Mushakhas karun, *v. t.* to confirm, to establish, to ratify, to determine.

Mushghúl, *adj.* occupied.

Mushik, *n. m.* smell.

Mushik, *adj.* black.

Mushik hyun, *v. t.* to smell; mushik hyutun, mushik hewán, mushik hyutmut, mushik heyih.

Mushk, *n. m.* a pleasant smell, fragrance.

Mushkaberrit, *adj.* fragrant.

Mushkabudij Dányí, see Dányí.

Mushkil, *adj.* difficult.

Mushrán, *n. m.* demon.

Musht, *n. m.* fist.

Músla, *n. m.* skin of animal.

Mustakh, *n. m.* a species of Chenopodium.

Mut, *adj.* mad.

Mútaragúts, *n. f.* bladder.

Múth, *n. m.* a species of leguminous plant.

Múth, *adj.* furious.

Muṭh, (*m.*) maṭh, (*f.*) *adj.* forgetful.

Muthar, *n. m.* urine.

Muthar karun, *v. t.* to make water, see 'Karun.'

Múthráṅ, *n. m.* Cyperus longus, rotundus.

Mutlab, *n. m.* meaning, purpose.

Muts, *adj.* useful.

Mutsáí, *n. f.* utility.

Mutsaráwun (kushádan), *v. t.* to detect, to open, to disclose, to cause to open, or be opened; mutsaranov, mutsaranáwán, mutsaránomut, mutsaranáwih.

Mutsárun (kholná), *v. t.* to open; mutsur, mutsàrán, mutsurmut, mutsàrih.

Mutwál, *adj.* silly.

Múzavara, *n. m.* a dish consisting of rice and poppy water, which is given to the sick in certain conditions.

Myáda, *n. m.* stomach.

Myĕng, *n. f.* temple (of head).

Myón, *adj.* my, mine.

Myul, *n. m.* reconciliation.

Myun, *v. t.* to measure.

Myúnd, *n. m.* morsel, mouthful, piece.

Myund, *n. m.* leprosy.

Myúnd, *adj.* leprous.

Myúṭ, *n. m.* kiss.

Myúṭ, *adj.* delicious, sweet.

Myúṭh, *adj.* sweet.

Myúṭh karun, *v. t.* to kiss.

Myuts, *n. m.* profit, gain.

N.

N: the letter *n* in Kashmírí is pronounced exactly as in English.

N is the enclitic form of the singular objective case, masculine and feminine, of the third personal pronoun, and also of the case of the agent of the third personal pronoun singular number.

Nab, *n. m.* sky, heaven, firmament.

Nábad *n. m.* sugar, sugar candy.

Nabír, *n. m.* a proper name.

Nabíra, *n. m.* a proper name.

Nabistán, *n. m.* navel.

Nabukár, *n. m.* twilight.

Nád, *n. m.* voice, a cry, exclamation, noise, summons, sound.

Nádán, *n. m.* fool.

Nádárí, *n. f.* poverty.

Nád dyun, *v. t.* to cry aloud, to call; nád dyut, nád diwán, nád dyutmut, nád diyih.

Nadeor, *adj.* poor.

Nádí, *n. f.* vein.

Nadir, *n. m,* the stalk of the Lotus (Nilumbium), which grows abundantly in the extensive lakes of Kashmir. The Hindus cut up the stalk of the Lotus into small pieces, cook it with oil and condiments, and eat it along with flesh or dál.

Nadir, *n. m.* a vegetable growing in the city lake. It is eaten by the natives in winter because of its heating qualities.

Nãdir, *adj.* wonderful.

Nafa, *n. m.* plenty, enough. It is enough, nafa chhu.

Nafadár, *adj.* useful.

Náfah, *n. m.* navel.

Nafak, *n. m.* flatulence.

Nafarust, *adj.* useless.

Nafrat, *n. m.* disgust.

Nág, *n. m.* serpent, lead, fountain, spring of water.

Nágah, *adv.* suddenly, unawares.

Nágám, *n. m.* a pargana, or inferior division of Maraz, also the chief village of the Nágám pargana.

Nagamah, *n. m.* female dance.

Nagar, *n. m.* town, city.

Nagár, *n. m.* a drum.

Nagára, *n. m.* drum.

Nágarád, *n. m.* water spring, fountain.

Nágawóiň, *n. m.* spring water.

Nagár wáyanwol, *n. m.* a drummer.

Naghma, *n. m.* song.

Nah, *adv.* not, no.

Nah-nah, *conj.* neither, nor.

Nahakk, *adj.* unjust.

Naháwun, *v. t.* to obliterate.

Nahĕkanwol, *adj.* unable.

Nái, *n. f* Arundo donax.

Náí, *n. m.* barber.

Nai, *conj.* unless.

Nai (nahin to) *adv.* if not. Nai is made up of *nah* and *ai*, "not if." Nai is never placed first in a sentence.

Naid, *n. m.* barber.

Naih, *n. m.* a flat, wide, cultivated headland in the mounds.

Nair, *n. f.* fore-arm.

Naishakar, *n. m.* sugar-cane. It does not grow in the valley.

Nakad, *n. m.* cash.

Nakal, *n. m.* translation.

Nakal karun, *v. t.* to translate.

Nakáthí, *n. m.* thread-winder.

Nakawár, *n. m.* nostril.

Naka wálun, *v. t.* to repay.

Nakc̆hickni, *n. f.* Myriogyne minuta.

Nakha, *prep.* near.

Nakhás, *n. m.* cattle-dealer.

Nakha wálun, *v. t.* to pay; nakha wólun, nakha wálán, nakha wolmut, nakha wálih.

Nakhra, *n. f.* coquetry, blandishments.

Nakhra karinyi, *v. i.* to coquet; nakhra kar, karán; nakhra kãrmats; nakhra karih.

Nakhral, *adj.* elegant.

Nákh ṭang: see 'Ṭang.'

Nakh ṭangakul: see 'Ṭangakul.'

Nakkásh, *n. m.* painter, either of houses or of papier maché articles; shawl-pattern drawers also are called nakkásh.

Nakkãshi, *n. f.* painting, papier maché; drawing of shawl patterns. There are said to be one hundred houses engaged in the papier maché business. On the other hand, there are but eight houses engaged in drawing patterns for shawls.

Nakót, *n. m.* thread-winder and woof-preparer.

Naksha, *n. m.* map.

Naksh karun, *v. t.* to paint.

Nál, *n. m.* horse-shoe.

Nál, *n. f.* bosom, including neck.

Nál, *n. m.* collar (literally the border of the garment called the kurta, round the neck and down the breast).

Nal, *n. m.* leg (anatomically).

Nál, *n. m.* a ring.

Nála, *n. m.* stream, canal.

Nálah, *n. m.* grief.

Nálamut, *n. m.* embrace.

Nálamut karun. *v. t.* to embrace.

Nálband, *n. m.* horse-shoer.

Nalchiband, *n. m.* a pipe-stalk-maker.

Nálish, *n. f.* complaint (accusation).

Nam, *n. m.* the prow or stern of a boat. Upon the stern, Namas pĕṭh.

Nam, *n. m.* nail of finger or toe.

Namanamat, *adj.* ninety-nine.

Namanamatyum, *adj.* ninety-ninth.

Namaskár, *n. m.* compliment.

Namat, *adj.* ninety.

Naṃath, *adj.* ninety.

Namatyum, *adj.* ninetieth.

Namáz, *n. f.* prayer.

Nambal (guzargah) *n. f.* ferry, ford.

Namut, *adj.* prone.

Namdagur, *n. m.* rug-maker. Islamabad is famous for its manufacture of rugs.

Námósdár, *adj.* famous, renowned.

Namúd, *adj.* visible.

Namun, *v. i.* to nod, to lean, to bend, to stoop, to be crooked; nameo, namán, nameomut, namih.

Namúna, *n. m.* sample.

Nang, *n. f.* impropriety.

Nanga, *adj.* naked.

Nanwun, *v. i.* to be pleased, to be fresh, (táza hona).

Nányí, *n. f.* grandmother, either on the father's or mother's side.

Nànz, *n. m.* house. This is the word in use towards Báramúla.

Náo, *n. m.* name. On the name, náwas pĕṭh.

Náo, *n. f.* boat, ship.

Náo Kaḍun (nám kashídan), *v. t.* to defame.

Náo karun, *v. t.* to name.

Nár, *n. m.* a glen, defile.

Nár, *n. m.* Rhamnus virgatus.

Nár, *n. m.* fire, light, flame.

Nãr, *n. f.* arm, vein, tendon.

Nar, *n. m.* the arm (the whole upper extremity, reed.

Nár, *n. m.* precipice.

Nar, *adj.* male.

Náragaj, *n. f.* furnace.

Narain, *n. m.* God.

Nárakur, *n. m.* a village in the Dúns pargana, where excellent rice grows.

Nárang, *n. m.* orange. It does not grow in the valley.

Náratĕngul, *m. n.* fire.

Nárawáo, *n. m.* a village of the Kruhin pargana,

Nargis, *n. m.* Narcissus tazetta: It grows in Kashmir.

Narívár, *n. m.* silk embroidery over the lower part of the sleeves of the 'pheran' worn by the women.

Nar-kachur, *n. m.* Zinziber zerunbet.

Nar kãnyí, *n. f.* a reed found chiefly in the Anchar lake, of which the weaver's brush is made.

Narkoṅ, *n. m.* pen.

Narm, *adj.* delicate, tender, soft.

Narmdil, *adj.* gentle, kind.

Nártraṭ, *n. f.* thunder bolt.

Nár tráwawun, *n. m.* incendiary.

Naruk, *n. m.* hell.

Náruts, *n. f.* hook.

Naryi, *n. f.* a sleeve of the pheran.

Nár zálun, *v. t.* to make a fire.

Nashráwun, *v. t.* to spoil, to mar.

Nashun (bigaṛná), *v. i.* to spoil, to go wrong, to be spoilt.

Nasíhat, *n. f.* admonition, advice.

Nasíhat karinyi, *v. t.* to advise, to admonish.

Nasím bágh, *n. m.* a large garden on the southern shore of the city lake, and composed of old sturdy chunar trees. It is said to have been planted by one of the servants of Álí Mardán Khán, who once ruled Kashmir.

Nast, *n. f.* nose.

Nást, *n. m.* snuff. Most of the snuff used in the valley is imported from Peshawar. The snuff manufactured in the valley is much cheaper, but greatly inferior.

Nastawáj, *n. f.* a nose ring worn by the Panditánees.

Nástigur, *n. m.* snuff-seller.

Naṭ, *n. m.* shaking palsy, shaking, shivering.

Náṭá, *n. m.* flesh.

Nata, *conj.* or.

Natah, *conj.* or.

Naṭh, *n. m.* shaking, trembling, paralysis agitans.

Natha, *conj.* either.

Natíja, *n. m.* result.

Natsun (náchná), *v. i.* to dance; núts, natsán, nútsmut, natsih.

Naṭun, *v. i.* to be afraid, to tremble; naṭeo and nauṭ, natán, naṭeomut and nauṭmut, naṭih.

Nau and nauṅ, *adj.* nine.

Nau, *adv.* recently.

Nau, *adj.* fresh.

Naukar, *n. m.* servant.

Nankarí, *n. f.* service.

Ná-umedí, *n. f.* despair, disappointment, hopelessness.

Ná-ummed karun, *v. t.* to frustrate.

Nauṅ, *adj.* nine.

Naur, *n. m.* vein.

Náür, *n. m.* sleeve.

Naurávwun, *v. t.* to increase.

Nauṭ, *n. m.* a bucket made of clay, and used for lifting water out of wells.

Nauṭ, *n. m.* jar, pitcher, a jug with a long neck.

Nauwun, *v. i.* to be new, to be fresh, to be born.

Navir, *n. m.* newness.

Navyum, *adj.* ninth.

Náwak, *n. m.* arrow.

Nazar, *n. m.* sight.

Nazm, *n. m.* verse.

Náznín, *n. f.* a beautiful woman.

Náznún, *adj.* elegant.

Nazuk, *adj.* slender.

Názuk, *adj.* soft (of cotton goods).

Neb, *n. m.* trace, mark, token, address.

Nebar (báhar), *adv.* without, outside.

Nĕbar karun, *v. t.* to draw out.

Nebar-kun, *adv.* outwards.

Nebrum, *adj.* outer.

Nechú, *n. m.* son, infant, child, a boy.

Neknáo, *adj.* famous, illustrious.

Nephis, *n. f.* a proper name.

Nerun (nikalná), *v. i.* to go out, to come out, to rise (as sun); nyúr, nerán, nyúrmut, nerih, also, dráo, nerán, drámut, nerih.

Nesbat, *adj.* convenient.

Nethanun, *adj.* naked, bare.

Nethar, *n. m.* marriage.

Newala, *n. m.* vine (Vitis).

Niamat, *n. m.* favour.

Nichar, *n. m.* leanness, thinness.

Niká, *n. m.* marriage.

Nikráwun, *v. t.* to make thin.

Níkú, *n. m.* Rhododendron Campanulatum.

The Rhododendron Campanulatum is found growing on the ridge between Bráng and Shahbad. On the Himalayas, the rhododendron is a tree of from forty to fifty feet in height.

Nílakrai, *n. f.* Crozophora tinctoria, Trichodesma indica.

Nílam, *n. m.* sapphire.

Nílawaṭ, *n. m.* marble, said to be found in a quarry behind the famous Shálimar Gardens.

Nílúj, *n. m.* a bird, of whose skin postins are made for the wealthy. In its tail are two feathers, which are worn by the Panjábí and Hindustáni women. Konḍal is the name given to them.

Ním garm, *adj.* lukewarm.

Ním-khanda, *n. m.* smile.

Níndar, *n. f.* sleep. From sleep, Níndarih.

Nindará, *n. f.* sleep.

Nindar-karinyi, *v. i.* to sleep.

Nindarih wŏthun, *v. i.* to be awake, lit. to rise out of sleep.

Ningalun, *v. t.* to swallow.

Ninyi, *n. f.* flesh, mutton.

The mutton of Nandipur is said to be the finest in Kashmir.

Ninyi mondij, *n. f.* frog.

Ninyimonduk, (*m.*) ninyimondich (*f.*) *n.* frog.

Niradhar, *n. m.* Cuscuta reflexa.

Nirásh, *n. m.* disappointment.

Nirásh karun, *v. t.* to frustrate.

Nish, *prep.* near, to.

Nishán, *n. m.* sign, mark.

Nishána, *n. m.* aim, mark.

Nishánah, *n. m.* proof.

Nishána karun, *v. t.* to aim, to take aim.

Nishát Bágh, *n. m.* beautiful gardens, situated on the northern shore of the city lake. They are said to have been laid out by one of the servants of Áli Mardán Khán, a former ruler of Kashmir.

Nishi (pás), *prep.* to, properly beside. Go to him, Yimis nishi gatsh.

Nishi, *prep*, from, than.

Nishi, *adv.* near.

Nishih, *prep.* beside, with.

Nithar (chashm), *n. m.* eye.

Níyat, *n. f.* resolution.

Níz, *conj.* also.

Nizám, *n. m.* a proper name.

Nizám Dín, *n. m.* a proper name.

Nízík and nízik, *adj.* near, close, contiguous.
Nók, *n. m.* Canthus of the eye.
Nókar, *n. m.* servant.
Nókhun, *n. m.* pterygium.
Nŏn, *adj.* apparent.
Nŏsh, *n. f.* daughter-in-law.
Noṭh, *n. m.* thumb.
Nú, *adj.* new.
Núar, *n. m.* posture.
Nú kadal, *n. m.* a bridge over the Jhelum in Srínagar.
Nuksán, *n. m.* damage, loss.
Nuksándár, *adj.* destructive.
Nuksán karun, *v. t.* to injure.
Nuksánlad, *adj.* destructive.
Nuksánzad, *adj.* destructive.
Núl, *n. m.* rat, weazel.
Numráwun, *v. t.* to bend, to make to nod.
Nun, *n. m.* salt. Two varieties are found in the bazárs of Kashmir: viz. rock salt, from the Punjab, and powder salt, called Boṭa nun, from Ladak. Twelve pounds of the latter are sold for the rupee chilki, while only six pounds of the former are given for the same sum.
Nun, *adj.* famous, renowned.
Nunar, *n. m.* a village in the Lár pargana, said to be fruitful, populous, and salubrious.
Nundbón, *adj.* pretty.
Núr, *n. m.* light.
Nur, *n. m.* sleeve.
Nur, *n. m.* arm (the whole upper extremity).
Núra, *n. m.* a proper name.
Núrí, *n. f.* a proper name.
Núr Shah, *n. m.* a proper name.
Nuṭ, *n. m.* a small water vessel or pot of earthenware.
Nyáí, *n. m.* tumult, quarrel, fight.
Nyáí karun, *v. t.* to fight.
Nyaṭ, *n. m.* thumb.
Nyauṭ, *n. m.* big toe.
Nyáwun, *v. t.* to cause to take; nyov, nyáwán, nyomut, nyáwih.
Nyerásh, *n. m.* despair.
Nyerbal, *adj.* weak, unable.
Nyerláb, *adj.* useless.
Nyeṭ, *n. m.* thumb, big toe.
Nyethar, *n. m.* marriage.
Nyethar karun, *v. t.* to marry.
Nyetun, *v. t.* to shear (as sheep).
Nyeza, *n. m.* spear.
Nyikun, *v. i.* to be thin, to waste; nikeo, nyikán, nikeomut, nikih.
Nyío, *n. m.* a flower of Kashmir.
Nyingal, *n. m.* swallowing.
Nyuk, *n. m.* fist.
Nyuk, *adj.* mean, ignoble (haqír), worthless, lean, fine, thin, (nyuk, the opposite of vyuṭh).
Nyúl, *adj.* blue, green.
Nyun (lena, lejáná), *v. t.* to take,

to take away, to bring, to support, (a burden), to carry away; néo, niwán, nyúmut, niyih; also nyún, nyiwán, nyiyih.

Nyúr, *n. m.* cleft hoof, meadow,

Nyúr, *adv.* near.

Nyuṭ, *n. m.* thumb.

Nyuṭ, *n. m.* the big toe.

O, Ŏ.

O: this letter is pronounced as *o* in the English word prone.

Ŏ: this letter is pronounced as *o* in the English word pot.

Obré, *n. m.* dignity, honour.

Obúl, *n. m.* Rumex acutus.

Ŏbur, *n. m.* cloud.

Óḍ, *adj.* half.

Ŏdur, *adj.* wet, moist.

Odurr, *adj.* moist, wet.

Ois, *pron.* we.

Ókhun, *n. m.* religious teacher.

Ól, *n. m.* nest, shelf, recess in a wall.

Olchí, *n. m.* Prunus domestica (plum). The wood of the tree is used in making papier-maché boxes.

Óm, *adj.* uncooked, raw.

Ŏn, *adj.* blind, probably derived from andha.

Ŏn sapanun, *v. i.* to be blind.

Oṅkár, *n. m.* a kind of heron peculiar to Kashmir.

Oryór pakun, *v. i.* to wander.

Ós (*m.*), *v.* was.

Óṭ (áṭá), *n. m.* flour.

Ot, *adv.* only.

Ótrah, *adv.* the day before yesterday.

Ótruk, *adj.* of or belonging to the day before yesterday.

P.

P: this letter is pronounced exactly as in English.

Pach, *n. m.* a Hindu space of time consisting of fifteen days. There are two periods of fifteen days each in the Hindu month. These are respectively called Gatah pach, and Zúnah pach, *i. e.* the pach of darkness, and the pach of the moon or light.

Pachhin, *n. m.* water-fowl of Kashmir.

Pachhum, *n. m.* west.

Pád, *n. m.* foot, step.

Pádamadat, *n. m.* said to have been one of the ancient kings of Kashmir. He is said to have caused Pámpúr to be built, which was called after him, Pádamápúr, which at last became Pámpúr.

Padi pat padi, *adv.* step by step, by degrees.

Pádir suh, *n. m.* lion.

Pádshah, *n. m.* emperor, king, lord.

Pádshãhí, *n. f.* kingdom.

Paḍur, *n. m.* uncloven hoof.

Pagah, *adv.* to-morrow.

Pagah do kárit, the day after to-morrow.

Pagir, *n. f.* man's turban.

Pah, *n. m.* human manure, which is used for enriching ground prepared for the growth of vegetables. Animal dung, on the other hand, is used for the same purpose in the case of grain-land. See 'Guh.'

Pahaj, *n. f.* shepherdess.

Pahan, an affix signifying a little, being equivalent to the English affix -ish.

Pahár, *n. m.* hill.

Páhar, *n. f.* a small cottage.

Pahrawol, *n. m.* watchman.

Páhú, *n. m.* Wych hazel (Parrotia Jacquemontiana).

Paida, *adj.* created.

Paidah, *adj.* created.

Paida karun, *v. t.* to create.

Paida karanwol, *n. m.* creator.

Paiḍun (chakídan), *v. i.* to drop.

Paiját, *n. m.* trousers.

Paijáma, *n. m.* trousers.

Paijámah, *n. m.* drawers, trousers.

Painch, *n. m.* council, assembly.

Paintre, *adj.* thirty-five.

Paiṅtsah, *adj.* twenty-five.

Pantsahyum, *adj.* twenty-fifth.

Pairi pat pairi, *adv.* step by step.

Paitawa, *n. m.* bandage for the legs on a journey, worn both by Hindus and Muhammedans.

Paitila, *n. m.* a Mussulman vessel corresponding to the Hindu bhogun, or teapot.

Paiwand, *n. m.* connection.

Paizár, *n. m.* slipper, shoes made of leather.

Paizár dyun, *v. t.* to give the shoe, to dishonour.

Páj, *n. f.* the largest of all the baskets made in the valley.

Pák, *n. m.* pus, matter, boiling.

Pak, *n. f.* feather.

Pak, *n. m.* wing.

Pák, *adj.* clean, hallowed, pure, holy.

Pakanáwun, *v. t.* to make to go, to drive, to make to walk; pakanóv, pakanáwan, pakanomut, pakanáwih.

Pákanáwun, *v. t.* to cause to cook; pákanov, pákanáwán, pákanomut, pákanáwih.

Pakání, *n. m.* Rubus lasiocarpus.

Pakanbed, *n. m.* Gentiana root.

Pákawun, *v. t.* to cook.

Pakh, *n. f.* wing (of a bird), feather.

Pakha, *n. m.* wing of bird.

Pákhur, *n. m.* Himalayan honeysuckle (Lonicera quinquelocularis).

Pakúá, *n. m.* Euonymus Fimbriata and Hamiltonii.

Pakun, *v. i.* to go, to walk; pauk, pakán, paukmut, pakih.

Pál, *n. m.* abstinence, shepherd.

Pal, *n. m.* large stone or rock.

Pálak, *n. m.* spinach.

Pálgám, *n. m.* the shepherds' village, for such is the translation of the word. It is romantically situated at the head of the Lidur valley.

Paliyár, *n. m.* hedge.

Palṭan, *n. f.* a detachment, regiment.

Pám, *n. f.* reproach, a rebuke.

Pambach, *n. m.* nut of the lotus. It is eaten as a delicacy, both by Hindus and Mussulmans.

Pambahák, *n. m.* rhubarb, which grows on the mountains surrounding Kashmir.

Pambalokhir, *n. m.* the nut case of the lotus.

Pambatsálan, *n. f.* rhubarb. It grows abundantly on the mountains of Kashmir. There is said to be no tax on it. The dried root is found in the bazár. The triturated root mixed with oil is used as an application to wounds and ulcers. Both Hindus and Mussulmans are fond of the stalks. The stalk is called Pambahák. It is also used as a purgative.

Pamposh, *n. m.* the Lotus (Nelumbium speciosum). Grows abundantly in the lakes of the valley. The seeds, stalks, and roots are eaten by the natives. The petals of the lotus are remarkably acceptable to Vishan. The Hindus, when performing their devotions on the banks of the Jhelum, throw handfuls of the lotus petals into the river. The lotus is in bloom in August and September. The nuts are regarded as a great delicacy. The broad leaves are used as plates. The stalk of the lotus is ripe in October.

Pámúkh, *n. m.* Verbena officinalis.

Pámpúr, *n. m.* moth.

Pámpúr, *n. m.* the chief town of the Véhí pargana. Its population is perhaps about 10,000. In the neighbourhood of Pámpúr are the famous saffron fields. The town is said to have been built by the ancient king Pádamadat, after whom it was originally called Pádamapúr. The word is also said to be derived from padma, lotus, and púr, a city. The limestone strata of the Karewah, on which Pampúr is built, are very remarkable. In some places they rise to a height of thirty and forty feet, close to the river. The saffron fields are said to cover an area whose circumference is from ten to twelve miles. The soil is said to be the richest in the valley. The roots of the crocus sativus are planted in June, and the saffron is picked in October. Saffron is extensively used in cookery and dyeing. A large proportion of the saffron is exported to Yarkand.

At the foot of a mountain five miles from Pámpúr is a slightly warm spring, whose waters are impregnated with sulphuretted hydrogen, and the rock from which it issues is composed of limestone.

Pan, *n. m.* thread, a leaf, properly, of a tree.

Pán, *pron.* one's self.

Pán (badan), *n. m.* human body.

Pána, *pron.* self.

Paná, *adj.* broad.

Panah, *n. m.* width.

Pánah, *pron.* self.

Pánai, *pron.* self.

Panapómpur, *n. m.* a moth: see next word.

Pánapŏpur (fr. pan, a leaf, and popur, a moth), *n. m.* a species of moth, whose favourite resting-place is the leaf of some tree, where it gives forth a prolonged and very shrill noise.

Pánas yitsawun, *adj.* selfish.

Pánawuiń, *adv.* together.

Pand, *n. m.* Loranthus longiflorus.

Pán dach, see 'Dach.'

Pandah, *adj.* fifteen.

Pandãhyum, *adj.* fifteenth.

Pandrenton, *n. m.* a beautiful little temple near to the city of Srínagar. The building is in the centre of a small pond of water, which is surrounded by willows and plane trees. The structure is small, square, and pyramidal. It is built of limestone. The word Pandrenton is supposed to be derived from Pandu and Durendun, the father of the Pandus.

Panjah, *n. f.* claw.

Panjãlí, *n. f.* yoke.

Panjara, *n. m.* window, the wooden trellis work which takes the place of glass in the windows of Kashmir. Some of it is very beautiful. When the weather becomes cold and rainy, paper of different colours is pasted over the inside of the trellis work.

Panjí, *n. f.* talon, as of the tribe Filo.

Panjih, *n. m.* the five fingers.

Pánkhí, *n. m.* bird.

Páṅsah, *adj.* fifty.

Pãṅsah, *n. m.* a paise, cash, money.

Pántraṭ, *n. f.* waterspout. The water which falls from the clouds is said to be hot and bad-smelled.

Pántsádar, *n. f.* waterfall, literally translated, sheet of water, pánich tsádar.

Pántsah, *adj.* fifty.

Pántsahéṭh, *adj.* sixty-five.

Pántsahaiṭhyum, *adj.* sixty-fifth.

Pántsãhyum, *adj.* fiftieth.

Pántsanamat, *adj.* ninety-five.

Pántsanamatyum, *adj.* ninety-fifth.

Pántsasatat, *adj.* seventy-five.

Pántsasatatyum, *adj.* seventy-fifth.

Pántsashít, *adj.* eighty-five.

Pántashítyum, *adj.* eighty-fifth.

Pántsatãjih, *adj.* forty-five.

Pántsatatãjihyum, *adj.* forty-fifth.

Pántsatràh, *adj.* thirty-five.

Pántsatràhyum, *adj.* thirty-fifth.

Pántsawanzah, *adj.* fifty-five.

Pántsawanzãhyum, *adj.* fifty-fifth.

Pántsawuh, *adj.* twenty-five.

Pántsh, *adj.* five.

Pántshyum, *adj.* fifth.

Pánts tah pántsah, *adj.* fifty-five.

Pántsum, *adj.* fifth.

Pántsyum, *adj.* fifth.

Panun, *adj.* own.

Pányúr, *n. m.* water-carrier.

Panzál, *n. m.* the range of mountains on the south-west of Kashmir.

Pánzavyun, *n. m.* the weight of six pounds.

Pánzú, *n. m.* six pounds' weight of something.

Páo, *n. m.* (equal to four gira), span.

Páo, *n. f.* half-a-pound weight.

Páo, *n. m.* a quarter.

Páp, *n. m.* crime, fault, sin, vice.

Pápadráo, *n. m*, flesh, mutton.

Paphlú, *n. m.* Marsilea quadrifolia.

Papun, *v. i.* to be ripe (of fruit).

Par, *n. m.* wing.

Párádú, *n. m.* mercury, which is greatly abused as a medicine in Kashmir.

Párah, *n. m.* a shortened form of the word pargana.

Paramántsun, *n. m.* the third day after a marriage.

Pára-pára, *adj.* in pieces.

Paraspór, *n. m.* a pargana of the Kamráz division of the valley.

Parbat, *n. m.* hill.

Parda, *n. m.* partition, screen.

Pardah, *n. m.* a curtain, screen.

Pardeshí, *n. m.* traveller.

Pareshán, *adj.* dishevelled, perplexed.

Pareshán karun, *v. t.* to perplex, to puzzle, to scatter.

Pargana, *n. m.* district.

Parganah, *n. m.* district, division of Kashmir. Nágam and Deosir are the two largest parganas in the valley.

Pãri, *n. f.* sacrifice.

Parí, *n. f.* fairy.

Parinda, *n. m.* a long state barge with the boatmen seated behind a raised canopy for the passenger.

Parmán, *n. m.* a weight for weighing.

Parmandij, *n. f.* rectum.

Parnáwun, *v. t.* to teach to read.

Pársá, *adj.* temperate.

Pársang, *n. m.* equipoise.

Párúd, *n. m.* mercury, quicksilver.

Parud, *n. m.* stranger, foreigner.

Parud, *adj.* strange.

Párun, *v. t.* to make, to complete, to finish, to perform.

Parun, *v. t.* to read; purun, parán, purmut, parih.

Parur, *n. m.* last year.

Parus, *adv.* last year.

Parvés, *adj.* Persian.

Parwa, *n. m.* care, regard.

Parwah, *n. m.* care.

Parwána, *n. m.* warrant, moth.

Paryun, *n. m.* a sieve, generally made of a broad wooden hoop with a bottom of perforated sheep's skin.

Parzán, *n. m.* acquaintance, knowing.

Parzanáwun (pahchánná), *v. t.* to recognize; patzanov, parzanáwán, parzanomut, parzanáwih.

Parzanun, *v. t.* to recognize.

Parzanun (pahchánná), *v. t.* to recognize; parzun, parzanán. parzunmut, parzanih.

Parzun, *n. m.* a servant.

Parzun, *v. t.* to know, to recognize.

Pás, *prep.* for the sake of. Pás is always used with names of God.

Pasár, *n. m.* rest.

Pash, *n. m.* roof, mat cover, or roof of a boat. On the roof, pashas peṭh.

Pãsh, *n. f.* a kind of wood of which the skewer-like little sticks, on which is wound the shawl-thread, are made.

Pashemán sapadun, *v. i.* to repent.

Pashpun (chakídan), *v. i.* to drop, to ooze; pashpeo, pashpán, pashpeomut, pashpih.

Pashm, *n. m.* shawl-wool. A considerable quantity of shawl-wool is conveyed on the backs of sheep to Rámpúr, from which it is afterwards distributed to Amritsar, Loodiana, and Gujerat. 3,200 mounds, or 128,000lbs. of shawl-wool are annually imported into Kashmír from Ladak.

Pashmína, *n. m.* a fine kind of woollen cloth manufactured in Kashmir. Over 30,000 persons are said to be engaged in this manufacture.

Paṭ, *n. m.* plank.

Paṭ, *n. f.* a small shelf.

Paṭ, *n. m.* the board on which the wool is spread to have a paste of rice and water rubbed into it.

Pãṭ, *n. m.* worship, manner, mode.

Pat, *prep.* & *adv.* behind, back. Stand back, pat roz.

Patah, *prep.* & *adv.* after, behind. After me, mih patah. After two days, doyi doho patah. Behind the door, darwázas patah kanyih. After evening, shámah patah. Remain behind, patah roz.

Patákí, *n. m.* Gymnosporia spinosa.

Paṭan, *n. m.* a village in the Bángil pargana.

Patang, *n. m.* moth.

Patar, *n. m.* a leaf or blade of a vegetable.

Pãtau, *n. m.* a bandage for the legs, generally worn by sportsmen. A couple of bandages, pãtauhur.

Pata yun (dar pas ámadan), *v. i.* to follow.

Pãt-guts, *n. f.* silk cocoon.

Paṭh, *n. m.* a board or plank on which the dead body of a Hindu is placed and carried away to the place of cremation.

Pãṭh, *n. m.* manner.

Pàthar, *n. m.* leaf.

Pathar pyun, *v. i.* to fall. See 'Pyun.'

Páthul, *n. m.* valley.

Pathur, *n. m.* bare ground.

Pãṭ-pandáo, *n. m,* silk thread.

Pãtigur, *n. m.* silk braid maker.

Patij, *n. f.* matting (towards Islamabad).

Patila, *n. m.* teapot.

Pãṭ-kyum, *n. m.* silkworm.

Pat-kun, *adv.* backwards.

Patolákain, *n. f.* the end.

Patolákan, *adv.* in fine, in short, in a word, at last, shortly, finally.

Patra, *n. m.* leaves of the Cinnamomum albiflorum.

Patraj, *n. m.* leaves of the Cinnamomum albiflorum.

Pats, *n. f.* faith, trust, confidence, dependence, reliance, certainty.

Patsaláz, *n. f.* entertainment, hospitality.

Patsaláz karinyi (mahmándárí kardan), *v. t.* to entertain.

Patѐ karinyi, *v. t.* to confide, to trust, to believe, to depend on.

Pats nyinyi, *v. t.* to trust.

Pats tháwinyi, *v. t.* to believe.

Pãṭ-thán, *n. m.* silk cloth.

Paṭṭú, *n. m.* a coarse woollen cloth manufactured in Kashmir. There are two kinds: yeripauṭ paṭṭú, all of wool, and sutrapauṭ paṭṭú, partly of wool and partly of cotton. Such cloth is washed in Kashmir in exactly the same way as blankets are sometimes washed in Scotland. The washer tramples them under feet.

Patum, *adj.* last.

Patwárí, *n. m.* an official belonging to a village, whose duty is to keep an account of the various crops reared by the villagers.

Paṭyini, *n. f.* Panditáni's lock of hair.

Patyum, *adj.* last.

Paud, *n. m.* sole of foot, step, foot of camel or elephant.

Pauh, *n. m.* spleen.

Paus (kaf), *n. m.* foam.

Paus tráwun, *v. i.* to foam, see 'Tráwun.'

Pauṭ, *n. m.* paṭṭú, woollen cloth.

Pautkat, *n. m.* slander.

Pauṭ-manḍanwól, *n. m.* a

cleaner (lit. a kneader) of paṭṭú.

Paut phírit, *adv.* again.

Paut phírit gatshun, *v. i.* to return, to retreat.

Pauts (mihmán), *n. m.* guest.

Paut-tsháe, *n. f.* the human shadow.

Pawan, *n. m.* wind.

Páwathar, *adj.* pure, hallowed, clean.

Páwun, *v. t.* to fell, to lay low, to make to fall.

Páyir, *n. f.* stirrup.

Páz, *n. m.* ham.

Pãz, *n. m.* falcon, hawk.

Pazar, *n. m.* truth.

Pãzár, *n. m.* men's shoes.

Pazir, *n. m.* truth.

Pazpáth, *n. m.* truth.

Pazpãṭ, *adv.* verily, in truth.

Pech, *n. m.* gripe, screw.

Peḍun, *v. i.* to drop; peḍeo, peḍán, peḍeomut, peḍih.

Pekkar, *n. m.* Adhatoda vasica.

Pepás, *n. m.* thirst.

Perun, *v. t.* to ornament.

Pesháb, *n. m.* urine.

Peshabuk ṭhela, *n. m.* the bladder.

Peshan and peshnan, *adv.* one o'clock.

Peshat, *prep.* before thee.

Peshkár, *n. m.* magistrate.

Peshnan, *adv.* some point of time between one and three o'clock P.M. In the afternoon.

Peshnas, *adv.* in the afternoon.

Peshwá, *n. m.* a leader, a guide.

Pĕṭ, *prep.* above, on.

Peṭh, *prep.* on, upon, above. Upon the mountain, Kohas peṭh.

Pethun, *n. m.* walk, journey.

Peṭhyum, *adj.* upper.

Péts, *n. f.* a tall strong reed growing in the Kashmir lakes, of which matting is made.

Phágun, *n. m.* the twelfth month of the Hindu year, and corresponding to our month of February, and to Safar or Safar-u-l-muzaffar of the Islamic year, in order, not in time.

Phagan, *n. m.* February. This word is the same as Phágun.

Phaharghás, *n. m.* madder, (Rubia cordifolia).

Phailwàn (gurd), *adj.* brave.

Phak, *n. m.* stink, bad smell, stench.

Phák (near the city lake), *n. m.* a pargana of Maráz.

Phakalad *adj.* stinking, having a bad smell.

Phál, *n. m.* ploughshare.

Phal, *n. m.* fruit, result.

Phal, *n. m.* materials of which colours are formed.

Phalgur, *n. m.* seller of dyes.

Phalibungir, *n. f.* a kind of bracelet.

Phalabàrit, *adj.* fertile.

Phalhár, *n. m.* the Hindu name for the cooked water-chesnut, see 'Gáṛí.'

Phálnáwun, *v. t.* to tear.

Phalsatsan, *n. m.* pin. It has a large shining head. The Mussulman women adorn their head dress, called Kasába, with it.

Phalun, *v. i.* to bear fruit.

Pham, *n. m.* cotton.

Pham, *n. m.* cotton without the seeds. The cotton plant is sown in May, and the cotton is gathered in September and October.

In former days cotton was extensively cultivated in the valley.

Phamb-pan, *n. m.* shawl-thread. It is double. The finest thread brings one rupee chilki for one tola weight. Of a coarser kind, two and three tolas are given for one rupee chilkí, and a still coarser quality, called phír, is sold at the same price for four or five tolas. The women who clean the wool and spin the thread sell it to the thread-merchants, who in their turn sell it to the shawl manufacturers, making a profit of two or three annas on the rupee. The shawl manufacturers give the thread to the dyers, from whom it is given to the winders, and then dealt out to the weavers.

Phán, *n. m.* Rhus Cotinus.

Pháńsi, *n. f.* noose.

Phar, *n. f.* a kind of fish.

Pharaz, *n. f.* a proper name.

Pharj, *m. n.* anus.

Phãrsí, *n. f.* the Persian language.

Pharzain, *n. f.* a proper name.

Pharzand, *n. m.* son.

Pharzání, *n. m.* a proper name.

Pharzí, *n. f.* a proper name.

Phash dyun, *v. t.* to stroke.

Pháta, *n. f.* a proper name.

Pháṭanáwun, *v. t.* to split; pháṭanowun, pháṭanáwán, pháṭanomut, pháṭanáwih.

Pháṭawun, *v. t.* to cleave, to split, to burst, pháṭówun, pháṭawán, pháṭomut, pháṭawih.

Phaṭáwun, *v. t.* to drown.

Phátáwun, *v. t.* to cause to sink.

Phaṭeng, *n. m.* apricot. This is a Ladákí word.

Phatú, *n. m.* basket.

Phaṭun (ḍúbná, phaṭná), *v. i.* to drown, to tear, to sink, to split, to rend, to burst; phauṭ, phuṭ, phaṭán, phauṭmut, phuṭmut, phaṭih.

Phaul, *n. m.* grain (generic name).

Phaut, *n. m.* a basket lined with bójpatr.

Phauṭ, *adj.* drowned.

Phazl Bíbí, *n. f.* a proper name.

Phazlí, *n. f.* a proper name.

Phenḍasháj, *n. f.* fox.

Phĕphur, *n. m.* pimple, abscess.

Phephar-wephar, *n. m.* abscess, pimple.

Pheran, *n. m.* dress, the chief garment worn by the Kashmírís. Its shape is not very unlike that of a nightgown, with very wide sleeves. It is made either of cotton or wool. Pheran is manifestly a contraction of the Persian word Pairáhan, garment. The Pheran is worn by the women of the valley, as well as by the men. It is sometimes red, at other times blue. The sleeves of the women's pheran are wider than those of the men's. When it is manufactured of wool it is called lóch, when of cotton, póts.

Pheranáwun, *v. t.* to turn; pheranowun, pheranáwán, pheranomut, pheranáwih.

Phernáwun, *v. t.* to turn round to circulate.

Pherun, *n. m.* walking.

Pherun, *v. i.* to wander, to return, to crawl, to circulate, to turn round, to turn; phúr, pherán, phúrmut, pherih.

Phestid, *n. f.* a proper name.

Phihrawáo, *n. m.* file.

Phír, *n. m.* a coarse kind of shawl thread.

Phiranáwun, *v. t.* to surround.

Phiri, *n. f.* time (dafa). Three times. Trih phirih.

Phirun, *v. i.* to turn.

Phirun, *v. t.* to pour.

Phirit dyun, *v. t.* to repay.

Phírit gatshun, *v. i.* to return, retreat.

Phírit hyun, *v. t.* to take back.

Phírit yun, *v. i.* to return, to come back.

Phis, *n. f.* the penis of a child.

Phitní, *n. m.* zizyphus vulgaris.

Phŏk, *n. m.* breath.

Phŏkun, *v. i.* to blow (of the wind), phuk, phŏkán, phukmut, phŏkih.

Phol, *n. m.* grain.

Phólanáwun, *v. t.* to cause to flower, to cause to bloom, to cause to blossom.

Phólun, *v. i.* to flower, to blossom, to bloom, to blow, (as a flowe); phul, phŏlán, phulmut, phŏlih.

Phótah, *n. m.* a kind of composition of which necklaces are made.

Phrak (dam), *n. m.* breath.

Phras, *n. m.* white poplar, (Populus alba, Populus fastigiata).

Phrast, *n. m.* Italian Poplar, (Populus nigra). The poplar is very common in Kashmir. There are two species in the valley, one of which is called the Kashmir poplar, the other the Cabul poplar.

Phrĕk, *n. f.* breathlessness.

Phrúts, *adj.* auspicious.

Phú, *n. m.* a dog.

Phúd, *n. m.* the tail of a bird.

Phuhur, *n. f.* burnt bread.

Phúk, *n. m.* shoulder.

Phukh, *n. m.* blowing.

Phukh dyun, *v. t.* to blow.

Phul, *n. m.* a grain.

Phúl, *n. m.* Verbascum Thapsus.

Phul, *n. m.* a salt used in the infusion of tea. It is found in the Nubra valley in Ladák. The 'phul' contains the carbonate and the sulphate of soda, and a little of the chloride of sodium.

Phúlai, *n. f.* flourishing.

Phulai, *n. f.* spring time.

Phulsel, *n. m.* Viburnum Stellulatum.

Phulun, *v. i.* to flourish, bloom, to blossom, to blow.

Phúlwárí, *n. m.* white rose, (Rosa Brunonis).

Phúman, *n. m.* Leucas cephalotis and aspera.

Phur, *n. m.* a point.

Phúr, *n. m.* a drop.

Phúr, *adj.* coarse.

Phurílí, *n. f.* Deutzia staminea.

Phuṭ, *n. f.* wrinkle.

Phuṭarun, *v. t.* to break; phuṭar, phuṭarán, phuṭarmut, phuṭarih.

Phuṭun, *v. i.* to break; phuṭ, phuṭán, phuṭmut, phuṭih.

Phuṭun, (tútná) *v. t.* to break; phut, phután, phutmut.

Phyuk, *n. m.* shoulder.

Phyur, *n. m.* drop.

Píádah, *n. m.* footman.

Pída, *n. m.* nuisance.

Píḍa, *n. m.* fever.

Pihchain, *n. f.* aunt, father's brother's wife.

Pihun, *v. t.* to grind; pyuhun, pihán, pyuhmut, pihih.

Pilanáwun, *v. t.* to extend (puhancháná).

Pilun, *v. i.* to arrive at or reach from below.

Pind, *n. m. f.* a bird of Kashmir.

Pind, *n. m.* a species of water fowl.

Pinga, *n. m.* millet-seed.

Pingí, *n. f.* Panicum Italicum (millet).

Pinj, *n. f.* wheel.

Pír, *n. f.* a low stool, which is used as a small table.

Pír, *n. m.* nut.

Pír, *n. m.* a Mussulman saint, a holy man.

Pír Pantsál, *n. m.* the range of mountains to the south-west of Kashmir. The height of the range is about 18,000 feet above the sea's level. The Pir Panjal range is composed of amygdaloid trap. In the south, south-east, and south-west, however, the surface in some places is composed of lime-stone, containing marine fossils. Belemnites and small shells were seen by Vigne.

Písh, *n. m.* flea.

Pishul, *adj.* delicate, soft (of woollen goods). Rurally, the form 'pishól' is used.

Pistán, *n. m.* nipple.

Pita, *n. m.* father.

Pítámbar, *adj.* yellow.

Pitar, *n. m.* uncle on father's side.

Pitarbinyí, *n. f.* cousin, father's brother's daughter.

Pitarboí, *n. m.* cousin, father's brother's son.

Pitáwul, *n. m.* blood stone.

Pits, *n. f.* bulrush, (Typha angustifolia and T. latifolia). This is the reed of which matting is made. It grows abundantly in the Ḍal, Anchár sar, and the Wulur Lake. The roots of the bulrush are eaten by the Kashmírís.

Piturboe, *n. m.* cousin.

Piyála, *n. m.* a cup used by the Mussulmans. It it either of clay or China.

Piyála, *n. m.* glass (vessel).

Po, *n. m.* Wych hazel (Parrotia Jacquemontiana).

Póf, *n. m.* a kind of wood, of which the skewer-like little sticks, on which is wound the shawl thread, are made.

Pŏh, *n. m.* the tenth month of the Hindu year, and corresponding to our month of December.

Poh, *n. m.* spleen.

Poh, *n. f.* bar.

Pohol, *n. m.* shepherd.

Pŏhul, *n. m.* shepherd who watches upon the remote mountain pasture-lands the flocks and herds of other people, spending the summer there with his family and dogs, until driven down into the valley by the snows of winter.

Poholú, *n. m.* a spring of water in the Divisar pargana.

Póiṅ, *n. m.* water. This is the word used by the Hindus of the valley.

Poit karun (nashándan), *v. t.* to extinguish.

Pokhráj, *n. m.* topaz.

Polád, *n. m.* steel.

Pómpur, *n. m.* moth.

Pón, *n. m.* anus.

Pónd, *n. f.* sneezing.

Ponz, *n. m.* monkey.

Pop, *adj.* ripe.

Pŏp, *n. f.* father's sister, aunt.

Popal, *n. m.* Saxifraga ligulata.

Pŏpatir - binyi, *n. f.* cousin, father's sister's daughter.

Pŏpaturbóí, *n. m.* cousin, father's sister's son.

Popur, *n. m.* moth.

Pór, *n. m.* side (direction).

Pósh, *n. m.* flower, rose, testes, scrotum.

Poshagund, *n. m.* wreath of flowers. When an old Pandit gets married he dons the poshagund.

Posháks, *n. m.* garb, habit, dress, clothes, wearing apparel, clothing.

Poshan hund táj, *n. m.* garland.

Poshanúl, *n. m.* a bird of Kashmir.

Poshkar, *n. m.* a species of Ligularia.

Poshibág, *n. m.* flower garden.

Poshídah, *adj.* hidden.

Poshídah sapadun, *v. i.* to disappear.

Poshnúl, *n. m.* mango bird.

Póshun, *v. t.* to gain a victory, to get the upper hand, to prevail; púsh, póshán, púshmut, póshih.

Post, *n. m.* skin of man.

Pósta khokhur, *n. m.* poppy head.

Postal, *n. m.* Taxus baccata (the common yew).

Pŏṭ, *n. m.* rectum, prolapsus ani, piles, hæmorrhoids.

Póṭ, *n. m.* silk. The zillah of Islamabad is especially famous for its silk. The Maharája buys all the silk produced from the natives at five rupees a seer, or 2 lbs. He gives the seller two and a-half rupees in cash, and two and a-half rupees' worth of grain. His Highness then sells it at twelve and a-half double rupees, for the full seer. One half of the silk produced in Kashmir is exported to the Punjab. A small portion of the other half is exported to Ladak.

The best silk to be had in the valley is produced in the Kotihár pargana, probably from the mulberry flourishing most luxuriantly there.

Potul, *n. m.* image (idol).

Póts, *n. m.* a cotton pheran.

Pŏts, *n. m.* guest.

Potsalo, *n. m. f.* fox.

oz, *n. m.* truth.

Póz, *adj.* true. He was the true light, Su póz gásh os. This word is true, yih kat pŏz chhih.

Poziyor, *adj.* true, sincere.

Prabát, *n. m.* dawn, sunrise, day-break, morning from sunrise to nine o'clock.

Prabátan, *adv.* early in the morning.

Prabátas, *adv.* early in the morning.

Prágásh, *n. m.* moonshine.

Prai, *n. f.* receipt.

Práj, *n. f.* straw.

Prakár, *n. m.* species.

Prakásh, *n. m.* light, glory, ray.

Prakásh Rám, *n. m.* a proper name.

Prálabad, *n. m.* fate.

Prán, *n. m.* onion. The Hindu inhabitants of the valley do not eat the onion. They say that the ancient Hindus would not eat the onion on account of its aphrodisiac effects, which they did not wish to experience, as they had given themselves to the worship of God. The onion is a favourite article of diet with the Mussulmans.

Prán, *n. m.* breath.

Pranun, *v. i.* to flow.

Prárun, *v. i.* to wait.

Prasand, *adj.* willing, contented, cheerful, happy, gay, glad, merry.

Prasandák, *n. m.* compliment.

Prasandákha, *interj.* welcome.

Prasand sapadun, *v. i.* to be happy, see 'Prasand.'

Prasandatáí, *n. f.* joy.

Prasun, *n. m.* birth.

Prasun, *v. t.* to bear, to bring forth.

Prastar, *n. m.* the close watch of the saffron growing near Pámpúr.

Prat, *adj.* every, each. Every man, prat mohanyú. Every day, prat doho, prat din.

Práts, *n. f.* corner of mouth.

Prats, *n. f.* a wooden spike on which shawl thread is wound. It is about three or four inches long.

Prat shái, *adv.* every where.

Prätshun, (púchhná), *v. t.* to inquire; prutsh, prätshán, prutshmut, prätshih.

Prau, *n. f.* sunshine.

Prauwa, *n. m.* ray, sunshine.

Prauwah, *n. m.* sunshine ray.

Práwun, *v. t.* to clothe, to don,

to embroider; prov, práwán, prómut, práwih.

Prayánand, *n. m.* saddle.

Prazalun, (chamakná), *v. i.* to shine; prazaleo, prazalán, prazaleomut, prazalih.

Prazaláwun (afrokhtan), *v. t.* to illuminate, to make to shine; prazalowun, prazaláwán, prazalomut, prazalomut, prazaláwih.

Prej, *n. f.* straw.

Prets, *n. f.* a proper name.

Pretsí, *n. f.* a proper name.

Prháṭ, *n. f.* a crack.

Prits, *n. f.* a little apparatus forming part of the spinning wheel and intended to receive the thread; when the distaff or yindertul has become full, the thread is then called Satra-miler (when of cotton), and yera-miler (when of wool).

Pritsagár, *n. m.* examination.

Pritshun, *v. t.* to ask, to inquire.

Pristinarust, *adj.* unjust.

Pritsun. *v. t.* to inquire, pruts, pritsán, prutsmut, pritsih.

Prón, *adj.* old.

Prón sapanun, *v. t.* to be old.

Prór, *adj.* deer, last year's.

Prót, *n. m.* Marlea begonifolia.

Prun, *adj.* white.

Prutsagár, *n. m.* inquiry.

Púdinah, *n. m.* peppermint, much eaten as a condiment by the Hindus. It is used as a remedy in the diarrhœa of children.

Púdína, *n. m.* mentha viridis.

Puhol, *n. m.* shepherd.

Púhul, *n. m.* shepherd.

Puhór, *n. m.* the river of the Loláb valley. In the cold weather it becomes a very insignificant stream.

Puhur, *n. m.* scorpion. Scorpions are said to be very numerous in the pargana of Dachanpára and in the Lár pargana. The bite is said to be fatal sometimes. The puhuris short, earth-coloured, venomous, and with a fine tail.

Púí, *n. f.* woollen thread spun by the women of Kashmir out of the shawl wool imported from Ladák.

Púí-wányí, *n. m.* shawl-thread seller.

Púí-wŏin, *n. m.* thread merchant. The thread merchants buy from the Kashmírí women the thread spun by them out of the goat wool imported into the valley from Ladák.

Púj, *n. m.* butcher. It is remarkable that the word 'butcher' is very often heard on the lips of the Kashmíris in Srínagar.

Pújain, *n. f.* butcher's wife.

Pukána, *n. m.* Rubus rotundifolius.

Púkhta, *adj.* complete.

Pukhta karun, *v. t.* to accomplish.

Púlahor, *n. m.* grass-shoes, worn by the Kashmíris on the mountains. On marriage days the women wear shoes of horse's skin or mule's. Those shoes for great occasions are adorned with silk work. In the winter and when it rains heavily, the women wear the Khráo which are shoes made of wood with thongs of straw, called ḍel.

Puláo, *n. m.* pilao; a favourite dish with the Kashmíris.

Púlla, *n. m.* Rubus tiliaceus.

Pún, *n. m.* rectitude.

Pun, *n. m.* carpenter's chisel, monkey.

Púnjan, *n. m.* Artemisia Indica and vestita.

Púr, *n. m.* step, pace, footstep, east.

Purzagur, *n. m.* a pashmina finisher.

Púsh, *n. m.* flower-seller.

Pusharun, *v. t.* to entrust.

Púshiráwun (Sapurdan), *v. t.* to entrust, to surrender.

Pushirun, *v. i.* to surrender.

Pushráwun, *v. t.* to consign, to give in charge.

Pusht, *n. m.* back (of body).

Pusht-i-pá, dorsum of the foot.

Pushurun, *v.* to consign, to entrust; pushur, pushurán, pushurmut, pushurih.

Pústúl, *n. m.* Himalayan spruce (Abies Smithiana).

Pút, *n. m.* a male chicken.

Púth, *adj.* fat.

Puthar, *n. m.* son.

Púthí, *n. f.* a Sanscrit religious book.

Púthibrár Dányí: see 'Dányí.'

Púthúr, *n. m.* earth.

Púts, *n. f.* a long piece of cotton cloth thrown over the head and allowed to hang down the back of the Mussulman women, the ordinary veil worn by the Kashmírí females.

Púts, *n. m.* a female chicken.

Putal, *n. m.* image, idol.

Pu,úr, *n. m.* step.

Puz, *n. m.* worship. It is derived from púja.

Púza, *n. f.* worship.

Puza karinyi, *v. t.* to worship: see 'Karun.'

Pyíhun, *n. m.* goad.

Pyuhun, *v. t.* to grind, to triturate.

Pyuk, *n. m.* shoulder.

Pyúl, *n. m.* testicle, testes.

Pyun (parná), *v. i.* to fall, to depart, to happen; peo, pewán, peomut, peyih; also, pyau, pyĕwán, pyomut, pyeyih.

Pyur, *n. m.* point, dot.

Pyush, *n. m.* flea.

Pyut, *n. m.* gall.

Pyut, *n. m.* point of a pointed instrument.

R.

R: there are two varieties of R. There is R, which is pronounced as a Scotchman pronounces the English R. And there is Ṛ which is sounded by rolling the tongue back upon itself and against the roof of the mouth. A euphonic R is not uncommon in Kashmiri: for example, shát̤ shrát̤, zóḍ and zróḍ, bont̤ and bront̤.

Rab, *n. m.* mud.

Rabáb, *n. m.* a musical instrument not unlike a banjo.

Rach, *n. f.* the charm contained inside the dólnah, and consisting either of God's names, Muhammad's name, the Mussulman Kalma, the names of the greatest Mussulman Saints or passages from the Qurán.

Rãch, *n. m.* watchman.

Rách, *n. m.* defender.

Rãchh, *n. m.* protection, preservation.

Rachhit, *n. f.* maintenance.

Rãchh-karun, *v. t.* to preserve, to protect.

Rachhun (pálná, hifázat karná), *v. t.* to nourish, to protect, to cherish, to maintain, to rear; ruchhun, rachhán, ruchhmut, rachhih.

Ráe, *n. f.* thought.

Rafík, *n. m.* companion, friend.

Ráfiz, *n. m.* Shi,a. The Shi,as are comparatively few in number. They say there are about 1000 houses of them. They are found chiefly at Zadibal, about two kos to the north of Srínagar, at Nandapor, and Hassanábád, near to the city lake.

Ráfiz-bái, *n. f.* a woman belonging to the Shi,a portion of Mussulmans.

Rafugur, *n. m.* a hand shawl-maker, a shawl-mender, shawl-repairer. The shawl-menders work with the needle, and are generally Mussulmans.

Rag, *n. m.* artery, vein. The Kashmíris call the cephalic vein the Kefál rag, and the basilic vein the Basilík rag.

Doubtless these names come to the Kashmíris from the Greek through the Arabic.

Ráginyá, *n.m.* a small island, see 'Tulamul.'

Ráh, *n.m.* fault.

Ráh, *n.m.* falling star.

Ráhat, *n. m.* rest.

Ráhatsán, *adv.* quietly.

Rahím, *n. m.* a proper name.

Rahímdár, *n.m.* a proper name.

Rahmán, *n. m.* a proper name.

Rahmat, *n. m.* mercy.

Rahmat Bíbí, *n. f.* a proper name.

Rahmí, *n.f.* a proper name.

Rahmrúst, *adj.* cruel, pitiless.

Raihán, *n.m.* Ocymum pilosum.

Raj, *n.f.* halter (for hanging with).

Rajaba, *n. m.* a proper name.

Rájá Kák, *n m.* a Pandit, who was over the shawl trade in Kashmir, and much respected by the people. He died about six years ago. Since his death the revenue from shawls has dwindled away to half its former amount, which was twelve lacs of rupees. On account of this great falling off in the revenue, Bod Rájá, son of Partáb Shah, a name well known in Kashmir, was removed from the office of Dewán of the Shawl Department, and Badrí Náth, Chief Judge of the valley, was put in his place. About two hundred Pandits are inspectors of the shawl weavers in their work shops.

Rájá Ram, *n. m.* a proper name.

Rakáb, *n. m.* a musical instrument not unlike a banjo.

Rakhshun, *v. i.* to shine.

Ráe, *n. m.* thought.

Rál, *n. m.* Mimosa rubicaulis.

Rámahádrindúiṅ, *n. m.* rainbow

Rámahál, *n. m.* a pargana in the Kamráz division.

Ramahúiṅ, *n. f.* wolf.

Ramahún, *n. m.* wolf. Wolves are numerous on the mountains of Kashmir, and often do great injury to flocks of sheep. They are not often seen in the valley.

Rám Chand, *n.m.* a proper name.

Rámpór, *n. m.* a village in the Wular pargana.

Rámrám - badrindúiṅ, *n. m.* rainbow.

Rámrám - badaraindún, *n. m.* rainbow.

Ramuz, *n. m.* a man's name. This is the familiar and endearing form of Ramzán. The vocative is Ramazeo.

Ramzán, *n. m.* November, the eleventh month of the Mussulman year, a proper name.

Ramzána, *n. m.* a proper name.

Rán, *n. m.* thigh.

Ranáwun, *v. t.* to cause to cook; ranov, ranáwán, ranomut, ranáwih.

Ránḍa, *adj.* vile.

Randah, *n. m.* carpenter's plane.

Rang, *n. m.* colour, dye, dyeing. The art of dyeing was introduced into Kashmir in the reign of Akbar the Great.

Rangatsur, *n. m.* pheasant.

Rang dyun, *v. t.* to dye.

Rang-ghás, *n. m.* Panicum miliaceum.

Rangi, *n. f.* colour.

Rangun (rang dená), *v. t.* to dye, to tinge; rúng, rangán, rungmut, rangih.

Rangur, *n. m.* dyer, who is generally a Mussulman.

Ranun (pakáná), *v. t.* to cook, to boil, to make ready food; rún, ranán, runmut, ranih.

Rányí, *n. f.* queen.

Rárá, *n. m.* Randia dumetorum.

Rarím, *n. m.* a proper name.

Ras, *n. m.* soup, serum, juice.

Rasm, *n. m.* model.

Rast, *n. m.* pension.

Rasul, *n. m.* a proper name.

Rasula, *n. m.* a proper name.

Rasul Khán, *n. m.* a proper name.

Rasul Shekh, *n. m.* a proper name.

Rát, *n. m.* night, the whole period of darkness, extending from sunset to sunrise. It is divided into four equal portions called pahar, or watch.

Rát, *n. f.* yesterday.

Raṭ, *n. f.* tardiness.

Rat, *n. m.* blood.

Ráta-doho, *adv.* by day and night.

Ráta krúl, *n. m.* bat.

Rátamoghul, *n. m.* owl.

Rátamogul, *n. m.* owl.

Raṭanáwun, *v. t.* to cause to seize; raṭanov, raṭanáwán, raṭanomut, raṭanáwih.

Ratanjog, *n. m.* the Anemone obtusiloba.

Ratankát, *n. m.* Andromeda ovalifolia.

Rátarăch, *n. m.* night-watchman, sentry.

Rátaráchí, *n. f.* guarding.

Rátaráchí karinyi, *v. t.* to guard.

Rátas, *adv.* by night, at night.

Ratel, *n. m.* brier-stone.

Rath, *n. m.* blood.

Rath kaḍun, *v. t.* to draw blood, to bleed.

Rát kyut, *adv.* at night.

Rats, *n. f.* a grain, the small red bean used in weighing.

Rats, *n. f.* a proper name.

Ratsah-ratsah, *adv.* very little.

Ratsar, *n. m.* kindness, goodness, benevolence, benevolent action, probity.

Rattan, *n. m.* ruby.

Raṭun (pakaṛná), *v. t.* to take, to lay hold of, to hold, to grasp, to catch, to detain, to seize, to take hold of; rúṭun, raṭán, rúṭmut, raṭih.

Rãtwángin, *n. m.* egg-plant.

Raun, *adj.* footless, handless.

Rawak, *n. m.* a long chamber for meeting and dining in, verandah.

Ráwarun, *v. t.* to lose.

Ráwun, *v. i.* to be lost.

Rãyil, *n. m.* cedar (deodar). This is the word in use out of Srínagar. See 'Divadár.'

Raz, *n. m.* string, rope. Ropes are made of rice-straw and the fibre of bang, or Indian hemp, which is very tough.

Ráza, *n. m.* king, emperor.

Rázabal, *n. m.* funereal pile.

Razák, *n. m.* a proper name.

Rázasi, *n. f.* kingdom.

Re, *n. m.* ant.

Reban dányí, see 'Dányí.'

Rĕk, *n. f.* dung of birds.

Rĕkh, *n. f.* bird's ordure.

Rénz, *n. m.* bow for propelling small stones.

Ré-ól, *n. m.* ant-hill.

Resh, *n. m.* beard, keeper of a Hindu temple.

Rĕt, *n. m.* month, sand.

Reṭa, *n. m.* pay, salary.

Rĕtakol, *n. m.* summer, hot season.

Rets, *adv.* early in the morning.

Rĕts, *n. f.* dawn.

Rewand, *n. m.* Rheum moorcroftianum, rhubarb.

Rewand chíní, *n. m.* Rheum moorcroftianum, rhubarb. It grows abundantly on the Kashmir mountains. The natives eat stalk and blade with great fondness. The root is used as a purgative, and, when pounded and mixed with oil, as an application to ulcers.

Rewun, *v. i.* to mourn.

Reza, *n. m.* bit, fragment, piece.

Riai, *n. f.* ant.

Riaul, *n. m.* Mimosa rubicaulis.

Ribás, *n. m.* Rheum moorcroftianum.

Ríchhábí kílmich, *n. m.* Viburnum cotinifolium.

Rih, *n. f.* flame, burning.

Rik, *n. f.* line.

Rikib, *n. m.* the vessel out of which the Hindu children eat. It is small, round, deep, and brazen.

Rimbiára, *n. m.* the river of

Shupiyon. It empties itself into the Veshau river which takes its rise from the Kosah Nág, and joins the Jhelum five miles below Bíj Bihára. TheRimbiára river flows close to Haripúr.

Ríng, *n. m.* Cratægus oxyacantha (hawthorn).

Ringa-kul, *n. m.* a tree of Kashmir.

Ringo, *n. m.* Cratægus oxyacantha (hawthorn).

Rish, *n. m.* spite, ill-will, Mussulman religious beggar.

Ríshi, *n. m.* saint, sage.

Rít, *n. m.* pomp, ceremony.

Ritha, *n. m.* Sapindrus emarinatus, the berry of which is used in washing the shawls of Kashmir. A decoction of it is said to be a specific for making the hair grow.

Ritsar, *n. m.* rectitude.

Riyai, *n. f.* a little ant.

Riyál, *n. m.* see 'Birre.'

Róchh, *n. m.* watchman.

Roda, *n. f.* bowels.

Rodang, *n. m.* madder.

Róe, *n. m.* face.

Rogánáthpúr, *n. m.* a village of the Phák pargana, where there is a prison.

Rógí, *adj.* miserable.

Rŏh, *n. m.* a man's name. This is the familiar and endearing form of Rahman. The vocative is Raheo.

Rŏk, *n. m.* hindering.

Rŏkh, *n. m.* cheek.

Róng, *n. m.* clove.

Rŏṅk, *n. m.* ileum, haunch-bone.

Rónkh, *n. m.* hip.

Rŏnyi, *n. f.* bell. In Kashmir, bells are hung about the necks of horses, cattle, and goats, and also about the ankles of the Panditánís. It is also used as a toy to amuse children.

Róp, *n. m.* mending, repair, especially of shawls.

Rŏp, *n. m.* silver.

Rŏpai, *n. f.* a rupee.

Rŏpalãṅk, *n. m.* the silver island in the Ḍal.

Ropiṭh gád, *n. m.* a species of fish with silver scales, found about the upper parts of the Jhelum.

Róp-karanwol, *n. m.* mender, repairer.

Rop-karawun, *n. m.* mender, repairer.

Ros, *n. m.* deer, stag.

Roshangar, *n. m.* cutler.

Roshan karun, *v. t.* to lighten.

Roshun, *v. i.* to be angry; rúsh, roshán, rúshmut, roshih.

Roskaṭ, *n. f.* doe.

Roza, *n.f.* fast.

Roza karinyi, *v. t.* to fast.

Roza tháwinyi, *v. t.* to fast.

Rozanáwun, *v. t.* to stop, to cause to stop, to cause to remain.

Rozun (rahná), *v. i.* to remain. to stop, to dwell, to halt, to continue, to live, to be left; rúd, rózán, rúdmut, rózih.

Rúd, *n. m.* rain.

Rúdahoń, *n. m.* a village in the Hamal pargana.

Rúd pynn, *v. i.* to rain.

Rufúgar, *n. m.* shawl-mender.

Rúg, *n. m.* sickness.

Ruhun, *n. m.* garlic, eaten by Mussulmans, but not by Hindus in the valley.

Rúíwángin, *n.f.* egg plant.

Ruk, *n. m.* a letter, an epistle.

Rukhsat, *n. m.* permission.

Rúl, *adj.* grey, applied especially to grey-coloured wool.

Rúlya, *n. m.* Rottleria tinctoria.

Rúm, *n. m.* Turkish Empire.

Rún, *n. m.* husband.

Rúp, *n. m.* image (of man), form.

Rúp, *n.f.* copy.

Rúph, *n. m.* disguise.

Rús, *n. m.* deer, stag, antelope? muskdeer.

Rúshwat, *n. m.* bribe.

Rúshwat karun, *v. t.* to corrupt.

Rús-kaṭ, *n.f.* doe.

Rust, *prep.* without.

Rusula, *n. m.* a proper name.

Rut (nek), *adj.* good, excellent, honest, propitious.

Ruts, *n. m.* a weight of about eight barleycorns.

Rutsar, *n.f.* excellence, goodness, kindness.

Rúwángún, *n. m.* tomáto, see 'Baṭa wángún.'

Ryiwun, *v. i.* to weep. This word is said to be obsolete.

Ryúg, *n. m.* plant of Kashmir. The juice of this plant mixed with honey is said to be efficacious in amenorrhœa.

Ryunz, *n. m.* pellet.

S.

S: this letter is pronounced as in English.

S is the enclitic form of the nominative and accusative singular of the first personal pronoun, and also of the dative and accusative singular of the third personal pronoun.

Sa, *n.* Sir. It is equivalent to jí, in Urdu. Come, sir,. aojí (Urdu). Walasa (Kashmírí),

Sabab, *n. m.* reason.

Sabar Shah, *n. m.* a proper name.

Sábinyigur, *n. m.* soap-maker.

Sabr, *n. m.* patience.

Sabr karanwol, *adj.* patient.

Sábun, *n. m.* soap. Two kinds of soap are manufactured in Kashmir: one kind from oil, which yields a coarse soap, another kind from fat. The former is called tela sábun, the latter sufed sábun. There are two manufactories of soap in Srínagar, the proprietors of which have a monopoly of the trade.

Sãbunsáz, *n. m.* soap-maker.

Sabz, *adj.* fresh.

Sabza, *n. m.* emerald.

Sãd, *n. m.* a descendant of Muhammad's, a holy man, a saint.

Sád, *n. m.* taste, flavour.

Sada, *n. m.* sound.

Sádah, *adj*, senseless.

Sadah. *adj.* seventeen.

Sadãhyum, *adj.* seventeenth.

Sadá,í, *adv.* always, eternally, ever.

Sadbag, *n. m.* Senecio?

Sadbarg, *n. m.* Senecio?

Sadbargí, *n. f.* Tagetes erecta.

Sadík, and Sidik, *n. m.* a proper name.

Sádik, *n. m.* a proper name.

Sádik, *adj.* sincere.

Saḍun (chahná), *v. t.* to wish for.

Sáf, *adj.* clean, smooth.

Safah kadal, *n. m.* a bridge over the Jhelum, in Srínagar.

Safapór, *n. m.* a village in the Sáírí pargana, where lime is made.

Safar, *n. m.* journey.

Safar karun, *v. i.* to travel.

Safed, *adj.* white.

Safeda, *n. m.* Dalbergia sissoo.

Safed dányi, see 'Dányí.'

Safrí, *n. m.* a proper name.

Ság, *n. m.* vegetables.

Sag, *n. m.* waṭer.

Saga, *n. m.* water-carrier.

Ságalar, *n. m.* a necklace composed of beads and pieces of glass or stone at intervals.

Sah, *n. m.* tiger, sir. It is derived from the Sanscrit 'Sahá.'

Sahal, *adj.* soft, easy.

Sahí, *n. f.* signature.

Sahidív, *n. m.* said to have been one of the ancient kings of Kashmir.

Sáhil, *n. m.* ease.

Sahul-hul, *adj.* pliable.

Sai, *n. f.* earnest money.

Saidmakár, *n. m.* fortune-teller.

Sail, *n. m.* flood.

Sailáb, *n. m.* inundation, storm, flood, torrent.

Sáilí, *n. f.* a proper name.
Sair, *n. m.* a walk, journey.
Sáírí Mawázih Páín, *n. m.* a pargana in the Kamráz division of the valley.
Sá,ís, *n. m.* groom.
Saiyat, *n. f.* lamp, formed of oil, wick, and a small earthenware vessel.
Sak, *adj.* german (of the same germ), as cousin german.
Sakah, *n. m.* water-carrier.
Sákhí, *n. m.* witness, eye-witness.
Sakht, *adj.* difficult, ferocious.
Sakht-kan, *adj.* deaf.
Sakre, *n. f.* abstinence. To abstain, sakre karinyi.
Sál, *n. m.* invitation, banquet, entertainment, feast.
Sál, *n. f.* wife's sister, sister-in-law.
Sala, *n. m.* peace.
Salah, *n. m.* counsel.
Salah karanwol, *n. m.* counsellor.
Salah karun, *v. t.* to consult.
Salai, *n. f.* distaff.
Salám, *n. m.* compliment.
Salám, *n. f.* farewell.
Saláma, *n. m.* a proper name.
Salám dinyi, *v. t.* to bid farewell.
Salám karinyi, *v. t.* to bid farewell.
Salám karun, *v. t.* to salute, to compliment.
Sálí, *n. m.* a proper name.
Sallí, *n. m.* a proper name.
Samad, *n. m.* a proper name.
Samad Jú, *n. m.* a proper name.
Samagh, *n. m.* gum.
Sámagrí, *n. f.* furniture.
Samah, *n. m.* a song.
Samáí, *n. m.* time.
Samakhun, *v. i.* to associate, to agree, to suit, to meet.
Sámána, *n. m.* end, harness.
Sambálun, *v. t.* to repair, to adorn, to prepare, to mend, to arrange, to set in order; samból, sambálán, sambólmut, sambalih.
Sambul, *n. m.* spikenard. It grows in Kashmir.
Samdí, *n. f.* a proper name.
Samdú, *n. m.* a proper name.
Samrat, *n. f.* glory.
Samrut, *n. m.* strength.
Samsár, *n. m.* world.
Samsáras-prazaláwanwol. *adj.* world-illuminating.
Samúd, *n. m.* a proper name.
Samun (jama honá), *v. i.* to meet together, to assemble; samiyo, samán, samiyomut, samih.
Samundar, *n. m.* sea.
San, *n. f.* burglary.
Sán, *prep.* with.
Saná, the sign of a question (?).

Sandal, *n.f.* chair.
Sandij, *n.f.* mustard.
Sandimán, *n. m.* said to have been one of the ancient kings of Kashmir.
Sandiya, *n. m.* evening.
Sandra, *n. m.* a proper name.
Sandramma, *n. m.* moon.
Sandrí, *n.f.* a proper name.
Sangal, *n. m.* Taxus baccata (the common yew).
Sangkaṭ, *n. m.* defeat.
Sangur, *n. m.* hill.
Saniyás, *adj.* intoxicated.
Sannarkat, *n. m.* Daphne Cannabina.
Sáṅs karun, *v. i.* to cough.
Santán, *n. m.* son.
Santuk, *n. m.* contentment.
Sántúsh, *adj.* confident.
Santush, *n. m.* patience.
Santushi, *adj.* patient.
Sanyar, *v.f.* descent, declivity.
Sanyer, *n.f.* beak.
Sanyir, *n.f.* ditch.
Sanyitsúr, *n. m.* burglar.
Sáó, *adj.* rich.
Sapadáwun, *v. t.* to finish; sapadowun, sapadáwán, sapadomut, sapadáwih.
Sapadun, *v. i.* to be; sapud sapadán, sapudmut, sapadih.
Sar, *n. m.* pond, lake.
Sara. *n. m.* test, trial.
Saráf, *n. m.* banker.
Sarái, *n.f.* inn.
Saragí, *n.f.* temptation.
Sara karun, *v. t.* to try, to test.
Sargí, *n.f.* experiment.
Sargaul, *n. m.* the Shagdar's superior.
Saṛhad, *n. m.f.* frontier.
Sári, *adj.* all.
Sarkash, *n. m.* chief.
Sarpéch, *n. m.* a long narrow piece of red woollen cloth, which the Panditanís bind round their heads.
Sarráf, *n. m.* banker, exchanger (of money), money-changer.
Sarruph, *n. m.* serpent.
Sarshár, *adj.* brimful.
Sartal, *n. m.* brass. All the cooking, eating and drinking vessels of the well-to-do Hindus are made of this or some other metal. If a Hindu eats or drinks out of an earthenware vessel he breaks it, or at least he will not eat or drink out of it again.
Sarú, *n. m.* cypress. The Kashmírí cypress is a distinct species.
Saruf, *n. m.* snake, serpent.
Saruf-ráṭanwol, *n. m.* snake catcher.
Sárun, *v. t.* to touch.
Sás, *adj.* thousand.

Sas, *n. m.* dál, made of mong.
Sàsar, *n. f.* heat sufficient to cause perspiration.
Sás karun, *v. i.* to cough.
Sãt (city term), *n. f.* wick.
Sát, *n. m.* moment of time.
Sat, *adj.* seven.
Satahéṭh, *adj.* sixty-seven.
Satahaiṭhyum, *adj.* sixty-seventh.
Satajih, *adj.* forty.
Satanamat, *adj.* ninety-seven.
Satanamatyum, *adj.* ninety-seventh.
Satár, *n. m.* a proper name.
Satarand, *n. m.* a carpet.
Satarát, *n. m.* the third day after a marriage.
Satasatat, *adj.* seventy-seven.
Satasatatyum, *adj.* seventy-seventh.
Satashít, *adj.* eighty-seven.
Satashítyum, *adj.* eighty-seventh.
Satat, *adj.* seventy.
Satatãjih, *adj.* forty-seven.
Satatãjihyum, *adj.* forty-seventh.
Satatrâh, *adj.* thirty-seven.
Satatrâhyum, *adj.* thirty-seventh.
Satatút, *n. m.* lapwing,
Satatyum, *adj.* seventieth.
Satawanzah, *adj.* fifty-seven.
Satawanzãhyum, *adj.* fifty-seventh.
Satáwun, *v. t.* to teaze.
Sath, *adj.* true.
Sãth, *n. m.* companion.
Sathir, *n. m.* cotton.
Sathir, *n. m.* thread.
Sãthí, *n. m.* companion.
Satówuh, *adj.* twenty-seven.
Satówuhyum, *adj.* twenty-seventh.
Satrakón, *n. m.* the cotton thread wound round the distaff.
Satur, *adj.* flat.
Satyum, *adj.* seventh.
Sauda, *n. m.* merchandise.
Saudágar, *n. m.* tradesman, merchant.
Saudeá, *n. m.* see 'Sham.'
Saukhí, *n. f.* evidence.
Saun, *adj.* profound, deep.
Saut, *n. m.* roasted grain, either rice, wheat, barley, or Indian corn.
Sawáb, *n. m.* reward.
Sawál, *n. m.* question.
Sawálí, *n. f.* alder (alnus).
Sawár, *n. m.* rider, horseman.
Sawárí, *n. f.* retinue.
Sawár sapadun, *v. i.* to ride.
Sáwísan, *n. m.* quietly.
Sáwun, *v. t.* to put to sleep; sóv, sáwán, sómut, sáwih.
Sáwun, *n. m.* see 'Shráwun.'
Sayad, *n. m.* prey.
Sáyam, *n. m.* sunset.
Sáyi, *n. f.* shadow.
Sayyád, *n. m.* hunter.

Sáz, *n. m.* harness.

Sáz, *n.* woof.

Sázandar, *n. m.* musician.

Sáz Rám, *n. m.* a proper name.

Seda-seda, *adv.* face to face.

Sefeda, *n. m.* Populus fastigiata.

Seham, *n. m.* tiger.

Sejpán, *n. m.* asparagus (asparagus racemosus).

Sĕk, *n. f.* sand.

Semin, *n. f.* lioness.

Sĕp, *n. f.* chalk, found abundantly in different parts of the valley.

Seri-karanwol, *n. m.* brick maker.

Serish, *n. m.* fringe.

Serriping, *n. f.* serpent.

Sĕs, *n. f.* tumour, a wart.

Set, *prep.* with.

Set, *n. f.* epilepsy.

Set, *n. f.* lamp. See 'Saiyat.' Set is the word in use out of Srínagar.

Setárah, *n. m.* a kind of guitar. This word is only another form of the Persian word Sihtár, literally, the three strings.

Seth, *prep.* with. With him. Yimis seth.

Seṭha, *adj.* & *adv.* much, many, abundant, very, extremely.

Séṭhah, *adj.* & *adv.* very, extremely, much, many, abundant.

Sĕṭhah ásun (bisiyár búdan) *v. i.* to abound.

Seṭha báúḍ, *adj.* enormous.

Seṭha thaud, *adj.* enormous.

Seṭhah báúḍ, *adj.* enormous.

Seṭhah thaud, *adj.* enormous.

Set-pakawun, *n. m.* fellow-traveller.

Shábash, *interj.* well done, bravo!

Shabí, *n. f.* a small band, adorned with beads and worn by the Mussulman women.

Shabid, *n. m.* voice.

Shabit, *n. m.* echo.

Shabnam, *n. m.* dew.

Shád, *adj.* merry.

Shádí, *n. f.* a proper name.

Shádipor, *n. m.* a village in the Sáírí pargana. Near to this place is an island, formed by the junction of the Jhelum and the Sind rivers, which is regarded by the Hindus as a very sacred spot.

Shafak, *n. m.* twilight.

Shafkat karun, *v. t.* to forgive.

Shagdar, *n. m.* an officer whose duty is to watch the crops while growing, and the Government portions after they have been reaped.

Shágird, *n. m.* pupil.

Shah, *n. m.* breath, king, prince.

Shahár, *n. m.* a village in the

Véhí pargana, Here iron and flints are found.

Shahár, *n. m.* a mountain near to the village of Khrú, where iron is found.

Shahbád, *n. m.* a pargana of Maráz.

Shahbád, *n. m.* the chief village of the pargana of the same name. Shahbád, or the abode of the king, was once a place of great importance, but it is now a ruin. The strata in the vicinity of Shahbad are composed of a bluish grey limestone. The apples of Shahbád are said to be the finest in this part of the valley, and the wheat grown here is said to be unrivalled. Iron and copper are said to exist in the neighbourhood.

Shahbán, *n. m.* a proper name.

Shah hyun, *v. i.* to breathe.

Sháhid, *n. m.* witness.

Sháhidí, *n. f.* evidence, testimony, witnessing.

Shah kaḍun, *v. t.* to draw a breath.

Shah khárun, *v. i.* to breathe.

Shahmár, *n. m.* serpent.

Shahmát, *n. m.* checkmate.

Shahnishín, *n. m.* a dormitory with trellis work for walls.

Shahr, *n. m.* city, town.

Shahsawár, *n. m. f.* a rider.

Shah túl, see 'Túl.'

Shah Tulakul, see 'Tulakul.'

Shahzádah, *n. m.* prince.

Shái, *n. f.* place.

Shaitán, *n. m.* Devil.

Sháj, *n. f.* jackal.

Shakk, *n. m.* suspicion.

Shakakol, *n. m.* Sium? Dr. Stewart has proved that some specimens of Shakakol are the root of a species of Convallaria.

Shakar, *n. m.* sugar.

Shakdár, *n. m.* a village official whose duty is to see that the villagers do not steal the grain, that the Maharaja's share may not be diminished.

Shakhdar, *n. m.* a spy over the shawl-weavers.

Shakdãrí, *n. f.* the duties of the Shakdár.

Shákhá, *n. m.* lock of hair on top of Hindu's head.

Shakht, *n. m.* power.

Shakl, *n. m.* disguise, image (of man), form.

Shál, *n. m.* jackal. Said to be numerous in Kashmir.

Shálakát, *n. m.* Myricaria Germanica.

Shálbáf, *n. m.* shawl-maker, shawl-weaver.

Shálí, *n. f.* millet (Panicum Italicum.

Shálimár, *n. m.* the name of

the famous royal gardens on the shores of the lake near Srínagar. The word Shálimar is probably derived from Márat-i-Shah Álam, which has been first shortened into már shála; and this, according to the genius of the Kashmírí, read Shála már, the habitation of the king of the world.

Shalpa, *n. m.* trade.

Shalúk, *n. m.* poetry, verse.

Shám, *n. m.* Damascus, Syria, evening, fourth division of the day, extending from three o'clock till sunset.

Shamá, *n. m.* candle.

Shamál, *n. m.* north.

Sháman, *adv.* in the evening.

Shámas, *adv.* in the evening.

Shámat, *n. m.* spot, blemish.

Shainsher, *n. m.* sword.

Shána, *n. m.* shoulder.

Shanachar, *n. m.* the planet Saturn.

Shánd, *n. m.* pillow for head.

Shándagunḍ, *n. m.* pillow for head, a cushion.

Shángas, *n. m.* a village of the Kúṭahar pargana, notorious for its strumpets.

Shankarátsári, *n. m.* the name of a Hindu devotee, who is said to have lived some four hundred years ago, and to have taken up his abode for a time in the small temple, originally built by the ancient Kashmírí king, Sandeman, on the top of the hill now called either the Takht-i-Sulaimán, or the hill of Shankarátsárí. This remarkable temple is supposed to have been built about 220 years before the birth of our Saviour. The spring on the top of the hill is said to have dried up after this devotee's death!

Shankarlechár, *n. m.* See the preceding word.

Sháṅsh, *n. f.* breathlessness.

Sháṅtun, *n. m.* death.

Shánuk, *n. m.* dog.

Shanyiwáṛ, *n. m.* Saturday.

Sharáb, *n. m.* wine.

Sharábasán, *n. m.* a cup-bearer.

Sháradá, *n. m.* the name given to the Kashmírí alphabet, which is but a modification of the Sanscrit, in honour of Sháradá Nandan, the person who is said to have first reduced the Kashmírí language to writing.

Sháradá, *n. f.* the name of a Hindu goddess who has a shrine on the Hari Parbat, near to the city of Srínagar.

Sharbat, *n. f.* a manufactured beverage.

Sharík, *n. m.* accomplice, partner.
Sharík, *adj.* common.
Sharík sapadun, *v. i.* to connive at, to share, to be a party to.
Sharkar, *n. m.* sugar.
Sharminda, *adj.* ashamed, confounded, modest.
Sharphí, *n. f.* a proper name.
Shart, *n. m.* treaty.
Shásh, *n. f.* lung.
Shashbarg japhiri, see 'Japhiri.'
Shastar, *n. m.* armour.
Sháṭ, *n. m.* falls (of a river), ford.
Shathar, *n. m.* enemy.
Shatíl, *adj.* frigid, cold.
Shatrut, *n. m.* discord.
Shau, *n. m.* corpse, dead body, God.
Shauk, *n. m.* desire, love.
Shawálah, *n. m.* temple.
Shayitãjih, *adj.* forty-six.
Shayitãjihyum, *adj.* forty-sixth.
Shayitráh, *adj.* thirty-six.
Shayitráhyum, *adj.* thirty-sixth.
Sháyum, *adj.* sixth.
Shĕch, *n. f.* message, news, notice.
Shĕch anawun, *n. m.* an apostle, messenger, prophet.
Shĕch-anawúin, *n. f.* prophetess.
Sheheṭ, *adj.* sixty-six.
Shel, *n. m.* rock.
Shela, *n. m.* rock, stone.
Shenamat, *adj.* ninety-six.
Sheṅk, *n. f.* doubt, suspicion, shell, blown as part of the worship in Hindu temples.
Shenk ninyi, *v. i.* to doubt.
Sher, *n. m.* arrangement, head.
Sheriph, *n. m.* a proper name.
Sheriphí, *n. f.* a proper name.
Sher Khán, *n. m.* a proper name.
Sherun, *v. i.* to accomplish, to arrange, to set in order, to repair, to mend, to prepare, to finish, to adorn; shúr, sherán, shúrmut, sherih.
Shesatat, *adj.* seventy-six.
Shetaráz karinyi, *v. t.* to oppose.
Shéṭh, *adj.* sixty.
Shéṭhyum, *adj.* sixtieth.
Shewanzah, *adj.* fifty-six.
Shewuh, *adj.* twenty-six.
Sheyishít, *adj.* eighty-six.
Sheyishítyum, *adj.* eighty-sixth.
Sheyitajih, *adj.* forty-six.
Sheyitãjihyum, *adj.* forty-sixth.
Sheyitruh, *adj.* thirty-six.
Sheyitruhyum, *adj.* thirty-sixth.
Shía, *n. m.* a follower of Alí. There are said to be between five and six thousand Shías in Kashmir. Their great masjid is at Hasanábád.

Their great íd, or mela, is held in the month called Zéth. Its name is Ashurá (mátam), grief.

Shich, *n. f.* information.

Shichh, *n. f.* news.

Shih, *adj.* six.

Shihaiṭhyum, *adj.* sixty-sixth.

Shihéṭh, *adj.* sixty-six.

Shihposh, *n. m.* a quilted coverlet, made of cotton-cloth, and stuffed with cotton-wool.

Shihul, *n. m.* shadow, shade.

Shikam, *n. m.* belly, abdomen.

Shikamdár, *adj.* pregnant.

Shikár, *n. m.* hunting, prey, game.

Shikárí, *n. m.* hunter. The Kashmírí hunter has not a very good character. He is said to be lazy, cowardly, and unskilful. There are exceptions.

Shikárí, *n. f.* a light swift sailing boat.

Shikár, karun, *v. t.* to hunt.

Shikaslad, *adj.* unfortunate, unlucky.

Shilighá, *n. m.* Chrysopogon glaucoptis.

The sieves used in paper making are made of the stems of this plant.

Shimál, *n. m.* north.

Shín, *n. m.* snow.

Shinamat, *adj.* ninety-six.

Shinamatyum, *adj.* ninety-sixth.

Shínawóin, *n. m.* snow water.

Shindar, *n. m.* Pyrus variolosa.

Shinya, *n. f.* a desert.

Shinya, *adj.* desolate.

Shinyí, *n. f.* air.

Shíp (súp), *n. m.* sieve.

Shír, *n. m.* medicine.

Shíri Cháí, see 'Cháí.'

Shírín, *adj.* sweet.

Shírín, *n. m.* Colchicum illyricum.

Shirwans, *n. m.* mat cover of a boat.

Shisatat, *adj.* seventy-six.

Shisatatyum, *adj.* seventy-sixth.

Shísha Nág, *n. m.* the lake to the north-east of the valley of Kashmir, from which the river Lidur takes its rise.

Shishí, *n. f.* a kind of bracelet.

Shíshí, *n. f.* looking glass.

Shishigar, *n. m.* bottle-maker.

Shishirgánṭ, *n. m.* icicle.

Shishít, *adj.* eighty-six.

Shishítyum, *adj.* eighty-sixth.

Shistur, *n. m.* iron (σιδηρος).

Shistir, *n. m.* iron, found in the Shahár hill near to the village of Khrú, and also in the hill of Sóp situated towards the Bannihal Pass, in the Brang pargana, and at Achabal, in the Kuṭahár pargana.

Seven hundred Kharwárs

of iron are extracted from the mine of Sop. The native Government give a Kharwár of rice for every Kharwár of iron. The people are compelled to agree to these terms, to which they very strongly object.

Shít, *adj.* eighty.

Shithar, *n. m.* enemy, rival.

Shitil, *n. m.* small-pox.

Shitilyí, *n. m.* small-pox.

Shítraj, *n. f.* Plumbago Europea.

Shitrut, *n. m.* enmity, hostility, resistance.

Shitrut karun, *v. t.* to hate.

Shítyum, *adj.* eightieth.

Shív, *n. m.* a village in the Zainager pargana.

Shiwalura, *n. m.* a village in the Rámahál pargana. Here is a well built fort.

Shiwanzah, *adj.* fifty-six.

Shiwanzähyum, *adj.* fifty-sixth.

Shiwŏhyum, *adj.* twenty-sixth.

Shób, *n. m.* mercy.

Shoga, *n. m.* parrot. Not indigenous to the valley.

Shógah, *n. m.* crow. This is the word in use towards Báramula.

Shogal, *adj.* diligent.

Shogla karun, *v. t.* to employ.

Shók, *adj.* stupid.

Shŏkhur, *n. m.* the planet Venus.

Shŏkshŏk, *n. m.* paper. This is a Ladákí word.

Shól (arzan), *n. m.* millet seed. (Panicum italicum).

Shóla, *n. m.* a dish consisting of rice, flesh, and condiments.

Shoncha, *n. m.* a wooden spoon.

Shŏngun, *v. i.* to recline, to lie, to sleep, to lie down; shong, shongán, shongmut, shongih.

Shónṭ, *n. m.* ginger. It does not grow in Kashmir.

Shŏnt, *adj.* abstemious, temperate, honest, devout, pious.

Shora, *n. m.* gun-powder. The nitrate of potash is found in Kashmir, the sulphur is imported from Tibet, and the charcoal is made from the pine tree.

Shoragur, *n. m.* a gun powder maker.

Shorah, *adj.* sixteen.

Shrád, *n. m.* worship for the dead.

Shrád karun, *v. t.* to perform worship for the dead.

Shrák, *n. m.* knife.

Shrákah-púch, *n. m.* pen-knife.

Shrákapúch, *n. m.* pen-knife.

Shrán, *n. m.* bath.

Shrán karun, *v. t.* to bathe, see 'Karun.'

Shrapun, *n. m.* digestion.

Shrapun, *v. i.* to digest, (hazm

honá); shrup, shrapán, shrupmut, shrapih.

Shráṭ, *n. m.* falls (of a river).

Shráwún, *n. m.* the fifth month of the Hindu year, and corresponding to our month of July, and to Rajab or Rajabu-l-murajjab, the seventh month of the Mussulman year.

Shruk, *n. m.* binding, tying.

Shrúk, *n. m.* poetry, verse.

Shruk karun, *v. t.* to tie.

Shrúts, *adj.* clean, pure, legal.

Shrúts karun, *v. t.* to clean.

Shubanáwun, *v. t.* to cause to be got ready, be prepared, be fitted.

Shubání, *n. f.* a shepherd's functions.

Shúbawun, *adj.* worthy, becoming, beautiful.

Shúbun, *v. i.* to be beautiful, to be becoming, to be fit, to be proper, to suit, to be worthy; shúb, shúbán, shúbmut, shúbih.

Shuhrat, *n. f.* report.

Shuhul, *n. m.* shade, shadow.

Shuhul, *adj.* cold.

Shukharwár, *n. m.* Friday.

Shukr, *n. m.* praise.

Shukr Baṭ, *n. m.* a proper name.

Shukrguzár, *adj.* thankful.

Shukr karawun, *adj.* thankful.

Shukr karun, *v. t.* to praise.

Shukrú, *n. m.* a pargana of Maráz.

Shukrwoiṅ, *n. m.* a proper name.

Shúm, *n. m.* miser.

Shúmí, *n. f.* avarice.

Shúmir, *n. m.* miser.

Shúmrí, *n. f.* avarice.

Shumshán, *n. m.* the place where Hindu corpses are burned.

Shungun, *v. i.* to sleep.

Shunt, *n. m.* hermit, saint.

Shúp, *n. m.* fan. It is used for cleaning grain.

Shupiyon, *n m.* the chief town of the Bátú pargana. In former days it was called Shahrah, the king's way, a name probably given by the Moguls. The population is about 6000, and the houses are in a most dilapidated state. The hill of Shupiyon is a formation of trap.

Shur, *n. m. f.* infant, child.

Shurah, *adj.* sixteen.

Shurãhyum, *adj.* sixteenth.

Shurí, *n. f.* a little girl, girl.

Shuribãts, *n. m.* family. This is a plural.

Shuripúr, *n. m.* a village in the Dúns pargana.

Shúsh, *n. m.* lung.

Shúshanor, *n. m.* lung.

Shúshnor, *n. m.* lung.

Shuwuh, *adj.* twenty-six.

Shyúp, *n. m.* a sieve or flat basket used for winnowing grain with.

Siálú, *n. m.* Marlia begonifolia. It is found in the Wardwan valley.

Sidun, *v. i.* to be straight.

Sihal, *adj.* easy.

Sihim, *n. m.* Leo (zodiac sign).

Sihmin, *n. f.* tigress.

Síhra ṭánj, see 'Ṭánj.'

Síjú, *n. m.* ash, (Fraxinus xanthoxylloides).

Sikandar, *n. m.* surnamed Butshikan, or Image breaker, was the sixth Mussulman King of Kashmir, and reigned in 1396 A.D.

Síkí, *n. m.* Euonymus Fimbriata and Hamiltonii.

Silah, *n. m.* pulmonary consumption.

Síla supárí, *n. m.* acorn of the Quercus incana.

Sílein, *n. m.* alder (Alnus).

Síling, *n. m.* a kind of pashmina manufactured in Ladak.

Símáb, *n. m.* mercury, quicksilver.

Símiń, *n. f.* tigress.

Síming, *n. f.* tigress, lioness.

Símlí, *n. m.* zizyphus flexuosa.

Sína, *n. m.* chest, breast.

Sína, *n. f.* army.

Sínaband, *n. m.* inner garment worn by Hindus.

Sinan, *n. m.* bath.

Sinán karun, *v. t.* to bathe, see 'Karun.'

Sind, *n. m.* name of an abutting valley, and a river in a northerly direction from Kashmir. The waters of the Gangabal lake flow into it. It joins the Vĕṭh at Shádapór.

Sindawóiń, *n. m.* Sind water.

Sínjlí, *n. m.* zizyphus flexuosa.

Singára, *n. m.* a small red cap worn by the Mussulman women.

Singhpór, *n. m.* a village in the Dúńs pargana, where there are about twenty families of Sikhs.

Sipah, *n. m.* soldier.

Sipáhí, *n. m.* soldier. The majority of the Maharaja's soldiers are Hindus, not belonging to Kashmir, but to the Punjab. His Mussulman soldiers belong to the Punjab, Hindustan, and the neighbouring states. Few are of Kashmir.

Sipar, *n. f.* shield.

Siparish karinyi, *v. t.* to entrust.

Sir, *n. m.* secret, mystery.

Sír, *n. f.* brick. There are two

kinds of bricks manufactured in Kashmir—the baked and the unbaked. The unbaked are made of earth, and dried in the sun. The baked are made of clay, and burned in a furnace. The Maharaja retains the monopoly of making bricks. The baked brick is called 'pach sír', the unbaked brick is named 'om sír.' The tomb of Bàudshah (Great King in Kashmírí), or Zín-nl-ab-u-Dín in Srínagar, is built of brick, is octagonal in shape, and is surmounted by a large dome surrounded by four small ones. Baudshah lived in 1422, and was the eighth and most illustrious Mussulman king of Kashmir.

Siráj, *n. m.* saddler.

Siram Khirahom, *n. m.* a village of the Dachanpór pargana. Vessels of stone are hewn here.

Sirhúl, *adj.* moist.

Sirí, *n. m.* sun.

Siriyi, *n. m.* sun.

Sirka, *n. m.* vinegar made from the vine.

Sis, *n. f.* a passing wind backwards.

Sisar, *n. f.* heat.

Sit, *n. f.* a sound.

Sitam, *n. m.* tyranny.

Sithar, *n. m.* cotton without the seeds.

Sitsan, *n. m.* needle.

Sium, *n. m.* shakakol.

Siwáí, *prep.* except, without.

Síwun, *v. t.* to boil, to sew.

Siyah-posh, *adj.* dressed in black.

Siyahtarah, *n. m.* the pattern of a Kashmir shawl intended for the weaver, that he may learn from it the different colours, and their proper places in the shawl. The man who makes the siyahtara is called nakkásh. There are said to be five different houses engaged in making patterns for the shawl-manufacturers of Srínagar.

Sódá, *n. m.* traffic.

Sódágar, *n. m.* merchant.

Sodágarí, *n. f.* trade.

Só,e, *n. f.* common nettle.

Sof Ahun, *n. m.* a village where, in Vigne's time, were the chief and only iron works of the valley. Veins of copper, lead, silver, and gold were said to be found there. The iron of Kashmir is said to be of inferior quality.

Sogandár, *adj.* fragrant.

Sóí, *n. f.* peppermint.

Soiyĕt, *n.f.* wick (rural name).

Sŏk, *n. m.* rest, leisure.

Sŏkabul, *adj.* lukewarm.

Sŏkh, *n. m.* peace.

Sŏkhabŏl, *adj.* lukewarm.

Sokhabaul, *adj.* lukewarm.

Sokhdá dányí, see 'Dányí.'

Sokhasán, *adv.* quietly.

Sokhawushun, *adj.* lukewarm.

Sokhsar, *n. m.* a beautiful bird frequenting Kashmir.

Solei, *n. f.* Plectranthus rugosus.

Sombráwun, *v. i.* to lie with (a man with a woman).

Somráwun (andokhtan), *v. t.* to gain.

Sŏn, *n.f.* a rival wife. Polygamy does not appear to be very common among the Hindus of the valley. The Mussulmans, on the other hand, are generally polygamists if their means will admit of it.

Sŏn, *n. m.* gold, riches.

Sóná, *n. m.* a proper name.

Sónalãuk, *n. m.* the golden island in the Ḍal.

Sŏnâr (Fr. sónár), *n. m.* goldsmith, silversmith.

Sóng, *n. m.* lamp.

Sŏn láwun, *v. t.* to gild.

Sóṅṭ, *n. m.* the season of spring, hot season.

Som, *adj.* level.

Sóp, *n. m.* a village in the Shahbád pargana. There is an iron mine here, which is said to be at present worked.

Soph, *n. m.* a mountain in the Brang pargana, where there is a rich iron mine. Eight hundred kharwárs of the ore are extracted annually. Copper, too, is said to be found there.

Sŏpun, *n. m.* a dream.

Sopun wuchhun, *v. i.* to dream.

Sopúr, *n. m.* a town in the Zainager pargana. Its pupulation is about 5,000. The town is in a very dilapidated state.

Sor, *n. m.* slow music.

Sór, *n. m.* boar.

Sŏr, *n. m.* carefulness, watchfulness.

Sór, *adj.* all, trustworthy.

Sorag, *n. m.* paradise.

Sor karun, *v. t.* to think, see 'Karun.'

Sóruí, *adj.* all.

Sŏruph, *n. m.* serpent.

Sosan, *n. m.* the iris (Iris nepalensis). There are at least four species of iris to be found in Kashmir: the yellow, the white, the red, and the blue. The Iris is the great graveyard flower with the Mussulmans of the valley. The root of the red species is bruised, mixed with honey, and given in cases of amenorrhœa. An infusion of this same root, mixed with olive oil, is dropped into the ear for noises in the ear.

The graveyards of Kashmir are covered with the blue and the white Iris. These flowers are in their glory in the months of April and May, beautifying and rendering fragrant the abodes of the departed.

Soṭka, *n, m.* crystal.

Sŏtsal, *n. f.* mallows.

Sov, *adj.* rich, wealthy.

Soyat, *n. m.* candle.

Soyet, *n. m.* wick, which is made of cotton.

Sóz, *n. m.* music.

Ṣozanáwun, *v. t.* to cause to be sent.

Sozun (bhejná), *v. t.* to send; súzun, sozán, súzmut, sózih.

Sóz wáyun, *v. i.* to play music.

Srán, *adj.* clean.

Sranḍah, *n. m.* buffalo.

Srang, *adj.* cheap.

Sré, *n. f.* love.

Srí, *n. f.* Lakshmí.

Srínagar, *n. m.* the capital of Kashmir. This word is derived from Srí, or Shrí, the name of Lakshmí, the wife of Vishnu, and goddess of prosperity, and nagar, a city. The city of Srínagar was built by Pravarasena, who invaded Gujerat, A.D. 59.

Srol, *n. m.* Alder (Alnus).

Srug, *adj.* cheap.

Srúts, *adj.* clean.

Su, *pron.* he. The pronoun Su is sometimes used as a definite article.

Subah, *n. m.* morning.

Subh, *n. m.* morning from sunrise to 9 o'clock.

Subhan, *n. m.* morning, dawn, in the morning.

Subhán, *n. m.* morning, daylight, a proper name.

Subhána, *n. m.* a proper name.

Subhanas, *adv.* early in the morning, at the dawn.

Subhas, *adv.* in the morning.

Subul, *n. m.* a man's name. This is the familiar and endearing form of Subhán. The vocative is Subuleó.

Subur, *n. m* a proper name.

Subúra, *n. m.* a proper name.

Suchh, *n. m.* abundance.

Súd, *n. m,* interest on money.

Sufédar, *n. m.* Himalayan poplar (Populus ciliata).

Suh, *n. m.* lion, tiger.

Suh, *f.* of 3rd pers. *pron.* she.

Suhai, *pron.* she, emphasized.

Suhul, *adj*. easy.

Suí, *pron*. that very.

Sukré, *n*. *f*. abstinence.

Sukúj, *n*. *f*. buttock.

Sul, *n*. *m*. spare time.

Sulahar, *n*. *m*. kitchen.

Sulaimání, *n*. *m*. onyx stone.

Sulálí, *n*. *f*. Himalayan poplar (Populus ciliata).

Súlí dinyi, *v*. *t*. to crucify.

Sultán, *n*. *m*. a proper name.

Sultána, *n*. *f*. a proper name.

Sultán Shekh, *n*. *m*. a proper name.

Sum, *adj*. flat, smooth.

Sumburmut, *adj*. assembled.

Súmráwunwol, *n*. *m*. collector.

Súmráwun (jama kardan), *v*. *t*. to collect.

Sumun, *v*. *i*. to assemble, to come together.

Súmwár, *n*. *m*. Monday.

Sun, *n*. *m*. flesh, whatever is eaten along with boiled rice.

Sun, *adj*. deep.

Sunáwun, *v*. *t*. to clothe another.

Sund, *prep*. of.

Sundabrãr, *n*. *m*. a spring of water in the Brang pargana, which is an object of worship to the Hindus on the 11th of June. The Brahmans call the spring Trisaudiya.

Súndarmál, *adj*. pretty.

Sundrí, *n*. *f*. a proper name.

Sungal, *n*. *m*. yew tree (Taxus baccata), Himalayan spruce (Abies Smithiana).

Sungmut, *p*. of shongun, asleep.

Suniyár, *n*. *m*. goldsmith.

Súnú, *n*. *m*. Amygdalus Persica (peach).

Sunun, *v*. *t*. to clothe one's self.

Suprúsaman, *n*. *m*. a pargana of Maráz.

Supun, *n*. *m*. dream.

Súr, *n*. *m*. hoar-frost, ashes.

Súradag, *n*. *m*. dew.

Suraiya, *n*. *m*. Pleiades.

Súrat, *n*. *f*. a copy, image (of man), form, shape, disguise.

Surgauch, *n*. *m*. Rubus lasiocarpus.

Súrín, *n*. *f*. sow. Guláb Singh is said to have introduced them. Till lately, the Hindus of Srínagar were allowed by government to keep swine, to the great disgust of the Mussulman inhabitants. Recently, however, the city was entirely cleared of the swine by order of His Highness the Maharaja.

Surma, *n*. *m*. antimony.

Súrú, *n*. *m*. a village near to Bawun. Here is a statue in black marble of Sri, Shrí, or Lakshmí, the Indian Ceres.

Súrug, *n. m.* heaven (bihisht).

Sust, *adj.* slow.

Sút, *adj.* lazy.

Suth, *n. m.* embankment.

Sut pakun, *v. i.* to creep.

Súts, *n. m.* tailor, generally a Mussulman, sometimes a Hindu Pandit.

Sutsan, *n. m.* needle.

Sutsanyipoh, *n. m.* eye of a needle.

Suttur, *adj.* level, smooth.

Suwun (síná), *v. t.* to sew (cloth); suwun, suwán, sumut, suwih.

Swád, *n. m.* taste, flavour.

Swád, *adj.* one and a-quarter.

Swád zah, *adj.* two and a quarter.

Swoi, *n. f.* tamarisk, which grows abundantly in Kashmir.

Syud, *adj.* straight.

Syun, *n. m.* what is eaten along with rice, and is either vegetables, meat, or fish.

Syut, *n. m.* bee's wax.

T.

There are two varieties of T, one of which is represented by the English T, and is pronounced as in English. The other is represented as in English, but with a dot underneath it, thus Ṭ, and is pronounced by rolling the tongue back upon itself against the roof of the mouth. T is the enclitic of the singular objective case of the second personal pronoun.

Tab, *n. m.* fever.

Ṭabar, *n. m.* family.

Tabar, *n. m.* a small axe.

Tabardár, *n. m.* woodman.

Tabatú, *n. m.* Nicotiana tabacum.

Tabela, *n. m.* stable.

Tabra (gálí), *n. m.* abuse.

Tabra Kaḍun, *v. t.* to abuse.

Tabra wanun, *v. t.* to abuse.

Táchhar, *n. m.* love.

Tachhun, *v. t.* to dig, to shave or plane (wood), to excoriate; tuchh, tachhán, tuchhmut, tachhih.

Tadbír, *n. m.* counsel, advice.

Tadrelú, *n. m.* Coriaria Nepalensis.

Tadrú, *n. m.* Rhamnus virgatus.

Tafáwat tháwun, *v. i.* to differ.

Tah, *conj.* and. It connects single words; beyib connects clauses.

Tahalyí, *n. m.* groom.

Tahar, *n. m.* a dish eaten by the Kashmírís, consisting of rice, colouring matter, salt, and oil.

Tahsíldár, *n. m.* collector, the chief magistrate of a tahsíl, or large division of Kashmír.

Táj, *n. m.* a crown.

Taj, *n. m.* bark of Cinnamomum albiflorum.

Tajallí, *n. f.* lustre.

Tajíl, *n. m.* haste.

Táj Shah, *n. m.* a proper name.

Tájtáruk, *n. m.* a comet, the tail of which points upwards. It is considered a star of a good omen.

Ṭaich, *n. f.* a bird of Kashmír.

Ṭâirṭair, *n. f.* chattering woman.

Taiyár, *adj.* ready.

Ṭak, *n. f.* running.

Takabúr, *n. m.* pride, haughtiness.

Takán, *n. m.* celerity, quickness, swiftness, haste.

Ṭakán, *adv.* quickly, instantly.

Takanár, *n. f.* Tendo Achilles.

Takán karun, *v. i.* to be quick, to make haste, to hasten.

Takạn-ṭakán, *adv.* hastily.

Tákat, *n. f.* power.

Takatrust, *adj.* unable.

Tákhána, *n. m.* an underground apartment where goods and valuables are stowed away.

Takht, *n. m.* throne.

Takht-i-Suliman, *n. m.* a hill of amygdaloid trap rock near to Srínagar, some 800ft above the level of the valley. It is called by the Hindus Sir-i-Shur, or Siva's head, or Sankarachár. See 'Shankarátsárí.'

Takhta, *n. m.* plank.

Takiya, *n. m.* pillow.

Taksír, *n. m.* sin, vice.

Tal, *prep.* & *adv.* under, below, down.

Tal anun, *v. t.* to bring down.

Tál, *n. m.* palate, roof of mouth, crown of head, cymbal.

Talab, *n. m.* wages.

Tálai, *n. m.* success, fortune, destiny.

Talák, *n. f.* divorce.

Talakatur, *n. m.* ice formed on the surface of water.

Taláo, *n. m.* tank.

Talásh, *n. m.* effort, exertion.

Talásh karun, *v. i.* to endeavour.

Tálatsúk, *n. m.* a circular piece of woollen or silken stuff worn above the kalaposh by the Pandítanís.

Tálau, *n. m.* roof of house, ceiling.

Talawúl karun, *v. t.* to harass.

Tal gatshun, *v. i.* to go down, to descend.

Tãlím, *n. f.* learning, instruction.

Tálím, *n. m.* the paper on

which are depicted the curious hieroglyphics denoting the different coloured threads to be used by the shawl-weaver at every step of his work.

Talkh, *n. m.* Colchicum illyricum.

Tál márinyi, *v. t.* to beat a cymbal, to play with a cymbal; tál mãrin, tál márán, tál mãrmats, tál márih.

Talordach, *n. m.* vine (Vitis).

Tálpód, *n. m.* sole of foot.

Talyum, *adj.* lower.

Tám, and támat, *prep.* as far as, up to.

Tama, *n. m.* covetousness, greed.

Tamáí, *adj.* covetous, greedy.

Tama karun, *v. t.* to covet.

Tamála, *n. m.* leaves of the Cinnamomum albiflorum.

Tamanná, *n. m.* longing desire.

Tamarí, *n. m.* date (fruit).

Tamáshá, *n. m.* spectacle.

Támat, *prep.* till.

Tambuláwun, *v. t.* to deceive, to perplex; tambulov, tambuláwán, tambulomut, tambuláwih.

Tambalun, *n. m.* fraud, delirium.

Tambalun, *v. t.* to astonish.

Tambulun, *v. i.* to be perplexed, to be deceived.

Tamíz, *n. f.* civility, courtesy.

Tamih patah, *adv.* afterwards.

Tamok, *n. m.* tobacco. Small quantities of tobacco are exported from Kashmir to Ladak. The tobacco of Jehámu is said to be the finest in Kashmir.

Támut, *prep.* up to, as far as.

Tamí, *conj.* then.

Tan, *n. f.* body.

Tan, *n. m.* breast (mamma).

Tan, *adj.* thin (of cloth).

Tan, *n. m.* pear.

Tana, *n. m.* nipple.

Tánatána karun, *v. t.* to despise

Tanaur, *n. m.* vine (Vitis). According to Cayley, fifteen maunds of currants were imported into Leh from Kashmir in 1867.

Tandarustí, *n. f.* health.

Táng, *n. m.* braying of an ass, lowing of cattle.

Tang, *n. m.* girth.

Tang, *adj.* light, narrow.

Táng, *n. m.* pear.

Tánjakul, *n. m.* pear tree.

Ṭang, *n. m.* pear. The following varieties of pear grow in the valley: Goshibeigi ṭang, Nákh ṭang, Gulábi ṭang, Hápat ṭang, Kotarnal ṭang. Pears are ripe in Kashmir in the month of September.

Tangakul, *n. m.* pear tree. The following are the varieties: Goshabab ṭangakul, Nakh ṭangakul, Kotarnal ṭangakul, Gulábí ṭangakul, Tánjakul.

Tang-wang, *n. m.* a pear.

Tanha, *adj.* solitary.

Táni, *n. f.* Oryza sativa.

Ṭánj, *n. f.* a species of pear? There are the following varieties: Tsŏk ṭánj, Mŏder ṭánj, Khar ṭánj, Síhra ṭánj. The country people cook the ṭánj in warm water. The skin is thick.

Tanun, *v. i.* to be thin.

Tanyar, *n. m.* thinness.

Táo, *n. m.* a small pan, twist, coil.

Táp, *n. m.* sunshine.

Tápadán, *n. m.* umbrella.

Tapasia, *n. m.* devotion.

Tápdán, *n. m.* umbrella.

Tapun, *v. i.* to warm one's self.

Tár, *n. m.* eyelid.

Tăr, *n. f.* tenderness, slowness, delay.

Tarámusha, *n. m.* Mentha incana.

Taranga, *n. m.* a long piece of cotton about three inches broad, which the Panditanís bind round their heads. In the hot season it is white.

Táranwol, *n. m.* ferryman.

Tárats, *n. m.* a small balance.

Taraugdar, *n. m.* an official whose duty is to weigh the grain when the government's share is taken from the cultivators.

Tárawun, *n. m.* ferryman.

Tarbíbawarái, *adv.* disorderly.

Ṭárich zih, *n. f.* edge of eyelid.

Táríf, *n. m.* praise.

Táríf karun, *v. t.* to praise.

Tarjuma karanwol, *n. m.* interpreter, translator.

Tarjuma karun, *v. t.* to interpret.

Tarkárí, *n. f.* vegetables.

Tárkhanḍ, *n. f.* lower jaw.

Táruk, *n. m.* star.

Tarun, *v. i.* to cross (as a river or ferry).

Tárun, *v. t* to ferry, to benefit, to assist.

Ṭáryí, *n. f.* eyelid.

Taryiák, *n. m.* opium. The poppy grows in the valley.

Tasbí, *n. f.* Mussulman necklace.

Tasbíh, *n. f.* Mussulman rosary.

Tasht, *n. f.* basin.

Ṭasna, *n. m.* jest.

Ṭaṭ, *n. f.* a pony mare.

Tát, *n. m.* gleet.

Tataur, *n. m.* Artemisia Indica and vestita.

Tati, *adv.* there.

Tatih, *adv.* thence.

Tatit, *adv.* there.

Tatsar, *n. m.* heat.

Tatsaráwun, *v. t.* to heat to a red heat (of metal).

Tattúr, *n.m.* Datura stramonium.

Tatun, *v. i.* to become hot, to be hot; tateo, tatán, tateomut, tatih.

Tatur, *n. m.* smarting of a wound.

Tatúra, *n. m.* balsam (Balsamina impatiens).

Tatwen, *n. m.* Artemisia sacrorum and vulgaris.

Taun, *adj.* thin.

Taup, *n. m.* ringlet.

Taut, *adj.* hot.

Tawai (usi waste), *conj.* therefore.

Tawai, *conj.* there.

Táwakal (mutawakal), *adj.* confident.

Táwí, *n. m.* Grislea tomentosa.

Tāwiza, *n. m.* charm, amulet. These consist of the names of God, the name of Muhammad, the names of Mussulman saints, or verses from the Quran. The paper on which these are written is usually sewed into a piece of cloth, generally of a red colour, and then tied round the arm, or attached to the wearer's dress.

Táwun, *v. t.* to heat, to a red heat (of metals). This is a shortened form of Tatsaráwun.

Táza, *adj.* fresh.

Táza, *adv.* recently.

Tázak-tsun, *n. m.* Rhododendron anthopogon and lepidotum.

Tázihun, *n. m.* greyhound.

Tázun, *n. m.* a horsewhip.

Tazzar, *n. m.* fever.

Tĕb, *n. m.* stitch.

Tech, *n. m.* a species of waterfowl.

Techihor, *adj.* spotted.

Techibor suh, *n. m.* leopard.

Tejpat, *n. m.* leaves of the Cinnamomum albiflorum.

Teka bataiṅ, *n. m.* a flower of Kashmir.

Tél, *n. m.* sesame. Grows abundantly in the valley. Bread is made of it.

Telawoin, *n. m.* an expresser of oil.

Tembir, *n. m.* spark, flame.

Ṭeng, *n. m.* ostentation, a rising ground, eminence.

Tĕngul, *n. m.* fire.

Tentol, *n. m.* top or summit (of mountain).

Ter, *n. m.* sheep.

Ṭĕṭ, *n. f.* intoxication.

Tetar, *n. m.* Rhus Buckiamela.

Ṭeṭha shakir tsúnṭ, see 'Tsúnṭ.'

Teṭha tsera, *n. m.* a species of apricot.

Téz, *adj.* sharp.
Téz, *adv.* swiftly.
Thadun (thŏd), *v. i.* to be high.
Ṭhagil, *n. m.* forgery.
Thaharanáwun, *v. t.* to cause to remain.
Tháí, *n. m.* Grislea tomentosa.
Ṭhaimij, *n. f.* the little wooden pillars of the spinning wheel.
Thain, *n. f.* butter.
Thaing, *n. f.* butter.
Thainyi, *n. f.* butter.
Thaj Tulakul, see 'Tulakul.'
Thakun, *n. m.* fatigue.
Thakun (máṇḍa hoṇá), *v. i.* to be tired (from manual work), to be weary; thauk and thuk, thakán, thaukmut and thukmut, thakih.
Ṭhãkur, *n. m.* a proper name.
Thál, *n. m.* the vessel out of which the Hindu men eat. It is round in shape, and made of brass. It is not used by the Mussulmans.
Tham, *n. m.* pillar, column.
Than, *n. m.* udder.
Ṭhán, *n. m.* cork.
Thánadár, *n. m.* the chief majistrate of a pargana.
Ṭhán dyun, *v. t.* to cork.
Ṭhánṭhir, *n. m.* coppersmith.
Thanyi, *n. f.* butter.
Thanyibagaira, *n. m.* a dish composed of butter and vegetables.
Thap, *n. m.* handle of plough.
Thápur, *n. m.* thump, blow, slap.
Thapul, *n. m.* snatching.
Thar, *n. f.* back (of body).
Thar-kaub, *adj.* hump-backed.
Thar kúnḍ, *n. m.* spinal column.
Ṭhas, *n. m.* noise.
Ṭhasabar, *n. m.* a door that closes of its own accord, making a noise while so doing.
Ṭhaṭha, *n. m.* jest.
Thaud, *adj.* high, tall.
Thaud karun (bardashtan), *v. t.* to exalt.
Thauí, *n. f.* butter.
Thaup, *n. m.* a plug.
Thaur, *n. m.* fig tree, (Ficus reticulata).
Tháwanáwun, *v. t.* to cause to be put or placed.
Tháwun, *v. t.* to place, to possess, to have; thówun, tháwáṇ, thomut, tháwih.
Thazar, *n. m.* height, ascent, acclivity, size.
Thekawun, *n. m.* fop.
Thĕkun (shekhí karná), *v. t.* to boast; thyuk, thĕkán, thyukmut, thekih.
Ṭhelah, *n. m.* a cotton sack.
Ṭhela, *n. m.* large bag, purse.
Thílí, *n. f.* small bag.
Thinya, *n. m.* field.
Thŏd, *adj.* high, tall, erect.
Thod túlun, *v. t.* to raise.

Thŏd wathun, *v. i.* to stand up; thŏd wuth, thŏd wathán, thŏd wuthmut, thŏd wathih.

Thŏk, *n. m.* saliva.

Ṭhókur, *n. m.* image (idol).

Ṭhokur-kuṭ, *n.m.* god-chamber, generally placed on the second floor.

Thóm, *n. m.* Allium sativum.

Thong, *n. m.* tower, minaret.

Thosh, *n. m.* the name of the goat from which the finest shawl wool is obtained.

Thŏt, *n. m.* nettle-rash.

Thuj, *n. f.* the mulberry, the leaves of which are considered the best of all the varieties for silk worms. The tree is said to be fruitless.

Thukmut, *adj.* wearied.

Ṭhúl, *n. m.* egg.

Thúng, *adj.* foppish.

Thung, *n. m.* mountain pass.

Thup, *n. m.* closing.

Ṭhúr, *n. m.* partition.

Thur, *n. f.* bush.

Thurun, *v. t.* to shape (said of potter).

Tih, *adv.* also even.

Tihir, *n. m.* a feather, wing.

Ṭíka, *n. f.* translation.

Ṭíka karinyi, *v. t.* to translate.

Ṭikar, *n. f.* earthenware cooking pot.

Tika Rám, *n. m.* a proper name.

Ṭikipúts, *n. f.* spotted-veil worn by the Panḍitánís, or Hindu females, but not by the female Mussulmans.

Ṭikir, *n. m.* a village in the Loláb pargana.

Tíl, *n. m.* oil.

Til, *n. m.* oil.

Til, *n. m.* sesamum orientale.

Tílabagaira, *n. m.* a dish composed of oil and vegetables.

Tílagám, *n. m.* a village in the Kruhin pargana.

Tilapyut, *n. m.* gall-bladder, bile.

Tilawóiṅ, *n. m.* an oil-expresser. Oil is expressed from mustard, walnuts, almonds, and linseed in Kashmir.

Tili, *adv.* then.

Tilih (tab), *conj.* then.

Tilih tih, *conj.* nevertheless.

Tilok Chand, *n. m.* a proper name.

Tílpatar, *n. m.* the maple (acer).

Tilur, *n. m.* bee.

Tilyim, *n. f.* a bit, part, portion.

Tilyun, *n. m.* fragment.

Tímbar, *n. m.* Xanthoxylon hostile.

Timbir, *n. f.* spark.

Tímbrú, *n. m.* Xanthoxylon hostile.

Tím ṭám, *n. m.* ostentation.

Tír, *n. m.* arrow.

Tíranor, *n. m.* quiver.

Tír-tráwunwol, *n. m.* archer.

Tirun, *adj.* cold.

Títabaterí, *n. f.* Himalayan Honeysuckle (Lonicera quinquelocularis).

Títãjih, *adj.* forty-three.

Títãjihyum, *adj.* forty-third.

Títar, *n. m.* partridge, which has been lately introduced into Kashmir by his Highness the Mahárájá.

Tithar pãṭ, *adv.* in that manner.

Tithanhyú, *adj.* such.

Tithanhyú, *adv.* so.

Tithúí, *adv.* so.

Tithai, *adv.* in that manner.

Ṭiṭhun (ṭyuṭh), *v. i.* to be bitter.

Títráh, *adj.* thirty-three.

Títrâhyum, *adj.* thirty-third.

Títrí, *n. m.* Rhus Buckiamela.

Tíyitãjih, *adj.* forty-three.

Tíyitãjihyum, *adj.* forty-third.

Tŏh, *n. m.* chaff.

Tohi, *pron.* you.

Ṭŏhul. *n. m.* pony-herd. The Mahárájá has numerous herds of ponies, which graze especially towards the north-west end of the valley, in the direction of the Wulur Lake.

Ṭokur, *n. f.* basket.

Tól, *n. m.* a contrivance consisting of a long wooden pole, so placed upon another fixed perpendicular pole, that one end shall be nearly equal in weight to the other end, with a vessel full of water. It is employed in raising water out of a stream.

Tól, *n. m.* weight.

Toḷun (tolná), *v. t.* to weigh; túl, tolán, túlmut, tolih.

Tomul, *n. m.* rice stripped of its husks.

Tomula-tsauṭ, *n. f.* rice-bread.

Tón, *n. m.* turban. This is an old Kashmírí word.

Tŏn, *adj.* thin.

Tongur, *n. m.* a hand spade.

Tónt, *n. m.* beak, bill.

Ṭóp, (fr. ṭápú), *n. m.* island.

Ṭŏp, *n. f.* sting, pulsation or beating of an abscess, Mussulman's lock of hair, lancet.

Tŏp, *n. m.* gun.

Ṭopagar, *n. m.* cap-maker.

Ṭŏp-dinyi, *v. t.* to sting.

Ṭópi, *n. f.* skull cap. This is often all the covering the poor Mussulmans have for their heads. In the case of those who are better off the ṭópi forms the foundation and support for the ample folds of the voluminous turban.

Ṭopigur, *n. m.* a cap maker.

Ṭŏp láyinyi, *v. t.* to sting.

Ṭŏp taiyár karun, *v. t.* to load a gun.

Tor, *n. m.* adze.
Tór (udhar), *adv.* thither.
Ṭór, *n. m.* eyelid.
Torkachhán, *n. m.* cabinet maker.
Ṭóṭ, *adj.* beloved, precious, dear, loved, generous, venerable, magnificent, splendid.
Tŏt, *adj.* hot.
Tota, *n. m.* parrot. Not indigenous to the valley.
Tŏtámat, *adv.* as far as that.
Tóta Rám, *n. m.* a proper name.
Ṭóṭ tháwun, *v. t.* to prefer.
Tówarun, *v. t.* to make red hot, to heat (exclusively of metals).
Traft, *adj.* full.
Tragám, *n. m.* a village in the Táírí pargana.
Tráh, *adj.* thirty.
Trahaiṭhyum, *adj.* sixty-third.
Trahal, *n. m.* a pargana and village to the north-east of Awántipúr. Here are settled the Sikhs who accompanied Rájá Sukh Jawán, whom Timur Shah of Kabul sent to govern the valley for him. The pargana of Trahal is perhaps the most barren and uninteresting part of Kashmír.
Trahéṭh, *adj.* sixty three.
Tráhyum, *adj.* thirtieth.
Trai, *n. f.* woman.
Trak, *n. m.* a grain measure containing four and three quarter seers full (pakka). A seer is equal to two English pounds.
Trak, *n. m.* back (of body).
Tarkajár, *n. m.* plot.
Trakajár karun, *v. t.* to plot.
Trakár, *n. f.* weighing scales of middling size.
Trakir, *n. f.* a pair of small scales.
Trakkur (shokh), *adj.* dissolute.
Trakur, *n. m.* Libra (Zodiac sign).
Trakúr, *adj.* coarse, ferocious, hard.
Traḳur, *n. f.* a balance, weighing scales.
Trál, *n. m.* a town in the Wular pargana, where there is a large colony of Sikhs. Three thousand Sikhs are said to have been settled here in the time of Ranjít Singh. Their women dress like Kashmírí women. The men are chiefly cultivators of the soil. A few have become soldiers in the Maharájá's army. By order of His Highness, about one hundred of these Sikhs left Trál and settled on the Karewah of Maṭan, to people and cultivate it.
Tram, *n. m.* the hole in the forepart of the prow Mahtábí for the peg to go into, to

which the rope is attached by which the boat is dragged along.

Trám, *n. m.* copper. The Mussulman inhabitants make use of vessels made of this metal; the Hindus do not.

Trãm, *n. m.* the vessel out of which the Mussulmans eat. It corresponds to the Thál of the Hindus: the trãm is of copper.

Tránamat, *adj.* ninety-three.

Tránamatyum, *adj.* ninety-third.

Trápajár, *n. m.* ophthalmia.

Trasatat, *adj.* seventy-three.

Trasatatyum, *adj.* seventy-third.

Tráshit, *adj.* eighty-three.

Tráshityum, *adj.* eighty-third.

Trashúl, *n. m.* trident.

Traṭ, *n. f.* meteorite, thunderbolt.

Trát, *n. m.* rent.

Trát dyun, *v. t.* to rend, to tear.

Trauṭh, *n. m.* a collar either of gold, silver, or iron.

Tráwanáwun, *v. t.* to make to leave off, to make to let off.

Trawanzah, *adj.* fifty-three.

Trawanzãhyum, *adj.* fifty-third.

Trawa-tráwa, *adj.* full.

Tráwit tsunun, *v. t.* to throw away.

Tráwun (chhoṛna), *v. t.* to let go one's hold of, to pour out, to pour, to abandon (tark kardan), to resign, to forsake, to quit, to leave, to discharge, (as an arrow), to shoot, to leave off, to let off, to dismiss, to release, to liberate, to cast down, to cast, to throw, to doff, to spill, to strew; tróv, tráwán, trómut, tráwih,

Tráwun, *n. m.* divorce.

Trayi laṭi, *adv.* thrice.

Trayi phiri, *adv.* thrice.

Treheṭ, *adj.* sixty-three.

Tréí, *n. f.* wife.

Trek, *n. m.* back (of body).

Trel, *n. f.* a small species of apple.

Trela, *n. m.* apple? There are the following varieties of this species of apple. Wazají trela, Chatsa trela, Jámbáz trela, Khotunyi trela.

Trelakul, *n. m.* a kind of apple tree.

Trenamat, *adj.* ninety-three.

Tresatat, *adj.* seventy-three.

Tresh, *n. m.* thirst.

Tresh lagun, *v. i.* to be thirsty (with dative of person thirsty).

Treshahut, *adj.* thirsty.

Tresh-wesh, *n. m.* thirst.

Trewanzah, *adj.* fifty-three.

Trewuh, *adj.* twenty-three.

Treyih phirih, *adv.* thrice.

Treyishít, *adj.* eighty-three.
Treyitruh, *adj.* thirty-three.
Treyum, *adj.* third.
Trhas, *n. m.* matting, (towards Baramúla).
Trí, *n. f.* wife.
Trih, *adj.* three.
Trihagám, *n. m.* a village in the Wutar pargana.
Trihyum, *adj.* third.
Trit, *n. m.* slit, rent, fissure.
Troahyum, *adj.* thirteenth.
Tromba, *n. m.* Fagopyrum esculentum.
Trŏshur, *n. m.* conjunctivitis, ophthalmia.
Trŏwuh, *adj.* twenty-three.
Trŏwuhyum, *adj.* twenty-third.
Trúal, *n. m.* Balsam (Balsamina impatiens).
Truh, *adj.* thirty.
Truk, *adj.* quick, clever, ingenious, acute, sharp-witted, intelligent.
Truk, *n. m.* a Turk.
Trúmba, *n. m.* Fagopyrum esculentum.
Trúnts, *n. m.* panther.
Trús, *n. m.* prick.
Trús dyun, *v. t.* to prick.
Trushi, *n. f.* fire stick.
Ṭruṭ, *n. m.* necklace.
Truwah, *adj.* thirteen.
Truwāhyum, *adj.* thirteenth.
Tsáḍanáwun, *v. t.* to cause to seek.
Tsádar, *n. f.* sheet, woollen shawl, veil.
Tsádir-wádir, *n. m.* chadar, shawl.
Tsádun, *v. t.* to request, to demand.
Tsáḍun (justan), *v. t.* to examine, to search; tsoḍun, tsáḍán, tsoḍmut, tsáḍih.
Tsáhun (chukná), *v. t.* to taste; tsuh, tsáhán, tsuhmut, tsáhih.
Tsáí, *n. f.* shade.
Tsak, *n. f.* rage, passionateness, anger.
Tsak khasinyi, *v. i.* to be angry, (with dative).
Tsak yinyi, *v. i.* to be angry (with dative).
Tsakar, *n. m.* the handle for moving the large wheel of the spinning wheel.
Tsákawár, *n. m.* a state barge, with the rowers seated before and behind the raised canopy for the passenger.
Tsakij, *n. f.* hip.
Tsalanshái, *n. f.* a place of refuge, an asylum.
Tsalanwol, *n. m.* a deserter.
Tsálun, *n. m.* the small spade used to stir up the fire of the Kángrí.
Tsalun, *v. i.* to run away, to escape, to flee; tsol, tsalán, tsolmut, tsalih.

Tsam, *n. m.* skin of human body, volume.

Tsáman, *n. m.* cheese.

Tsamar, *n. m.* shoe-maker.

Tsamaṭhun, *v. i.* to wither, to decay; tsamaṭheo, tsamaṭhán tsamatheomut, tsamaṭhih.

Tsámp, *n. m.* dimness of vision, of sight.

Tsámp yun, *v. i.* to be dim sighted, to have dim vision.

Tsáṅ, *n. m.* salt, which is imported into Kashmir from Ladak and the Panjab. Tsáṅ is a Ladákí word

Tsandar, *n. m.* new moon, crescent-shaped moon.

Tsandarwár, *n. m.* Monday.

Tsánḍun, (ḍhunḍhná), *v. t.* to seek for, to search for; tsonḍ, tsánḍán, tsonḍmut, tsándih.

Tsandun, *n. m.* sandal wood. There is said to be a forest of sandal wood in Wama Díví in the Kútahár pargana beyond Islamabád.

Tsángij, *n. f.* a round piece of matting.

Tsangun, *v. i.* to be happy; tsingeo, and tsung, tsangán, tsingeomut and tsungmut, tsangih.

Tsánṭ, *n. f.* swimming.

Tsánṭal, *n. m.* swimmer.

Tsánṭ láyinyi, *v. i.* to swim.

Tsántul, *n. m.* swimmer.

Tsánṭ wáyinyi, *v. i.* to swim; woyun, wáyán, woimut, wáyih.

Tsanun, *n. m.* internal malleolus.

Tsánun, *v. t.* to bring in.

Tsap, *n. f.* a sheaf of grain.

Tsăpanáwun, *v. t.* to cause to gnaw.

Tsápun, (dandídan), *v. t.* to gnaw, to bite, to chew, to masticate; tsóp, tsápán, tsŏpmut, tsápih.

Tsáṅs, *n. f.* cough.

Tsar, *n. f.* hen-sparrow.

Tsareṭ, *n. f.* spectacle.

Tsarir, *n. m.* increase.

Tsári túl, see 'Tul.'

Tsari Tula Kul, see 'Tulakul.'

Tsárun (chunná), *v. t.* to gather, to pick, to select, to separate, to pick up (as birds); tsórun, tsárán, tsórmut, tsárih.

Tsás, *n. m.* cough.

Tsáṭahál, *n. m.* school, college.

Tsatajih, *adj.* forty.

Tsatajihyum, *adj.* fortieth.

Tsaṭanáwun, *v. t.* to cause to eat; tsaṭanov, tsaṭanáwán, tsaṭanomut, tsaṭanáwih.

Tsáṭawăr, *n. m.* the smallest, lightest and swiftest of all the boats used on the Kashmir lakes. It is so light and small that it is not at all endangered by the prevalent wind-storms which are often very violent on the Wulur and other lakes. It has but one or two boatmen in it.

Tsaṭawun, *n. m.* a cutter.

Tsátsa, *n. m.* a village where paper is made. It is situated in the Phák pargana.

Tsaṭun, *v. t.* to cut, to gather (grapes), to clean (grain), to tear, tsuṭ, tsaṭán, tsuṭmut, tsaṭih.

Tsáuḍ, *n.* a large earthenware vessel for milk.

Tsauk, *adj.* sour, acid.

Tsáúl, *adj.* escaped.

Tsaur, *adv.* more, much.

Tsauṭ, *adj.* torn, little, short.

Tsauṭ karun, *v. t.* to shorten.

Tsáwij, *n. f.* goat.

Tsáwiji-mongir, *n. f.* kid.

Tsáwiji-mongur, *n. m.* kid.

Tsáwil-máz, *n. m.* goat's flesh.

Tsawuh, *adj.* twenty-four.

Tsáwúl, *n. m.* goat.

Tsáya, *n. m.* shadow.

Tsĕḍ, *n. f.* patience.

Tseda, *n. m.* patience, endurance.

Tsĕḍ karinyi, *v. i.* to be patient.

Tsĕí, the emphasised form of tsih.

Tsĕl, *n. m.* shampooing, squeezing.

Tsenawain dinyi, *v. t.* to point out, to shew.

Tsenta, *n. m.* the funeral pyre on which a Hindu corpse is burned to ashes.

Tsenṭh, *n. f.* the noise of wind passing backwards.

Tsepan *n. m.* protection.

Tser, *n. f.* lateness, delay.

Tser, *n. f.* apricot.

Tser, *n. m.* Pinus excelsa.

Tséra, *n. m.* apricot. Large quantities of dried apricots are imported into Kashmir from Ladák. The following are the different varieties of apricot growing in Kashmir: Boṭa tsera, tsoki tsera, modari tsera, ṭeṭha tsera, khas tsera, gordol.

Tserakul, *n. m.* apricot tree.

Tserawinyi, *n. m.* a village in the Loláb pargana.

Tseta karun (nashândan), *v. t.* to extinguish.

Tséṭanáwun, *v. t.* to cause to pulverize; tseṭanov, tséṭanáwán, tseṭauomut, tseṭanáwih.

Tsetas, *n. f.* remembrance, recollection.

Tsetas pyinyi (yád paṛná), *v. i.* to remember, to recollect.

Tsetas tháwinyi, *v. t.* to remember, to recollect.

Tsetas yinyi (yád áná), *v. i.* to remember, to recollect.

Tseṭun (kuftan), *v. t.* to crush, to pound, to mince; tsyúṭun, tseṭán, tsyúṭmut, tseṭih.

Tsháe, *n.f.* shadow.

Tshál, *n.f.* running.

Tshalarawan, *n. m.* temptation.

Tshánḍun (ḍhúnḍhna), *v. t.* to search for, to search.

Tshar, *n. f.* a small basket which is generally carried on the head.

Tshauṭ, *adj.* short, small.

Tsháwúl, *n. m.* goat.

Tsháwij, *n.f.* goat.

Tshenun, *v. i.* to be torn, to break (of thread); tshun, tshenán, tshunmut, tshĕnih.

Tshetah karun, *v. t.* to extinguish.

Tshóg, *n. m.* the arrangement of the hair, as worn by the Kashmírí women.

Tshŏpah, *n.f.* silence.

Tshŏpah karinyi, *v. i.* to keep silence.

Tshunun, *v. t.* to cast, to throw.

Tshur, *adj.* empty.

Ṭshuṭ, *n. m.* remainder.

Tshuṭ, *adj.* low.

Tshuṭun (tshuṭ), *v. i.* to be low.

Tsih, *pron.* to thee.

Tsihun, *v. t.* to suck; tsuhun, tsihán, tsuhmut, tsihih.

Tsintabal, *n. m.* funeral pile, place of funeral pile.

Tsinya, *n. m.* charcoal.

Tsinyaráwun, *v. t.* to point out, to shew.

Tsinyin, *n.f.* coal.

Tsipun, *v. i.* to hide.

Tsiran, *n.f.* hole.

Tsíri, *n. f.* bird.

Tsirir, *n. f.* abundance.

Tsitar, *n. m.* the first month of the Hindu year, corresponding to our March, as to time.

Tsithar, *n. f.* March (=Rabi-u-l-awwal, the third month of the Mussulman year).

Tsŏchar, *n. m.* shortness.

Tsŏdah, *adj.* fourteen.

Tsŏdãhyum, *adj.* fourteenth.

Tsog, *n. m.* lock of hair on top of Hindu's head.

Tsŏhaiṭhyum, *adj.* sixty-fourth.

Tsŏhéṭh, *adj.* sixty-four.

Tsŏk bamtsúnṭ, see 'Bamtsúnṭ.'

Tsŏk dáṅ, see 'Dáṅ.'

Tsokalaḍar, *n. m.* a vegetable found on the mountains.

Tsŏka tsúnṭ, see 'Tsúnt.'

Tsŏker, *n. m.* acidity.

Tsŏki-tsera, *n. m.* a species of apricot.

Tsŏk ṭánj, see 'Ṭánj.'

Tsŏkun, *v. i.* to be acid.

Tsŏl, *n.f.* fire place, hearth.

Tsombun, *v. t.* to bore; tsúmb, tsombán, tsúmbmut, tsombih.

Tsomor, *n. m.* cobbler.

Tsŏn (chároṅ) four.

Tsong, *n. m.* lamp.

Tsopah, *adj.* dumb.

Tsŏpah, *n. f.* silence.

Tsŏpah karinyi, *v. i.* to keep silence.

Tsor, *adj.* four.

Tsŏr, *adv.* very.

Tsoras, *n. f.* wedge (as for splitting wood).

Tsorats, *n. f.* wedge.

Tsorit, *n. m.* essence.

Tsor karanwol, *n. m.* conqueror.

Tsŏruí, *adv.* very.

Tsorúí, *adj.* whole.

Tsor karun, *v. t.* to conquer.

Tsoryishít, *adj.* eighty-four.

Tsoryum (*m.*) tsoryim (*f.*) ord, *adj.* fourth.

Tsósatat, *adj.* seventy-four.

Tsŏt, *n. m.* the Ladákí name for Mazet, which see.

Tsot, *n. f.* pudendum muliebre.

Ťsoṭ, *n. m.* ash-pit.

Tsŏṭ, *n. f.* bread, loaf.

Tsot, *n. m.* anus.

Tsoṭa, *n. m.* a club. This is the word used in Srínagar.

Tsóts, *n. m.* adultery.

Tsóts karun, *v. i.* to commit adultery.

Tsŏwanzah, *adj.* fifty-four.

Tsŏwanzãhyum, *adj.* fifty-fourth.

Tsŏwuh, *adj.* twenty-four.

Tsŏwuhyum, *adj.* twenty-fourth.

Tsŏyitãjih, *adj.* forty-four.

Tsŏyitãjihyum, *adj.* forty-fourth.

Tsŏyitràh, *adj.* thirty-four.

Tsŏyitràhyum, *adj.* thirty-fourth.

Tsráṭ, *n. f.* trembling.

Tsraṭ dyun, *v. t.* to fret, see 'Dyun.'

Tsrauṭ, *n. f.* potter's wheel.

Tsról, *n. m.* jailer, the ancient name for the functionary called Mahalladar, which see.

Tsruṭ, *n. m.* potter's wheel.

Tsuḍ, *n. m.* a middle sized water vessel.

Tsugul, *n. m.* a village in the Machipor pargana.

Tsuh, *pron.* thou.

Tsúheṭ, *adj.* sixty-four.

Tsushít, *adj.* eighty-four.

Tsushítyum, *adj.* eighty-fourth.

Tsuhun, *v. t.* to taste.

Tsuk, *adj.* acid.

Tsún (reza), *adj.* broken finely.

Tsúń, *n. f.* filings, gold-filings, Sonatsúń.

Tsunamat, *adj.* ninety-four.

Tsunamatyum, *adj.* ninety-fourth.

Tsunanáwun, *v. t.* to clothe another, to cause to be clothed.

Tsúns or tsŏns, *n. f.* female slave. In olden times the Kashmírí kings gave two or three tsúns, or female slaves to their daughters at marriage, to be their maids for life.

Tsúnṭ, *n. m.* apple. The following are the numerous varieties of apple growing in Kashmir: Ambir tsúnṭ (large and red), Kuduseri tsúnṭ (small and good), Modur tsúnṭ (small and sweet), Tsŏka tsúnṭ (sour and small), Ṭeṭha Shakir tsúnṭ (very unpalatable), Markhambiri tsúnṭ (large).

Tsúnṭ-kul, *n. m.* apple tree.

Tsúnú, *n. m.* Amygdalus Persica (Peach).

Tsunun, *n. m.* ankle.

Tsunun, *v. t.* to pour, to put on, to clothe one's self, to throw.

Tsunun, *n. m.* peach. There are two varieties of the peach in Kashmir, the sweet (Mŏdur), and the sour (tyut).

Tsúp, *n. m.* bite.

Tsúp hyun, *v. t.* to bite; see 'Hyun.'

Tsur, *n. f.* hen sparrow.

Tsúr, *n. m.* Xanthium strumarium.

Tsur, *adj.* abundant, superfluous.

Tsúré, *n. m.* burglar, thief.

Tsúri, *n. f.* theft.

Tsúrih, *adv.* furtively, stealthily.

Tsur, *adv.* furtively.

Tsúri karinyi, *v. t.* to steal.

Tsúri ninyi, *v. t.* to steal.

Tsúryum *adj.* fourth.

Tsŭsatat, *adj.* seventy-four.

Tsusatatyum, *adj.* seventy-fourth.

Tsuṭ, *n. f.* loaf, bread.

Tsúṭ, *n. m.* a chief.

Tsut, *n. f.* podex (kún).

Tsuṭ, *adj.* cut,

Tsút, *adj.* little, light.

Tsuts dúṅ, see 'Dúṅ.'

Tsyun, *n. m.* pillar.

Túbra, *n. m.* a leathern bag out of which horses eat their fodder.

Túda, *n. m.* granary.

Túfán, *n. m.* storm.

Tuh, *n. m.* chaff of rice.

Tuhund, gen. case of 2nd. pron. of thee, thy, thine.

Túj, *n. f.* a long wooden spike on which the shawl-wool-thread is wound of which the famous Kashmir shawls are made.

Tuj, *n. f.* clod.

Tújigur, *n. f.* a maker of the túj, which see.

Ṭuk, *n. m.* cutting.

Ṭukanáwun, *v. t.* to make to run; ṭukanowun, ṭukanáwán, ṭukanomut, ṭukanáwih.

Ṭukar, *n. m* part.

Ṭúkin, *n. m.* a club used in playing hockey on horseback.

Ṭukra, *n. m.* bit, piece.

Tukun, *v. i.* to run; ṭuk, ṭukán, ṭukmut, ṭukih.

Túl, *n. m.* mulberry. The mulberry grows very abundantly in Kashmir. There are at least six varieties of mulberry tree in the valley, viz. Boṭa túl, the Ladák mulberry, Shah túl, the fruit of which is large, acid, and deliciously flavoured, Chhata túl, Bedána tul, Tsári túl, Krihun túl, which is said not to be edible: Thaj túl. The silk worm, therefore, has abundance of its proper food, and gives a good return for it in an excellent silk. During the mulberry season the Kashmírís eat largely of the fruit, of which they are very fond.

Túl, *n. m.* measure.

Túl, *n. m.* weight.

Tul, *n. f.* collyrium.

Túl, *adj.* cold.

Tulakatar, *n. m.* ice on surface of water.

Tulakul, *n. m.* mulberry tree. There are the following varieties; Shah Tulakul, Bedana Tulakul, Tsari Tulakul, Boṭa Tulakul, Chhata Tulakul, Thaj Tulakul. This last variety of mulberry is said to be fruitless. The silk produced by the worms that feed on its leaves is said to be the finest in the valley.

Túlakutur, *n. m.* ice.

Tulamul, *n. m.* a village and a small lake about ten miles to the north of Srínagar. There is also a small island called Ráginyá, where a Hindu festival is held in the month of May.

Tulanáwun, *v. t.* to cause to lift; tulanov, tulanáwán, tulanómut, tulanáwih.

Tular, *n. f.* wasp.

Tulatál karinyi, *v. t.* to harass.

Tulun, (uṭháná), *v. t.* to raise, to lift, to exalt, to excite, to support, (pain, etc.) to hold up, to sustain, to lift; tul, tulán, tulmut, tulih.

Tumul (Cháwal), *n. m.* rice without the husks.

Tumul, *n. m.* uncooked rice.

Tumla-óṭ, *n. m.* rice-flour.

Tún, *n. m.* novel.

Tun, *adj.* slender, thin, lean.

Ṭúng, *n. m.* the cry of the jackal.

Túng, *n. m.* mountain pass.

Túng, *n. m.* yew tree (Taxus paccata, Picea Webbiana). See 'Birre.'

Ṭúnga, *n. m.* sob.

Tungarú, *n. m.* small pick-axe, the iron part of which is placed at an angle of forty-five to the wooden handle.

Tungul, *n. m.* a live coal.

Túní, *n. m.* the Toon tree (Cedrela Toona).

Tun-kóḍ, *n. m.* cerebellum.

Túr (tesha), *n. f.* adze, axe.

Túr, *n. f.* cold.

Túr, *n. f.* fever.

Ṭúr, *n. m.* the dish out of which the Hindu women eat: it is round, deep, and brazen.

Turela, *n. m.* one of the Cucurbitaciæ.

Turjuma, *n. m.* translation.

Turjuma karun, *v. t.* to translate.

Turun, *adj.* frigid, cold, cool.

Ṭuṭ, *adj.* bitter.

Tut, *adv.* there.

Tút, *n. m.* mulberry.

Tut, *adj.* warm.

Ṭuṭ, *n. m.* seeds of cotton.

Tutám, *conj.* then. Tutám is correlative of Yutám.

Ṭuṭh, *adj.* bitter.

Tútú, *n. m.* noise in the ears.

Tutut, *adv.* there.

Ṭyuk, *n. m.* mark on the forehead of a Hindu. The colour varies: it is generally yellow or red.

Tyúr, *n. m.* a flock of sheep.

Ṭyuṭ, *adj.* bitter.

Tyút, *adj.* so many, so much. This is the correlative of yút.

Tyuth, *adj.* such.

Tyuth, *adv.* so.

U.

U: there are three varieties of U. There is U̇ which is formed far down the throat; there is U, which is pronounced as in the English word "put"; and there is Ú which is pronounced as in the English word "rule."

Uḍar, *n. m.* a plateau. This word answers to the Persian word "karewah."

Udaráwun, *v. t.* to wet; udrowun, udaráwán, udromut, udaráwih.

Udur, *n. m.* otter, which is found pretty numerously about the ruins and wooden piers of the bridges in Kashmir.

Uktsor, *n. m.* fireplace.

Umar, *n. m.* age, lifetime. What is his age? umar kya chhus?

Umr, *n. m.* age, lifetime.

Ummed, *n. f.* hope.

Ummedrúst, *adj.* desperate.

Ummed tháwinyi (ummed dáshtan), *v. t.* to expect, to hope.

Ungàj, *n. f.* finger, toe.

Ungustaiń, *adv.* hitherto.

Unṭ, *n. m.* camel. There are

said to be about 2000 camels in the valley, all of which belong to His Highness the Maharaja. I doubt the correctness of this large number. Guláb Singh is said to have introduced them into the valley.

Untham is made up of unut and mih.

Unṭín, *n. f.* she-camel.

Upháún, *n. m.* bird.

Ur, *adj.* healthy, in good health.

Urí, *n. m.* Cæsalpinia sepiaria.

Us-gagar, *n. m.* flying fox, or flying squirrel.

Ush, *n. m.* tears. Many tears flow, ush seṭha pakán.

Ush tráwun, *v. i.* to weep, see 'Tráwun.'

Usmàn, *n. m.* a proper name.

Ushna, *n. m.* Barrera ushna.

Ustád, *n. m.* teacher, especially of the shawl-weaving apprentices. There are 780 ustáds, or overseers, in Kashmir. They are nearly always Mussulmans.

Ustakhán, *n. m.* bone.

Ustukhudus, *n. m.* Prunella.

Utáwul, *n. m.* fickleness of disposition.

Uzmal, *n. m.* lightning.

Uzr, *n. m.* excuse.

V.

V: this letter is pronounced as in English.

Vái, *interj.* oh!

Vãìs, *n. f.* age.

Vãr, *adj.* spiteful.

Varshun, *n. m.* rain.

Vasa, *n. m.* Adhatoda vasica.

Vatalur, *n. m.* inn.

Vauwun, *v. t.* to sow.

Věchhar, *n. m.* fatness.

Vediva, *n. f.* widow.

Vehatir, *n. m.* neighbourhood.

Véhí, *n. m.* a pargana of Maráz.

Vélah, *n. m.* time, age (not of individual).

Vemán, *n. m.* a board, see 'Paṭh.'

Venna, *prep.* without.

Verái, *prep.* without.

Vernág, *n. m.* a celebrated fountain at a little distance from Shahbad, in the southern end of the valley. The word is made up of Ver, or Wer, the ancient name of the pargana in which the fountain it located, and nág, a fountain. In the year 1619, the Mogul Emperor, Jehán Gír, caused this beautiful fountain to be enclosed with a wall.

Vĕs, *n. f.* a female friend, a woman's female confidant.

Vesarun (afsardan), *v. i.* to fade.

Véshih, *prep.* upon.

Vĕṭh, *n. m.* the Jhelum river, in its course in Kashmir. The Hindu priests call it Vedasta. This is the ancient classical Hydaspes. According to the Hindus of the valley, the Vĕṭh has four sources, or streams, which go to form it. They are: (1) the Vishau, which rises in the Kaisaring Kuṭhar, and flows near to Shupiyan; (2) the Rimiyárá, which also flows from the south-east; (3) the Lidar, so called from the colour of its waters, for lidar, in Kashmírí, means yellow. It takes its rises in a lake called Társar, and then flows in a southerly direction; (4) the Arapoth, which takes its rise at Achabal, and flows past Islámabad.

Vetharan, *n. f.* a sack made of grass, and generally used by the poor cultivators of the soil in Kashmir.

Veṭhawóiñ, *n. m.* Jhelum water.

Veṭhráwun, *v. t.* to fatten, to increase; veṭharowun, veṭharáwán, veṭharomut, veṭharáwih.

Veṭhun (fr. vyuṭh), *v. i.* to be fat, to become fat, to increase; veṭheo, veṭhán, veṭheomut, veṭhih.

Vetsanun, *v. t.* to tease out (as wool).

Vetsár, *n. m.* thought, meditation.

Vetsár karun, *v. t.* to fancy, to imagine.

Vetsár Nág, *n. m.* a fountain or spring two kos from Srínagar, towards the north.

Vetsun, *v. i.* to be contained; vyuts, vetsán, vyutsmut, vetsih.

Veva, *n. m.* marriage.

Vevahár, *n. m.* trade.

Veva karun, *v. t.* to marry.

Vidyawán, *n. m.* philosopher.

Vien, *n. m.* Mentha incana and royleana.

Viganí, *n. f.* fairy.

Vih, *n. m.* poison, venom.

Vijibrór, *n. m.* a town some two-and-a-half kos from Islamabad, situated on the river Jhelum. Vijibrór is said to be derived from Viziyapúr, the city of Viziya, whose idol was worshipped here.

Vil, *n. m.* a short space of

time—the word used towards Islamabad.

Vír, *n. m.* white willow (Salix alba). Two varieties of willow grow in the valley: the musk willow, Muska vír, and the Boṭa vír. The weeping willow does not grow in Kashmir. The twigs are used in basket-making, and as tooth-sticks. The native hakims regard a pediluvium of the leaves as very efficacious in cholera. The Hindus of the valley clean their teeth with small twigs of the willow. They also chew them to sweeten their breath, and improve their stomachs. The leaves of the willow are stored up as fodder for oxen, sheep, and goats in the winter-time.

Virám (kaṛí), *n. f.* beam.

Vis, *n. m.* a short space of time. The word in use in Srínagar.

Vishan, *n. m.* a proper name.

Viz, *n. f.* moment of time.

Vrad, *n. m.* old man.

Vreshib, *n. m.* bull.

Vúlr, *n. m.* Verbascum thapsus.

Vyauṭh, *adj.* fat.

Vyendun, *v. t.* to practise; vyendun, vyendán, vyund-mut, vyendih.

Vyĕt, *n. f.* the portion of the river Jhelum within the valley of Kashmir. See 'Vĕṭh.'

Vyúg, *n. m.* a figure or picture drawn on the ground with chalk or flour, on which the newly married couple are seated the morning after their marriage.

Vyuṭ, *adj.* swift, fat, gross, coarse.

Vyuṭh, *adj.* fat.

W.

W: this letter is pronounced as in English.

Wach, *n. m.* chest, breast.

Wachakányi, *n. f.* hypochon-drium.

Wachh, *n. m.* breast.

Wád, *n. m.* answer.

Wáḍ, *n. m.* hedge; word in use towards Islamabad.

Wã̄ḍ, *n. m.* garden plot. The form of the word wã̄r, in use towards Islamabad.

Wadam, or wadĕm, *n. m.* exertion.

Wadás, *n. m.* grief.

Wadanáwun, *v. t.* to make to weep.

Wadawun, *adj.* lamenting, weeping, bewailing.

Wadhyug, *n. m.* exertion, effort.

Wadhyug karun, *v. i.* to endeavour.

Wádí, *n. f.* plain.

Wadun, *v. i.* to sob, to weep, to mourn; wod, wadán, wodmut, wadih.

Waḍur, *n. m.* belly, abdomen.

Wádwád karun, *v. t.* to answer.

Wadyúg, *n. m.* exertion.

Wãe, wãe! *interj.* alas!

Wafádár, *adj.* faithful, trustworthy.

Wafádárí, *n. f.* fidelity.

Wafá karanwol, *adj.* faithful.

Wag, *n. f.* tether, bridle, reins.

Wagívgur, *n. m.* mat-weaver.

Wagivigur, *n. m.* mat-maker, or weaver.

Wagivwonanwol, *n. m.* mat-weaver.

Wagú, *n. m.* matting (chaṭáí). This is the word in use in Srínagar.

Wagun, *v. i.* to flow.

Wágúr, *n. m.* a village in the Kruhin pargana.

Wáhab, *n. m.* a proper name.

Wáhaba, *n. m.* a proper name.

Wahal, *n. m.* mistletoe (Viscum album).

Waharáwun, *v. t.* to spread (phailáná).

Wáharun, *v. t.* to open.

Wahek, *n. f.* April. It corresponds to the Rabí'-u-l-Ákhir, the fourth month of the Mussulman year.

Wahrát, *n. f.* rainy season.

Wahwaila, *n. m.* lamentation.

Wáhyik, *n. m.* the second month of the Hindu year, and corresponding to our month of April.

Waid, *n. m.* physician.

Waiharát, *n. f.* rainy season.

Wáímats zamín, *n. m.* arable land.

Wainádat, *n. m.* said to have been one of the ancient kings of Kashmir.

Wair, *n. m.* enmity.

Wàir, *n. f.* a dish composed of rice, fat, and seasoning.

Wairán, *adj.* ruined.

Wairánah, *adj.* desolate.

Wairán karun, *v. t.* to desolate, to ruin.

Wáj, *n. f.* a stoned ring.

Wãj, *n. f.* ring.

Wáj, *n. f.* a proper name.

Wajud, *n. f.* vulva.

Wajun, *v. i.* to ring, to sound.

Wakána, *n. m.* reason.

Wakíl, *n. m.* deputy, substitute.

Wãkrisar, *n. m.* a lake near to Káwapor, the city of crows: in it grows the Nelumbium, or Lotus.

Wakt, *n. m.* time.

Wál, *n. f.* a hole (as that of a serpent).

Wál, *n. m.* hair.

Wála, *n. m.* See 'Dálá.'

Walád, *n. m.* son.

Walanáwun (poshanídan), to dress another, or cause another to dress, to cause to clothe; walanáo, walanáwán, walanomut, walanáwih.

Walás karun, *v. t.* to flatter.

Walí, *conj.* nevertheless, but then.

Walí, *n. m.* a proper name.

Walí Jú, *n. m.* a proper name.

Wãlinj, *n. f.* heart.

Waló, *interj.* come!

Wálraz, *n. m.* See 'Kí.'

Walun, *v. t.* to put on one's own clothes, to bind, to entangle, to wrap up, to roll up in something, to cover, to clothe; wol, walán, wolmut, walih.

Wálun, *v. t.* to bring down, to strip off, to ruin, to take off, to strip; wol, wálán, wolmut, wálih.

Walwal, *adv.* quickly.

Wámarí, *n. m.* a proper name.

Wamáwo, *n. m.* the name of the Kashmírí alphabet, so called from the name of the first letter in it.

Wámik, *n. m.* a proper name.

Wán, *n. m.* shop, workshop.

Wan, *n. m.* forest.

Wánawol, *n. m.* shopkeeper.

Wanda, *n. m.* heart, disposition, winter.

Wandah, *n. m.* winter.

Wandakhosh, *adj.* cheerful, happy, comfortable.

Wandakhosh karun (dilshad kardan), *v. t.* to comfort.

Wandakumal, *adj.* gentle.

Wanda-narm, *adj.* kind.

Wandaprasand karun, *v. t.* to rejoice, to gladden.

Wandaprasand sapadun, *v. i.* to rejoice, to be glad.

Wanda-rúdmut, *adj.* disgusted.

Wándelí, *n. f.* a kind of rush, used by merchants for tying up small parcels.

Wanduh, *n. m.* winter.

Wanduk dokh, *n. m.* remorse.

Wándúr, *n. m.* bear.

Wándur, *n. m.* monkey.

Wángat, *n. m.* a village in the Lãr pargana. At a distance of some three or four miles, there is a lake called Náranág, near to which there are several temple ruins of very ancient date. Venomous serpents are said to be numerous in the vicinity.

Wángún, *n. m.* the egg-plant, which is dried and eaten when winter has come. The Kashmírís are very successful in preserving fruit and vegetables for future use.

Wánk, *n. m.* a curl.

Wánk, *n. f.* long plaited hair hanging down behind, worn by women.

Wánkapan, *n. m.* the name of the peculiar arrangement of the hair, as worn by the Kashmírí women.

Wanmat, *n. m.* madman.

Wanmath, *adj.* furious.

Wãṅs, *n. f.* age.

Wantipór, *n. m.* a village of the Wular pargana. In ancient times, this was the capital of Wainádat, after whom, no doubt, the city was called Wainádatpúr, which has been shortened into Wantipór.

Wãnts, *n. f.* curse, partiality.

Wanun (kahná, bolná), *v. t.* to say, to speak, to explain, to tell; wunun, wanán, wunmut, wanih.

Wanut, *adj.* tall.

Wányain, *n. f.* shopkeeper's wife.

Wányi, *n. m.* shopkeeper.

Wányi, *n. f.* sound, proverb.

Wáo, *n. m.* air, wind, a strong wind, a wind-storm on the lakes.

Wapáí, *n. f.* cure.

Wapáí karinyi, *v. t.* to cure.

Wãr, *n. m.* garden.

Wãr, *n. f.* a plot of kitchen garden.

Wár, *n. m.* hedge.

Wãr, *n. m.* earthenware loṭa, or water-vessel.

Wárah, *adv.* thoroughly, excellently (bakhúbí), attentively, in an excellent manner, skilfully.

Waráí, *prep.* except. Eat every thing except salt, sãrí chiz khyun nun wará,í.

Warakúr, *n. f.* a daughter by husband's first wife.

Waramúl, *n. m.* native name of Báramúla, a town situated at the west-end of the valley. See 'Báramúla.'

Warawara, *adv.* slowly.

Warch, *n. m.* Acorus calamus.

Warchak, *n. m.* the zodiac sign Scorpio.

Warísh, *n. f.* Taurus (zodiac sign).

Warm, *n. m.* swelling.

Warshá, *n. m.* rainy season.

Warshun, *n. m.* rest, rain.

Waruk, *n. m.* page of a book.

Wáryin, *n. f.* midwife.

Was, *n. m.* marrow of bones, brain.

Wásak Nág, *n. m.* a fountain in the Divisar pargana.

Wasawun, *n. m.* a descender.

Washán, *n. m.* Adiantum caudatum, venustum.

Wasl, *n. m.* meeting, interview.

Wasta, *n. m.* a kind of vegetable.

Wasúl, *n. m.* arrival.

Wasun, *v. i.* to descend, to come down; wuth, wasán, wuthmut, wasih.

Waswã, *n. m.* surprise.

Waswas, *n. m.* sorrow.

Waswa tráwun, *v. t.* to surprise.

Wat, *n. f.* way, road, path, method.

Watahávwuk, *n. m.* guard, guide, conductor.

Watalar, *n. m.* caravansary, inn.

Wáṭamúj, *n. f.* a species of radish.

Watan, *n. m.* native country.

Wátanáwun, *v. t.* to convey, to deliver, to cause to arrive; wátanov, wátanáwán, wátanomut, wátanáwih.

Wátanáwuwun, *n. m.* conveyer.

Wátanáwuwun, *adj.* conveying.

Wata sámána, *n. m.* travelling expenses.

Wath, *n. f.* way, journey.

Wàthar, *n. m.* leaf.

Watharun, *n. m.* a carpet.

Watharawun, *v. t.* to spread, as a carpet (bichháná); wathur, watharán, wuthurmur, watharih.

Watharáwun, *v. t.* to spread; wàtharowun, watharáwán, wàtharomut, watharáwih.

Wat háwinyi, *v. t.* to conduct.

Wathir, *n. m.* a blade, leaf.

Wáṭh-sapadun, *v. i.* to cling.

Wathun, *v. i*, to stand; woth, wathán, wothmut, wathih.

Watiráwarun, *v. t.* to mislead; ráwurun, ráwarán, ráwurmut, ráwarih.

Watirust, *adj.* impassable.

Wat-phúta, *n. m.* Saxifraga ligulata.

Watsir, *n. f.* calf.

Wattúr, *n. m.* north.

Wátul, *n. m.* a sweeper, a mihtar. The sweepers are a very low class in Kashmir, as every where else in India, and are said to sell their daughters to be prostitutes. The Wátul has been called the gipsy of Kashmir. He has no caste, and is generally most degraded. Has the Wáṭul of Kashmir any relation to the gipsies of other lands?

Wátun, *v. i.* to arrive at, or reach; wot, wátán, wotmut, wátih.

Waṭun, *v. t.* to restrain, to close (of the eyes and mouth), to fold; wuṭun, waṭán, wuṭmut, waṭih. Close the eye, àch waṭ. Close the mouth, ãs waṭ.

Wáúr, *n. m.* weaver.

Waut, *n. m.* the groundfloor of a house, where the tenants live in the winter, for warmth's sake.

Wauts, *n. f.* pincers.

Wauts, *n. m.* forceps.

Wáwamál, *n. m.* sail. The boats on the Kashmir lakes and rivers have no sails. They are either towed along, or are propelled by means of paddles.

Wáwat, *n. m.* borax.

Wawun, *v. t.* to plant, to sow, to strew; wau, wawán, womut, wawih.

Wãwur, *n. m.* weaver, either of cotton or wool. The weavers in the valley are generally Mussulmans, and are the most miserable and despised class of the population.

Wáwura, *n. m.* a village in the Wular pargana.

Wáyí, *n. m.* wind.

Wáyun, *v. t.* to make to go, to ring, to sound, to plough, to play upon an instrument; woyun, wáyán, woimut, wáyih.

Wáza, *n. m.* cook.

Wazagar, *n. m.* cooking-house.

Wazají trela, see 'Trela.'

Wazan, *n. m.* measure.

Wazanáwun, *v. t.* to wet; wazanowun, wazanáwán, wazanomut, wazanáwih.

Wazír, *n. m.* minister.

Wazírí, *n. m.* counsellór.

Wazn, *n. m.* weight.

Wazra, *n. m.* a proper name.

Wazul, *adj.* red.

Wazum, *n. m.* loan.

Wazum dyun, *v. t.* to lend.

Wazum hyun, *v. t.* to borrow.

Wazum tháwun, *v. t.* to owe.

Wazumwól, *n. m.* debtor.

Wazun, *n. m.* debt.

Wazun, *v. i.* to ring, to sound (bajná).

Wazun, *v. t.* to lend.

Wazun hinawol, *n. m.* debtor.

We, or Wenat, *n. m.* the shaking palsy.

Wenath, *n. m.* Paralysis agitans.

Wens, *n. m.* age, lifetime.

Weri, *n. m.* year.

Wiharát, *n. f.* rainy season.

Wínrí, *n. f.* Corylus colurna.

Wit, *n. m.* river.

Wŏd, *n. f.* crown of head.

Wodás, *n. m.* sorrow.

Wódín, *n. f.* the marriage veil, which is made of finer materials than the ordinary veil (púts).

Wŏdur, *n. m.* stomach.

Wŏga, *n. m.* a window or opening on the roof of a house.

Wógun, *adj.* shallow.

Wohau, *n. m.* curse.

Wŏhawun, *v. t.* to curse.

Wóiṅ, the form which 'poin' (water) takes in composition.

Wŏiṅ, *n. m.* oilman, shopkeeper, a eulogistic hymn, sung at the death of a Panḍit or Panḍitání, gentleman, a noble, a grocer.

Woin, *adv.* now.

Wokhajár, *n. m.* plot.

Wokhajár karun, *v. t.* to plot.

Wokhij, *n. f.* a small mortar.

Wŏkhul, *n. m.* mortar, a large, round stone trough, in which woollen garments are washed.

Wŏlo, *exclam.* come!

Wŏlun, *v. t.* to bind,

Wolyómut, *adj.* drunk.

Wónṭ dúṅ, see 'Dúṅ.'

Wónun, *n. m.* woof, short wool.

Wonun (banná), *v. t.* to weave; wún, wonán, wúnmut, wonih.

Wŏpáí, *n. f.* remedy, cure.

Wŏpar, *n. m.* foreigner, stranger.

Wŏpar, *adj.* different, jealous.

Wopúdáwun, *v. t.* to create; wopúdov, wopúdáwán, wopúdómut, wopúdáwih. This word is said to be peculiar to the mountainous districts remote from Sirinagar. The expression current in the capital is Paida karun.

Worun, *v. i.* to bark; wúr, worán, wúrmut, worih.

Wosh, *interj.* oh!

Wŏsh, *n. m.* grief, sigh.

Wŏsh kaḍun, *v. i.* to sigh.

Wŏsta, *n. m.* teacher.

Wosta, *adj.* skilful.

Woṭ, *n. f.* leap.

Wotam, *adj.* propitious.

Wŏth, *n. m.* leap.

Wŏthun, *v. i.* to blow (of the wind); wauth, wŏthán, wauthmut, wŏthih.

Wŏthun (uṭhná), *v. i.* to rise (as from a bed); wuth, wŏthán, wuthmut, wothih.

Wŏṭ, láyinyi, *v. i.* to leap; wŏṭ láyin, wŏṭ láyán, wŏṭ láimits, wŏṭ láyih.

Wŏttar, *n. m.* answer.

Wótun, *v. i.* to rise.

Wŏtur, *n. m.* north.

Wówúr, *n. m.* a weaver of cotton and coarse woollen cloth, see 'Wãwur': spider. This word properly means weaver.

Wozanáwun, *v. t.* to waken, to rouse up.

Wuch, *n. m.* sight.

Wuchhun, *n. m.* eyesight.

Wuchhun, (dekhná) *v. t.* to see, to look, to behold; wuchh, wuchhán, wuchhmut, wuchhih.

Wuḍán, *adj.* flying.

Wuḍanáwun, *v. t.* to make to fly; wuḍanowun, wuḍanáwán, wuḍanomut, wuḍanáwih.

Wuḍar, *n. m.* plain, a plateau raised a little above the level of the valley. These plateaus are numerous, and point to the fact of their being of aqueous origin. In Persian the corresponding word is Karewah. The following are the great plains of Kashmir: Painpur, Báwun, Daḍun, Dámdár. See 'Karewah.'

Wuḍun (uṛná), *v. i.* to fly; wuḍeo, wuḍán, wuḍmut, wuḍih.

Wuh, *adj.* twenty.

Wuhur, *adj.* of so many years. The word 'wuhur' corresponds exactly to the word 'Sála' in Persian.

Wuhyum, *adj.* twentieth.

Wúin, *adv.* immediately.

Wúinkin, *adv.* now.

Wuinkinas, *adv.* now.

Wúlag Dányí: see 'Dányí.'

Wular, *n. m.* a pargana of Maráz.

Wular Ráza, *n. m.* the largest lake in the valley of Kashmir; hence it has received the name of Ráza, or prince, by way of pre-eminence. It is about twelve miles long by nine in breadth.

Wúmpúr, *n. m.* a village in the Dúns pargana.

Wunar, *n. m.* mist.

Wunir, *n. m.* mist.

Wúnṭ, *n. m.* camel. Camels enter the valley of Kashmir by the Banihal route, which is reserved by His Highness the Maharaja for himself.

Wúntinyi, *n. f.* camel.

Wunyi, *adv.* still, now.

Wunyuk tám, or munyuk támat, *adv.* till now.

Wuphanáwun, *v. t.* to make to fly; wuphanowun, wuphanáwán, wuphanomut, wuphanáwih.

Wuphun, *v. i.* to fly; wupheo, wuphán, wuphmut, wuphih.

Wurun, *n. m.* bed-clothes,

Wúsawás, *n. m.* perspiration.

Wushka, *n. m.* oats, barley. Not eaten by the Hindu inhabitants of the valley except in times of scarcity, but largely eaten by the Mussulman Kashmiris.

Wushnáwun, *v. t.* to warm, or make warm.

Wushnun, *v. i.* to become warm, to be warm.

Wushun, *adj.* warm, hot.

Wusuṭ, *adj.* loose.

Wuṭ, *n. m.* lip.

Wutar, *n. m.* a pargana in the Kamráz division of the valley.

Wuṭh, *n. m.* lip.

Wuṭhan, *n. f.* screw.

Wuṭhin, *n. f.* a twist, coil.

Wuthun, *v. i.* to rise up.

Wuṭhun (pechídan), *v. t.* to twist, to coil, to entangle; wuṭhun, wuṭhán, wuthmut, wuṭhih.

Wútín, *adj.* supine.

Wúts, *n. m.* calf.

Wútsagagur, *n. m.* flying fox.

Wutsah-gagur, *n. m.* the flying fox. (literally, the swift rat).

Wutsai, *n. f.* necessity.

Wuzamal, *n. f.* flash.

Wuzmal, *n. m.* lightning.

Wuzmala, *n. m.* lightning.

Wuzun, *v. i.* to be awake.

Y.

Y: this letter is pronounced as in English.

Yá, *conj.* or.

Yach, *n. m.* one of the parganas or inferior divisions of Maráz. The rice produced in Yach is said to be the finest in the valley.

Yach, *adj.* wicked, bad, hideous, ugly, dissolute, depraved.

Yachh, *n. m.* hyena.

Yachhar, *n. m.* badness, evil, depravity.

Yachhí, *n. f.* evil.

Yach karun, *v. t.* to disable.

Yach kom karawun, *n. m.* evil doer.

Yach-rúp, *adj.* deformed.

Yach-shakl, *adj.* deformed.

Yãḍ, *n. m.* fir tree. This is the form of the word yãr in use towards Islamabád where there is a great tendency to change r into ḍ as they do towards Báramúla also.

Yaḍ, *n. f.* stomach, abdomen, belly.

Yàd, *conj.* athough.

Yaḍabàuḍ, *adj.* big-bellied.

Yadante, *conj.* although.

Yadat, *n. f.* a proper name.

Yaḍ-barit, *adj.* full (as to food).

Yád, *n. m.* memory, remembrance.

Yád karun, *v. t.* to remember.

Yád pyun, *v. i.* to remember.

Yád tháwun, *v. t.* to remember.

Yád yun, *v. i.* to remember.

Yahya, *n. m.* John.

Yain (púd), *n. f.* warp.

Yain yerinyi, *v. t.* to prepare the warp.

Yáj, *n. f.* biscuit.

Yakbál, *n. m.* a proper name.

Yakh, *n. m.* ice, formed from snow.

Yakjazámut, *adj.* equal in age.

Yakrah, *adv.* in the east.

Yaksán, *adj.* same.

Yakúb Khán, *n. m.* a proper name.

Yal, *n. m.* jolting.

Yala, *n. m.* assault.

Yalat, *n. m.* disease.

Yám, *conj.* when.

Yam, *n. m.* angel.

Yaman, *n. m.* Yemen in Arabia.

Yámat, *conj.* when.

Yanai, *adv.* gratis.

Yandan, *n. m.* spinning wheel.

Yandar-tul, *n. m.* the little wheel of the spinning wheel on which the thread being spun is wound.

Yáne, *adv.* that is to say, to wit.

Yang, *n. m.* Assafœtida (Ferula Assafœtida).

Yangar, *n. m.* the charcoal used by goldsmiths and blacksmiths.

Yangtash, *n. m.* Fragaria vesca (Strawberry).

Yangú and yanga, *n. m.* assafœtida. It does not grow in the valley, but is imported from the Punjab. It is eaten by the Hindus, but not by the Mussulmans. The former use it as a condiment.

Yányi, *conj.* when.

Yányit, *conj.* when.

Yáo, *adv.* yesterday.

Yár, *n. m.* companion, friend.

Yār, *n. f.* pine, fir tree.

The Yār is very common on the Himalayas. The most wide spread species of pine is the Pinus longifolia.

In the Vehí pargana is a very extensive pine (yār) forest. The rosin of the pine is applied to wounds; it is called Yāri kilum.

Yáraz, *n. f.* friendship.

Yárbal, *n. m.* quay, landing place, Go to that landing place, Hut yárbalas gatsh.

Yárí, *n. f.* assistance, help, Pinus excelsa.

Yāri kilum, *n. m.* the rosin of the pine.

Yárí karinyi, *v. t.* to relieve, to help, to assist.

Yár sapadun, *v. i.* to befriend, to connive at, to share, to be a party to.

Yat, *adv.* more.

Yátai, *conj.* or.

Yat andar, *adv.* herein.

Yat manz, *adv.* herein.

Yáts *adv.* very, more, much.

Yatsanwol, *adj.* eager.

Yatshá, *n. f.* will.

Yatsha, *n. m.* decision.

Yatshun (chahná), *v. t.* to wish, to desire, to long for; yutsh, yatshán, yutshmut, yatshih.

Yátu, *conj.* except.

Yauwa, *adv.* yesterday.

Yauwah, *n. m.* yesterday.

Yawai (kalhi), *adv.* yesterday.

Yawai (isi waste), *conj.* therefore.

Yazat, *n. m.* honour, reverence.

Yel, *n. f.* command, order.

Yĕn, *n. f.* warp.

Yer, (ειρος) *n. f.* wool.

Yérákón, *n. m.* woollen thread wound round the distaff.

Yero, *n. m.* Pinus excelsa.

Yerun, *v. t.* to sort (as the warp); yírun, yerán, yírmut, yerih.

Yesham, *n. m.* agate.

Yetsa, *n. m.* power, (Hindu God's).

Yetsa, *n. f.* wish. intention.

Yetsha, *n. f.* resolution.

Yetsun, *v. t.* to wish.

Yezár, *n. m.* drawers, the flowing or wide trousers of the Mussulman.

Yí for yi, emphasised.

Yiḍabàuḍ, *n. m.* a glutton.

Yiḍal, *n. m.* a glutton.

Yih, *pron.* this, he (near and present).

Yihánat, *n. f.* abuse, rebuke, contempt.

Yihánat karinyi, *v. t.* to abuse, to rebuke, to contemn.

Yihoi, *pron.* this very.

Yihsán, *n. m.* kindness.

Yihuí, *pron.* this very.

Yihwah, *adv.* yesterday.

Yikawaṭain, *adj.* equal in age.

Yili, *adv.* when.

Yilih (jab), *conj.* when.

Yili tili, *adv.* now and then.

Yim, *plur. m.* of yih.

Yimah, *plur. f.* of yih.

Yímám, *n. m.* priest.

Yimbarzal, *n. m.* the narcissus.

Yimberzal, *n. m.* narcissus.

Yimbirzal Dányí, see 'Dányí.'

Yimih patah, *adv.* since.

Yimi jáí nishi, *adv.* hence.

Yimi khátra, *adv.* therefore.

Yin, *n. m,* fringe.

Yindertul, *n. m.* the part of the spinning wheel corresponding to the dístaff (salai).

Yipor, *adv.* this side.

Yira, *n. m.* bulrush, (Typha angustifolia and T. latifolia).

Yiran, *n. f.* anvil.

Yírun, *v. i.* to float.

Yit and yiti, *adv.* here.

Yitai pãṭ, *adv.* in this manner.

Yiten, *adv.* here.

Yithah pãṭ, *adv.* in this manner, thus.

Yithapãṭ, *adv.* again.

Yithai, *adv.* gratis, gratuitously.

Yithanhyú, *adj.* such.

Yiti, *adv.* here.

Yitih pĕṭhah, *adv.* from here, hence.

Yitit, *adv.* here.

Yits, *adv.* very, more.

Yitsha, *n. f.* desire.

Yúvawun, *adj.* future.

Yiza, *n. m.* nuisance.

Yŏd, *n. m.* war, fight.

Yod karun, *v. t.* to fight, to war.

Yónyi, *n. f.* bowstring; the thick thread going round the the two wheels of the spinning-wheel. The Brahminical thread, consisting of several fine cords, is worn by all the Kashmírí Pandits: it passes from the left shoulder down to the right side.

Yór, *adv.* hither.

Yór (Hindee, chír, pinus longifolia), *n. m.* fir-tree.

Yót, *adv.* only.

Yud, *conj.* if.

Yud for yut, *conj.* that, in order that.

Yúduwane, *conj.* moreover.

Yudwai, *conj.* if.

Yudwanai, *conj.* if.

Yuhus, *adv.* this year.

Yun (áná), *v. i.* to come, to blow (of the wind); áo, yiwán, or íwán, ámut, yiyih.

Yúp, *n. m.* flood, inundation, storm, torrent.

Yúr, *adv.* hither.

Yúri, *adv.* hither.

Yus, *pron.* who.

Yút (tákí), *conj.* that, to, in order that. I have come to bear witness, Boh ámut chhus yut sháhidí dimah; Thou hast come to bear witness, Tsuh ámut chhuk yut sháhidi dikh; We have come to give testimony, Ais ámiti chhih yut sháhidi dimau; You have come to give testimony, Tohi ámiti chhú yut sháhidí diyú; They have come to give testimony, Yim ámiti chhih yut sháhidi din; He came to bear witness of the light, Su gáshas peṭh sháhidi dinih áó.

Yut, *adj.* such.

Yút, *adj.* such as this, so many, so much.

Yut, *adv.* here.

Yutám, *conj.* whilst, while, until.

Yutámat, *conj.* so long as, till when.

Yuth, *conj.* as, that, in order that.

Yúth, *adj.* so much, so, such.

Yuthui hyu, *adv.* thus.

Yuthyu, *adv.* thus.

Yútoi, *adv.* enough.

Yutui, *adj.* so much, enough.

Yutut, *adv.* here, hither.

Z.

Z: this letter is pronounced as in English.

Zaba, *n. m.* killing, slaughter.

Zaba karun, *v. t.* to kill, to destroy.

Zabar, *adj.* good.

Zabar, *adv.* well.

Zabar gatshun, *v. i.* to improve.

Zag Dányí, see 'Dányi.'

Zagat, *n. m.* world.

Zah, *adv.* ever, always.

Záh, *adj.* two.

Zahar, *n. m.* venom, poison.

Záhir, *adj.* evident, visible.

Záhir pãt, *adv.* ostensibly.

Záhir sapadun, *v. i.* to exist.

Zahir karun, *v. t.* to publish.

Zahír, *n. m.* dysentery.

Zahr, *n. m.* poison, venom.

Zainager, *n. m.* a pargana in the Kamráz division of the valley.

Zaiṭ (*f*) *adj.* old, tattered. Said to have no masculine.

Zaitun, *n. m.* olive.

Zak, *n. m.* revenge.

Zakham, *n. m.* scar, wound.

Zakhmakh, *n. m.* flint.

Zal, *n. m.* water. This word is used sometimes by the priestly section of the Hindus in Kashmir.

Zál, *n. f.* fever.

Zál, *n. m.* net, spider's web.

Zálanáwun, *v. t.* to cause to burn, or be burned; Zálanov, zálanáwán, zálanómut, zálanáwih.

Zalamai, *n. m.* storm.

Zála Parbat, *n. m.* a hill near to the village of Khrú. On this hill is a stone which the Hindus of the valley go and worship on the fourteenth of June, presenting money, gold, silver, clothes, and eatables.

Zalawun, *adj.* hot, warm, boiling.

Zaldeo, *n. m.* the name of the monster whose attacks on the dwellers of the surrounding mountains led to the draining of the lake of Kashmir by Kashaf. See Kashmir.

Zálim, *n. m.* tyrant.

Zálun, *v. t.* to burn, to kindle; zol, zálán, zolmut, zálih.

Zálun, *n. m.* firewood. The word in use towards Bárámúla.

Zalur, *n. m.* spider.

Zaman, *n. m.* day.

Zambchule, *n. m.* Prunus padus (bird cherry).

Zámatur, *n. m.* son-in-law.

Zamín, *n. f.* country, the earth, land.

Zamín khananwol, *n. m.* a ploughman.

Zamzam, *n. m.* the name of a famous spring or fountain in Mecca.

Zán, *n. f.* knowledge, acquaintance, discovery, ascertaining.

Zan, *conj.* and *adv.* as if, as, as you would say, that is to say, so to speak.

Zang, *n. m.* leg, in common parlance, lower extremity.

Zangahur, *n. m.* a pair of legs.

Zangár, *n. m.* rust.

Zanjír, *n. f.* chain.

Zánun, *v. t.* to recognise, to

know, to understand; zónun, zánán, zónmut, zányih.

Zaorun, *v. t.* to curdle.

Zápitah, *n. m.* custom.

Zar, *n. m.* deafness.

Zȧr, *adj.* deaf.

Zár, *n. m.* respect, dice, game, gambling.

Zar, *n. m.* the ephemeral fever of children.

Zār, *n. m.* gambler.

Zárah, *adv.* respectfully.

Zárah-párah, *adv.* respectfully.

Zárapar, *n. m.* excuse.

Zárapára, *n. m.* apology.

Zarar, *n. m.* damage, loss.

Zarar karun, *v. t.* to hurt.

Zard, *adj.* yellow.

Zarer, *n. m.* deafness.

Zár gindun (kamár kardan), *v. t.* to gamble.

Zārí, *n. m.* gamester.

Zar kakú, *n. m.* pheasant. Found on the mountains of Kashmir.

Zárpár, *n. m.* intercession, request.

Zarun, *v. i.* to be.

Zaṭ, *n. f.* the loose hair found in the hand or comb when dressing hair.

Zatāwuh, *adj.* twenty-two.

Zatówuh, *adj.* twenty-two.

Zatāwuhyum, *adj.* twenty-second.

Zauḍ, *adj.* stupid.

Zauk, *n. m.* love.

Zaun, *n. m.* a person.

Zauv, *n. f.* louse.

Záyul, *adj.* soft (of cotton goods).

Záza, *n. m.* lord.

Zĕchhar, *n. m.* stature, length.

Zĕl, *n. m.* cream.

Zen, *n. f.* a small wooden basket.

Zenah Kadal, *n. m.* a bridge over the Jhelum, in Srínagar.

Zenajáe, *n. f.* birthplace.

Zenána, *n. f.* wife, woman.

Zenánah, *n. f.* woman, wife.

Zénun, *v. t.* to win, to conquer, to earn one's living, to gain at play.

Zeo, *n. f.* tongue.

Zeo dapinyi, *v. t.* to speak a language.

Zeo karinyi, *v. t.* to speak a language.

Zeo waninyi, *v. t.* to speak a language.

Zéṭh, *n. m.* the third month of the Hindu year, and corresponding to Jamaḍa-l-awwal, or Jamada-l-úla, the fifth month of the Muhammadan year. It corresponds to our month of May.

Zéwan-zowur, *n. m.* a village in the Vehí pargana, where

a spring exists whose waters are said to be the best in the valley.

Zí, *n. f.* profit.

Zí,áfat, *n. m.* feast.

Zichhar, *n. m.* seniority.

Zidd, *n. f.* envy.

Zih, *adj.* two.

Zillah, *n. m.* district.

Zilun, *v. t.* to shave, to scrape; zulun, zilán, zulmut, zilih.

Zimah, *adj.* necessary.

Zín, *n. m.* saddle. The present kind of leather saddle is said to have been introduced into the valley by Akbar the Great.

Zinda, *adj.* alive.

Zindagí, *n. f.* life.

Zinda Rám, *n. m.* a proper name.

Zín gaṇḍun, *v. t.* to saddle.

Zín ladun, *v. t.* to saddle.

Zír, *n. f.* a sign.

Zirát, *n. m.* cultivated field.

Zirin, *n. m.* old man.

Zitáwuh, *adj.* twenty-two.

Ziṭher, *n. m.* a fountain on the hill behind the Takht-i-Salaiman.

Zitish, *n. m.* astrologer.

Zitsah, *n. m.* ray of light.

Ziza, *n. m.* ray.

Zóḍ (guzargah), *n. m.* ferry, ford.

Zoin, *n. f.* a proper name.

Zók, *n. m.* love.

Zŏl, *n. f.* rural name for a woman's head-dress.

Zŏlah, *n. f.* drowsiness.

Zŏn, *n. m.* a person, a man.

Zón, *n. f.* a proper name.

Zórah, *adv.* strongly.

Zoras set anun (bazor kardan), *v. t.* to force.

Zoráwar, *adj.* overcoming, powerful.

Zór karun, *v. t.* to make an effort.

Zórwàr, *adj.* strong.

Zótun, *v. i.* to shine (especially of metals).

Zowaráwun, *v. t.* to beget (lit. to cause to be born); zowarov, zowaráwán, zowaromut, zowaráwih.

Zówur, *n. m.* a fountain in the Vehi pargana.

Zránd, *n. m.* Cuscuta pedicellata.

Zróḍ, *n. m.* a ford.

Zú, *n. m.* spirit, life.

Zubún, *adj.* bad.

Zud, *n. m.* hole, cavity.

Zúd karun, *v. t.* to pierce.

Zúj, *n. f.* a long piece of cloth, extending from the crown of the head down to the small of the back.

Zúl, *n. m.* an illumination.

Zulaf, *n. m.* lock of hair.

Zulf, *n. m.* ringlet.

Zulm, *n. m.* violence, tyranny.

Zulm karun, *v. t.* to oppress.

Zulum, *n. m.* tyranny, violence.

Zulun, *v. t.* to shave or plane wood.

Zún (ξυλον), *n. m.* firewood.

Zún, *n. m.* moon.

Zúní, *n. f.* a proper name.

Zuntí, *n. f.* a proper name.

Zúr, *adj.* deaf.

Zur, *n. m.* the great trochanter of femur.

Zúr, *n. m.* a lamp-stand made of wood.

Zurú, *n. m.* a spring of water in the pargana of Máchhá-mah.

Zúrust, *adj.* insensible, life-less.

Zúṭh, *adj.* long, tall, elder. Elder brother, zúṭh boi.

Zúṭh karun (daráz kardan), *v. t.* to extend, to draw out.

Zyun, *v. i.* to be born; záo, ziwán, zámut, ziwih, ziwih.

Zyun (jinná), *v. t.* to give birth, to bear; záo, zĕwán, zámut, ziwih.

Zyun, *n. m.* firewood.

Zyun, *v. i.* to curdle.

Zyur, *n. m.* anise? caraway-seed.

Zyúṭh, *adj.* long, tall, elder.

Zyúṭ, *adj.* long, tall, elder, chief, main, principal.

Zyút, *n. m.* magistrate.

Zyút karun, *v. t.* to super-annuate.